PERSONNEL MANAGEMENT LAW

Personnel Management Law

FRANK W ROSE

Gower Press

First published in 1972 in Britain by Gower Press Limited
140 Great Portland Street, London W1N 5TA

© Frank W Rose 1972
ISBN 0 7161 0072 X

Printed in Britain by
Clarke, Doble & Brendon Ltd, Plymouth

Preface

The aim of this book is to give a straightforward explanation of the law affecting the employer and the employee. The personnel manager is often charged with the responsibility of complying with the law in so far as it affects his employer and it is hoped that this book will assist in the understanding of these requirements. Over simplification of the law can give a misleading impression of the precise obligations involved, consequently many of the important statutory obligations are dealt with in detail. At the same time every effort has been made to explain complex legal concepts in as simple a form as possible so that they may be readily understood by the non lawyer.

It would be presumptuous to claim that the book is a complete statement on the law of employment in England and Wales, but if the personnel manager and company secretary are able to solve some of their everyday problems by reference to the text then the main purpose behind this undertaking will have been achieved. In complex cases where it is necessary to take professional legal advice, the book may help the manager to appreciate more readily the legal background to the problem that is confronting his employer or one of the employees.

I am deeply indebted to Mr Derek French for editing the text and making innumerable useful suggestions on the content and form of the book. Finally, I must thank my wife, Andrina, for so patiently transforming my illegible handwriting into a comprehensible type-written script: without her help and encouragement I could not have completed this task.

Contents

Introduction:
The English Legal System

EVOLUTION OF COMMON LAW AND EQUITY

THE NORMANS DID NOT ATTEMPT TO IMPOSE THEIR OWN LAWS IN England, instead they took positive action to bring uniformity to English customary laws which had varied from one part of the country to another. This was achieved by sending judges from Westminster to tour the country and determine disputed issues in accordance with local customary law. The judges consulted with each other on their return to Westminster and chose the best customs from various parts of the country for application uniformly throughout the realm. Eventually the varied customary laws were moulded into a single system of rules for universal application. This was called the common law of the land.

Although the development of the common law was rapid, its growth was accompanied by many serious drawbacks, and by the middle of the fourteenth century its approach had become very conservative, technical and inflexible. Formalities surrounding application of the law took precedence over the granting of justice. Two examples are given as illustrations. At common law the only remedy was damages, but some situations demanded precise performance of a binding contractual promise where damages were an inadequate remedy; for example, if a seller had backed out of an agreement to sell a unique work of art, monetary compensation for a breach of contract was unlikely to satisfy the disappointed buyer. In some instances the common law refused to grant a remedy of any kind, though justice required one: in his will a man might leave legal title in his property to a friend on trust to manage the estate and account for the profits and benefits produced for the enjoyment of his widow and children in circumstances where they were unable to manage the property themselves. At common law, the friend (or trustee) with the legal title could regard the property as his own and keep the profits produced to the exclusion of the widow and children who were the intended beneficiaries.

Origins of equity

Aggrieved persons not granted redress by the common law courts addressed a petition to the King in Council, asking him to exercise the royal prerogative of justice and to grant them relief. As the number of petitions grew, the King referred them to the Lord Chancellor for just settlement, on the basis of legal principles and concepts derived from sources other than the common law. The overriding requirement was observance of the requirements of good conscience. Derived from this source is the remedy of specific performance of contractual obligations and also enforcement of a trust. These remedies deal with the two problems already outlined where the common law was defective. This new form of justice was called "equity," a term best understood as meaning "fair." A person has acted equitably if his conduct is fair and reasonable, as being in accordance with the dictates of conscience. Principles of equity came to be administered in a separate court known as the Court of Chancery.

Equity assumed the existence of common law rules and remedies by improving upon them, filling in gaps, and rectifying any defects, without seeking to replace or usurp common law principles. Equitable remedies are granted only at the court's discretion, but there is a right to demand a common law remedy for infringement of a right recognised by common law. If A trespasses on B's land, B may demand damages at common law as compensation, though the injury suffered and consequently the sum recoverable will be merely nominal. B may seek an injunction instead, but he cannot demand it as of right. This is an order from a court administering equity which directs the trespasser not to violate B's right in the future. An injunction will be granted if it is the only effective way of preventing A from continually trespassing on B's land, but not otherwise.

Until the middle of the last century a litigant had to seek common law and equitable remedies in different courts, but today either type of remedy may be granted by any court where circumstances demand.

JUDICIAL PRECEDENT

With the exception of law emanating from Parliament in the form of a statute or delegated legislation, most of the law is derived from case law or judicial precedent, that is, the law as laid down by judges in disputes referred to them for decision.

If Harris trespasses on Brown's land, Brown may bring a civil action to recover damages from Harris as compensation for the harm allegedly caused. In reaching its decision the court may make an important statement on the law in so far as it relates to trespass. This establishes a guide or precedent and in a later dispute between Robinson and Green where the facts are similar, the court may be referred to the earlier case as an authority to be followed.

Law reports

The doctrine of judicial precedent depends upon accurate recording of important decisions through a system of regular law reporting. It will be easy for the court deciding the dispute between Robinson and Green to rely on the earlier decision in Brown and Harris if an accurate report of those proceedings can be referred to. Since 1865, barristers have been employed to record proceedings of significant cases. Their reports (revised by the judges who conducted the cases) are published by the Incorporated Council of Law Reporting for England and Wales. Other reports are issued by commercial publishers usually giving shorter summaries but issued sooner than the Council's reports. The volume and page numbers of the report in which each case mentioned in this book is summarised are given on pages 523–8.

The report of Brown and Harris's case would be cited as Brown v Harris, with the date of publication of the report appearing in brackets. Brown is the plaintiff or party bringing the action, and Harris is the defendant or party being sued. If the court gives judgement in favour of Brown, then Harris may appeal against this decision to a higher court. In civil proceedings, with which this book is mainly concerned, the appeal will lie from the County Court or High Court to the Court of Appeal (Civil Division). The report of the appeal proceedings will still be referred to as Brown v Harris, though Harris is bringing the appeal. Previously it was customary to place the name of the party appealing first, whether this was the original plaintiff or the original defendant. If Harris appeals from an adverse decision in the Court of Appeal to the House of Lords as the ultimate appeal court, the case is cited as Harris v Brown. Harris is now referred to as the appellant, that is the person making the appeal, while Brown is called the respondent. In reports of House of Lords proceedings the name of the appellant is always placed first.

Why previous decisions are followed

When reaching his decision the judge may prefer to follow a previously decided case on the same issue, in order to give some support to his own views. If precedents are followed, the law is given an element of continuity and certainty. Failure to follow an earlier decision upsets dealings that have taken place in reliance on that decision, based upon the belief that it was a valid and correct statement of the existing legal position. With a system of precedent it is possible to predict within limits what the court's ruling will be, if a new set of facts arise similar to those in a previous decision, without incurring the expense of bringing a dispute to court.

As new decisions emerge, the law grows and develops to meet changing conditions and ideas. By adhering to the doctrine of precedent it is possible to keep the law flexible and up to date.

Original and declaratory precedents

Today there is a direct or analogous precedent for most situations that arise in any dispute. Legal principles have been built up over the years by the ever increasing number of decided cases that have been reported. These precedents constitute the common law. If an entirely new situation arises— a case of first impression—the judge may make his decision without reference to any previously decided case. The creation of a new rule derived from the application of general legal principles to a novel situation is called an original precedent. A declaratory precedent is further evidence of an existing rule of law by its application to the situation that has arisen.

Determining which part of a decision is binding

Only the principle upon which the judge decided a case is binding as a judicial precedent upon a judge deciding a subsequent case. When reaching his decision, the judge will not usually distinguish between those parts which are to be regarded as binding in subsequent cases (ratio decidendi) and those parts that may be disregarded as remarks made in passing and not directly related to the facts in issue (obiter dicta). This means that the ratio decidendi or binding part of a precedent is that part which is ascertained and approved by a judge deciding a later case where the precedent is cited as an authority. Binding authority is not accorded to those statements of the law made in the course of a decision if unaccompanied by a judicial application of those principles to the facts in dispute: judges may make the law by applying it to a dispute referred to them for decision, but they cannot make a mere declaration of what the law is.

Obiter dicta do not bind any court, but they may have persuasive authority if the facts of a later case resemble the facts of an earlier decision in which the remarks obiter dicta were made. The obiter dicta of a distinguished judge will often have persuasive authority.

Binding precedents may not be followed

A court may refuse to follow a precedent otherwise to be regarded as binding under the rules outlined. This is permissible for a number of reasons.

The ratio decidendi of a case is based upon its material facts and a later case may be distinguished by some material fact that was not present in the earlier decision. It is impossible for the facts in two different cases to be identical, but if they are basically and essentially the same when stripped of all trivial or insignificant distinctions (on all fours) then the doctrine of precedent must be observed.

A court need not follow a decision given per incuriam—that is, without consideration of an important precedent or statutory provision. On the other hand, the passage of time does not reduce the authority accorded to a precedent; in fact the courts are reluctant to overrule a well-established precedent, unless it is clearly erroneous and based upon a misunderstanding of the law. A statute may have the effect of overruling an unpopular judicial decision and restating the law in more acceptable terms (see Priestley v Fowler on p. 12).

Sometimes the court is faced with a number of binding precedents of equal authority where the actual decisions are in conflict, and then the most appropriate precedent will be followed. The conflicting decisions may exist because of the differing facts in each individual case, though collectively they all have some basic similarities.

Disadvantages of a system of judicial precedent
A binding precedent may have to be followed even though it is generally regarded as an incorrect or inappropriate statement of the law. Reluctance to follow a precedent may lead the courts to make illogical distinctions by concentrating attention on the differences between the case being heard and the undesirable precedent, even though the distinctions are without real substance and force. This can lead to a mass of irreconcilable precedents which makes it difficult to ascertain what the law is and how a future court will react when applying the precedents to a new set of facts.

The growing number of cases reported makes it difficult to determine the precise content of the law on a given subject, except by a detailed analysis of all relevant decisions. This is a lengthy, tedious and specialised task which must be done by a trained lawyer.

COURTS

A brief summary of the hierarchy of courts of civil and criminal jurisdiction will assist in the appreciation of the relative significance and authority accorded to the many decided cases that will be discussed. It will also indicate the court to which any legal dispute involving the employer will be assigned. The system of courts that is described is that introduced by the Courts Act 1971, which is expected to take effect on 1 January 1972. The aim of the Act is to speed the administration of justice.

Courts of civil jurisdiction

County Courts. County Courts, of which there are over four hundred, are unrelated to the geographical areas of the counties. They are organised in a way that will best serve the needs of the population. The informal and relatively inexpensive procedure makes the County Courts the busiest civil courts in the judicial system, with jurisdiction in the following matters:

1   Claims in contract and tort, except libel and slander, up to a limit of £750, unless the parties agree to waive the monetary limitation when claims over £750 may be heard
2   Equity matters up to a limit of £5000, unless the limit is waived—for example, trusts, partnerships, company matters and some revenue and bankruptcy claims
3   Actions concerning title to and recovery of possession of land where the rateable value does not exceed £400

High Court. The High Court is divided into a number of separate divisions. The Queen's Bench Division hears actions in contract, tort and recovery of land that are beyond the jurisdiction of the County Courts because of the sum of money involved. These are common law matters formerly heard in the old common law courts. The Chancery Division deals with claims in equity. A dispute may be heard in London or at places outside London as indicated by the Lord Chancellor.

Court of Appeal (Civil Division). An appeal lies from a decision in the High Court or County Court to the Court of Appeal. The original decision may be upheld or it can be reversed, in which case judgement is given for the party unsuccessful in the original proceedings. The court consists of the Master of the Rolls and thirteen Lords Justices of Appeal. A quorum is three, with each judge giving a separate and independent judgement. In cases of dissent the majority view prevails.

House of Lords. The House of Lords sitting in its judicial capacity is separate and distinct from the House when sitting as a legislative body. It is an independent Court of Law consisting of the Lord Chancellor, eleven Lords of Appeal in Ordinary (Law Lords) and peers who hold or have held high judicial office. Appeals are usually heard by five judges and the majority view prevails. Appeals may be heard from:

1   The Court of Appeal (Civil Division), Court of Session in Scotland and the Supreme Court of Northern Ireland, provided the House or the lower court grants leave to appeal
2   The High Court, by-passing an appeal to the Court of Appeal (Civil Division), if the case involves:
   (a) a point of law of general public importance, and
   (b) the issue concerns the construction of a statute which has been fully argued in the County Court before a judge who is bound by a previous decision of the Court of Appeal or the House of Lords

Judicial Committtte of the Privy Council. This body is separate and distinct from the courts discussed already. It does not form part of the hierarchy of civil and criminal courts in this country, but it is the final appeal court in civil and criminal disputes from some Commonwealth countries, including Australia, New Zealand, Ceylon, Sierre Leone, Jamaica, Trinidad, Tobago and Malaysia. The Judicial Committee is an eminent legal body with a composition similar to that of the House of Lords sitting in its judicial capacity, including the present and former Lord Chancellors, Lords of Appeal in ordinary and senior Commonwealth judges.

Courts of criminal jurisdiction

Less emphasis is placed on criminal matters in discussions of the personnel manager's duties than on civil liabilities, consequently this summary of the hierarchy of criminal courts will be brief. Criminal offences are classified as:

1   Summary offences triable only by the magistrates—for example, minor road traffic offences, such as speeding
2   Summary offences triable by jury: when, on conviction for a summary offence, the magistrate may order imprisonment of over three months, the accused is entitled to trial by jury on indictment if he wishes; if he does not, the offence is triable summarily by the magistrates—for example, dangerous driving
3   Indictable offences: an indictment is a formal, written accusation of a crime; serious criminal offences like murder,

robbery, conspiracy and perjury must be tried on indictment; some indictable offences are triable summarily, such as offences under the Theft Act 1968, with the exception of the more serious crimes like robbery

Magistrates' Courts. Magistrates have power to:

1 Make a preliminary investigation into indictable offences to determine whether there is a prima facie case (some evidence to support the charge) justifying trial by the Crown Court
2 Try, and give judgement for, petty offences with a maximum penalty of:
   (*a*) Six months' imprisonment
   (*b*) Twelve months' imprisonment for Custom and Excise offences, or on conviction for two or more indictable offences tried summarily
   (*c*) A fine of £400

Appeal lies, on a point of law only, to a Divisional Court of the Queen's Bench Division.

The Crown Court. This is a newly constituted court forming part of the Supreme Court, replacing the courts of assize and quarter sessions as from 1 January 1972. The court may sit anywhere in England and Wales.

When the Crown Court sits in the City of London it will continue to be known as the Central Criminal Court ("Old Bailey").

The jurisdiction of the Court may be exercised by a High Court judge, a Circuit judge, or a recorder. Between two and four magistrates will sit as full members of the Crown Court with a judge or recorder when the court is:

1 Hearing an appeal from a Magistrates' Court
2 Dealing with committal for sentence, and,
3 Hearing the type of case previously tried at quarter sessions, if the Lord Chief Justice so directs.

In such cases the court's decision may be by majority, and if there is an equal division the judge or recorder has a second, casting vote.

Appeals may be heard from Magistrates' Courts at the instance of the accused, on questions of law or fact, against sentence or conviction. The Crown Court may confirm, reverse, vary or remit any decision appealed against. There is power to reduce or increase the sentence appealed against, provided the punishment is one that the Magistrates' Court could have awarded.

An appeal lies from the Crown Court, on a question of law, to a Divisional Court of the Queen's Bench Division or to the Court of Appeal (Criminal Division).

Divisional Court of the Queen's Bench Division. A Divisional Court has appellate jurisdiction, exercised by two or more judges sitting without a jury. It hears an appeal by way of case stated, on the ground that the decision is wrong in law or in excess of jurisdiction, from:

1   A Magistrates' Court, even if the accused has pleaded guilty
2   The Crown Court

A case stated is a written statement by the lower court giving the relevant facts and reasons for its judgement.

A further appeal to the House of Lords is possible provided:

1   The Divisional Court or the House of Lords gives leave, and
2   In the view of the Divisional Court the case involves a point of law of general public importance requiring consideration by the House of Lords

Court of Appeal (Criminal Division). There is a right of appeal from the Crown Court:

1   On a matter of law
2   On any ground by leave of the Court of Appeal (Criminal Division) or on the certificate of the judge of the Crown Court
3   Against sentence, unless it is fixed by law, if the Court of Appeal (Criminal Division) gives leave

The court may allow or dismiss the appeal, vary but not increase sentence, quash conviction or order a new trial. There may be a further appeal to the House of Lords if:

1   Either the Court of Appeal (Criminal Division) or the House of Lords gives leave
2   The Court of Appeal (Criminal Division) certifies that a point of law of general public importance is involved

9

House of Lords. Appeals in criminal cases may be heard from :

1   The Court of Appeal (Criminal Division)
2   A Divisional Court of the Queen's Bench Division

BINDING FORCE OF A JUDICIAL PRECEDENT

House of Lords

Decisions of the House of Lords in civil and criminal matters are binding upon, and must be followed by, all other courts. Although the House of Lords is no longer bound to follow its own previous decisions, refusal to do so will usually occur in very few instances. It could happen, for example, where a previous decision is erroneous, made without consideration of a relevant statute or case (a decision per incuriam), or socially unacceptable in the light of changed circumstances. Nonetheless, the House must bear in mind the danger of disturbing retrospectively the basis upon which contracts, property settlements and financial arrangements have been made and also the need for certainty in the law, especially criminal law.

Court of Appeal

The Civil Division of the Court of Appeal is bound by its own decisions, unless they conflict (when it can choose which one it follows), but it has to give way to decisions of the House of Lords. Court of Appeal decisions are binding on all inferior courts with civil jurisdiction. The Criminal Division of the Court of Appeal is bound by decisions of its predecessors, the Court of Criminal Appeal (abolished in 1966) and the Court of Crown Cases Reserved (abolished in 1907), its own previous decisions and decisions of the House of Lords. The Court may depart from its own previous decisions if individual liberty of the accused is involved and a full court can overrule its own previous decisions. Decisions of one division of the Court of Appeal do not bind the other.

Divisional Courts of the High Court

In civil cases, a Divisional Court of the High Court is bound by decisions of the House of Lords, the Court of Appeal (Civil Division) and its own previous decisions. In a criminal case, a Divisional Court of the Queen's Bench Division will not now be bound by previous decisions of the Court of Appeal (Criminal Division) or the former Court of Criminal Appeal, since it is possible to appeal direct to the House of Lords from the Divisional Court. Previous House of Lords cases are binding.

High Court

High Court judges hearing civil cases are bound by decisions of the House of Lords and Court of Appeal (Civil Division). They are not bound by previous High Court decisions although they have strong persuasive authority if the decision is well established or given by an eminent judge.

A County Court judge is bound by the decisions of all superior courts of civil jurisdiction.

Judicial Committee of the Privy Council

These decisions have persuasive authority only, since they relate to appeals from overseas jurisdictions, but they are often followed in English courts because of the eminent composition of the Committee.

STATUTE

It is a fundamental principle of the British constitution that a statute (also referred to as an Act of Parliament or legislation) binds all persons within the sphere of its jurisdiction. It is immaterial that a person disagrees with the policy that lies behind the law being enforced against him.

Procedure for passing a bill through Parliament

A statute begins life as a bill introduced into either the House of Commons or the House of Lords. Most bills are drafted and sponsored by the government of the day, often implementing some change in the law that was foreshadowed in the party's election manifesto. The government then claims to have a mandate from the electorate for the proposed new law, since it was voted into office on the basis of its electoral promises.

A private member of Parliament may introduce his own bill, but there is only a remote chance of it becoming law since Parliament's time is devoted largely to the passage of government bills.

A bill passes through several stages in each House before receiving the Royal assent and being placed on the statute book to become binding and enforceable law. Assuming that the bill is introduced first in the House of Commons, its first reading is a mere formality. At second reading a government-sponsored bill is fully debated with speeches from government and opposition, usually with a vote being taken at the conclusion of the debate; if the government failed to secure a majority it would have to resign. At no stage is the bill read out clause by clause. Second reading is merely a debate on general principles, amendments are out of order.

The bill is then referred to a committee for detailed consideration and amendment of its wording and effect. Important bills, such as the Industrial Relations Bill in 1971, are discussed by a committee consisting of the whole House giving every member of Parliament a chance to make a contribution. More usually, committee proceedings take place in one of the small committee rooms at Westminster, with only between twenty and fifty members under a chairman taking part. The bill is referred back with amendments by the committee to the House, and at report stage further amendments may be proposed and accepted. The final stage is the third reading, which is another debate on general principles. The bill is then referred to the House of Lords and the same procedures are repeated. The final requirement to make the bill into law is the giving of the Royal assent, but this is a mere formality.

Reasons for enacting new laws

Statutes are an important source of law in modern times, because of Parliament's ever increasing control over the nation's affairs in social and economic matters. There has been an unprecedented rise in statute law since the last war, with the increased significance of social security, town and country planning, rent control, and nationalisation.

A statute may be used by Parliament for one of the following purposes:

1   To provide laws that would not come into existence by the slow development of legal principles through the medium of judicial precedent—for example, a comprehensive system of statutory rent control of premises leased by landlord to tenant, fixed periods of notice for employees continuously employed for a stated period

2   To abolish or amend common law principles that are hampering the administration of justice—for example, the doctrine of common employment enunciated by the House of Lords in Priestley v Fowler (1837) was abolished by the Law Reform (Personal Injuries) Act 1948; this unjust doctrine prevented an employee who was injured because of the negligence of a fellow employee while they were both acting within the scope of their employment from recovering damages from the common employer.

3   To amend, or completely repeal, existing legislation that is deemed to be undesirable on technical grounds or for political reasons. For example, a Labour government nationalised the

steel industry, a succeeding Conservative government de-
nationalised it, and later a Labour government renationalised it

Interpretation of statutes

Great care is required when drafting the wording of a statute so that it
clearly expresses the law which Parliament intended to make. The precise
meaning of the words used must be determined by those judges who are
called upon to apply the statutory provisions to cases brought before them
for decision. The meaning of the detailed provisions of statutes like the
Factories Act 1961, the Offices, Shops and Railway Premises Act 1963, the
Contracts of Employment Act 1963 and the Redundancy Payments Act
1965 have all been the subject of judicial assessment, explanation and
interpretation. Over the centuries the courts have developed recognised
techniques to assist them in this function of interpretation.

Sanctions against persons breaking the law

Failure to observe a statutory requirement or the principles of common
law and equity will usually lead to imposition of a sanction following legal
action. Liability for the commission of a wrong may be established in a
court of criminal or civil jurisdiction, as appropriate in the circumstances
of the case. A criminal conviction may involve a fine, or deprivation of
personal liberty as by commitment to a prison or borstal. Violation of the
civil law may result in:

1   The payment of damages as monetary compensation to the
    aggrieved person
2   Specific performance of the promise made in the case of a
    contractual obligation
3   Injunction to restrain continuance of the wrongdoing that
    gave rise to the complaint

Delegated legislation

Parliament has time to discuss only the essential principles of any bill that
proposes to introduce changes in the law. The power to make regulations,
rules and orders dealing with subordinate matters of detail (statutory
instruments) is delegated by Parliament to other persons and bodies.
Several statutes empower local authorities to make by-laws for their own
administrative area, but the recipient of power to make subordinate legislation is often the Minister whose department is most concerned with the
subject in issue. For example, the Factories Act 1961 and the Industrial

Relations Act 1971, both of which will be discussed in detail, give power to the Secretary of State for Employment to issue regulations as and when necessary, to give effect to the policy implicit in the parent statute. The Industrial Relations Act empowers the Secretary of State to draw up and submit a draft code of industrial practice to Parliament for its approval. Regulations may be numerous and far greater in bulk than the Act itself.

Reasons for the wide use of subordinate legislation. Pressure of time is not the only reason for recourse to delegated legislation on such a vast scale. Bills are confidential until their text is disclosed on first reading in Parliament, thereafter amendment is possible only at committee and report stage. Delegated legislation is drafted and amended informally with the help of expert advice without any need for secrecy. Unlike broad issues of policy which can be effectively discussed in Parliament by politicians, technical matters are best dealt with through the medium of subordinate legislation. Delegated legislation also provides a degree of flexibility that is vital in cases where experiment is desirable. Changes can be made in the light of experience, by revoking existing statutory instruments and introducing new ones, without the need to amend the parent statute by lengthy or formal procedures.

There is no general rule requiring delegated legislation to be laid before Parliament for examination and approval. The parent Act granting the power to make statutory instruments sets out the precise procedure for Parliamentary approval to be followed by the Minister or other body responsible for drafting it in order that it may become binding and effective.

Publication of statutory instruments. Ignorance of the existence and effect of the law is no excuse to a person charged with breaking it, thus the whole of the law applicable at any given moment should be accessible to the citizen or his legal adviser, so that he may regulate his conduct in order to avoid committing a wrong. All statutory instruments made are published by HM Stationery Office. In any proceedings against a citizen for contravening a regulation, it is a good defence to prove that it had not been issued by HM Stationery Office when the offence was committed, unless reasonable steps had been taken to bring it to the attention of the general public, or persons likely to be affected, or the person charged with the contravention. A collected edition of all statutory instruments is published annually containing those instruments made during the year that are still effective.

Consultation when drafting regulations. A government department intending to make any new statutory instrument usually consults interested bodies affected by the proposal and in some instances there may be a statutory duty to consult. This procedure helps to ensure that the new regulations are acceptable to those persons and bodies who are most affected. The government department has the advantage of hearing expert representations on its proposals.

Challenging the validity of delegated legislation. The courts exercise control over delegated legislation by declaring ultra vires and void any regulation unauthorised by the parent Act granting the power. The term ultra vires means acting in excess of the powers conferred. This type of defence may be raised by an individual charged with contravention of the statutory instrument. When drafting a regulation, great care is taken to determine the precise scope of any power to make delegated legislation, to avoid it being declared ultra vires by the courts. The courts will never entertain any claim by a litigant that a statute or a section of it is ultra vires. Parliament is legally omnipotent and supreme. It may make any law it pleases, however extreme, undesirable or unpopular. In practice, governments do not sponsor legislation that offends the majority of voters for fear of losing office after a general election.

ONE

Creating

Contracts of Employment

THIS BOOK EXAMINES THE LEGAL IMPLICATIONS OF EMPLOYING PEOPLE. The relationship between employer and employee is governed by the contract of employment and it is natural to begin by examining what happens when a new employee is taken on and a contract of employment is created.

For some personnel managers, engaging staff may be a part of the everyday routine, but it is important to be aware of the precise legal implications of such actions as advertising a vacancy, discussing terms with an applicant and concluding a verbal or written agreement. An awareness and understanding of the legal rights involved may enable the personnel manager where necessary to insist on implementation by the employee of the terms of a contract, or its termination by giving the appropriate period of notice. Recourse to legal proceedings by the employer should be necessary only in exceptional circumstances. It is often cheaper and more effective to take a firm stand from a position of strength in the confident knowledge of the legal remedies available, if the other party, usually the employee, refuses to be bound by his contractual obligations. Section 1:2 examines the legal implications of each stage of the negotiations. The Contracts of Employment Act requires the employer to provide written details of important points in the contract after it has been created. Section 1:6 describes the precise rules that employers must follow to comply with this Act.

In general, people are free to make any kind of contract with anyone they please: however, for various reasons the courts may refuse to enforce certain contracts—important cases of this are:

1   Contracts containing terms that are illegal or contrary to
     public policy (1:8 and Chapter 2)
2   Contracts with people younger than eighteen (1:9)

The Race Relations Act prevents people from not making contracts if the sole reason is an irrational prejudice that operates against the public interest; Section 1:11 discusses this Act's implications for the personnel manager's work.

The chapter ends with a discussion of the distinction between a contract of *service* and one *for services*—in other words, the difference between being an employee and being a contractor.

1:1 WHO IS THE CONTRACT BETWEEN?

When an employee negotiates a contract of employment, the employer may be a sole trader, a partnership or a company. Reference will be made in the majority of cases simply to the "employer," for often the legal position is exactly the same, whatever legal characteristics the individual employer may possess in any given instance. A short explanation of the legal status of these different types of possible employers may be useful at this stage.

The sole trader. A sole trader is an ordinary individual trading on his own account for his own benefit, usually in a small way with only a handful of employees working for him. In law a person is subject to various rights and liabilities, a distinction being made between different groups of persons. An individual has his own personal status, which may mean that his rights and obligations are more limited than those attaching to the normal adult person. Aliens, bankrupts, infants and persons of unsound mind are subject to special provisions in law by reason of their status. If an individual employer or employee falls within one of these groups, then the contract of employment and the rights and duties it gives rise to will be affected in a number of ways (see 1:9 on minors, and 13:3:2 on bankruptcy).

Partnership. Partnership is a relationship that exists between two or more persons carrying on business in common, with the object of making a profit. This relationship usually arises between a relatively small group of people, which in a business partnership is limited to twenty, with exceptions to this legally permitted maximum for solicitors, accountants, members of the stock exchange, patent agents, surveyors, auctioneers, valuers and estate agents.

Legal formalities are not essential when a partnership is formed: it may be the result of an oral agreement or even inferred from conduct, though often the mutual rights and liabilities of partners are set out in a formal deed of partnership or in a written agreement. In the absence of any contrary agreement, the Partnership Act 1890 sets out detailed provisions on the more important matters of concern, such as contributions to capital, division of profits, dissolution, and rights and duties of partners.

A partnership is not a separate legal entity distinct from the partners who comprise it, though the firm may sue and be sued in its own name. The rights and liabilities of the firm are merely those of the individual partners. Partners are fully liable for payment of the firm's debts, including arrears of salary due to employees. If the partnership assets are insufficient to meet the firm's liability, creditors have recourse against the individual personal estates of each partner in order to satisfy their debts. The liability of a limited partner is confined to the amount of capital he has contributed to the business, but there must always be a general partner fully liable for the firm's debts.

When one partner dies the partnership ends automatically and a new partnership must be formed if the remaining partners wish to continue the business, perhaps with a new partner replacing the deceased partner. On dissolution of a partnership, existing contracts of employment are terminated, but a new contract is usually offered on the same terms and the employees should accept it (see 13 : 3 : 1, Brace v Calder).

The corporate entity. A company is an artificial legal person with a legal existence separate and distinct from that of persons who are members of the company. The death of a member and his replacement by a new member does not affect the company's existence. A company has perpetual succession and continues until its affairs are wound up.

Power is conferred on the company to carry out the objects specified in its constitution (memorandum of association) and to further those objects the company can carry on business, make contracts and own property. A contract of employment is made between the employee and the company itself. Members and officials of the company are not parties to the agreement, consequently they have no rights or obligations in relation to it. Actions for breach of contract are brought by and against the company and the employee concerned. A company must act through the medium of human agents, its affairs being controlled by directors and effected by other officials and employees.

There are several different types of company and it is necessary to give a brief explanation of each one. A *chartered company* is formed when the Crown grants a charter, following a petition by the promoters praying for the grant. Only a few trading enterprises fall into this category, but they include banks and insurance companies. This form of incorporation is more usual for professional bodies (such as the Chartered Institute of Secretaries) colleges or universities and borough councils.

A *statutory company* is formed by a special, private Act of Parliament, this having been used in the past as a method of company formation by public utilities; undertakings concerned with the supply of water still use this particular form. When the most important public utilities were nationalised, the necessary powers were granted by a public Act of Parliament.

Registered companies are numerically the largest group, being bodies registered under the Companies Acts 1948 and 1967, by the deposit of specified documents giving details of the company's constitution with the Registrar of Companies in London or Edinburgh. In order to trade, a registered company will need capital. In the case of a public company this will be provided by investors in return for a share in the company proportionate to the extent of their investment. The capital can take the more usual form of money, or it can be land, machinery or any other form of property that the company needs.

If the company makes a profit, a dividend is usually declared and each shareholder will receive a payment dependent upon the number of shares he holds. A *limited company* is one in which the liability of members to make cash payments to the company when in need of financial support is limited to the amount of money still unpaid on their shareholdings. Many shares are fully paid for when first allotted to the shareholder, consequently he cannot be asked to make a further contribution if the company is wound up and its assets do not realise a sum sufficient to pay its debts. An *unlimited company* is one in which the liability of members is not limited in this way. The unlimited liability of members may be advisable in those cases where clients of the company may wish to pursue their claims to the full extent of the members' ability to pay, for example, where the business is that of stockbroker or bookmaker.

It may be advisable for a sole trader or partnership to became a *private registered company*. The business assets are sold by the owner or owners to the company, in return for an allotment of fully paid shares. The main advantage is that the liability for any losses incurred by the company is not the responsibility of the former proprietors, since their liability is limited to assets already transferred. In many cases a private company is formed to run a family business, and then all shares are held by a few members of the same family.

1:2   OFFERING AND ACCEPTING EMPLOYMENT

Like any other contract, a contract of employment comes into existence only when an offer is made and accepted. In practice there may be several intermediate stages starting with a newspaper advertisement, continuing with negotiations about salary and periods when both parties go away to think about their attitudes to the terms of employment.

It is essential to appreciate the legal implications of each stage of the negotiation so that both parties know exactly when they have committed themselves and what they are committed to.

From the negotiations it must be possible to extract an offer in precise terms made by either employer or employee which is then accepted without qualifications by the other party. A contract of employment is binding even if concluded only by word of mouth, but for greater clarity it is advisable for the employer to make a definite written offer, clearly stating all terms and conditions, which the potential employee is then expected to accept in writing. To prevent any misunderstandings, the oral negotiations may be made conditional upon a written offer and acceptance. If the terms of a written contract of employment are unambiguous then oral evidence is generally inadmissable to vary or contradict those terms, unless there has been fraud or illegality.

The Contracts of Employment Act 1963 requires an employer to provide an employee with a written statement of the most important terms of the contract. A binding contract of employment may exist quite independently of this written statement, which need not be handed over to the employee until some time after the conclusion of the contract of employment itself (see 1 : 6 : 1).

The parties are free to negotiate the terms applicable to their contract, but in many cases important matters such as wages, hours and holidays have been settled already by collective bargaining. Even if the employer is not a member of an employers' association he may wish to observe the terms negotiated by the trade unions. In addition, there are many duties imposed by statute upon all employers: for example, restrictions on the number of hours of work by women and young persons. Those matters will be discussed more fully at a later stage.

Throughout this section, the word "employer" is used for the person playing the role of hirer. In law the actual employer will often be a corporation—such as a limited company—or someone who has delegated the negotiating function to a personnel manager: the latter will then be acting as an agent and his precise legal position as an agent is explained in Section 1 : 4.

1 : 2 : 1   *When is an offer of employment first made?*
An advertisement by an employer, giving details of a vacancy he wishes to fill, is an invitation to interested persons to make an application for the post. It is not an offer of a job, capable of acceptance by the first person to reply who has the requisite qualifications.

A person applying for a job may offer his services to the potential employer orally, in writing or by implication from his conduct. Acceptance of the offer by the potential employer will bring a contract into existence.

Alternatively, and more usually, it may be the employer who is the offeror making an offer on given terms, which the applicant (the offeree) is free to accept or reject. These terms do not have to correspond with those set out in the advertisement.

1:2:2 Acceptance of any offer made

A mere intention by the offeree to accept an offer is insufficient. The acceptance must be brought expressly to the notice of the employer before a contract comes into existence, for example, by writing a letter of acceptance. A postal communication of an acceptance is permissible whenever the parties can be taken to have contemplated this possibility: where, for example, the employer allows the offeree to consider the offer of employment for a few days before reaching a decision. The acceptance is complete as soon as the letter of acceptance is posted, and a legally binding contract exists even if the letter is lost in the post and is never received by the employer. Before offering the job to another applicant, the employer should, in the absence of any communication from the first applicant, determine whether he intends to accept the offer, for if the letter has been lost in the post he may well finish up with two binding agreements for one vacancy.

1:2:3 Where the mode of acceptance is specified

An employer may request acceptance of his offer in some particular form such as a telephone message or a telegram, a likely possibility where a speedy answer is required. Acceptance by any other method, for instance a letter, would be invalid. If the method of acceptance was quicker than the one prescribed by the employer, such as a telegram instead of a letter, this would probably be a valid acceptance. In cases where a speedy reply is not required but the employer stipulates a particular method of acceptance, it does not always follow that use of an alternative method will be invalid, for the circumstances may suggest that a choice was open to the offeree. For example, the employer may require the offeree to sign a standard written agreement containing the terms of the contract, but pending execution of the document an informal letter accepting the contract and its terms may suffice, especially if in consequence the employer expressly or by conduct waives the condition as to the special mode of acceptance.

1:2:4 Acceptance by silence

The offeror cannot impose contractual liability on the offeree by stating that silence on the offeree's part will be regarded as consent to the terms of the offer. A person cannot offer his services to an employer and effectively bind him to a contract by stating "unless I hear to the contrary within seven days I will take it that you have accepted my terms." It follows that the employer cannot hold a potential employee to a contract of employment simply by making him a firm offer and attempting to dispense with the need for an acceptance by him.

1:2:5 *Unauthorised notification of acceptance*
An employer may decide to appoint a certain applicant from among a number of candidates applying for a post. An unauthorised notification to that applicant (probably by a member of the employer's staff) that his offer has been accepted will not result in a binding contract of employment. The employer is free to re-open discussions and select another candidate until an official notification of acceptance is sent to the chosen applicant.

1:2:6 *Making a counter-offer*
During negotiations a definite offer may be made by one party, but if the other party then proposes terms different from those contained in the offer, the new terms constitute a counter-offer and also a rejection of the original offer.

Appelby v Johnson (1874)

Appelby set out terms upon which he was to be employed in a letter to Johnson, who replied to the offer made in the following words: "Yours of yesterday embodies the substance of our conversation and terms. If we can define the terms a little more closely, it may prevent mistakes. We shall therefore expect you on Monday."

The court decided that Johnson's reply to the offer was not clear and certain; it left some matters still to be arranged, and so it did not constitute a binding definite acceptance and a contract of employment did not exist. Johnson's letter was a counter-offer and a rejection of Appelby's offer.

It may be unwise for an employer to make a counter-offer in the hope of inducing better terms, for the potential employee's original offer is rejected by this action, and he is free to abandon the negotiations altogether. If the employer makes the original offer, then the potential employee may ask for a higher salary or shorter working hours. The employer may use the counter-offer as a means of terminating negotiations, if he so wishes.

An offeree may ask further questions concerning the employment being offered to him in the hope of inducing the employer to offer better terms but without intending to reject the original offer. For example, he may inquire about the possibility of working later than usual on one day in order to leave earlier on another day, but a refusal by the employer to allow this may not mean that the original offer has been rejected.

1 : 2 : 7   *Keeping the offer open for a stipulated time*

It is not unusual for a person who has been offered employment on stated terms to ask for a period of time to reach a decision, at the end of which he is expected to accept or reject the offer. He may reach his decision before the time allowed has elapsed and if he accepts, a binding contract comes into existence. An employer may feel morally bound to allow the offeree the stipulated period of time for reflection, but he is legally entitled to revoke the offer at any time he wishes before he receives notification of acceptance, even if the stipulated period has not ended. This right may be exercised where changed circumstances in the business or fresh knowledge about the offeree render the conclusion of the contract undesirable.

An offer lapses if it is not accepted within the stipulated time. Where a given period of time for acceptance is not prescribed in the offer, there must be an acceptance within a "reasonable" time.

An offer is automatically terminated by the death of either offeror or offeree.

1 : 2 : 8   *Binding obligation to keep the offer open*

An employer may wish to engage someone, but make a final decision dependent on the satisfactory settlement of other important factors. For example, if Smith & Co are negotiating the acquisition of the business of Brown & Co it may be important, if the negotiations are successful, to install a new management team to make Brown & Co more profitable. To achieve this objective Smith & Co may have to engage several professional men of high calibre, but if the takeover does not go through their services will not be required. The employer can safeguard his position by taking an option on the services of the prospective employee. It is necessary to negotiate a separate binding contract with the prospective employee whereby the employer is given a period of time during which to make a final decision one way or the other concerning the employment. If during the period of the option the prospective employer indicates his intention to conclude a contract of employment, but the prospective employee refuses to accept his decision, then the employer may sue for breach of contract and recover damages.

One vital factor must be remembered: since the option itself is a contract it must satisfy all the essential requirements of a contract and be supported by consideration. This usually means that a payment must be made to the prospective employee for granting the option to the employer.

1:2:9 *Revoking an offer*

An offer may be revoked any time before acceptance, but it is an effective revocation only when it is actually communicated to the offeree. If an employer wishes to withdraw an offer of employment already made prompt action is vital. It is also important to make sure that the means of communication chosen are reliable, so that the offeree will not be able to claim that he has not heard of the revocation. If the post is used, a revocation is effective only when it is actually received by the offeree. If the communication is lost in the post the revocation is ineffective.

Notification of the revocation need not be made by the offeror himself, it is only necessary that the offeree hears of the revocation from some reliable source, for example, the employer's secretary or personal assistant. The same principles apply when the potential employee wishes to withdraw an offer made to work for an employer. Where the employer wishes to accept the offer made to him, delay in so doing may result in loss of the contract.

1:3 PERIOD OF PROBATIONARY SERVICE BY THE EMPLOYEE

It may be difficult for an employer to assess the potentialities of a person to whom he offers employment on the strength of a short interview and a reference. The new employee may be required to undergo a period of probationary service before being offered employment for an indefinite time. There now exists a contract of employment for the trial period agreed upon, at the end of which the contract is terminated automatically. The services of an unsuitable probationer may then be dispensed with, by paying wages up until the end of the stipulated period.

If the employer dismisses the employee summarily without lawful justification before the end of the trial period, then a breach of contract is committed and damages are recoverable. The employer must pay a sum equivalent to the wages that would have been earned during the unexpired part of the probationary period. The employee must reduce the loss suffered as a result of his dismissal by securing another position as soon as he can. Any remuneration earned by the employee from his alternative employment during the remainder of the probationary period will be deducted from the damages payable by the employer who dismissed him. If the probationary period is relatively short, for example, three months, and dismissal occurs at the end of six weeks, then the full three months' wages will probably be payable, since it may be difficult for the employee to find alternative work during the remaining part of the trial period. If the employee has been dismissed for some lawful reason he cannot make such a claim (see 13 : 4).

1:4 LEGAL POSITION OF THE
PERSONNEL MANAGER WHEN ENGAGING NEW STAFF

The negotiation of a contract of employment is a function often delegated to a paid official, such as a personnel manager, employed by a person trading on his own account, a firm or a limited company. In this case, the relationship of principal and agent exists between the employer and his personnel manager. When engaging staff the personnel manager may deal with all necessary details, but any contract of employment concluded will be between the employer and the new employee. Consequently the employer is liable for any of the personnel manager's actions that result in a breach of contract.

1:4:1 Express delegation to the
personnel manager of authority to negotiate

The personnel manager is usually given express authority, verbal or written, by his employer to negotiate a contract of employment with an applicant for a job, on the employer's behalf. The employer is bound by the agreement so concluded, unless the personnel manager has exceeded the powers conferred on him (referred to as acting "ultra vires") in which case he is personally liable for any loss caused to the applicant.

Sometimes the personnel manager may be unaware of the limitations on his authority, but even where he makes an honest mistake he is still liable to the other party to the purported contract with the employer. Such liability is called breach of warranty of authority, the personnel manager being responsible for making a promise (or warranty) that he had authority to bind his employer in a stated manner, a promise which later turns out to be untrue. It is in the personnel manager's own interests to seek precise instructions on such important matters, and then keep within the limits of any power so conferred.

Where the personnel manager is employed by a limited company, it is necessary, as an added precaution, to be satisfied that any contract of employment negotiated is within the powers of the company: otherwise it does not bind the company. There is usually an express provision in the company's constitution (articles of association) empowering the company to engage staff as required; alternatively, such a power is often necessary or ancillary to the objects of the company.

1:4:2   Implied delegation of authority to negotiate

If a personnel manager's duties involve conducting business for his employer, an implied general authority exists which allows him to contract on his employer's behalf in fulfilment of that authority. Such authority is in addition to any authority expressly delegated. If it can be shown that the personnel manager was acting within the scope of his authority and also that the contract was closely connected with his work, then any contract of employment so negotiated binds the employer to the exclusion of the personnel manager. But since it may be difficult to establish an implied power to act in this way it is advisable to rely upon express instructions only.

1:4:3   What happens if the personnel manager acts without the necessary authority?

Many personnel managers are able to seek immediate instructions directly from the employer or other official with authority and get express permission for a proposed course of action. There may be occasions, however, when it is wise to act promptly for fear of irretrievably losing an opportunity that has arisen, but it is impossible to seek any prior approval. For example, John Jones, an accountant, with an interview fixed for Friday may present himself at Grey & Co's place of business on Wednesday stating that he has been offered elsewhere a post carrying a salary of £2500 which he will accept, unless Grey & Co can offer better terms immediately. The personnel manager may not have authority to engage staff at a salary over £1000 a year unless the employer expressly sanctions the appointment. If Grey & Co desperately need an accountant with the experience, qualifications and ability of John Jones, the personnel manager may on his own initiative make an offer of employment at £2750 a year if he cannot contact his employer (who might be touring abroad with his precise whereabouts unknown).

It is open to the employer later to ratify or adopt the contract and this will undoubtedly happen if the contract is advantageous. The contract is capable of ratification, however, only if it was originally made on the employer's behalf. It is important that the personnel manager makes this point clear during discussions with an applicant.

The danger here for the personnel manager who acts without or in excess of his authority is that the employer may repudiate the contract made, in which case the personnel manager himself is liable for damages for deceit to the other party to the contract. The personnel manager has made a representation of the extent of his authority which he knows to be untrue, and the motive for so acting, though apparently reasonable, is an irrelevant consideration.

1:4:4   *Where the employer is a firm of partners*

When a person is offered employment in a firm, the contract may be negotiated by one of the partners, particularly if the firm is a small one. Sometimes one of the partners may carry out the functions of a personnel manager. Any contract of employment so concluded will be legally binding, since every partner is an agent of the firm and of his co-partners for the purpose of carrying on the firm's business in the usual way, which includes engaging employees. If the partner negotiating the contract does not have authority to so act, where, for example, the co-partners have forbidden a junior partner to engage staff, any contract of employment concluded contrary to this limitation is nonetheless binding on the firm, since an act of that type is within a partner's apparent authority (Partnership Act 1890 s5).

In a large firm with numerous employees, a personnel manager may be employed to deal with staffing and have power, within limits, to engage staff on his own initiative. Any act done by a personnel manager in these circumstances, which relates to the firm's business and is done in the firm's name, will bind the firm and all the partners (s6).

1:5   ESSENTIAL ELEMENTS OF A CONTRACT OF EMPLOYMENT

A contract is an agreement intended to have legal consequences which comes into existence when one party, the offeror, makes an offer which the other party, the offeree, accepts. A contract of employment is a legally binding agreement between employer and employee, whereby the employee is under a duty to serve the employer in accordance with the terms set out, while in return the employer promises, among other things, to pay the stipulated wages. A contract of employment is subject to the general principles governing the law of contract; consequently the essential elements of a legally enforceable contract must be present.

1:5:1 *Valuable consideration is*
essential to make an agreement legally binding

A contract of employment is not binding on either party unless it is supported by *consideration*. This has been defined as "some right, interest, profit or benefit accruing to one party or some forbearance, detriment, loss or responsibility given, suffered or undertaken by the other." (Mr Justice Lush)

In a contract of employment, consideration will take the form of an exchange of promises. The employee will give a promise to carry out certain duties, in return for which the employer will promise to pay the agreed wages, sometimes coupled with other benefits such as food and lodgings. If the employee then refuses to report for work in fulfilment of his promise, he commits a breach of contract and the employer may sue for the damage suffered.

When the employee has completed his duties the consideration that he has provided is then executed. The employer's consideration remains *executory* (not yet carried into effect) until he pays over the wages due.

Not only is it essential for consideration to be present in a contract, that consideration must also be *valuable*, meaning that it must have an economic character. Use of the word "valuable" here is not a reference to how much the service rendered is worth. The adequacy or inadequacy of the price paid by an employer for an employee's services is irrelevant to the validity of the contract; any payment, however slight, is sufficient. Persons of full age may enter into any contract they like and it is for them to decide whether or not the terms are satisfactory.

Enforcing a promise to work without payment. Where one party agrees to work for another party without receiving any benefit in return, the promise is gratuitous and is unenforceable for lack of consideration if it is not carried out. A promise to work without payment by an employee will be a rare occurence, but to make such a promise legally binding it is only necessary for the parties to conclude the agreement by deed. A solicitor should be consulted if this is necessary.

Where the employee undertakes extra work. A promise by an employee to do something that he is already bound to do under his contract of employment, in return for a promise of extra money by the employer, does not amount to valuable consideration on the employee's part. If the employee tries to recover, by legal action for a breach of contract, the extra money not yet paid his claim will fail. For example, if one typist out of six in a typing pool leaves her employment and cannot be replaced immediately, a promise by the employer to pay extra money to the remaining five typists if they share the extra burden of work during office hours is unenforceable; the employee's original contract obliges her to meet the normal emergencies connected with her work, and fulfilling extra duties during a temporary staff shortage is such an emergency. Where a department is seriously undermanned because of staff shortage, so that it is unreasonable to expect employees to carry the burden of the extra work, then the employees are free to negotiate a fresh agreement with the employer and a promise to pay a higher wage for increased productivity is then legally binding (Stilk v Myrick (1809), Hartley v Ponsonby (1857)).

It may seem strange that an employer should make a promise of extra payment to his employees, and then try to evade his responsibility to pay it, but there are two important possibilities here. The promise may not have been made by the employer personally, but by some official acting on his behalf, such as the personnel manager, when work had been seriously disrupted and in danger of not being completed by the stipulated date, unless an added inducement was given to employees. In such circumstances the employer may wish to dispute his liability to pay and if he is successful it must be determined whether the official making the unauthorised promise is personally liable (see 1 : 4).

The employer may become bankrupt, and his employees' entitlement to wages due but unpaid will depend upon the extent of their legally maintainable claim. A right to extra payment for additional work may be rejected on the ground that the employer would not have been liable to pay it, consequently the trustee in bankruptcy may reject the claim also.

1 : 5 : 2 *Is a contract of employment intended to be legally binding?*
If an agreement is supported by consideration it is presumed that the parties intended it to be legally enforceable one against the other, especially if it relates to a commercial matter, such as a contract of employment. The parties are free, however, to state expressly that their agreement is not intended to be legally binding, in which case it is an obligation binding in honour only. Such a statement is unusual in a contract of employment. The following case raised this issue in the context of the employer–employee relationship.

Edwards v Skyways Ltd (1964)

Edwards, a pilot employed by Skyways Ltd, was declared redundant. At a meeting between representatives of the company and Edwards' trade association, it was agreed that any pilot leaving the company's employment because of redundancy would receive "ex gratia" a payment "approximating to" the company's contributions to the contributory pension fund, of which Edwards was a member. Because of financial difficulties the company did not pay over the sum promised. The company admitted that Edwards had provided consideration for the sum promised to him and that at the time of the meeting the company intended to keep their promise.

The court decided that the subject matter of the agreement related to business affairs, and the company was unable to discharge the heavy burden of showing that it was not intended to create legal relations. The use of the phrase "ex gratia" did not by itself justify the assumption that the company's promise was not intended by the parties to be legally enforceable. The fact that the payment to Edwards was to be of a sum "approximating to" the amount of the company's contributions did not make the terms of the contract too vague to be enforceable.

It is likely that this decision will be limited in its application to circumstances involving a single employer dealing with representatives of a small number of employees in a defined section of the work force, whose position is well known to the employer. In cases involving the wider form of collective agreement it is unlikely to be authoritative.

1:5:3 Breach of contract

If the terms of a contract are not observed by one of the parties, the innocent party is entitled to sue for breach of contract. The court determining the issue will grant a remedy to the person aggrieved, provided that breach of contract has been established by satisfactory proof. In most cases damages will be the usual and most appropriate remedy, that is monetary compensation for any loss suffered, to place the innocent party in the same financial position that he would have been in if the contract had been duly performed (see 13:5). A decree will not be granted to order a defaulting party to carry out those obligations which he has promised to discharge by the terms of the contract of employment. A decree of specific performance is inappropriate in relation to a contract for personal services, since the court is not in a position to supervise the actions of employer and employee, whichever party is at fault, to ensure that the decree is obeyed. There are important qualifications to this principle, however, and in some cases a reluctant employee may be persuaded to perform his contract of employment by the court granting an injunction preventing him from being engaged elsewhere, on similar work to that stipulated in the original contract of employment, for the period during which that contract was intended to last (see 13 : 6).

Depending upon the individual circumstances of any given situation, a contract of employment may be:

1   Valid, and fully enforceable by either party against the other
2   Voidable, in which case one party has an option: he may regard the contract as binding, or refuse to carry out the terms agreed upon by exercising his right to rescind. If a person under the age of eighteen negotiates a contract of employment that is not beneficial to himself, it is voidable at his option by reason of his minority; in such cases the party rescinding the agreement cannot be sued for a breach of contract.
3   Void and without any legal effect, for example, an illegal contract is void (see 1 : 8)

1 : 6   OBSERVING THE REQUIREMENTS OF THE CONTRACTS OF EMPLOYMENT ACT 1963 s4

Even though a legally binding contract of employment exists, the statutory requirements of the Contracts of Employment Act s4 must be satisfied. An employer is not allowed to evade the requirements of the Act by "contracting out" of it. An employee who does not receive the particulars as required may report this failure to an industrial tribunal, established under s12 of the Industrial Training Act 1964, which has power to fine the employer up to £20 for failure to comply.

An employer may be unable to enforce a contract of employment against an employee who has not been supplied with written particulars of his contract as required by the Act.

Grantham v Harford (1968)

A deed of apprenticeship was executed by Grantham, the employer, a female apprentice and her father, the defendant. Grantham refused to supply the defendant with a copy of the deed, nor was the apprentice herself given a reasonable opportunity to read it during the course of her employment. The employer sued for a breach of the apprenticeship agreement.

The court decided that the employer had failed to comply with s4 of the Contracts of Employment Act by not supplying the apprentice with a statement of the terms of her employment; consequently the contract was unenforceable against her.

1:6:1 *Every employee must be supplied with written particulars*

The employer must, within thirteen weeks after the beginning of an employee's period of employment, supply him with written particulars of his work, unless these are contained in a written contract of which the employee has a copy or reasonable access to a copy.

Trial periods of thirteen weeks or less are not covered by the Act, so that particulars need not be given if the employee is dismissed within thirteen weeks. But if employment continues beyond the trial period written particulars must be given immediately.

The particulars required by s4 are set out below. They are extremely important and should be carefully studied by all personnel managers delegated with the responsibility of complying with the Act. Details must be given of:

1   The name of the employer
2   The name of the employee
3   The date when the employment began
4   The rate of remuneration, or the method by which it is calculated
5   The intervals at which remuneration is paid—that is, weekly, monthly, quarterly, yearly etc.
6   Any terms and conditions relating to
    (a) Hours of work, including times of meal breaks and overtime
    (b) Holidays and holiday pay
    (c) Incapacity for work because of sickness, and provisions for sick pay if any
    (d) Pensions and pension schemes, except where pension rights are determined by a statutory provision which requires new employees to be informed of their rights
7   The length of notice which the employer must give, and which he is entitled to receive, when the contract of employment is terminated: if the contract is for a fixed term, a statement to that effect should appear giving the date on which the contract expires

It should be noted that if there are no particulars to be entered under any of the above-mentioned headings, this fact should be included in the statement of details.

1:6:2 Amendments by the Industrial Relations Act 1971

Every statement of particulars given to an employee under s4 must include:

1 Not only entitlement to holidays (including public holidays) and holiday pay, but sufficient particulars to enable the employee's entitlement to be precisely calculated, including any entitlement to accrued holiday pay on the termination of employment

2 The nature of the employee's rights as regards joining or refusing to join a union, and the effect on those rights of any agency shop agreement or an approved closed shop agreement, since the employee may be required to pay a sum equivalent to his union contribution to the trade union itself in lieu of membership, or to a charity

3 An indication of the person to whom the employee must apply to secure a redress of any grievance relating to his employment and the manner in which the application should be made; or reasonable access to a document explaining these matters

4 An explanation of the procedure available to an employee with a grievance in relation to the employment covered in the statement, or a reference to a reasonably accessible document explaining that procedure

After an employer has given his employee a written statement of particulars as required by s4 there may be a change of:

1 The name of an employer, but without any change of identity, where for example the name of a limited company is changed, or

2 The identity of an employer,

without causing any break in the continuity of the employee's period of employment. Where such changes do not involve any other change in the terms contained in the statement of particulars already given, then a further statement of particulars need not be given (Industrial Relations Act 1971 schedule 2).

1:6:3 Changes to the particulars given

The employer must provide his employee with a written statement of any change in the terms of service within one month of that change. Alternatively, the employee must be given a reasonable opportunity of reading about such changes during the course of his employment: for example, a notice could be posted or some other method adopted to make the information personally accessible to him. The original statement of the terms of employment, or the statement of a change, may indicate that future changes will be entered in a document which the employee has a reasonable opportunity of reading in the course of his employment. The document may, for example, be kept readily available in the personnel manager's office or the works manager's office.

If within six months after the termination of his employment the same employee begins another period of employment with the same employer, then it is unnecessary to give a statement of particulars of employment if they have remained unchanged.

The written statement given in compliance with s4 is neither a contract of employment nor conclusive evidence of the terms of the employment. The terms of the written contract will probably prevail if they differ from the particulars in the written statement.

1:6:4 Examples of written particulars

1   Dear Mr Robinson,

I confirm that your appointment as Company Secretary with the Associated Gramophone and Wireless Co Ltd began on 1 January 1972. Your salary is £2400 per annum, payable monthly at a rate of £200. You will be expected to observe the normal office hours, namely, 9 30 a.m.–12 30 p.m. and 1 30 p.m.–5 15 p.m. on Mondays to Fridays.

You will be entitled to the following public holidays with pay: Good Friday, Easter Monday, Spring Bank Holiday, Summer Bank Holiday, Christmas Day and Boxing Day. In addition you may take three weeks a year as annual leave, during which time your salary will be paid in full. Entitlement to annual leave is calculated at the rate of 1¼ days for every month's service with the company. If your employment is terminated before taking annual leave due, then one working day's salary will be paid for any day's leave that has not been taken.

Any grievance relating to your employment may be referred

to the Personnel Manager direct and he will arrange a private interview. If the Personnel Manager cannot remove the cause of your grievance, the matter may be referred to the Joint Managing Directors for consideration and further action, if any.

You are entitled to join or refrain from joining any trade union. If you become a trade union member you may take part in union activities and seek election to office, but such activities will not be allowed during working hours.

Full salary will be paid up to four weeks during any absence because of illness, provided a medical certificate is produced to cover such absences. Full details of the company's pension scheme are given in the booklet enclosed.

Determination of the contract of employment is subject to four weeks' notice on either side.

Yours sincerely,

J J Johnson

Personnel Manager

2   *Details of the terms and conditions of the contract of employment as required by the Contracts of Employment Act 1963*

Date of statement   1 January 1972

Employer   The Readyfix Gum Co Ltd

Employee   John Davies

Date of commencement of employment   30 November 1971

Rate of pay   50p per hour for a forty-hour week, eight hours daily from Monday to Friday. Wages are payable weekly. Overtime worked on a weekday, Monday to Friday, will be at the rate of time and a half, double time for work on Saturdays.

Hours of work   8 00 a.m.–12 00 noon. 1 00 p.m.–5 00 p.m. Any change will be posted on the notice boards throughout the offices and works.

Holidays and holiday pay   Employees are entitled to holidays with pay for ten working days, to be taken between 1 June and 30 September in any given year by arrangement. Entitlement will be calculated as follows: five-sixths of a day per month after fifteen months' employment with the company; two-thirds of a day for every full month's service for employees who have not completed fifteen months' service with the company. Employees terminating their employment before taking any annual leave to which they are entitled will receive payment of wages for each day's holiday not taken at the normal, current hourly rate for the normal, current hourly number of working hours a day.

Employees are also entitled to the following public holidays with pay: Good Friday, Easter Monday, Spring Bank Holiday, Summer Bank Holiday, Christmas Day and Boxing Day.

Sickness pay Payment is not made for time lost because of sickness.

Pension scheme At present, arrangements have not been made for a pension scheme.

Grievances relating to employment Trade union members should approach a union representative during working hours. The method agreed between the company and the trade union for investigating such grievances is set out on notice boards posted throughout the works. Non-union members should contact the Personnel Manager at his office, which is situated on the first floor of the main office block. He will investigate any alleged grievance with a view to securing its removal.

Trade union membership Employees may choose whether to join or refrain from joining a trade union. Since the Company has an agency shop agreement with the Allied and General Factory Workers' Union, an employee is required to become a member of that union within one month from the commencement of employment here. Employees not wishing to join the union must pay to the union a sum equivalent to the subscription payable by union members. An employee who objects to making such a payment to union funds may make a donation to charity instead. Full details of your rights in this respect are available from the Personnel Manager.

Trade union members may take part in union activities and seek election to office, if desired, but such activities will not be allowed during working hours.

Notice of termination of employment Unless the employment is terminated as a result of misbehaviour, an employee is entitled to the following periods of notice: one week's notice after thirteen weeks' continuous service, two weeks' notice after two years' employment, four weeks' after five years', six weeks' after ten years', and eight weeks' after fifteen years'. An employee must give one week's notice during the first two years of employment; after two years' service two weeks' notice is required.

Reference to some other document. A statement such as the above may under all or any individual headings merely refer the employee to some other document which he has a reasonable opportunity of reading in the course of his employment. An example is the booklet giving details of a pension scheme quoted in the first example.

1 : 6 : 5   *Employees outside the protection of the Act*

For the purpose of the Act, an employee is defined as a person working under a contract with an employer, whether it be a contract for manual labour, clerical work or apprenticeship. The Act does not apply to the following categories of employees:

1   Crown servants, that is, civil servants and members of the armed forces
2   Dock workers under the Dock Workers (Regulation of Employment) Act 1946, unless they are engaged on work other than dock work
3   Independent contractors
4   An apprentice under the Merchant Shipping Act 1894 s108
5   Skippers and seamen on fishing boats required to be registered under s373 of the Merchant Shipping Act 1894
6   Persons whose hours of employment are less than twenty-one hours a week
7   Employees engaged on work wholly or mainly outside Great Britain, unless they ordinarily work in Britain and the work outside Britain is for the same employer: a person employed in Northern Ireland will be outside Great Britain for this purpose
8   An employee who is the father, mother, husband, wife, son or daughter of the employer
9   A partner

The Act does cover the following categories of employees:

1   Employees of local authorities
2   Members of the police force
3   Employees of national corporations
4   Directors of a company
5   Apprentices

1:6:6   *Directors are usually employees for the purposes of the Act*

Not every person who is employed is within the protection of the Act, which applies to a contract of service, but not a contract for services. A partner cannot be employed by a partnership, since it is legally impossible to be employed under a contract of service with oneself and other partners. It does not affect the situation if a salary is paid for services rendered to the partnership business.

The Contracts of Employment Act 1963 does normally apply to a company director on the ground that he is an employee of the company, but the exact nature of his relationship with the company has to be determined by examining the facts in a particular situation. A working director will be deemed to be an employee of the company benefiting from his services. Mr Justice Cohen has stated the position as follows: "When I find a man who is bound to devote his whole time to the affairs of the company, to do all in his power to develop and extend the business of the company, not to engage in any other business, and who is engaged on terms that his employment may be determined by the company by notice in writing, I find it impossible to say that he is not employed by the company." This will cover the majority of the cases arising in practice.

On the other hand, if the director is also the controlling shareholder it may be held that he is not an employee of the company he controls. In Robinson v George Sorby Ltd (1966), a case concerned with redundancy payments, the industrial tribunal made the following decision: "Although we appreciate that a company is a separate legal entity, distinguishable from the shareholders and directors, all the applicant did was to give such services as he thought fit to the company to suit his purpose as being by far the largest shareholder and the person to whom nearly all the profits would go . . . as regards his being a servant of the company, we feel that there was no control by the company, he controlled himself . . . he was not working under a contract of service with the company."

1:6:7   *The right to inspect a director's service contract*

A company must keep a copy of every director's service contract or, alternatively, a written memorandum specifying the terms of his employment, together with a record of variations as they occur, at one of the following places:

1   The registered office of the company
2   The principal place of business
3   The place where the register of members is kept, if it is not kept at the registered office

The Registrar of Companies must be notified of the intention to keep the information at a place other than the registered office (s26 Companies Act 1967).

These records must be open to inspection by any member of the company for at least two hours during usual business hours. The company is not obliged to allow a copy to be made or notes to be taken, if they do not wish it. This duty of disclosure covers public and private limited companies and also unlimited companies. The company and every officer in default commits an offence, punishable with a fine of up to £500 plus £5 for every day the default continues by either:

1   Not allowing inspection, in which case the court may order immediate inspection to be made possible, or,
2   Not notifying the Registrar within fourteen days that the records are being kept at a place other than the registered office

These provisions do not have to be observed where the director's term of employment:

1   Has less than twelve months to run
2   Can be terminated within the next twelve months, if it is deemed desirable, without the existence of any legal obligation to pay him compensation for loss of office, other than redundancy money: this provision covers a director employed on terms whereby he may be given notice of less than twelve months

It is unnecessary to record:

1   Any change in an existing contract of employment if it has less than twelve months left to run, or,
2   A contract, or its changes, where the director is required to work wholly or mainly outside the United Kingdom

1:7 RECIPROCAL DUTIES BETWEEN EMPLOYER AND EMPLOYEE IMPLIED IN A CONTRACT OF EMPLOYMENT

The contract of employment may deal with the rights and duties of the parties in the express terms of the agreement. Where these rights and duties have not been clearly set out, or are not dealt with at all, then the relationship between the employer and employee will be based upon those terms that may be implied by law or custom, and the presumed intention of the parties.

The employee is under a duty to his employer:

1   To take care (see 9 : 3 : 1)
2   To show good faith and fidelity (see 2 : 10)
3   To work at such times as he may reasonably be required to work (see 13 : 5 : 5, National Coal Board v Galley)
4   To obey lawful instructions (see 13 : 4 : 2)
5   To conduct himself properly (see 13 : 4 : 7)
6   To account for money received in the course of his employment (see 10 : 4)

The employer is under a duty to his employee:

1   To provide a safe system of work (see Chapter 5)
2   To pay the remuneration agreed upon (see Chapter 3)
3   To provide work (see below)
4   To indemnify him against expenses and losses suffered in the course of his employment (see 9 : 6)
5   To retain him for the period agreed upon (see 13 : 1)
6   To pay redundancy money where appropriate (see Chapter 12)

1 : 7 : 1   *Employers have no general duty to provide work*
An employer does not commit any breach of the contract of employment if he refuses to supply his employee with any work, provided the salary agreed upon has been paid over. If the employee is dissatisfied with the situation he can terminate the contract by giving notice.

Turner v Sawdon and Co (1901, Court of Appeal)

Turner was engaged by the defendant company to act as a salesman for a period of four years, at an agreed salary. He brought an action for an alleged breach of contract when they stopped supplying him with work, though his salary was still being paid.

The court decided that if the employer is willing to pay an employee's salary, he is not under any obligation to provide work, even though the employee is thereby prevented from acquiring experience and practice in his chosen occupation.

1:7:2 Employer's duty to supply piecework

An employer must supply his employees with a reasonable amount of work, where their wages are determined by reference to the amount of work completed.

Devonald v Rosser & Sons (1906, Court of Appeal)

Devonald was employed by Rosser & Sons at their tinplate factory on a piecework basis. The defendants closed their factory because of adverse trading conditions, and two weeks later they gave Devonald a month's notice, as required by the contract of employment. Devonald contended that his employers were bound by an implied term to provide work during this six-week period, and he claimed damages for the wages that he would have earned during that period if work had been provided.

The court decided that there is no distinction in principle between wages calculated by reference to time and wages calculated by reference to piece. Piecework is only a method of ascertaining the amount of wages payable to the employee. The necessary implication to be drawn from this contract is that the employer will provide a reasonable amount of work up until the time when the period of notice expires. The measure of what was reasonable could be determined by reference to the average amount of the plaintiff's earnings before the stoppage of the works. There is not an absolute obligation to find work in all events, where for example there is a breakdown of machinery or a lack of materials. But it is not a sufficient excuse for the employer to show that he could not produce his goods at a profit, either for the fulfilment of orders received or for stockpiling.

1:7:3 Employees receiving a
commission must be given the opportunity of earning it

If an employee under a contract of service is paid solely by commission, which is intended to replace his salary, there may be an express term, or alternatively an implied obligation, that his employer will give him the chance of earning that commission. The contract cannot be determined prematurely without payment of compensation to the employee.

Turner v Goldsmith (1891, Court of Appeal)

Turner was employed for a period of five years as agent, canvasser and traveller, to sell various goods manufactured or sold by Goldsmith, a shirt manufacturer. Goldsmith's factory was destroyed by fire two years later and he did not resume business.

The court decided that Turner was entitled to claim damages for breach of contract, since there was a definite agreement to employ him for a fixed period of five years. "On the face of the agreement, there is no reference to place of business and no condition as to the defendant's continuing to manufacture or sell." (Lord Justice Lindley)

An employee may be required to work almost exclusively for one employer, at a salary that is paid mainly on a commission basis for work completed. In such cases there is an implied obligation that the employee will be supplied with sufficient work to enable him to earn whatever salary the parties to the contract of employment contemplated, though they failed to specify a definite sum.

Bauman v Hulton Press Ltd (1952)

Bauman, a colour photographer, employed by the defendant company, was paid a fixed weekly retaining fee of £10, and also a fee at a fixed rate for any work completed. He promised:

1   Not to work for any British weekly periodical other than *Picture Post*, a magazine published by the defendants
2   To be available at all reasonable times to carry out different commissions
3   To give his employers a first option on all his ideas

He sued for wrongful dismissal when the defendants terminated the agreement at a fortnight's notice, and discontinued payment of the retaining fee after two weeks.

The court decided that a contract of service existed under which the employee was to be paid, partly by way of salary and partly at fixed rates, for any work actually carried out for the defendants. To give business efficacy to this contract of employment, there was no difficulty in implying a term that the employers were bound to supply Bauman with a reasonable amount of work, to enable him to earn whatever sum the parties contemplated, throughout the duration of the contract. On that basis Bauman was entitled to damages for loss of salary and remuneration.

The contract was terminable on reasonable notice, which was deemed to be six months in this case. Damages were awarded for loss of the retainer, loss of remuneration for work that would have been done, and loss in respect of work completed that would not now be accepted.

If the so-called contract of employment is in essence an agreement between an agent and a principal, without any element of service or subordination, with the agent being allowed to work for other principals at the same time, then usually there is no obligation on the principal to supply the agent with the means of earning his commission.

Rhodes v Forwood (1876, House of Lords)

Forwood was appointed the sole selling agent of coal produced at Rhodes' colliery for seven years. The contract was determinable by Forwood if Rhodes failed to supply 75 000 tons of coal in any year, while Rhodes could terminate the agreement if Forwood did not sell 50 000 tons in any year. Rhodes sold his colliery after the contract had been in existence for four years.

The court decided that Forwood was not entitled to damages against Rhodes for breach of contract, since there was no term in the contract implying that the colliery would not be sold within the seven-year period. "The parties seem to me to have entered into a simple contract of agency which necessarily determines when the subject-matter of the agency is gone . . . the contract is brought to an end by the course of events . . . by that happening which might necessarily have been expected to happen, and which would have the effect of putting an end to the contract." (Lord Hatherley)

1:7:4 Payment of wages while
work premises are closed for essential repairs

If the employer has to close down his work premises to facilitate the completion of essential repairs to make them safe, there is no term in the contract of employment which implies that he will be liable to his employees for non-provision of work during the period which causes a loss of wages.

Browning v Crumlin Valley Collieries Ltd (1926)

Without any fault on the part of the defendants their mine became unsafe, and it was necessary to close it down while repairs were carried out. The employees affected claimed payment of their wages during this period, alleging an implied term in the contract of employment, by which the employers were obliged to provide work to enable wages to be earned.

The court decided that it was not intended by either party to the contract of employment that the employers should be responsible for all the loss attributable to the operation of natural forces that caused the mine to become unsafe. Consequently, the loss should be divided between the parties. The employees were entitled to withhold their labour under these circumstances, but subject to the condition that they should not be entitled to their wages.

A situation of this type may not be conducive to good labour relations, but in the absence of an express contractual term protecting the employee against loss of wages during the period of repairs to work premises, he is not entitled to relief.

1:7:5 Where publicity is
important to an employee work must be provided
The employee may be entitled to publicity for his work: some employees, such as actors, dancers, singers or writers, depend very much on publicity. Thus the employer must supply the work promised by the terms of the contract which will bring with it the publicity required.

Herbert Clayton & Jack Waller v Oliver (1930, House of Lords)

Oliver was engaged to play a leading part in one of the appellant's productions, and when he was offered only a minor role instead he refused to accept it.

The court decided that Oliver was entitled to damages for breach of contract, since, as a result of being deprived of the part stipulated in the contract, the opportunities of enhancing his reputation were reduced.

1:7:6 Employers may be
contractually bound to retain employees in a specified post
An employee may claim damages for breach of contract if the particular post to which he was appointed is abolished in cases where the employer is obliged by the contractual terms to retain the employee in that post.

Collier v Sunday Referee Publishing Co Ltd (1940)

Collier was engaged by the defendant company as the chief sub-editor of the Sunday Referee for a two-year period. The newspaper was sold to another publishing company which abolished Collier's position, though payment of his salary continued until he failed to report for work, which action the defendants regarded as a repudiation of the contract of employment. Collier sued for damages for a breach of contract.

The court decided that Collier had not been engaged to carry out the type of work usually executed by a chief sub-editor, he had been appointed to this position in respect of a particular newspaper. By disposing of this paper, the defendant committed a breach of contract, entitling Collier to claim damages for the destruction of the office to which he was appointed. The salary payments already received by him were accepted on account of those damages, not as a waiver of the defendants' breach of contract.

1:8 POSITION OF THE EMPLOYER WHERE THE CONTRACT OF EMPLOYMENT CONTAINS ILLEGAL TERMS

If a contract of employment has for one of its objects an illegal purpose, neither party to that contract can enforce it by legal action, subject to the exceptions noted below, for this would be contrary to public policy. Acts contrary to public policy have a mischievous tendency, being injurious to the interests of the state or the community. Illegal contracts may be divided into three groups, those which are illegal at the time of their formation, those which are lawful but are performed in an illegal manner, and those void on grounds of public policy.

1:8:1 *Contracts illegal at the time of formation*

Use of the word "illegal" in this context does not mean that a criminal offence has necessarily been committed, but some degree of moral wrong or the violation of a statute is involved. For example, it is contrary to public policy to permit the employer to contract out of those duties imposed on him by a statute, such as the Factories Act 1961 which secures the safety of his employees.

If both parties realise that the contract of employment involves violating the laws of a foreign friendly state, it is not enforceable, even though the acts in question would be legal if they were committed in this country where the contract was negotiated.

Foster v Driscoll (1929, Court of Appeal)

Agreements were concluded with the object of smuggling whisky into the USA, contrary to their prohibition laws. One party sued the other for payment in respect of these undertakings, and the court decided that the contract was against public policy and void.

To assist the employee in avoiding payment of tax due to the Inland Revenue, the employer may support a false claim by the employee in relation to the expenses incurred in connection with his job. Where such an arrangement is contained in a contract of employment the whole agreement will be illegal, consequently neither party can enforce even the legal terms of the contract against the other.

Napier v National Business Agency Ltd (1951, Court of Appeal)

Napier was employed by the defendants at a salary of £13 weekly from which tax was deducted, plus £6 weekly for expenses from which tax was not deducted. Both parties knew that expenses rarely exceeded £1 weekly. The court decided that the agreement was illegal. Consequently, Napier's action against his employer for wages of £13 in lieu of notice, though in itself perfectly legal, failed on the ground that the whole agreement was tainted with illegality.

1:8:2   *Consequences of contracts illegal at the time of formation*
If a contract cannot be lawfully performed it is void and neither party can claim any right in respect of it. Where an illegal contract is concluded, like the agreement in Napier v National Business Agency Ltd, then if the employer has paid wages in advance he cannot recover the money if the work is not completed, and the decision in that case clearly shows that the employee cannot recover salary arrears otherwise due to him. The principle applicable in such a situation is that where both parties are equally in the wrong the possessor of the property has the right to retain it.

Where the parties are not equally in the wrong, the less guilty party may recover what is due to him, provided he can establish that the party in possession committed a fraud or abused a position of trust. For example, if the object of a statute is to protect the employee's interests he may recover property or money improperly in the possession of his employer in violation of the statutory enactment. An employee may agree in his contract of employment to receive a portion of his wages in some form other than current coin of the realm, such as goods sold to him by the employer. This agreement may be illegal and void as contravening the Truck Acts; consequently the employee can recover the sum not yet paid in current coin of the realm.

If a person is employed to violate either the laws of a friendly nation, as in Foster v Driscoll (see 1:8:1), or a trade embargo imposed by this country against another, and his employer hands over property so that the illegal purpose can be put into operation but then repents before the illegal purpose has been fully performed, the employer may recover the property he handed over, provided the repentance is genuine and voluntary. It does not suffice if the claimant has merely been prevented from completing the wrongful purpose by the intervention of a third party, such as the police, or by a change in circumstances such as the repeal of the prohibition law or lifting of the trade embargo.

1:8:3   *Lawful contracts performed in an illegal manner*
Although a contract of employment appears to be legal, one party may perform part of it in an illegal manner. The party committing the illegality cannot sue the other party for any breach of contract that may be committed, though the breach is unconnected with the illegality, nor can property handed over in pursuance of the contract be recovered. In this situation the innocent party can sue for money earned but not yet paid. For example, if an accountant refuses to accede to his employer's request to make false returns to the tax inspector, he can recover salary earned until the time of leaving the employment. The employer, on the other hand, cannot sue his accountant for any breach of the contract of employment unconnected with the illegal purpose: if, for example, he refuses to work overtime as agreed upon in his contract. Further, if wages have been paid in advance they are irrecoverable, though the employee refuses to work for the period covered by the advance payment.

The doctrine of severance discussed below (1:8:5) does not apply to the illegal contracts referred to under this heading.

1:8:4   *Contracts void on grounds of public policy*
The group of contracts to be discussed under this heading are often referred to as being illegal, but this description is not always appropriate. It is better to regard them as void contracts. The most important contract of this type is the contract in restraint of trade (see Chapter 2).

A contract of employment must not include restraints upon the liberty of the employee as an individual. "The law of England allows a man to contract for his labour or allows him to place himself in the service of a master, but it does not allow him to attach to his contract of employment any servile incidents" (Lord Justice Bowen). This principle prevents a contract of service from being assigned.

51

A party to a contract may be allowed in some cases to transfer the benefits to which he is entitled under the agreement to another person. A contract for personal services is not assignable in this way, since it would have the effect of altering the burden imposed on the employee.

Nokes v Doncaster Amalgamated Collieries Ltd (1940, House of Lords)

Nokes was employed as a miner by the Hickleton Main Colliery Co Ltd. That company was dissolved and its assets were transferred to Doncaster Amalgamated Collieries Ltd. Nokes, who was unaware of the change, was charged with wrongfully absenting himself from work contrary to s4 of the Employers and Workmen Act 1875.

The House of Lords decided that Nokes had not committed a breach of contract, since the transfer of assets from one company to another did not include an assignment of the employees' contracts of service.

Lord Atkin said, "I had fancied that ingrained in the personal status of a citizen under our laws was the right to choose for himself whom he would serve, and that this right of choice constituted the main difference between a servant and a serf."

Very often one company loses its separate legal identity and becomes the subsidiary of another company that buys a controlling interest in the shareholdings. The existing directors of the subsidiary are usually replaced by nominees of the parent company. In this case an employee is obliged to continue working under the terms of his contract of service with the subsidiary. If he is dissatisfied with his position because of the policies of the new management, notice may be given in accordance with the contractual terms: if he has a long-term contract, his freedom to do this is, of course, more effectively curtailed.

An employee may assign to another person, usually a creditor, the right to receive the salary payable by his employer, unless it deprives the employee of all means of support. It is not considered to be in the public interest that the salary of a public officer, such as a judge or clerk of the peace, should be so assigned, for the salary is deemed necessary to uphold the dignity and ensure the performance of the duties of the office held. The restriction applies to the salaries of officials payable from national but not local funds.

An agreement is void whereby an employee who borrows money promises the lender in return that he will not terminate his present contract of employment with his employer, unless the lender consents to such action.

Horwood v Millar's Timber Trading Co Ltd (1917, Court of Appeal)

Horwood lent money to Bunyan in return for his promise:

1   To assign the salary due or becoming due to him by virtue of his employment with the defendants or any other employer, and
2   Not to leave his present employment without Horwood's permission or do anything to get himself dismissed

The court decided that the contract of loan was illegal and unenforceable as being contrary to public policy, and therefore Horwood could not recover from the employer the salary so assigned. The part of the contract dealing with assignment of the salary, which was legal, could not be severed from the terms restricting the employee's freedom to leave his present employment, which was void.

1 : 8 : 5   *Severing the good parts of contracts of employment from the bad*
If a contract is void on grounds of public policy it is impossible to sever the bad clauses and then uphold the good clauses, unless the consideration for the contract is not an entire consideration, but is split into separate parts one of which can be allocated to the good clauses and the other to the bad clauses. In Horwood's case, Bunyan's two promises were supported by one entire consideration, the loan made to him, and thus severance was not possible. There is a general reluctance to allow severance at all in respect of illegal contracts, thus doubtful terms of this nature should be omitted. The doctrine of severance is discussed more fully in relation to contracts in restraint of trade (see 2 : 8).

1 : 9   EMPLOYING PEOPLE UNDER EIGHTEEN

A person attains majority and has full contractual capacity, that is the power to make an agreement which is binding in law, at the first moment of his or her eighteenth birthday (Family Law Reform Act 1969). A reference to a "minor" or an "infant" means a person under the age of eighteen.

1:9:1 Contracts binding on a minor

Although a minor is subject to certain contractual disabilities, all contracts for the instruction (that is, apprenticeship) or employment of a minor are enforceable against him on the ground that it is essential to allow him to earn his livelihood, provided such contracts are for his benefit. The burden of proving that the contract as a whole benefits the minor lies on the party alleging it, usually the employer, but as in any other contract there will be stipulations that benefit the employer, as well as stipulations that benefit the minor. Consequently, it is not necessary to establish that every single term of the contract benefits the minor. The contract should contain only clauses that are usual and customary in the type of employment undertaken.

In the absence of any unfair terms that are detrimental to the minor's interest, the employer may safely engage a minor and expect to pursue the normal contractual remedies against him if the terms of the employment are broken. The element of give and take that may be present in a minor's contract of employment without making it invalid is well illustrated in the next case.

Clements v L & N W Railway (1894, Court of Appeal)

Clements, a minor employed as a porter by the defendant company, agreed in his contract of employment to join the company's insurance scheme and forfeit his rights under the Employers' Liability Act 1880. The company's scheme covered more injuries than the statutory one, but the scale of compensation was lower. It was also agreed that disputes between employer and employee should be referred to arbitration. Clements was injured in the course of his employment and sued to recover damages from the defendants.

The court decided that the contract was binding on Clements, since taken as a whole it was advantageous to him. He was bound by the clause prohibiting proceedings in an ordinary court of law. There should instead have been a reference to arbitration, as agreed upon.

1:9:2 Contracts not binding on a minor

A contract of employment which is not beneficial to a minor is voidable at his option. This means that the minor can either regard the contract as binding, in which case the employer must observe his part of the bargain, or rescind it during minority or within a reasonable time after attaining majority. What length of time is considered to be "reasonable" depends upon the circumstances of each case. The minor will be in a position to terminate his employment without giving the length of notice to his employer required under the contract of employment.

1:9:3 *Rejecting an unreasonable term and upholding the rest*

It is impossible to frame a contract of employment between employer and a minor "in which some of the stipulations are not in favour of one and some in favour of the other. But if we find a stipulation . . . which is of such a kind that it makes the whole contract an unfair one, then that makes the whole contract void." (Lord Esher)

If one term in the minor's contract of employment is detrimental to his interests but the rest is perfectly fair, then the unreasonable term can be severed from the contract and the other terms enforced by either party against the other.

Bromley v Smith (1909)

Bromley, a baker, engaged Smith, a minor, to deliver bread. The contract of employment provided that Smith would not be engaged in the business of miller, baker, hay, straw or corn merchant or restaurant keeper for three years after leaving Bromley's employment. Bromley hoped to open a restaurant at some time in the future. Smith left Bromley's employment and traded in competition as a baker and confectioner some three miles away. He also canvassed some of Bromley's customers.

The court decided that since Bromley was not a restaurater, the stipulation in restraint of trade was wider than necessary to protect his business, even though he hoped eventually to extend his activities in this direction. This part of the restraint clause was severable from the rest however, since each prohibited trade was stated separately. With the offending part of the clause removed Smith was bound by the remaining restraints since he would not have been able to secure employment on better terms. It was for his benefit to be employed on those terms and also quite fair that he should forgo the right of soliciting customers whom he would never have known but for his previous employment with Bromley.

1:9:4 *Contracts of employment not yet performed*

A binding beneficial contract of employment or apprenticeship may exist between an employer and a minor, but performance of that agreement may not yet have been undertaken by the minor (an executory contract) for example, where the date of commencement of employment has not arrived. The employer is entitled to sue the minor for damages for breach of contract if he refuses to carry out its terms.

Roberts v Gray (1913, Court of Appeal)

Gray, who wished to become a professional billiards player, agreed to undertake a world tour with a leading professional, Roberts, in the course of which they would compete against one another in matches. After Roberts had organised the tour, the parties disagreed on the type of billiard balls to be used and Gray repudiated the contract.

The court decided that Roberts was entitled to £1500 damages for Gray's breach of a beneficial contract of employment, since in essence it was an agreement for teaching and education from which the minor would benefit by association with an established professional.

1:10 CONTRACTS OF APPRENTICESHIP

An understanding of the legal effects of the relationship of an employer and his apprentice may be as important to the personnel manager as a working knowledge of the legal consequences of the employer–employee relationship. The more important aspects of the relationship will be discussed in this section.

The essential elements of a valid contract must be present in a contract of apprenticeship, namely, offer and acceptance; consideration; capacity; legality and intention to create legal relations. The contract will be one of apprenticeship where teaching is the primary purpose, even if it contains an element of service and both parties are adults. In many cases it is a condition of the contract that the apprentice shall undertake some course of further education, either in the employer's time, or the employee's own time, or both. Conversely, where work is the primary object it is a contract of employment, though some teaching will be provided for the employee's benefit. The difference between the two types of contract should be clearly appreciated since the legal consequences vary according to the type of contract in issue in a given situation.

In determining whether a contract is one of apprenticeship or employment, the general intention of the parties will be considered, but the presence of terms like "master" and "apprentice" do not necessarily make a contract one of apprenticeship. A clear statement in the contract that it is intended to be one of employment or apprenticeship is advisable. In fact, many employers have a written contract readily available, embodying those terms deemed important in this type of agreement. Reference to a contract in the remainder of this section is a reference to a contract of apprenticeship.

1:10:1 *Consent of the apprentice*
The apprentice must genuinely consent to the contract, even if he is a minor, and anything in the nature of undue influence will make the agreement voidable at the option of the minor. It is essential therefore that the apprentice should be a party to the contract, so that the employer has an additional remedy if the contractual terms are broken. The apprentice's parent or guardian is often joined as a further party to:

1   Guarantee due performance of the agreement by the apprentice, and
2   Indemnify the employer against all losses and damage suffered because of the apprentice's misconduct (see 1 : 10 : 5)

1:10:2 *Form of the apprenticeship contract*
The contract must be in writing and signed by the apprentice, but a deed is not essential. A properly authorised person, such as a personnel manager, may sign on behalf of a limited company undertaking the responsibilities of acting as an employer (Companies Act 1948 s32).

An oral contract will not be enforced in any circumstances. An improperly executed written agreement is enforceable, if it has been acted upon by the parties on the understanding that it is valid.

McDonald v John Twiname Ltd (1953, Court of Appeal)

McDonald, aged fifteen, was apprenticed to the defendant company, but a deed was not executed by the boy and his father, until some time later. The company added its name to the deed by means of a rubber stamp, but never executed it in the required manner. Eventually the company forwarded a copy of the agreement to the Ministry of Labour, to enable McDonald to defer his call-up for national service until completion of his apprenticeship. When McDonald was later dismissed for misconduct, he sued for damages alleging a breach of the apprenticeship agreement.

The court decided that the company was bound by a contract of apprenticeship with McDonald, though it was never formally executed in the required form, since it had been affirmed by taking the benefit of Mc-

Donald's services and sending a copy of the agreement to the Ministry of Labour.

1:10:3 *Termination or suspension of the apprenticeship contract*

The employer may wish to be relieved of his obligations under the contract if the agreement becomes disadvantageous, where, for example, the apprentice is not making satisfactory progress or misconducts himself. Conversely, there may be circumstances when the employer will wish the apprenticeship to remain unaffected, though events have taken an unexpected turn: for example, where the firm is dissolved and a new one constituted in its place. These contingencies must be carefully considered, so that appropriate clauses may be drafted for inclusion in the contract, making whatever provision is required.

Death and illness. The death of either employer or apprentice terminates the contract, unless the apprentice has expressly agreed in the contract to serve the employer's personal representatives. The illness of the apprentice may be used by the employer as a means of discharging the contract. For example, an express term of the agreement may provide that if the apprentice is absent from work because of sickness or injury for a continuous period of twenty-six weeks or more, then the employer will be entitled to terminate the apprenticeship, by notice in writing to the apprentice and the guardian.

Bankruptcy of the employer. In these circumstances either employer or apprentice may give written notice to the trustee in bankruptcy discharging the apprenticeship, though the contract may be transferred to some other employer.

Change in the firm's composition. Dissolution of a partnership, whether caused by the death, resignation or retirement of a partner, terminates the contract. But if a new firm is formed, the contract may be continued by that firm, especially if the change in composition of the partners is a formality as far as the apprentice is concerned. The apprentice cannot be forced to serve the new partnership, unless a term in the contract makes express provision to that effect.

A dissolution may amount to a breach of the contract for which damages are recoverable by the apprentice, for example, for loss of wages and postponement of the opportunity to qualify for the trade or profession concerned.

Change in the place of business. The contract is subject to an implied term that the apprentice shall be required to work only at his employer's place of business as at the date of executing the agreement. He cannot be required to work at any other place to which the business is transferred at a later date, unless an express term of the contract provides to the contrary. Sometimes there is an express provision whereby the apprentice is expected to work away from the usual place of business, but only for short periods of time.

Change in the character of the firm. Any change in the fundamental character of the employer's business releases the apprentice from his contract, if the employer is thereby prevented from giving instruction, in accordance with the terms of the agreement, in those aspects of the business that have been discontinued. An express clause may provide that inability to provide work or instruction, because the concern or a section of the concern is closed down for a period of time, will cause the apprenticeship agreement to be suspended, without liability on the employer to make any wage payments to the apprentice. The apprentice is usually allowed to terminate the contract if work or instruction is not provided for a stipulated period of time, for example, two months out of a twelve-month period.

Misconduct. As a general rule the employer cannot dismiss his apprentice for misconduct, unless power to do so has been expressly reserved in the contract. There are cases, however, where contracts of apprenticeship have been discharged, even in the absence of an express power to do so; for example, where the apprentice:

1 Misbehaved and made teaching impossible
2 Was a habitual thief and the nature of the apprenticeship gave him access to valuable property (see 13:4:6, Learoyd v Brook)
3 Was a danger to the community, as in the case of an apprentice to a chemist who was too drunk to dispense medicine

The concept of misconduct may be extended by the express terms of the contract to cover misbehaviour of many varied kinds, including:

1 Wilful disobedience of lawful orders
2 Wilful neglect of studies connected with the apprenticeship
3 Failure to make satisfactory progress in learning his trade

59

There are significant differences between the status of the apprentice and the employee in relation to acts of insubordination. Insubordination, even if it embarrasses staff as well as management, does not justify summary dismissal of the apprentice, though it would suffice in the case of an employee. Even if the employer reserves the right in the contract to dismiss his apprentice for misconduct, a more lenient view is taken of the apprentice's conduct than of the employee's.

Newell v Gillingham Corporation (1941)

Newell, a minor, apprenticed to the defendants for five years, registered as a conscientious objector during the last war. His attitude towards the efforts of this country in the war and his pro-German, defeatist views were likely to irritate fellow workers and lead to loss of working time. The deed of apprenticeship enabled the corporation to dismiss Newell for disobedience, neglect or other gross misbehaviour.

The court held that while the plaintiff's conduct might justify the dismissal of an adult from employment, it did not entitle the defendants to terminate the contract of apprenticeship.

1:10:4   Minor's right to rescind a contract of apprenticeship

An infant apprentice may rescind a contract if it is not substantially for his benefit, where, for example, it includes unfair terms such as the following:

1   That wages will not be paid during a strike, though the apprentice may work elsewhere in the meantime
2   That wages or maintenance are not to be paid
3   That the infant makes himself liable to pay a penalty
4   That the employer exempts himself from liability for negligence

An infant may also rescind the contract on attaining his majority or within a reasonable time thereafter, what is "reasonable" depending upon the circumstances of the individual case. The employer is entitled to notice of intention to rescind and the length of such notice must again be reasonable. Any person guaranteeing performance of the contract is bound by all the promises embodied in it, even though the apprentice renounces the agreement on attaining majority. The apprentice may be given the right to terminate the contract if for some reason, such as lack of work or industrial unrest, the employer requires him to work a given number of shortened weeks within a stipulated period—for example, twenty weeks in a period of one year.

1:10:5 *Employer's remedies for his apprentice's breach of contract*
The employer cannot sue his infant apprentice for damages in respect of any breach of contract, but an action can be maintained against the other party to the contract, that is the parent or guardian, who guaranteed due performance of the agreement by the apprentice. In such cases, the employer is entitled to damages based upon loss suffered as a result of the apprentice's refusal to serve up until the time when the action is brought. Damages will not be awarded in respect of the time between the beginning of the action and the end of the contract of aprenticeship. "The apprentice may come back tomorrow; and the master cannot therefore recover . . . damages beyond the time of the action." (Mr Justice Byles)

When the apprentice attains majority he is fully liable on the contract in the normal way.

Gadd v Thompson (1911)

The infant defendant bound himself by deed as an apprentice to the plaintiff architect for a period of four years. The defendant promised that after termination of the apprenticeship he would not compete with the plaintiff for ten years within a radius of ten miles of the town where the architect resided. There was evidence to show that other architects in the area would insist on a similar promise from an apprentice.

The court decided that the promise was reasonable in the circumstances and could be enforced against the defendant by an injunction, though it was made while he was still an infant.

Neither party to the contract can specifically enforce its terms against the other. Lord Justice Fry said in De Francesco v Barnum (1890), "I should be very unwilling to extend decisions . . . the effect of which is to compel persons who are not desirous of maintaining continuous personal relations with one another to continue those personal relations . . . It is not in the interests of mankind that the rule of specific performance should be extended to such cases."

1:10:6 *Apprentice's remedies against his employer*
An employer wrongfully dismissing his apprentice may be sued for dam-

ages to compensate the apprentice for the loss suffered, up until the beginning of the action. If the apprentice absents himself from work or otherwise makes instruction impossible, the employer may use such conduct as a defence, if sued by the apprentice for failure to teach him properly in accordance with the contract.

Dunk v George Waller & Son Ltd (1970, Court of Appeal)

Dunk, aged 18, entered into an apprenticeship for four years with the defendant company, to be trained as an engineering technician. The defendant employer terminated the contract, fifteen months before the date fixed for its expiration, on grounds of lack of initiative and a report from a local technical college that Dunk was unlikely to pass the required examination. After being unemployed for fifty-seven weeks, Dunk secured unskilled work and earned more than he would have done had he remained an apprentice. He claimed damages for a breach of the apprenticeship agreement.

The court decided that Dunk was entitled to damages totalling £500. This reflected his short-term losses caused by unemployment, calculated as £10 a week for fifty-seven weeks, less £270 unemployment benefit received. A further £20 was added for the expense of trying to find employment. He had also lost that status in the labour market that he could have secured by completing his apprenticeship with an established employer. It was difficult for the court to assess the loss of long-term future prospects, but an award of £180 was made.

1:11 RACE RELATIONS ACT 1968

Generally speaking, an employer is free to contract with any person he chooses by way of offering employment. Total freedom would allow discrimination that is socially unacceptable; consequently the Race Relations Act 1968 contains many important provisions, of vital significance to the employer, preventing such conduct.

1:11:1 Advertising a vacancy and offering employment

When advertising a vacant position, it is unlawful to include any wording indicating that it will not be open to stated groups of persons on grounds of their "colour, race, national or ethnic origins"—for example, "coloureds need not apply." Much of the discrimination encountered is connected with colour, and the Act's main object is the prevention of this. Many of the examples in this section refer to this type of discrimination, but the broader scope of the law should be remembered.

It is also unlawful to discriminate on the grounds set out when offering employment to an applicant, provided he possesses the necessary qualifications for the job. If several people apply, including a coloured person, and all possess similar qualifications, the Act is not violated if a white applicant is engaged. On the other hand, if there are more vacancies than applicants, refusal to employ a coloured applicant, on the face of it qualified for the post, must be justified by sound reasons, as for example that he will be unable to control his subordinates or that he lacks the requisite practical experience.

If an employee such as a personnel officer discriminates when interviewing, the employer is still liable, unless he has taken reasonably practical steps to prevent such conduct. The personnel officer himself is also regarded as acting contrary to the Act.

1:11:2 Promotion; working conditions; dismissal

There are similar protections in respect of promotion. It has been alleged that coloured transport workers are rarely promoted to the rank of inspector. If a coloured employee is the obvious candidate for promotion by reasons of his qualifications, experience and personal characteristics, the Act may be invoked as a protection.

The same terms of employment (that is, hours, wages and the like) and conditions of work must be offered to the groups covered by the Act as are offered to other workers acting in the same capacity. The term "discrimination" denotes treatment less favourable than that given to other persons. Separate but equal treatment counts as less favourable treatment. Examples would be different toilets or canteen facilities for different racial groups, if they are sited or labelled in a way that enforces segregation. It is obviously sensible to provide Asian-style lavatories if they are required, but they should be in the same place as other lavatories—a notice saying "Europeans only" would be unlawful. Similarly provision of alternative menus in one canteen is a good idea, but not two separate canteens.

It is unlawful to discriminate when dismissing workers, by making redundant all coloured workers before other employees engaged on the same job, where all such workers are equally well qualified.

1:11:3 Justifiable refusal to employ an immigrant

Discrimination is lawful if done in good faith to secure a reasonable balance between different racial groups. Thus an employer with a labour force of a hundred, may decide not to engage more Pakistanis if he already has twenty-five such employees. No fixed proportion is laid down: each case must be considered on its own merits. The purpose of this provision is to promote integration, which may be hindered if certain types of employment became recognised as immigrant jobs. The protection of this provision is not available to an employer unless a substantial proportion of immigrants are employed in the particular section of the workforce in question. Thus, an employer cannot refuse to take a coloured accountant into his wages office, which comprises all white employees, on the ground that a substantial number of unskilled coloured workers are engaged on the factory's night shift.

It must be appreciated that second-generation immigrants are to be regarded as Englishmen, for the basic issue here is that of language and culture which should present an integration problem only in respect of the first-generation immigrant.

1:11:4 Discrimination not covered by the Act
Discrimination on grounds of religion, language or length of residence in this country are lawful, covering such groups as Jews and Sikhs, since they are not primarily ethnic or racial. Conciliation committees will, however, be wary of ostensible religious discrimination which in reality is motivated by racial prejudice.

It is also lawful to employ only persons of a particular nationality if they possess special qualities essential to that employment, for example, usually only Indian chefs and waiters will be engaged in an Indian restaurant.

1:11:5 Enforcement of the law on race relations
Complaints must be made by the person aggrieved within two months of the event in question to either an employment exchange, the Race Relations Board in London or a local conciliation committee. A person may complain on behalf of the aggrieved party with written authorisation from the latter. The Race Relations Board will refer complaints concerning employment to the Secretary of State for Employment. The alleged discrimination will be dealt with through the mechanism of any suitable negotiating machinery that exists, but if the complaint cannot be settled by such means, the Race Relations Board will take up the issue. In the absence of any negotiating machinery, a conciliation committee will make an investigation. Where an apparently genuine complaint exists, the employer will be persuaded to remove the cause of it and give a satis-

factory written assurance that the incident will not be repeated. If conciliation fails, then county court proceedings may be taken for an injunction to restrain continuance of the discrimination or damages for loss suffered or both. Any discriminatory terms in a contract of employment may be removed leaving the rest of the agreement valid and enforceable.

1:11:6 *Unfair dismissal and unfair industrial practices*

Some of the provisions in the Industrial Relations Act 1971 are basically similar in their scope to provisions in the Race Relations Act 1968. A complaint may be made to an industrial tribunal under s106 of the Industrial Relations Act complaining of either:

1   Unfair dismissal contrary to s22, or
2   An unfair industrial practice by an employer relating to an employee's right to join or refrain from joining a trade union, or take part in its activities

by reason of the complainant's colour, race, ethnic or national origins (s149(1)).

The Secretary of State or the Race Relations Board may act in order to secure a written assurance against a repetition of that action and to deal with breaches of that assurance (s149(2)).

1:12 DISTINCTION BETWEEN CONTRACTS OF SERVICE AND CONTRACTS FOR SERVICES

It is important for many varied purposes to distinguish between a contract of service, which is employment of an employee, and a contract for services, whereby an independent contractor is engaged to do certain work.

Salmond defines an employee as "an agent who works under the supervision and direction of his employer; an independent contractor is one who is his own master. [An employee] is a person engaged to obey his [employer's] orders from time to time; an independent contractor is a person engaged to do certain work, but to exercise his own discretion as to the mode and time of doing it—he is bound by his contract, but not by his [employer's] orders."

The intentions of the parties in this respect may be expressly stated, but the court does not allow the language used to be conclusive either way.

The substance of the agreement must be examined carefully before a decision is reached.

1:12:1 *Why it is important to make the distinction*

Tortious liability lies against both the employer and the employee, jointly and severally, where the employee's negligent conduct during the course of his employment causes injury to some other person (see Chapter 9). If an independent contractor is at fault in similar circumstances, an action does not usually lie against the employer, but only against the independent contractor responsible, subject to some exceptions (see 9 : 4).

Under the National Insurance Act 1965, persons between the age of fifteen and sixty-five (sixty in the case of women) must be insured. There are three classes and the difference between the first, covering employed persons, and the second covering self-employed persons or independent contractors, depends upon the distinction now under discussion. If the parties are paying the appropriate amount for employer and employee, it is presumed that a contract of employment exists.

The Redundancy Payments Act 1965 applies to a contract of service, but not to a contract for services (Chapter 12).

It is difficult in practice to draw a dividing line between a contract of service and a contract for services, but in making a decision one way or the other a number of guiding principles or tests may be used, though each particular case will turn on its own individual facts.

1:12:2 *"Control" test*

"The greater the amount of direct control exercised over the person rendering the services by the person contracting for them, the stronger the grounds for holding it to be a contract of service and, similarly, the greater the degree of independence of such control the greater the probability that the services rendered are of the nature of professional services, and that the contract is not one of personal service." (Lord Justice Fletcher Moulton)

Many cases fall between the two extremes of complete control by an employer over an employee under an undoubted contract of service, and the complete independence of an independent contractor under a contract for services. In many contracts of service the individual employee will be given a wide area of discretion and initiative by his employer, and in others it may be impossible for the employer to exercise any control at all, where, for example, a person is employed by a non-human legal entity, such as a limited company. Real and effective control over an employee often rests with another employee, such as a manager or foreman, but a superior employee is not liable at law for the actions of his subordinates: the employer himself remains responsible.

Where an employer wishes to use the services of a professionally qualified person, a contract for services is an appropriate arrangement where only a limited amount of work is to be completed. Where such services are required regularly, technicians with specialised knowledge, such as lawyers, doctors, engineers and chemists, may be employed full time under a contract of service, though the employer lacks the requisite degree of knowledge to supervise their work closely.

1:12:3 *"Organisation" test*

Persons who are employed as part of the business and integrated into it, such as office and factory workers, are deemed to be employees, while those performing related work which is accessory to the business are not employees. An independent contractor is not integrated into the organisation, since he works for the benefit of the undertaking only for a limited time and a specific purpose. Thus an engineer, architect, surveyor or lawyer, giving advice and practical assistance to an employer to help in the completion of some defined object, such as the building of a new factory, will be an independent contractor.

This test depends upon whether a person is part and parcel of the organisation, rather than upon his submission to orders, but the test has not been widely accepted and applied. The concept was expounded by Lord Justice Denning in the following terms: "It is often easy to recognise a contract of service when you see it, but difficult to say wherein the difference lies. One feature which seems to run through the instances is that, under a contract of service, a man is employed as part of the business; whereas, under a contract for services, his work, although done for the business is not integrated into it but is only accessory to it."

Whittaker v Minister of Pensions (1966)

Whittaker was injured during the course of her trapeze act at a circus, and she claimed industrial injury benefit as an employed person under a contract of service.

The court decided that she was entitled to recover, since she not only rehearsed and performed her act, but also spent half of her working day in moving the circus and acting as an usherette, this type of arrangement being customary among circus performers. She had no real independence, but had to carry out her contractual duties as an integral part of the business of the company during her engagement.

1:12:4 "Multiple" test

In the last twenty-five years, in place of the control test, the multiple test has been applied, which consists of four criteria set out by Lord Thankerton in Short v Henderson (1946). Even if these four elements are present in a given case, the contract may still be for the services of an independent contractor. Conversely, a contract may be deemed to be one of service, though one or more of the four elements is either absent, or present in an unusual form. In addition to the power of control the criteria are as follows.

Payment of wages or salary. A contract will usually be one of service if it either makes provision for the payment of an agreed wage or salary on a regular basis, or stipulates a method for determining how much will be payable, as in cases where the remuneration is solely upon a commission basis. A contract will usually be for services if the sum due for the service rendered is not stipulated in advance, though in cases where a professional service is discharged, the amount recoverable may be stated in the contract, or easily determinable by reference to a generally accepted formula. For example, an estate agent's fees for effecting a sale of property will be a fixed percentage of the purchase price.

Power of appointment and selection. Often the task of appointing new employees or selecting existing employees for a specific task is left by the employer to some official, probably the personnel manager or head of a section or department, but the employer remains liable for employees appointed or selected, as if he had personally discharged the task. Where this power of appointment or selection or the right to delegate it to another is absent, it is difficult to make one party responsible for the actions of another on the basis that a contract of service exists between them. In Cassidy v Ministry of Health (see 1:12:8) it was stated that the hospital authority would not be liable for the negligence of a doctor selected and employed by a patient himself for the purpose of supplying the medical attention required.

Right to dismiss. If a person has the right to dismiss another from performance of the work being carried out, this goes some way towards establishing the existence of a contract of service.

Morren v Swinton & Pendlebury
Borough Council (1965, Court of Appeal)

The defendant council engaged Morren as an engineer, with power to pay his salary, subsistence allowance, and National Insurance contributions, and also to dismiss him. Morren was selected by, and worked under, the general control and direction of a consulting engineer who had contracted with the council to execute sewage works.

The court decided that Morren was an employee of the defendants for the purposes of the Local Government Superannuation Act 1937, which was the point in dispute between the parties. Lord Parker said that although the cases have consistently stressed the importance of superintendence and control, it was clear that this was not the determining test. In this case the other considerations, outlined in the facts of the case, pointed to a contract of service. The terms of Morren's contract that he was to work under, and accept the direction and control of, the consulting engineer could not convert a contract of service into a contract for services.

1:12:5   *Other important tests*
Apart from the tests discussed above, the following considerations may be taken into account, in attempting to distinguish between a contract of service and a contract for services:

1 The right to fix the hours of working and the period during which holidays must be taken indicate that it is a contract of service
2 Provision by one party of large-scale plant and equipment for others to use usually suggests the relationship of employer and employee, but if a person supplies his own large-scale plant and equipment for the completion of a task for another then he is likely to be an independent contractor
3 If a person works on his own premises rather than at the premises of the person engaging him, then he is more likely to be an independent contractor than a person who always works at his employer's premises

1:12:6   *One contract may be both of service and for services*
There are instances where one person may work for another under a contract of service and also under a contract for services. In the case of Byrne v Statist Company (1914), a man on the regular staff of a newspaper

made a translation for the newspaper in his spare time. This work was held to have been done under a contract for services, not under the contract of service which regulated his day-to-day relationship with the newspaper. This decision meant that payment could be claimed for the work done under the contract for services, over and above the salary paid under the contract of service. The employee, not the employer, would be entitled to copyright in the translation. This was the point at issue in the next case.

Stevenson, Jordan & Harrison Ltd
v Macdonald & Evans (1952, Court of Appeal)

Mr Evans-Hemming, a former employee of the plaintiff firm of management consultants, wrote a textbook on budgetary control, and assigned the copyright to his publishers, the defendants. It was necessary to examine the legal nature of the plaintiff's relationship with its employee in respect of the book, to determine whether it was entitled to restrain the book's publication on the ground that it was entitled to the copyright.

The court decided that this case was an example of a mixed contract, being partly a contract of service and partly a contract for services. The plaintiff could restrain publication in the book of a report on a work assignment completed for them by Evans-Hemming as part of his service. But there was no right of restraint in respect of the texts of public lectures given in the course of employment at the plaintiff firm's request, since they were not a part of the employee's contractual duties. A man employed under a contract of service may sometimes perform services outside the contract. If a person employed to give lectures reduces them to writing, then the written work is not done under the contract of service.

1:12:7 Is an outworker an employee or an independent contractor?

An outworker who works on his own account without assistance from others, carrying out tasks for one employer only, may be deemed an employee under a contract of service. The position will be different if the outworker engages and controls his own section of employees. In that case he will be employed under a contract for services in respect of any work undertaken for another person, though in fact he tends to work permanently for one person.

Westall Richardson Ltd v Roulson (1954)

Roulson, a mirror polisher of cutlery, rented part of a room in a factory owned by the plaintiff company. He processed the materials supplied by the company, but he used his own tools, employed his own assistants, and determined his own and their conditions of employment. The company paid Roulson for his work on terms mutually agreed upon.

The court decided that Roulson was not employed by the company under a contract of service, but under a series of contracts, with the company as his customer. He was not entitled to holidays and holiday pay from the company under the Wages Council Act 1945 s10(1) and the Cutlery Wages Regulation. "While there may be (and indeed I think there is) some element of service or servitude in his position, there is a far greater element of independence and freedom. In the case of other outworkers, the balance may incline the other way." (Mr Justice Vaisey)

1:12:8 When is an employer liable for the acts of an independent contractor?

As a general rule an employer is not responsible for the torts of an independent contractor or his employees, if committed in the course of the work that they are employed to do. A hospital authority responsible for the organisation of hospitals is liable, however, for the negligence of doctors and surgeons, whether they are employees under a contract of service or independent contractors acting under a contract for services, although the authority cannot control the manner in which they perform their work. If an employer owes a duty of care to clients and customers who rely on proper performance of the responsibilities he has undertaken in relation to them, then responsibility cannot be evaded by delegating the discharge of those duties to an employee under a contract of service, or an independent contractor under a contract for services.

Cassidy v Ministry of Health (1951, Court of Appeal)

Cassidy had an operation on his left hand, which was performed by Dr Fahrni, a full-time medical officer employed by the defendants. After the hand had been bandaged, Cassidy repeatedly complained about the pain he was suffering, but neither Dr Fahrni nor Dr Ronaldson, a house surgeon attending Cassidy, did anything other than prescribe morphia to relieve the pain. When the splint was removed fourteen days after the operation, Cassidy had virtually lost the use of his hand. He sued the defendants for damages in negligence.

The court decided that the hospital authorities were liable to Cassidy for the negligence of the two doctors employed by them under a contract of service. Lord Justice Denning approached the problem from a different

angle: "If the patient himself selects and employs the doctor or surgeon
. . . the hospital authorities are of course not liable for his negligence,
because he is not employed by them. Where, however, the doctor or
surgeon, be he a consultant or not, is employed and paid, not by the
patient, but by the hospital authorities, I am of the opinion that the
hospital authorities are liable for his negligence in treating the patient. It
does not depend on whether the contract under which he was employed
was a contract of service or a contract for services. That is a fine distinction which is sometimes of importance, but not in cases where . . . the
hospital authorities are themselves under a duty to use care in treating
the patient."

1:12:9 *Transferring an employee from one employer to another*
An employee may be sent by his employer to work on a temporary basis
for some other employer, probably for the completion of specialised work
that the second employer cannot effect without outside help. Frequently
the first employer will supply the second employer with expensive and
complicated machinery, such as a crane, together with an employee skilled
in its operation. It may be important to determine whether the employee
is employed by his permanent or his temporary employer during the period
for which his services have been transferred, if one of the following situations arises:

1   Where a third party is injured as a result of the employee's
     negligence, since it must be determined whether his permanent
     or temporary employer is vicariously liable for his acts
2   At common law an employer must provide proper plant and
     equipment and safe working conditions and premises; the
     temporary employee may wish to ascertain whether the tem-
     porary employer is the party responsible for providing these
     amenities and if so to sue him for damages for failure to dis-
     charge his responsibilities, if the temporary employee is injured
     by a breach of this duty

1:12:10 *Situations where the temporary employer is liable*
It is presumed that the employee remains under the control of his permanent employer, unless the latter can discharge the heavy burden of
showing that his responsibilities have been effectively transferred to
the temporary employer. Where the employee is engaged on unskilled
work, or skilled work that does not involve the permanent employer in

supplying complicated machinery for the performance of the employee's task, then it is easier to find that control has passed to the temporary employer.

Garrard v Southey & Co and Standard Telephones & Cables Ltd (1952)

Two employees of Southey & Co, an electrical contractor, were sent to make electrical installations at a factory occupied by Standard Telephones & Cables Ltd. One of the electricians was injured while using some defective equipment owned by building contractors working at the factory. It was necessary to determine whether the factory occupier as temporary employer, or Southey & Co as permanent employer, was liable for the injuries sustained through failure to provide proper plant and equipment in fulfilment of the common law duty owed by employer to employee. The following factors were important in making this assessment:

1 The man worked exclusively at the factory and took meals in the factory canteen
2 The factory occupier supplied the plant, tools and materials used by the man with the exception of special tools supplied by the electrician personally
3 The factory occupier's foreman supervised the man's work in pursuance of the system laid down

The court decided that the factory occupier was liable in damages for failure to discharge the common law duty which he was deemed to owe to the electrician who had been injured. He could not only tell the electrician what work to do, but also instruct him on how to do it.

1:12:11 *Situations where liability remains with the permanent employer*
In order to resolve any doubts on the question of liability, an express term may be inserted in the contract of hire between the permanent and temporary employer, whereby the latter accepts responsibility for the negligent acts of an employee who has been engaged for a period of time to carry out a given project. A clause of this type is not conclusive on the question of liability, which may nonetheless remain with the permanent employer, in cases where the activities of the employee cannot be effectively controlled by the temporary employer.

Mersey Docks & Harbour Board
v Coggins & Griffith (Liverpool) Ltd and McFarlane (1947, House of Lords)

The Board hired out a crane and driver to Coggins & Griffith Ltd, with an express term in the contract of hire as follows: "The driver so provided shall be the servant of the applicant." The hirers had immediate direction of the driver's activities, since they could instruct him to move a particular cargo, but they had no control over the way in which he operated the crane. The driver started the crane negligently, causing injury to McFarlane, and the court had to determine whether it was the Board or the hirers who were to be held responsible.

The court decided that the Board was liable as the permanent employer, since they engaged, paid and had the power to dismiss the driver. They could only escape liability for his negligent acts by showing that their relationship of employer and employee had been suspended in favour of a similar relationship between the driver and Coggins & Griffith Ltd, on the ground that entire and absolute control had passed to the temporary employer. The negligence lay in the manner in which the driver's acts were performed, a matter upon which the temporary employers could give no direction, and for which they had no responsibility. The permanent employers were not present to dictate how directions given by someone else should be carried out, but they had given their employee discretion about the manner in which he carried out those directions.

By way of contrast, in the next case the hirer was held liable for the negligence of an employee hired from another employer, because of an express clause in the contract setting out the terms of the hire.

Arthur White (Contractors) Ltd
v Tarmac Civil Engineering Ltd (1967, House of Lords)

A White Ltd, the owner of a crane-excavator, entered into a written contract to hire the machine and a driver to the defendants. A clause in that contract provided that the driver "supplied by the owners to work the plant . . . shall be under the direction and control of the hirers. Such driver . . . shall for all purposes in connection with his employment in the working of the plant be regarded as the servant or agent of the hirers who alone shall be responsible for all claims arising in connection with the operation of the plant by the driver."

The driver's negligence while operating the plant caused injury to one

74

of Tarmac's employees, who successfully sued both White and Tarmac for damages: the court was asked to determine who was responsible for payment.

The court's decision turned on a construction of the clause set out above. Assistance could not be derived from other decisions, on the meaning of other contracts, couched in different language. The wording of the clause in this case was more explicit and went further than a similar clause in Mersey Docks & Harbour Board v Coggins & Griffith (Liverpool) Ltd. It was clear that the clause intended that any claim in connection with the operation of the plant by the driver should be the responsibility of the hirer, and consequently Tarmac was liable for the damages awarded to the injured employee.

Any employer hiring out equipment and drivers to other persons, who wishes to transfer responsibility for the driver's negligent acts to the temporary employer, should insert an express term in the contract of hire similar to that used in the above case. On such an important matter as drafting a clause of this nature, the professional advice of a solicitor should be sought.

TWO

Restraining an Employee's Competitive Activities

THE CONTRACT OF EMPLOYMENT OF ALMOST ALL EMPLOYEES CONTAINS only the items that s4 of the Contracts of Employment Act requires the employer to specify. However, there are some employees whose talents are so intimately connected with the objectives and success of the firm that the employer will want to make sure that he—and not a competitor or the employee on his own account—benefits from the work he has paid for.

The three parts of this chapter deal with the most common problems:

1   Where an employee makes a commercially valuable invention
2   Where the employee builds up personal contacts with the employer's clients and could take these clients with him when he goes to another job
3   Where the employee discloses commercially valuable information to a rival firm

The law relating to these problems is based on two concepts:

1   The contract of employment implies an obligation of "good faith" to the employer by his employee
2   The employer cannot be allowed to extend this obligation by adding terms to the contract of employment that would deny the community the benefits of the employee's talents

EMPLOYEES' INVENTIONS

2:1   PATENTS

If an employee is engaged on work, during the course of which he is likely to invent a new device, gadget, process or design, then the employer should include a term in the contract of employment explicitly giving himself ownership of that invention. In the absence of such an express term, the employer is still entitled to ownership, if it would be contrary to good faith for the employee to retain the invention for his own benefit. The next case clearly illustrates this point.

Triplex Safety Glass Co v Scorah (1937)

Scorah had been employed by the plaintiff company as an assistant chemist and during the course of his employment he had discovered a method of producing acrylic acid. Although the company had asked Scorah to embark on this invention they did not patent it. After leaving this employment, Scorah was granted a patent for his discovery, but the plaintiff company claimed it from him when they subsequently became interested in the commercial use of acrylic acid.

The court decided that although Scorah had covenanted in his contract of employment to assign to the plaintiff company any patents for his discoveries, this was void as being in restraint of trade. The covenant prevented Scorah from using any general knowledge he acquired in the course of his employment and it should have been limited to the protection of secret processes which was a reasonable restraint in the circumstances. Nonetheless, the employer was still entitled to the patent. "It is a term of all employment, apart altogether from any express covenant, that any invention or discovery made in the course of the employment of the employee in doing that which he is engaged and instructed to do during working hours and using the materials of his employer, is the property of the employer and not that of the employee, and that having made such a discovery or invention the employee becomes a trustee . . . of that invention . . . and is bound to give the benefit of such discovery or invention to his employer." (Mr Justice Farwell)

2 : 1 : 1 *Inventions not solicited by the employer*

If the invention is concerned with the employer's business and was made while the employee was bound by the terms of the contract of employment, it is the property of the employer. It is immaterial that the employee has not been asked to make the invention by his employer or that his job is unconnected with the making of inventions.

British Syphon Co Ltd v Homewood (1956)

Homewood was employed by the plaintiff company as their chief technician to give technical advice in relation to the design or development of anything connected with any part of the company's business. On his own initiative, without any request from the company, Homewood invented a low-pressure system of dispensing soda water, which was unrelated to his advisory work. He patented the invention, left the plaintiff company's employment and began working for a rival. The plaintiff company claimed that the patent should be assigned to them.

The court decided that the plaintiff company was entitled to have the patent assigned to them. It is inconsistent with the duty of good faith that exists between employer and employee that the employee should be entitled to invent something relating to his employer's business, then keep it for his own personal benefit or sell it to a rival. The employee "has a duty not to put himself in a position in which he may have personal reasons for not giving his employer the best advice which it is his duty to give if and when asked to give it." (Mr Justice Roxburgh)

Since Homewood was employed to give technical advice on design and development, he was placed in a position where he was more likely to invent something during the course of his employment than the majority of employees.

2:1:2 Employee's implied obligation
of good faith as a test for determining ownership

If the employee has made an invention during working hours or by using his employer's materials, the invention does not automatically become the employer's property. Conversely, an invention resulting from the employee's work in his own time, using his own materials or his own premises, does not necessarily belong to the employee. In such cases the benefit of the invention belongs to the employee only if this would be consistent with the implied obligation of good faith implicit in the contract of employment, otherwise the employee is a trustee of the invention for his employer.

2:1:3 Employees may be trustees of their inventions for the employer

A *trust* arises when one party, the trustee, although he is the legal owner of certain property, is forced to account to another party, the beneficiary, for all the benefits and profits that are produced by any use made of that property. Where the contract of employment gives the employer exclusive rights over inventions made by the employee, then that employee becomes a trustee and consequently accountable to his employer for all benefits resulting from his inventions, both during his employment and after its termination.

British Celanese v Moncrieff (1948, Court of Appeal)

Moncrieff was employed by the plaintiffs as a research chemist. His contract of employment provided that he would "obtain letters patent for the said inventions, in all such countries as the company may require and will vest such letters patent in the company." During his period of service, Moncrieff made inventions jointly with another employee, which were patented in Britain, the USA and Canada before he left the plaintiff's employment in 1945. Two years later Moncrieff was sued by his former employers for refusing to join with them in applying for patents for the inventions in other foreign countries, not covered by the first application.

The court decided that Moncrieff was a trustee of his inventions and was bound to account to his former employer for all benefits in relation to them, including joining in an application for the patents as requested. His obligations as a trustee continued to bind him even after the contractual relationship with his employer, under the contract of employment, had terminated.

2:1:4 Who is entitled to patent an invention?

Letters patent, conferring the exclusive use and benefit of a new invention, may be applied for by the first and true inventor or his assignee. The employer will be the first and true inventor, where the employee makes the invention as a result of guided research under the employer's instruction. Though the employee be the true and first inventor, he cannot claim the benefit of any patent where:

1   He agrees in his contract of employment to assign to the employer inventions made during the period of his employment
2   In the absence of express agreement it would be a breach of good faith for the employee so to act, as where:
  (a) Making inventions is his job or a by-product of his work
  (b) The invention results from the provision by the employer of all necessary facilities

An invention patented in the joint names of employer and employee belongs to the employer, since the employee is a trustee of his interest in the invention for the employer's benefit, unless there is an express agreement contradicting this implied assumption.

2:1:5 Procedure when applying for a patent

An employer applying for letters patent must send an application in the prescribed form to the Comptroller-General of Patents at the Patent Office, which is a branch of the Department of Trade and Industry. Since he will often be an assignee, the employer must name the person he believes to be the true inventor and file his consent to the application.

If consequent upon an application a dispute arises between an employer and employee about their respective patent rights to the invention, the Comptroller may, after giving each side an opportunity to be heard, determine the dispute and make orders to effect his decision. If the dispute raises issues which would be more properly dealt with by a court, the Comptroller may refuse to make a decision (Patents Act 1949 s56).

The patent when granted lasts for sixteen years, subject to an extension for a further five years or, where the patentee has not been adequately remunerated, for a further ten years.

2:2   COPYRIGHT

The author of a literary, dramatic, musical or artistic work is entitled to the copyright. This allows him to restrict any reproduction, performance, publication, broadcasting or adaptation of his work, unless permission is given. The employer is entitled to the copyright of a work made in the course of the author's employment or for the purposes of his employment unless there is an agreement to the contrary.

The employer may restrain publication of papers prepared by an employee in the course of his employment, where they form part of a literary work later published by the employee. This right of restraint does not extend to any literary work embodying the experience acquired by the employee in the course of his employment (see 1:12:6, Stevenson, Jordan & Harrison Ltd v McDonald & Evans).

Where the author is employed by a newspaper, magazine or periodical, the proprietor is entitled to copyright only in respect of publication in that newspaper, magazine or periodical. The author is entitled to the copyright in other media. Where a photograph, portrait or engraving is commissioned for valuable consideration, the copyright belongs to the person granting the commission.

Copyright extends over a period of fifty years after the calendar year in which the author died.

2:3   INDUSTRIAL DESIGNS

The Registered Designs Act 1949 s1(3) defines a design as:

1   Features of shape and configuration, such as the design given to clothes or shoes
2   A pattern or ornamentation, such as a design impressed upon wallpaper and textiles

When these designs are applied to an article by means of an industrial process, the appeal of the finished article is to the eye, by which the design is judged. The definition also covers the way in which goods are packaged, the shape of the container, the design and colouring of the label, and the jacket of a book. It does not cover a shape, configuration or construction which is dictated solely by the function of the article in relation to which it is used.

2:3:1   Application for registration of a design

A new or original design belongs to and may be registered at the Patent Office by:

1   The person who created it
2   The employer for whom it was made by the creator; this creator will often be an employee and the employer's rights to the design will be similar to his rights in respect of an employee's invention
3   The person to whom it has been transferred by the registered owner, but this change in ownership should be registered promptly in case there is a further attempted transfer by a fraudulent owner to some other party

The owner of a registered design is entitled to make changes which alter its appearance, and to apply for a registration to cover the changes made. In the past there have been around 6000 registrations annually, but this number may fall in view of the Design Copyright Act 1968 (see 2:3:2).

Since registration may take some time, the procedure to be followed should be set in motion three months before the item is marketed. This is especially important in cases where the design is easily copied when once it has been made public. In such cases registration is intended to act as an immediate and effective deterrent to those wishing to make copies.

Period of protection conferred. A design may be protected for five years from the time of filing an application for registration, with the possibility of a renewal for two further five-year periods, making a total of fifteen years. About one third of the registrations are renewed at the end of the first five-year period. After fifteen years, protection also ends for modifications to the original design and for the use of the original design in relation to articles not covered in the original application.

Action for infringement of these rights. Any person who either manufactures or deals in articles carrying a design that infringes the rights of its registered owner, may be sued by that owner in the High Court for:

1   An injunction to restrain continued infringement, and
2   Damages for losses suffered by its use, unless the infringement
     was committed without any knowledge that the design had
     been so registered

The question for determination is not whether the defendant's design is
an exact copy, but whether it substantially resembles the design registered
by the plaintiff to the action.

2:3:2   Copyright in an industrial design

Beginning at the date upon which an industrial design is first marketed,
its owner automatically has copyright in respect of it for the next fifteen
years, irrespective of registration (Design Copyright Act 1968). Nonetheless, a design should be registered if it is likely that some other person
may also produce the design independently, since registration prevents
the design from being marketed in competition. A copyright is infringed
and protection is conferred on the owner only if another person repro-
duces an exact copy. There is no protection for the owner if the so-called
copy is essentially the result of the maker's own independent thought and
research.

A person may be prevented from copying the design and infringing the
copyright if the owner promptly applies for an interlocutory injunction to
restrain such conduct. The fear of this action may be sufficient to prevent
anyone from copying a design, unless it is over fifteen years old, even
though it has not been registered. The copyright owner may, in addition
to seeking an injunction:

1   Demand any copies made and where appropriate the moulds in
     which they were made
2   Claim damages if copies have been sold already, unless the
     infringement of copyright has been innocent

An action for infringement will succeed only if a copyright artistic work
exists which has been copied by the person being sued, an issue to be
determined by examining the original item and the alleged copy. The
appropriate party to be sued is the person:

1   Producing the copy in this country, or
2   In possession of copies in this country, when they have been
     made abroad and imported

RESTRAINING AN EMPLOYEE'S COMPETITIVE ACTIVITIES AFTER TERMINATING THE CONTRACT OF EMPLOYMENT

One of the most important questions that an employer may have to deal with is the extent to which he can restrain his employee, after termination of the contract of employment, from:

1   Entering the service of a competitor
2   Operating a competing business
3   Divulging trade secrets acquired in the course of employment
4   Enticing away customers by use of a list compiled in the course of employment

The employer should bear in mind the area over which the restraint extends and the time during which it will operate. He should seek protection against any of the above-mentioned four contingencies through the insertion of an express term in the contract of employment. This precaution involves careful thought and appropriate action when the employee is first engaged. To determine the most suitable term for inclusion and to aid in the formation of a coherent policy on restraint of competition, the legal principles set out in this chapter may prove helpful. It is clear that reliance on an implied rather than an express term in the contract of employment will not usually give the employer the type of protection he requires (see 2 : 7).

The employer may be tempted to draft his restraint clause in very wide terms, to protect his proprietary interests against all possible forms of competition by the employee who has left his service. The danger is that by seeking too much protection he will lose the right to any protection at all. If, in the circumstances of the case, the covenant in restraint of trade is unreasonably wide, it is void and totally unenforceable against the employee who agreed to its terms unless the void promise can be cut out leaving the rest of the restraint clause fully enforceable.

Moreover, this particular issue is not solely the concern of employer and employee, since the general public is also vitally affected. It is important that individuals should be able to work for the benefit of the community as a whole, without undue restraint in respect of those tasks for which they are most suited. When drafting his restraint clause, the employer must consider whether it is reasonable not only as between the employer and the employee, but also from the point of view of the general public. These twin problems will be dealt with first.

2:4 WHAT IS MEANT BY
"REASONABLE IN THE PUBLIC INTEREST"

The general rule in favour of freedom to trade was clearly stated by Lord McNaghten in Nordenfeldt v Maxim Nordenfeldt Guns & Ammunition Co Ltd (1894). "The public have an interest in every person's carrying on his trade freely; so has the individual. All interference with individual liberty of action in trading, and all restraints of trade of themselves, if there is nothing more, are contrary to public policy, and therefore void." There are exceptions to this general rule and a restraint is binding if it is reasonable as between the employer and employee and also reasonable in the public interest.

In recent years attention has been concentrated on the reasonableness of the restraint as between employer and employee, but in Esso Petroleum Co Ltd v Harper's Garage (Stourport) Ltd (1968) the House of Lords re-emphasised that it is also necessary to consider whether it is in the interests of the public that the restraint of trade imposed by the employer on the employee should be upheld as being reasonable and enforceable. The concept of "public interest" is difficult to define with precision, as the next case clearly indicates.

Wyatt v Kreglinger & Fernau (1933, Court of Appeal)

Wyatt, aged sixty and about to retire from the defendant's employment, was promised a pension of £200 a year on condition that he did not compete with the defendants in the wool trade. Wyatt sued for damages for breach of this contract when the defendants stopped payment nine years later.

The court decided that even if a contract to pay the pension existed, and on this point there was some doubt, it was void as being in restraint of trade. It was contrary to public policy for the country to be deprived of the services of a person like Wyatt, since he was able to make a contribution to the national well-being by entering into a further period of employment.

This decision seems to allow an employer freely to negotiate an agreement which restrains the future competitive activities of an employee leaving his service, in return for the promise of payment. After receiving the benefits of this contract for a substantial period of time, the employer may then repudiate the agreement as being unduly wide, in restraint of trade and injurious to the community at large, presumably when the fear of competition has ceased to be a real threat to his business. The decision in Wyatt v Kreglinger & Fernau appears to give the employer an arbitrary and unfair power to reject an agreement acted upon by the parties, when he no longer fears the former employee's competitive activities.

2:4:1 Position held by the employee should be a relevant consideration

There may be some justification for refusing to uphold a restraint if the employee has held an important position, on the ground that it is un-reasonable for a person with high qualifications, wide experience and several years' service ahead of him to be prevented from contributing to the national well-being. On the other hand, restraints on ordinary em-ployees, like Wyatt, without special skills or qualifications, do not harm the national well-being, and any promise of payment by the employer in return for the employee's promise not to compete in the future ought to be binding on the employer and this view may prevail in any future dispute raising a situation of this type. Support for this view of public policy was expressed by Lord Lindley in 1899, "To allow a person of mature age, and not imposed upon, to enter into a contract, to obtain the benefit of it, and then to repudiate it and the obligations which he has undertaken is . . . contrary to the interests of any and every country."

2:4:2 Validity of a restraint clause contained in a pension scheme

In a more recent decision however, the view expressed in Wyatt v Kreg-linger & Fernau was supported, but the employer was obliged to forgo the benefits of the restraint clause imposed and pay the pension as well.

Bull v Pitney-Bowes (1966)

It was a condition of Bull's employment as a sales manager that he should join his employer's non-contributory pension scheme. Rule 16 provided that a retired member should be liable to forfeit his pension rights if he engaged in any activity or occupation which competed with the employer's business. Bull retired after twenty-five years' service, took up employment with one of the defendant's competitors and sued for a declaration that rule 16 was void as being in restraint of trade.

The court decided that the pension fund provisions were part of the terms upon which Bull was employed. The covenant in rule 16 was to be treated as a restraint of trade which was void on grounds of public policy, since it deprived the community of the services of a skilled person.

In this decision, while accepting the reasoning of the Court of Appeal in Wyatt's case, the judge was able to allow the employee to keep his pension, an important difference from the decision in Wyatt's case. The explanation of this apparent contradiction is that in Wyatt's case the covenant in restraint of trade was the only consideration that Wyatt provided in return for his employer's promise to pay the pension. When the covenant was held to be void, Wyatt ceased to provide any consideration upon which he could base his right to receive the pension. In Bull's case the void covenant was merely part of a wider agreement and when severed from the contract there remained other contractual terms to provide consideration to support the employer's promise to pay the pension.

If an employer wishes to insert a restraint clause in the terms of a contract of employment or pension scheme, he must be advised not to overstep the limits of what is reasonable in the circumstances of the case. This involves a close examination of such matters as:

1   The nature of the business to be protected
2   The extent of any competition which the employer must meet
3   The area of its operations
4   The position held by the employee agreeing to the restraint

2:5   WHEN A RESTRAINT IS
"REASONABLE BETWEEN THE PARTIES"

Covenants in restraint of trade taken by the employer from the employee are closely analysed, for in many cases they have not been freely negotiated. If an employee is in need of employment he cannot force his own terms on the employer and he may accept, at the insistence of the employer, a restraint on his future activities after leaving the employment. The guiding principle to be remembered is that the employer purchases the skills of the employee only for the time during which the employment continues. Thereafter the employee is free to offer his services elsewhere, even if it is to the employer's competitor. "A man's aptitudes, his skill, his dexterity, his manual or mental ability . . . may not be relinquished by an employee; they are not the employer's property, they are his own property." (Lord Shaw)

2:5:1 *Any restraint imposed by the employer must be reasonable*

It should be appreciated that any restraint taken to prevent mere competition by the employee after leaving the employer's service does not bind the employee. A restraint is valid only if the employer is restraining the employee's use of trade secrets and trade connections acquired while in his employment, in a manner contrary to the employer's best interests.

The employer must prove that the restraint imposed on the employee is no wider than is necessary to protect the employer's proprietary interest. In deciding whether a restraint is reasonable two factors are considered, the geographical area covered and the duration of the restraint, "As the time of restriction lengthens or the space of its operation grows, the weight of the onus on the covenantee to justify it grows too" (Lord Justice Younger). Whether any restraint will be valid or void depends upon the particular circumstances surrounding each individual case, and the type of interest that requires protection. It is difficult to lay down precise rules for the guidance of a personnel manager having to advise his employer on the validity of a covenant of restraint to be inserted into a proposed new contract of employment. A close analysis of the cases set out below may help him to avoid the more serious mistakes that have been made in the past.

2:5:2 *Area of restraint must be reasonable*

Since everything depends upon the circumstances of each individual case, a wide restraint covering, for example, the whole world, the Eastern Hemisphere or the UK may be held to be reasonable, where the business to be protected is carried on throughout the area stipulated. In Nordenfeldt v Maxim Nordenfeldt Guns & Ammunition Co Ltd, the world-wide restraint imposed on Nordenfeldt for the protection of the defendant company, which was engaged in the manufacture of guns and ammunition, was held to be reasonable, since the company's operations extended throughout the world and their customers were limited to foreign governments placing orders for weapons needed in warfare. In different circumstances, an employer operating only in a local area cannot prevent his employees from competing outside that area. Thus the following types of restraint have been held void:

1   Where an agent employed to canvass orders for clothing in Islington was restrained from trading within 25 miles of London (Mason v Provident Clothing & Supply Co Ltd (1913, House of Lords))

D

2   Where the manager of a butcher's shop in Cambridge pro-
     mised not to engage in a similar business within 5 miles from
     the shop, since a substantial number of the customers lived
     within a 2 mile radius (Empire Meat Co Ltd v Patrick (1939,
     Court of Appeal))

3   Where a junior reporter of a local newspaper in Sheffield was
     restrained from working for any other newspaper within a
     radius of 20 miles (Leng v Andrews (1909))

4   Where a traveller for a firm of brewers promised not to sell
     ale or porter brewed at Burton anywhere at all for a two-year
     period (Allsopp v Wheatcroft (1872))

2:5:3   Duration of restraint must be reasonable

Again individual circumstances are important, but there are fewer cases
that have been decided on this point. A restraint for the lifetime of the
employer is not necessarily void (see 2:7, Fitch v Dewes) but in such
cases, or where a time limit is not referred to, the burden on the employer
to establish the reasonableness of the restraint is increased considerably.
It is often a question of balance, for "If the restriction in respect of space
is extremely limited, it is evident that a very considerable restriction in
respect of time may be more acceptable than would otherwise have been
the case." (Lord Birkenhead)

Eastes v Russ (1914, Court of Appeal)

Eastes ran a pathological laboratory in Queen Anne Street, London, and
Russ, his assistant, covenanted in his contract of employment not to engage
in similar work within 10 miles of the laboratory. Eastes was carrying out
a new method of medical research and there were only three similar
institutions in London. Russ opened his own laboratory ½ mile away
from that of the plaintiff.

The court decided that the restraint was wider than was reasonably
necessary for the protection of the plaintiff and therefore void. In the
absence of a time limit in the covenant, the restraint on Russ was life-
long. Although the area of restraint was only 10 miles, it prevented Russ
from having any clients in the Harley Street area, which would be the
source of most of his work.

2:6 EMPLOYERS MAY PROTECT TRADE SECRETS ACQUIRED IN THE COURSE OF EMPLOYMENT

The employer may restrain the future competitive activities of his employee if he is thereby preventing the exploitation of trade secrets learned by the employee in the course of his employment.

Forster & Sons Ltd v Suggett (1918)

Suggett, the plaintiff's works manager, was instructed in confidential methods of glass and glass bottle making, including the correct mixture of gas and air in the furnaces. Suggett agreed that, for a five-year period after leaving the plaintiff's employment, he would not within the UK either carry on or be interested in glass bottle manufacture or any other business connected with glass making. The plaintiffs sued to restrain a breach of the covenant.

The court decided that the restraint was reasonable. The plaintiffs were entitled to the protection taken since Suggett could not have acquired this knowledge from any other sources.

A restraint is invalid if the employee has learned only part of the trade secret, so that he is not in a position to exploit it successfully for the advantage of the employer's competitors.

If the knowledge gained by the employee concerns a special manufacturing or organisational process that is not considered to be a trade secret, then any restraint imposed on him is unenforceable.

Herbert Morris Ltd v Saxelby (1916, House of Lords)

The company carried on business as engineers and leading manufacturers of hoisting machinery in the UK. Saxelby worked for the company for several years as a draughtsman and in various other capacities. He covenanted not to work in a similar capacity for his employer's competitors in the UK for seven years after leaving his present employment.

The court decided that the company was not entitled to an injunction to restrain Saxelby from working for a competitor in Manchester, since the restraint was wider than that required to protect the company's interests. Saxelby had gained knowledge of a special method of organisation developed in the business, but this was not an exceptional proprietary right requiring protection.

2:7 PREVENTING A FORMER EMPLOYEE FROM ENTICING AWAY HIS FORMER EMPLOYER'S CUSTOMERS

The employer is entitled to prevent his customers being enticed away by his former employee. To justify any restraint imposed, the employer must show that the employee has had close personal contact with the employer's customers, in consequence of which they have placed reliance upon the employee's skill and judgement, such that they will probably transfer their custom to him if he establishes his own business or joins the business of a competitor. This kind of contact exists where the employee holds a position akin to that of a stockbroker's clerk, an estate agent's clerk, a solicitor's clerk, a milk roundsman, or manager of a brewery.

Nicholl v Beere (1885)

Beere was employed by Nicholl, a tailor in Regent Street, as a cutter and fitter. Beere covenanted not to carry on business as a tailor within a radius of 10 miles of Charing Cross for three years after terminating his employment with Nicholl. Beere left Nicholl's employment and opened a tailors' business within 200 yards of Nicholl's business.

The court granted an injunction to restrain a breach of this undertaking since it was not unreasonable as regards area of operation or duration.

Fitch v Dewes (1921, House of Lords)

Fitch, a solicitor at Tamworth, employed Dewes first as his articled clerk, then as his managing clerk. Dewes covenanted that, if he left Fitch's employment, he would not at any time practise as a solicitor within 7 miles of Tamworth town hall. It was shown in evidence that Dewes personally dealt with the affairs of almost half of his employer's clients visiting the office. Fitch sued to restrain a breach of the covenant.

The court decided that the restraint was enforceable. "A person employed in such a practice as managing clerk must in the course of his duties acquire a knowledge of the affairs, the documents and the disposition of the clients of the business such as to give him a special equipment which he could, if not restrained by contract, use in obtaining employment as their legal adviser and that in this manner the goodwill of the employer's business might be impaired and perhaps destroyed." (Viscount Cave)

2:7:1 *Where the business protected does not have recurring customers*
The employer is not justified in imposing a restraint in the case of a business that does not have recurring customers, since then the employee does not have an opportunity to establish a personal relationship of confidence with the clientele.

Bowler v Lovegrove (1921)

Lovegrove, an outside canvassing and negotiating clerk, covenanted with his employers, who were auctioneers and estate agents, not to enter into a similar business in the borough of Portsmouth or the town of Gosport within one year after terminating his employment. Lovegrove left the plantiff's employment and immediately set up as an estate agent on his own account within the prohibited area.

The court decided that the covenant was wider than was reasonably necessary to protect the plaintiff's business, since the majority of the customers negotiated one transaction only.

2:7:2 *Where the employee has*
business contacts before taking up employment
Before entering employment, the employee may have established some connection already with customers who purchase goods of the type supplied by his new employer. Any restraint clause taken from the employee in such circumstances must not impinge on his rights in respect of those customers, otherwise it will be void.

M & S Drapers v Reynolds (1956, Court of Appeal)

Reynolds, a collector salesman, employed by M & S Drapers, agreed in his contract of employment that for five years after leaving he would not engage in the business of drapery with any of the customers inscribed on his former employer's books during the three years preceding termination of his employment there. Reynolds had brought customers with him when he entered the employment.

The court decided that the restraint clause was unreasonable and void. Reynolds should not be prevented from dealing with customers known to him before entering the employment of the plaintiffs, since his knowledge of and influence over them were due to his own efforts. Lord Justice Denning supported this decision: "Any other view would mean that, soon after employing him, they could dismiss him at a fortnight's notice, and then prevent him for five years thereafter from calling on his own customers who had been his long before he entered the employment."

2:7:3 *Mere contact with customers is insufficient*
A restraint imposed by the employer is not justifiable if the employee has contact with customers without gaining any influence over them such that they rely on his skill and knowledge. Another factor of importance is the employee's position in the hierarchy of employees: the lower the position the more difficult it becomes to justify the restraint imposed.

S W Strange Ltd v Mann (1965)

Mann, manager of the plaintiff company of bookmakers, covenanted in his contract of employment that he would not engage in any similar enterprise within 12 miles of Cheltenham upon termination of the contract. About three-quarters of the plaintiff company's customers lived within the stipulated area, but over 90 per cent of the bets were placed by phone and the remainder by letter or telegram. In breach of his covenant Mann became engaged in a similar business at Gloucester, some 9 miles from Cheltenham.

The court decided that there was nothing to show that Mann had established such a personal relationship or position of confidence with the plaintiff company's customers, as would make it likely that they would seek him out after he left his former employment. The covenant was void as being an unlawful restraint of trade.

Even if the employee does not come into personal contact with the employer's customers, he can be legitimately restrained from using for his own private benefit any list of clients known to him, for the purpose of canvassing orders for work.

2:7:4 *Where the employee has access to a list of his employer's clients*
The nature of the employee's work may be such that the employer is forced to disclose to him a list of clients' names and addresses, as in the case of a commercial traveller selling the employer's goods. The serious danger here is that, having established personal contact, the employee will be tempted to set up in business on his own account, then solicit the customers of his former employer. To protect his business interests, the employer must insert a restraint clause in the employee's contract of employment, and if this is broken after termination of the contract, seek an injunction to restrain the employee's activities.

Plowman & Son Ltd v Ash (1964, Court of Appeal)

Ash, a sales representative employed by the plaintiff company of agricultural and corn merchants, agreed in his contract of employment that for two years after leaving he would not solicit, for himself or other persons, any farmer or market gardener who had been a customer of his employer at any time during his employment. Ash was obliged under his contract to serve his employer anywhere in south Lincolnshire, but in fact he confined his attention to a much smaller area. He was never given a complete list of the company's customers, but he did call on those customers whose names appeared on a list given to him. On leaving the company's employment he solicited orders from the plaintiff's customers.

The court granted an injunction to restrain Ash from so acting.

When first engaging a salesman, the employer may not be able to state with certainty the exact area that the salesman will be expected to cover, since it will probably change from time to time because of staff changes and re-organisation. The problem for the employer is that he will wish to frame a restraint clause for the employee's approval that will cover all possible areas in which the salesman will operate, while at the same time prevent the restraint clause from becoming wider than is necessary to protect his proprietary interests and consequently being totally unenforceable. In Plowman & Son Ltd v Ash, the Court of Appeal made it clear that the terms of the restraint clause will be examined from the point of view of the parties' knowledge at the time when it was made. If a salesman is likely to engage, at one time or another, in selling activities that extend over a wide area, his employer may validly take a restraint clause covering the whole area and this will be enforceable against the salesman. If the salesman eventually confines his activities to a relatively small area, the validity of the restraint clause is unimpaired. The employer should divulge only a list of clients relating to that part of the total area in which the salesman operates. He may then be effectively restrained from soliciting their custom at a later stage. If a complete list for the whole area is handed over, the restraint will cover only those customers with whom the salesman had personal contact, though he now has knowledge of other possible clients.

2:7:5 *Employers can protect only present and potential clientele*
A restraint clause must be confined in its operation to customers and potential customers of the employer, otherwise it will be void.

Gledhow Autoparts Ltd v Delaney (1965, Court of Appeal)

Delaney, a travelling salesman, canvassed an area of fourteen counties in an attempt to sell his employer's goods. He was contractually bound for three years after the termination of his employment not to solicit orders for goods dealt in by his employer from persons, firms or companies within the area he had canvassed.

The court decided that if the employer imposes a covenant of restraint covering a wide area, he may restrain his former employee from soliciting within that area only those customers doing business with the employer or persons likely to do business some time as the result of being canvassed. He may not restrain him from soliciting persons within the area with whom the former employee did not establish any contact or relationship.

2:7:6 Restraints protecting legitimate purposes will usually be upheld

In practice, it is extremely difficult to frame restrictions which will adequately protect a trade connection, without also including some restrictions, the breach of which would not cause injury. If a restriction has been carefully framed for a legitimate purpose, it will not be deemed void as contrary to public policy on the ground that it can be interpreted as conferring a wider protection than that necessary in the circumstances.

Home Counties Dairies Ltd and Another
v Skilton and Another (1970, Court of Appeal)

Skilton left the service of the plaintiff employer and a few days later entered the employment of another dairy company in the same district. He immediately started to operate a milk round, covering the same area as the one he had worked in his former employment. An injunction was sought to restrain Skilton from breaking the terms of a restrictive covenant in his contract of employment with the plaintiff company. This covenant provided that Skilton must not within one year of leaving the plaintiff's employment serve or sell milk or dairy produce, on his own account or as a representative of another, to any person who during the last six months of his employment was a customer of the plaintiff company and was served by Skilton.

The court decided that the restraint clause must be read in the context of the whole agreement. Its intention was to protect the goodwill of the employer's business as a dairy company operating a milk round, against the employee's activities, if he engaged in a similar business after leaving that employment. It was not intended, nor did it purport to prevent, the employee from selling cheese or butter in a grocery business, thereby stretching the restriction beyond the protection of the employer's goodwill to make the whole restraint void. The injunction was granted.

2:8 SEVERING THE VOID COVENANT IN RESTRAINT OF TRADE FROM THE REST OF THE CONTRACT

It is important to appreciate the extent to which it is possible to sever from the contract of employment any covenant or part of a covenant that is void for being in restraint of trade, so that the remaining terms can be enforced. Only those cases that involve the relationship of employer and employee will be examined, since different considerations apply to restraints restricting future competition, taken by the purchaser of a business from the vendor. Three conditions must be satisfied before severance is permitted and each of these will be examined in turn.

2:8:1 *Promises must be separate and independent*
If an unreasonable restriction imposed upon the employee is contained in a promise separate and distinct from the other promises in the contract, such as the promise to work and the promise to pay wages, then the offending clause will be eliminated and the rest of the contract upheld. The employee may sue, where appropriate, for arrears of wages or damages for wrongful dismissal. If the employee is the party at fault, the employer may sue for failure to perform the contract in accordance with its terms, even though it was the employer who introduced the void covenant of restraint into the contract in the first place.

2:8:2 *Severed covenants must be subsidiary parts of the contract*
A covenant in restraint of trade may be severed from a contract of employment only if it is subsidiary to its main purpose, and provided that the employer's consideration remains unaffected by the severance. If a promise in restraint of trade is the sole subject matter of the contract and that promise is wholly or mainly contrary to public policy, then the whole contract is void. In Wyatt v Kreglinger & Fernau (see 2:4) the employee's promise not to compete with his employer in the wool trade was an unreasonable restraint and void. This promise was the employee's only consideration for the pension received from his employer. Thus removal of the restraint vitally affected the employer's consideration and the whole contract failed.

2:8:3   *Extent to which the restraint is unreasonable must be trivial*
The employer must be able to show that the extent of the unreasonableness of the restraint imposed on the employee is not of any great significance.

Attwood v Lamont (1920, Court of Appeal)

Attwood carried on business in Kidderminster as a draper, tailor and general outfitter. His shop was divided into several different departments, with a manager in charge of each. Lamont was head cutter and manager of the tailoring department, but he was not connected with the work in other departments referred to in the restraint clause, which provided that he must not engage in "the trade or business of a tailor, dressmaker, general draper, milliner, hatter, haberdasher, gentlemen's, ladies' or children's outfitter at any place within a radius of 10 miles of his employer's place of business." Lamont set up his own tailoring business in Worcester, which is over 10 miles away from Kidderminster, but he accepted orders in Kidderminster and did business with customers of his former employer, contrary to the terms of his covenant.

The court decided that only one composite covenant existed for the protection of his several businesses. It was possible to go through the covenant, remove the offending parts that were unreasonable and so separate the reasonable restraint that covered tailoring. Such action would alter entirely the scope and intention of the agreement and consequently severance was not possible.

2:9   COVENANTS IN
RESTRAINT OF TRADE BETWEEN EMPLOYERS

A covenant in restraint of trade may be made between two employers mutually agreeing that neither will employ for a given period of time anyone formerly employed by the other. The two tests of reasonableness discussed above must be satisfied if the covenant is to be enforceable. An employer cannot use indirect means to seek a protection against competition that he could not have taken directly from his employee in an express term in the contract of employment.

Kores Manufacturing Co Ltd
v Kolok Manufacturing Co Ltd (1959, Court of Appeal)

The two companies were manufacturers of carbon paper and typewriter ribbons and occupied adjoining business premises. They agreed that, in the absence of written consent, neither would employ any person who, during the previous five years, had been employed by the other. Kolok wanted to employ a chemist who had previously worked for Kores, and Kores sought an injunction to prevent such employment.

The court decided that the contract was unreasonable in the interests of the parties to it and unenforceable since it imposed a restraint in excess of that required to prevent a misuse of trade secrets and confidential information. Lord Justice Jenkins emphasised that "an employer has no legitimate interest in preventing an employee, after leaving his service, from entering the service of a competitor merely on the ground that the new employer is a competitor." Where a covenant in restraint of trade would be void if inserted in a contract of employment, there does not appear to be any sound principle why the same covenant should be enforceable if it is the subject matter of an agreement between two employers.

PREVENTING AN EMPLOYEE HELPING COMPETITORS

2:10   PROTECTION OF CONFIDENTIAL INFORMATION

Statements made above on restraint of trade show that, when drafting a contract of employment, the employer should carefully consider the insertion of a term to protect any confidential information such as a list of customers that will be disclosed to the employee in the course of his employment. It is advisable to define the employee's duties in this respect in unambiguous terms, but in the absence of an express clause in the contract of employment, duties of good faith and fidelity will be incorporated by implication. These duties prevent the employee from engaging in any activity which is injurious to his employer's business while in the service of the employer.

Robb v Green (1895, Court of Appeal)

Green, while employed as manager of the plaintiff's business, compiled a list of the names and addresses of his clients, with the intention of soliciting their custom after leaving the plaintiff's employment.

The court decided that the compilation of the list was a breach of an implied term in Green's contract of employment that he would show good faith and fidelity to his employer, for which damages were recoverable. An injunction was granted to restrain use of the list compiled.

99

Wessex Dairies Ltd v Smith (1935, Court of Appeal)

In the decision on this later case, it was clearly stated, on facts basically similar to those in Robb v Green, that the list so compiled must be handed back to the employer. In the absence of an enforceable covenant of restraint, however, the employee may, after termination of the employment, canvass his late employer's customers and send circulars to them giving details of his business, provided the employee can remember the relevant names and addresses without reference to the prohibited list.

Few employers will be content to rely on such an incomplete protection, and the implied term of good faith and fidelity in the contract of employment should be regarded only as a last hope when the protection of an express clause has not been taken. It should be remembered that where the employer has taken the protection of an express covenant in restraint of trade from his employee, but this is void for unreasonableness, the protection of the implied term is still available, if it offers a suitable restraint on the employee's activities (see 2 : 1, Triplex Safety Glass Co v Scorah).

2 : 10 : 1 Disclosure of confidential
information to outsiders by the employee
An employee owes a duty to his employer not to disclose confidential information coming to his knowledge during the course of employment to other persons interested in or requesting such information, for example, business rivals or trade unions, who might use the knowledge to the detriment of the employer.

Bents Brewery Co Ltd v Luke Hogan (1945)

A union sent to its members, who managed licensed premises, a questionnaire on such matters as terms of employment, takings, expenses, and wages bills, so that a programme of wages and conditions of service could be prepared.

The court decided that the brewery companies who owned the businesses involved were entitled to a declaration stating that their employees must not make these disclosures, since it would constitute a breach of the implied duty of fidelity in their contracts of employment. Details concerning the managers' contracts of employment could be given to the union, for the information was not acquired as the result of opportunities offered in the course of employment.

2:10:2 *Misconduct by the employer*
may be publicly disclosed by the employee

An employee is not bound by an implied term of fidelity not to disclose details of his employer's misconduct, provided the general public have some interest in the information given, and disclosure is made to a person having a proper interest in receiving it.

Initial Services v Putterill (1967, Court of Appeal)

Putterill had been employed as a sales manager by the plaintiff company of launderers. He resigned and gave information to the *Daily Mail* about the company's affairs, some of which was contained in papers taken from the company. A report in the *Daily Mail* alleged the existence of an agreement between different launderers to keep up their prices and that price increases represented as essential to offset the effects of selective employment tax had brought an increased profit.

The court decided that Putterill was not in breach of his implied duty of fidelity in disclosing to strangers confidential information of interest to the public, though doubts were expressed as to whether the press was the proper authority to receive the information (disclosure to a public agency like the National Board for Prices and Incomes might have been preferable).

2:11 RESTRICTION OF AN EMPLOYEE'S SPARE-TIME EMPLOYMENT

The employer may be reluctant to allow an employee to work in his spare time for another employer, where, for example, a reasonable salary is being paid and the demands of the work require the employee's maximum effort. In these circumstances, an express term must be inserted in the contract of employment, which prevents the employee from engaging in paid spare-time work.

Sometimes the employee accepts a job on condition that he will be allowed to engage in other remunerative work in his spare time, in which case the employer cannot object to such activities. For example, a tax expert working full time for a large company may wish to undertake private business out of office hours.

In many contracts of employment, the employer does not take the protection of an express term prohibiting spare-time employment, thus it is important to understand the legal position. An employee will be in breach of his implied duty of fidelity, and liable to summary dismissal or restraint by an injunction, if he works for his employer's actual or potential rivals or discloses to a rival confidential information or techniques made known to him by his employer.

Hivac Ltd v Park Royal Scientific Instruments Ltd (1946, Court of Appeal)

The plaintiff company were manufacturers of midget valves used in deaf aids, while the defendant company, a competitor new to the business, was engaged mainly in the assembly of deaf aids. Five employees of the plaintiff company, whose work was highly skilled, worked in their spare time for the defendant company, by helping in the assembly of midget valves. It could not be shown that the five employees had divulged any confidential information to the defendant company.

The court granted an injunction to restrain the employees' spare-time work, since it constituted a breach of the employees' duties of good faith and fidelity, owed to the plaintiff company and implied in every contract of employment. The employees' contract of employment did not contain any express restraint in respect of spare-time competitive activities.

The practical difficulty in any given case is to determine the precise limits of this seemingly vague duty of fidelity. This is a question of fact in the circumstances of each particular case, being more extensive in relation to some classes of employees than others. Restrictions should not be imposed on a manual worker to prevent him from utilising his spare time to earn extra money. "On the other hand, it would be deplorable if it were laid down that (an employee) could, consistently with his duty to his employer, knowingly, deliberately and secretly set himself up to do in his spare time something which would inflict great harm on his employer's business." (Lord Greene)

THREE

Wages and Payments to the Government

THIS CHAPTER DEALS WITH THE FINANCIAL RESULTS OF EMPLOYING people. Most of the chapter is taken up by the law relating to the payment of wages. The remainder is concerned with the employer's duty to make social security payments on behalf of his employees, to pay their income tax and make contributions to the Redundancy Fund and towards the cost of industrial training.

WAGES

The remuneration to be paid by the employer to the employee is usually fixed after negotiations. The sum payable is included in one of the principal terms of the contract of employment. A personnel manager must ensure that an employee clearly understands either the amount payable as wages or the method by which it will be calculated. Problems arise, in exceptional cases, where a reference to the terms of contract will not help to determine the amount the employee is entitled to receive.

3:1 WHERE THE CONTRACT OF EMPLOYMENT DOES NOT STIPULATE THE WAGES TO BE PAID

If the contract of employment does not fix the wages payable, the employer may be sued for a sum that is deemed to be reasonable after taking into account the circumstances of the individual case and the negotiations between the parties. An attempt will be made to determine the value that each party placed on the services to be rendered. This is called a quantum meruit claim, or a claim for what the services rendered are worth. In a situation involving employment, the inference is that some payment will be made for any work done. Where services of an unusual nature are to be rendered, the question of remuneration is often left in an indeterminate state by the parties negotiating the contract of employment.

Way v Latilla (1937, House of Lords)

Way alleged an agreement whereby he was to obtain and send to Latilla information relating to gold mines and concessions in West Africa, and also introduce concessions for acquisition. Way was to receive in return a customary or reasonable share of the value of the concessions and also a reasonable sum for any information supplied. It was claimed by Way that he had not received any share in respect of certain concessions obtained for Latilla, the profit on the sale of which amounted to £1 million.

The court decided that there was no concluded contract of employment between the parties as to the amount of the mining interest that Way was to receive and it was impossible for the court to complete the contract for them. A contract of employment did exist, however, clearly indicating that the work was not to be done without payment in return. Thus Way was entitled to a reasonable sum on an implied contract to pay him a quantum meruit. This sum was deemed to be £5000.

Lord Wright stated: "The appellant was employed on the basis of receiving a remuneration depending upon results. If he had been unsuccessful, he would have been entitled to no more than his expenses, but the respondent [Latilla] had led him to believe that, if the concessions he obtained were valuable, his remuneration would be on the basis of some proportion of their value. The precise figure can be only a rough estimate. If what the court fixes is either too small or too large, the fault must be ascribed to the parties in leaving this important matter in so nebulous a state."

3:1:1 Where the contract of employment is void

If a contract of employment which the parties believe to be valid later turns out to be void, as where the person making the appointment has acted without authority to do so, then the employee may claim payment of a quantum meruit for the services provided. The employee may also sue the official responsible for engaging him for loss suffered (see 1 : 4 : 3).

Craven Ellis v Canons Ltd (1936, Court of Appeal)

Craven Ellis was employed as the managing director of Canons Ltd, but his contract of employment turned out to be invalid because the directors negotiating it did not hold the necessary qualification shares in the company to allow them to act as directors.

The court decided that, in the absence of a valid contract, the managing director could recover a reasonable sum for the services rendered to the company on a quantum meruit claim.

3:1:2 Important limitation on a quantum meruit claim

If the original contract between the employer and employee has not been brought to an end (that is, discharged) then the employee cannot seek payment for work done, additional to that contemplated by the original contract, under a quantum meruit claim. This principle may cause hardship to the employee, as the next case illustrates.

Gilbert & Partners v Knight (1968, Court of Appeal)

Gilbert, a member of a firm of surveyors, was promised £30 by Knight for supervising building work, estimated to cost £600. Knight ordered additional building work, increasing the total cost to £2238, which Gilbert then supervised, but without requesting a higher fee until he had completed his task. Knight paid the £30 originally agreed upon, but refused to pay £105 for the extra work.

The court decided that the parties had not terminated their original express contract for one lump sum of £30, and it would be inconsistent with the terms of that express contract to imply the existence of a new contract to pay an extra sum for the additional work and allow it to be recovered on a quantum meruit claim.

3:1:3 Where the employer commits a breach of contract

The employee may also rely on the doctrine of quantum meruit to recover money for work done where the contract of employment has been discharged because of his employer's breach of contract. In this situation the employee's claim is, in reality, an alternative to a claim for a breach of contract. It is especially useful if it can be shown that the contractual payment agreed on between the parties underestimated the true value of the employee's work. The quantum meruit claim may allow a greater sum to be recovered by the employee, on the basis of being paid a reasonable sum for the value of his work.

Planchè v Colburn (1831)

Colburn engaged Planchè to write a book on ancient armour, to be published by Colburn in a weekly magazine that he intended to bring out. The magazine was abandoned after publication of a few editions.

The court decided that Planchè could recover payment for the work done under the contract on a quantum meruit claim.

The original contract was for £100 and Planchè recovered £50 for the work.

3:1:4 Agent's entitlement to a commission
on a repeat order after the agency agreement ends

The liability of an employer or principal to pay commission to his employee or agent does not cover repeat orders made by a third party after the contract of employment or agency has terminated, unless there is an express term in the contract to this effect. This same rule applies where the employer or principal does business with those customers introduced by the employee or agent. A term allowing a claim for commission by the employee or agent will not usually be implied, unless it is essential to give the contract business efficacy.

Levy v Goldhill (1917)

Levy obtained orders for other traders on terms of commission, while travelling around for his own business purposes. Goldhill agreed to pay Levy half of the profits made on orders and repeat orders given by customers introduced, provided the customer settled his debts. Goldhill terminated the relationship constituted by the agreement without notice. Levy sued for damages for breach of the agreement and payment of commission in accordance with the terms of the agreement.

The court decided that there was no contract of employment between the parties in the strict sense. Levy was not obliged to do work for Goldhill, nor was the latter obliged to provide any work for Levy to do. The relationship could be terminated without notice, but on a construction of the agreement between the parties Levy was entitled to commission on all orders, whenever they were received, if they came from customers introduced by him.

The principal's duty to pay commission may continue despite the death of the agent, where on a construction of the terms of the agreement commission is payable as long as the principal continues to do business with those customers introduced by the agent.

Wilson v Harper (1908)

Harper agreed to pay Wroe 5 per cent on all accounts introduced by him, so long as Harper did business with the persons concerned. Wroe died and his executors claimed payment of the commission as promised.

The court decided that the defendants must continue to pay the commission so long as they continued to do business with the persons introduced by Wroe, since his death did not relieve them of the obligation to pay. It was not an agreement for agency, terminated by the agent's death.

3:2 TRUCK ACTS: PAYMENT, BONUSES, DEDUCTIONS AND FINES

The word *truck* means the payment of wages in kind, whereby the employer supplies the employee with goods or services in place of a monetary payment. In the past, employers forced their employees to buy goods at a shop owned by the employer, where the goods were priced higher than elsewhere. The price of the goods bought was then deducted from the employee's wages, thus reducing the real value of the wages paid. The Truck Acts were passed to remedy this and other undesirable practices.

3:2:1 Who is protected by the Truck Acts?

The Acts do not protect all employees, only *workmen* as defined by the Employers and Workmen Act 1875—that is, all persons engaged in manual labour under a contract of service, excluding domestic or menial servants. While discussing the statutory provisions, it is necessary to use the word "workmen" instead of "employees." The term *manual labour* is important, since it refers to the exertion of physical effort. It is not enough to use one's hands in one's work. For example, a bus conductor is not a manual labourer, since "his real and substantial business is to invite persons to enter the omnibus and to take and keep for his employers, the money paid by the passengers." (Lord Brett)

The case law on this point makes it difficult to provide any clear and easy guide to the type of employee who is protected by the Act. The test seems to be whether manual labour forms a substantial part of the employment; if so the employee is protected by the Act, but not if manual labour is merely incidental to his work.

The following types of employee have been held to be workmen within the meaning of the Act:

1 A bus driver, who must execute repairs while he is in charge of the bus
2 A packer in a warehouse
3 A seamstress working a sewing machine and ironing dresses
4 Framework knitters

The following are not covered by the Act:

1 A tram-car driver
2 A goods train guard, where his principal task is to safeguard the train, though he sometimes helps with loading

3   A hairdresser
4   A grocer's assistant, though some manual work is involved
5   Professional footballers

It is important that the contract of employment embodies an agreement for personal service. A person is not protected by the Act if he contracts to do a given job for the completion of which he must employ other workmen.

3:2:2 *Employer must make wage payments in cash (Truck Act 1831)*

A contract will be illegal, null and void, if it provides for the payment of the wages of a workman in any other form than current coin of the realm (s1). The workman may recover any part of his wages that has not been paid in legal tender (s4). The provision of goods or services by the employer in part payment of wages due is illegal (s3), and the workman may claim the balance due to him in cash and also retain the goods. The employer is liable for a penalty for contravening the 1831 Act, even if he is unaware that the offence has been committed, unless he lays information against the person directly responsible for the illegality. If the offence has been committed by an agent of the employer, such as a personnel manager, then that agent is himself liable in the same way as if he were the employer (s9).

When paying the workman's wages, the employer cannot deduct a sum awarded to the employer by a court of law in respect of the employee's previous breach of contract, for this is forbidden by s3. It is permissible, however, for the employer to make a deduction in respect of bad workmanship, where this is not a deduction from wages rightly earned, but a loss which must be taken into account in ascertaining the true wage payable.

3:2:3 *Deductions that are legal under the Truck Act 1831*

An employer is authorised by s23 of the Truck Act 1831 to make deductions from his employees' wages for the following purposes:

1   The supply of medicine, medical attendance or fuel
2   The supply of food which is prepared and consumed on the employer's premises
3   The letting of a house by the employer to be occupied by the workman personally in return for payment of rent

Deductions for the above purposes are legal, only if the following conditions are observed by the employer:

1   The agreement concerning the deduction must be in writing and signed by the workman
2   The amount deducted must not exceed the real value of the goods or services supplied

The next case illustrates the serious consequences for an employer who ignores the provisions of the Truck Acts.

Pratt v Cook, Son & Co (St Pauls) Ltd (1940, House of Lords)

For fifteen years Pratt received a weekly wage of £2 13s from his employers, the defendant company. He was also provided with dinner and tea on the employer's premises, the weekly value of the meals being assessed at 10s. In 1935 Pratt's wages were increased to £3 3s, but meals were no longer provided unless he paid for them in cash. He sued to recover 10s a week extending over the period of his fifteen years' employment, on the ground that the free meals provided were considered to be part of his wages, but the employers had no written authority from Pratt to make this deduction as required by s23 of the Truck Act 1831.

The House of Lords decided that Pratt was entitled to recover £397 10s, being the wages for the fifteen-year period not paid in current coin of the realm in violation of the provisions of the Truck Acts. The employers should have employed Pratt at the rate of £3 3s per week, then deducted 10s a week for meals with Pratt's written consent.

3:2:4   Further protections
for the employee (Truck Amendent Act 1887)

If a workman is entitled, whether by custom in the trade or by agreement with his employer, to receive an advance of his wages before the fixed time for payment of the full sum, then it is illegal for the employer, either to refuse to make an advance or to charge interest for so doing (s3).

The employer cannot deduct from a workman's wages the price of goods supplied to him by a person ordered to do so by the employer. The person supplying the goods cannot sue the workman for payment (s5).

It must not be a condition of the workman's employment that he shall spend his wages, or part of his wages, at any particular place, or in any particular manner, or with any particular person, nor can the workman be dismissed for not doing these things (s6).

3 : 2 : 5 Valid contract of sale between employer and employee

The Truck Acts do not prevent the employer and workman from entering into an independent contract for the sale of goods in which the employer deals, which are often sold to employees at cost price. Similarly, the workman may buy shares in the company that employs him. In both cases, however, the contract of employment must not compel an agreement of this kind and any debt incurred by the workman must not be deducted from his wages direct. If, for example, a company agrees with its workmen to pay them £20 per week in cash and £2 more to be paid by allotting shares in the company to the workmen, such an agreement is void as an infringement of the Truck Acts.

As an added incentive, some firms give their employees shares in the company, so that they have an added interest in fostering the success of the enterprise. Any such arrangement must be independent of the payment of the agreed wages and the scheme should provide that such shares cannot be claimed as of right. If the essence of the agreement is that the share allotment is in substitution for payment of part of the wages, it is illegal.

3 : 2 : 6 Bonuses

If an employer regularly pays his employees a bonus, a usual occurrence at Christmas time in some firms, the danger for the employer is that the bonus may become, by implication, a part of the workman's wages, which must then be paid in cash. Where the bonus payment is not made at all, or made in a form other than cash, it becomes an illegal deduction.

3 : 2 : 7 Deductions in favour of a third party

If the workman requests the employer to pay his wages or part of his wages to a third party, any deduction and payment to that third party by the employer is legal. An example is the payment of trade union subscriptions. The workman must authorise this deduction in writing, whether it be for a single occasion, a stated period of time, or to remain effective until revoked. Where the employer is the creditor and the deduction from the workman's wages is an attempt to repay the employer, it is illegal. An employer cannot even make deductions for wages overpaid on a previous occasion, but if the workman refuses to refund the money, the employer may sue him (see also 10 : 5 : 2).

3 : 2 : 8 Deductions permitted by the Truck Act 1896

The Act authorises an employer either to make a deduction from a workman's wage, or require a payment to be made to him by the workman for:

1   A breach of discipline, by imposition of a fine
2   Bad or negligent work, or damage to property of the employer
3   Use or supply of materials, tools, machines, standing room, light, heat or any other thing to be provided by the employer in relation to the work of the workman

In each of the above three situations the deduction or payment is permissible if the following conditions have been satisfied by the employer:

1   The terms of the contract allowing the deduction or payment are either in writing and signed by the workman, or alternatively embodied in a notice that is continuously and conspicuously displayed, where it may be seen, read and copied by any person affected
2   Any deduction or payment made must be in accordance with that contract
3   The amount deducted or paid must be fair and reasonable in the circumstances of the case—for example, the wages earned must be related to the sum deducted
4   The workman must be informed in writing of the acts or omissions in respect of which the deduction or payment is imposed, together with the amount involved on each occasion when a deduction is made

There are other conditions that the employer must satisfy, depending upon the type of deduction made, and these will be discussed below under the appropriate individual heading.

Deduction by way of a fine. For the purpose of deducting a fine, the term "workman" also includes shop assistants, who are otherwise outside the scope of the Truck Acts. The fine imposed under the contract must be in respect of some act or omission which either actually causes, or is likely to cause, damage or loss to the employer. Fines are punishments intended to prevent any acts which harm the employer; thus they are not confined to those acts causing actual loss. If all the necessary conditions are satisfied by the employer, lighting a cigarette, for example, in the vicinity of inflammable material may be the subject of a fine, even though no harm was caused on the occasion in question.

     The most common offence for which an employer will deduct a fine from his workman's wages is late arrival for work, but fines for other more general acts and omissions showing a lack of discipline by workmen are frequently included.

Squire v Bayer & Co (1901)

A factory rule stipulated that workers should observe "good order and decorum." Some of the female workers danced around during mealtimes, creating a dust which was likely to damage the machinery. The court decided that a fine could be imposed for infringement of the disciplinary ruling.

Many employers hand out a rule book to their workmen, which clearly states the disciplinary offences for which a fine will be levied. The workman is then required to sign a statement whereby he agrees to the imposition of the fine in the circumstances set out in the rule book. This action makes it difficult for him to establish lack of knowledge of any relevant details, if an offence is committed at a later date.

Deductions for bad or negligent work or damage to the employer's property. Any deduction or payment must not exceed the actual or estimated damage or loss suffered by the employer as a result of the acts or omissions of the workman.

Deductions or payments in respect of materials. The amount to be deducted or paid for materials and tools supplied to the workman must not exceed the actual or estimated cost to the employer. Only a fair and reasonable rent may be charged for machinery, light and heat used by the employee.

3:2:9   *Enforcing the provisions of the Truck Act 1896*
A workman or shop assistant may recover sums deducted or paid contrary to the Act, but proceedings must be commenced within six months from the date of the deductions. If the workman has consented to the deduction or payment, he cannot recover the whole amount, but only the excess over and above the amount held to be fair and reasonable in the circumstances (s5).

The employer making the illegal deduction commits an offence under the 1831 Act and may be fined on conviction (s4). Factory inspectors may enforce the provisions of the Truck Acts against offending employers, by instituting any necessary proceedings. Inspectors may demand to see any written contract made between the workman and employer which authorises deductions, and may take a copy. The workman is entitled to a copy from his employer on request and free of charge. Where any deductions or payments have been made, the details must be entered in a register, which may be inspected at any time by a factory inspector (s6).

3:2:10   Shop Clubs Act 1902

It is an offence punishable by a fine to make it a condition of the employee's contract of employment that:

1   He must discontinue his membership of any friendly society registered under the Friendly Societies Act 1896
2   He must not join any friendly society, except a "shop club" or "thrift fund"—that is, a body which provides benefits for workmen in connection with a factory, shop, dock, workshop or warehouse
3   He must join a "shop club" or "thrift fund," unless it is one registered under the Friendly Societies Act 1896

Before a club or fund can be so registered it must:

1   Be one that provides substantial benefits to the workman, at the employer's cost
2   Be of a permanent character, without provision for a periodic share-out of funds
3   Be desired by 75 per cent of the workmen concerned, at the time when it is established

Unless it is contrary to the rules of the club, on leaving the employment, the individual workman who is a member must be entitled to:

1   Continue his membership, but without the right to vote or take part in the management of the club, or
2   Receive back the amount of his share of the funds

3:3   PAYMENT OF WAGES BY CHEQUE, MONEY ORDER, POSTAL ORDER, OR INTO A BANK ACCOUNT

The Truck Acts, requiring payment of a workman in "current coin of the realm," have been modified in their effect by the Payment of Wages Act 1960. Payment of wages by cheque makes possible increased mechanisation in the wages offices of the larger companies and removes the need for the transfer of large sums of money from the bank to the employer's place of business, with the attendant risk of theft. If the employer wishes to make a payment of wages by cheque, he must take care to observe scrupulously the provisions of the Act.

Methods of payment authorised by the Act (s1). The wages of all types of employees, not only those covered by the Truck Acts, may be paid in one of the following ways:

1   Into a bank account
2   By postal order or money order
3   By cheque

The employee must have given notice in writing requesting payment in one of those new forms and the employer must agree to that request, either by notice in writing to the employee, or by paying wages in the way specified in the request. It is clear that the employee cannot be forced to accept payment by one of these new methods. He must be willing to do so. Payment must be made in cash if the employee so wishes.

The employer may refuse the employee's request by written notice to that effect, given within fourteen days. The employee's request will also be ineffective if the employer simply ignores it for fourteen days after receipt. This is a useful safeguard for the employer of a small number of employees, where cash is readily available at the place of business, for example, a shop.

3:3:1   *Payment into a bank account (s2)*
A request for wages to be paid into a bank account must state:

1   The bank, the branch at which the account is kept, and whether it is a current or deposit account
2   The person or persons in whose name or names the account stands

Wages must be paid only into the account of the employee, as specified, or an account held jointly by the employee and another person or persons.

3:3:2   *Payment by cheque, postal order or money order*
A payment of wages by cheque must be:

1   Made payable to, or to the order of, the person to whom the wages are due

2   Without deduction from the gross amount of the wages to offset any expense incurred by the employer in making payment in this form (s2)

Although the employee may not have consented to payment into a bank account or by cheque, the employer is entitled to post the employee's wages to him in the form of a postal order or money order where the employee:

1   Is working away from the place where payments take place,
     or
2   Is absent from work because of injury or illness

unless the employee has given written notice to the employer that this method of payment is not acceptable (s4). A written statement of particulars of the payment must also be given (see 3 : 3 : 3).

The employer or employee may at any time, by written notice, cancel the agreement to be paid by any of the methods provided by the Act (s3). The notice takes effect four weeks after it is given.

3:3:3 *Every employee must receive particulars of his wages payment*
At or before the time of payment by one of these methods, the employer must give the employee a statement in writing containing the following particulars:

1   The gross amount of the wages, clear of all deductions
2   The amount of each deduction made from that gross amount with details of each deduction so made—for example, tax, graduated pensions, National Insurance
3   The net amount payable—that is, the gross amount less any deductions specified in the statement
4   Where the employee requests that *part* of his wages be paid in one of the new ways, the employer must give a written statement of:
   (a) The net amount payable in the way so requested, and
   (b) The net amount of the balance payable

If a mistake is made when giving the above-mentioned written particulars, but it is a clerical error or otherwise made accidentally in good faith, the written statement will be treated as complying with the Act (s2).

3:4 HOLIDAY PAY

The Industrial Relations Act 1971 Schedule 2 requires every statement of particulars of employment given to an employee under s4 of the Contracts of Employment Act 1964 to include details of entitlement to:

1   Annual holidays and public holidays
2   Holiday pay
3   Accrued holiday pay, if employment is terminated before the time arrives for taking the annual leave allowed

The provisions of the Holidays with Pay Act 1938 are incorporated into the Wages Council Act 1959. Wages Councils are given power to submit proposals to the Department of Employment to fix:

1   The duration of holidays
2   The times at which, or periods within which, such holidays will be allowed
3   The holiday pay to be given

These proposals may concern any workers for whom a minimum rate of wages is being or has been fixed. In the absence of an express direction to the contrary, the holidays granted must be in addition to any holidays or half-holidays to which the employee is entitled by virtue of any other enactment, for example, Bank Holidays. If an employee leaves his employment before taking his holiday with pay, then the employer must pay him the sum of money that has accrued, by way of holiday pay.

The personnel manager dealing with these problems must determine whether the particular industry or trade he is concerned with is covered by an order made under the 1938 Act. If the industry or trade is not covered, an employee's rights to holiday with pay, and accrued holiday remuneration, will depend upon the express terms of the contract of employment.

3:5 WAGE PAYMENTS DURING ILLNESS

An express term in the contract of employment may provide that during periods of illness wages will be paid at a given rate for a stated period of time, or alternatively that wages will not be paid. An agreement to pay wages during sickness also covers absence caused by an accident. The rights and obligations of the employer and employee will be governed by the provisions in the express term.

3:5:1 Where an express term
on wage payments during illness does not exist

Where an express term on wage payments during illness does not exist an employee is entitled to his full wages during illness, unless an implied term or trade custom provides otherwise. "A term can only be implied if it is necessary in the business sense to give efficacy to the contract: that is, if it is such a term that it can confidently be said that if at the time the contract was being negotiated someone had said to the parties, 'What will happen in such a case,' they would both have replied, 'Of course, so and so will happen; we did not trouble to say that; it is too clear.' Unless the court comes to some such conclusion as that, it ought not to imply a term which the parties themselves have not expressed." (Lord Justice Scrutton)

If the employer wishes to evade payment of wages during the employee's illness, he must prove the existence of an implied term to that effect.

O'Grady v M Saper Ltd (1940, Court of Appeal)

A commissionaire was absent from work because of illness and claimed payment of his wages for the period in question. He had been absent in similar circumstances on previous occasions, but he had not received any salary from his employer. The court decided that he was not entitled to any payment.

A clear statement is advisable on the position of each party to the contract of employment, since few employers will wish to rely upon an implication from the circumstances. The Contracts of Employment Act 1963 allows the employer to make whatever provision he feels to be necessary for wage payments to the employee during illness, but s4(1) states that any term relating to incapacity for work because of sickness or injury shall be included in the written particulars given to the employee. Approximately half of the working population are unprotected by sickness provisions and many employees who are protected receive less than the full wage, and then only for a limited period of absence. An employee unable to work may claim sickness benefit under the National Insurance scheme.

If an employee is likely to have a prolonged absence because of illness, the employer is free to terminate the contract of employment by giving the length of notice required in the circumstances. This ends the employee's

E

right to sick pay, whether his claim is made under an express contractual term or a mere implied term. As the next case shows, this course of action may be a better alternative for the employer than attempting to establish an implied term that wages are not payable.

Orman v Saville Sportswear Ltd (1960)

Orman, production manager in a factory owned by the defendant company, was absent from work for two months because of illness. The defendant company paid Orman his salary during this time, but not his bonus or commission. When he reported back to work he was paid his salary in lieu of notice, but not his bonus. Orman claimed £250 by way of bonus for the period between the beginning of his illness until the termination of his employment.

The court decided that when a written contract of employment does not make any provision for payment of salary during absence through illness, as in this case, the employer must pay the employee the full remuneration that would have been received, including bonuses. He must continue paying this until the contract is properly terminated, as by giving notice, unless he can establish an implied term to the contrary.

3:5:2 *National Insurance benefits*

An employee entitled to full pay during absence through illness may also claim sickness benefit under the National Insurance scheme or from a friendly society. Many employers include a term in the contract of employment stating that they will only supplement the sickness benefit received to make the total sum equivalent to a normal week's wage.

3:5:3 *Discharge of a contract because of illness*

If the illness will be protracted or if it goes to the root of the contract of employment, then the contract may be discharged completely (see 13:4:1).

3:6   SUSPENSION WITHOUT PAY

If the employer wants power to suspend an employee for misconduct he will usually have to include an express term to this effect in the contract of employment. In the absence of an express power any purported suspension will be wrongful and the employee may sue to recover wages lost during the period of suspension. There may be statutory power to suspend in some instances, depending upon the nature of the relationship between employer and employee. For example, the Municipal Corporations Act 1882 s191 empowers the watch committee of a local authority to suspend, without pay, a member of the police force whom they believe to have been negligent in the discharge of his duty, or otherwise unfit.

There may be a well-recognised and generally accepted practice in some types of employment that impliedly allow an employee to be suspended for misconduct.

Marshall v The English Electric Co Ltd (1945, Court of Appeal)

Marshall, an engineer employed by the defendant company, was suspended for three days without pay for a breach of discipline. There existed at the defendant's works a well-established and well-recognised practice of suspending workmen for breaches of discipline, including negligence in the performance of work. Marshall asked the court to declare that his suspension was contrary to the terms of his contract of employment.

The court decided that it was an implied term of the contract of employment that an employee could be suspended without pay for a reasonable period. This arose from a practice of which Marshall was aware and also from trade custom in the area where the factory was situated.

Such a suspension and deduction from wages does not make the contract illegal under the Truck Acts (see 3 : 2). During the period of the suspension the obligations of employer and employee are in abeyance and wages need not be paid for that period. "If the employed is suspended from his functions as an employed person . . . the effect is . . . to excuse the [employee] from performing his part of the contract, and at the same time to relieve the employer from performing his part of the contract. It would be a most extraordinary thing if suspension were to be so one-sided that the [employee] were to be excused from performing his part of the contract while the employer was to remain liable to perform his." (Lord Justice Warrington)

The employer cannot:

1   Suspend the employee, then dismiss him without paying wages covering the period of suspension, or,
2   Suspend the employee then continue the employer–employee relationship and treat the pay lost by suspension as the equivalent of damages for the employee's misconduct

unless necessary terms giving such powers are expressly or impliedly included in the contract of service. An express term of the contract may require payment of wages for the period of suspension if the employee is reinstated.

Gorse and Another v Durham County Council and Another (1971)

The plaintiff school teachers were suspended by their employers, the defendant county council, for refusing to supervise school meals. They were then reinstated, but payment of salary was not made for the period of the suspension.

The court decided that the teachers were entitled to succeed in their claim for payment. Their refusal to supervise school meals amounted to a repudiation of their contracts of employment, but by merely suspending the teachers the employers had not accepted their actions as a termination of the contractual relationship. The employers did not follow the procedure laid down in cases of suspension, nor had they paid salary for the period of suspension on eventual reinstatement as was required by an express term in the contract of employment.

3:7 EQUAL PAY FOR WOMEN (EQUAL PAY ACT 1970)

The object of the Equal Pay Act 1970 is to eliminate discrimination on grounds of sex respecting remuneration and other terms and conditions of employment.

3:7:1 Equal treatment of women (s1)
It will be a term of a woman's contract of employment that there be equal treatment of men and women, where they are engaged upon:

1   The same or similar work, or
2   Where the woman's job, though of a different nature to the man's, has been rated as equivalent to his, following job evaluation taking into account the demand on the worker of effort, skill and decision

In the absence of an express term securing these rights, a term will be implied. Employment wholly or mainly outside Great Britain is excluded. However, under s6, where

1   Terms and conditions of a woman's employment are affected
     by compliance with the law regulating their employment, or
2   They are specially treated in connection with birth, expected
     birth, retirement, marriage or death

then to that extent equal treatment for men and women is not required.

3:7:2 Disputes concerning equal pay (s2)

Either party to a dispute may refer the matter for a decision to an
industrial tribunal, established under the Industrial Training Act 1964 s12.
The term *dispute* covers any claim relating to the operation of an express
or implied term in a woman's contract of employment, including:

1   A claim for arrears of pay, or
2   Damages for failure to comply with an equal pay clause
     (s2(1)).

The Secretary of State for Employment may also refer to an industrial
tribunal an employer's failure to comply with an equal pay clause (s2(2)).

A court dealing with an equal pay clause dispute may, on its own
initiative, or that of a party to the proceedings, refer the matter to an
industrial tribunal, if that body might dispose of it more conveniently
(s2(3)).

Claims respecting an equal pay clause shall not be referred to an industrial tribunal, except under s2(3), if the claimant has not been employed
in that employment within six months preceding reference (s2(4)).

Damages or arrears of pay cannot be recovered for failure to comply with
an equal pay clause for any period over two years before instituting proceedings (s2(5)).

The onus of proof is on the employer to show that any pay difference
between the sexes results from material differences (other than sex) between
their cases (s2(6)).

3:7:3 Amending a collective agreement
and wages regulation orders to comply with the Act

Where clauses of collective agreement apply to men only or women only,
then any party to them or the Secretary of State may ask the Industrial
Arbitration Board to make necessary amendments to remove any discrimination. Any contract of employment dependent upon that collective
agreement is then effective, subject to those amendments (s3).

Any wages regulation order containing provisions applying to men only or women only may be referred by the Secretary of State for Employment to the Industrial Arbitration Board, so that any necessary amendment may remove the discrimination. He may make the reference either:

1   On his own initiative, or
2   If requested by representatives of either employers or workers on the wages council

The order is then effective subject to the amendments, where the Secretary of State so directs by statutory instrument, within five months of the Board's decision (s4).

3:7:4   Implementation of the Act (s9)

The Act is to become effective on 29 December 1975. The Secretary of State may provide by orders for an intermediate stage to be effective on 31 December 1973, at which date women will be entitled to treatment short of full equality, but ensuring orderly progress towards it.

3:8   PAYING A FAIR WAGE

A resolution passed by the House of Commons in 1946 states that in all government contracts a fair wage clause should be inserted, requiring contractors to:

1   Pay wage rates and observe hours and conditions not less favourable than those commonly accepted in the district; in the absence of a commonly accepted standard, then terms equal to those observed by other employers in the industry concerned should be granted
2   Comply in respect of all employees, not only employees directly engaged on the government contract; before being placed on the list of firms invited to tender for government contracts, the contractor must show compliance with those terms for the preceding three months at least
3   Allow his workers to join a trade union
4   Display a copy of the resolution in every work place used by the contractor during the continuance of the employment
5   Ensure the observance of the resolution by subcontractors employed by him in performance of the government contract

Any dispute concerning the implementation of the clause must be referred to the Secretary of State for Employment. If it is not settled, a further reference is necessary, usually to the Industrial Arbitration Board.

The main purpose of this resolution, which does not have the force of law, is to ensure that government contractors set a good example to other classes of employers, by paying the current wage expected by the employee for the type of work undertaken. The clauses set out above have been extended to employees in:

1 The film industry (Cinematograph Films Acts 1939, 1948, 1960)
2 Road haulage (Road Haulage Wages Act 1938)
3 The British Sugar Corporation (Sugar Act 1956)
4 Television, if employed by television programme contractors (Television Act 1954)

An employee is legally entitled to the wages he has agreed to accept under his contract of employment. He cannot demand the higher wage rates commonly recognised in his trade, by attempting to establish a legal right to enforce a fair wages resolution embodied in a contract between a government department and his employer.

Simpson v Kodak Ltd (1948)

Simpson was employed by Kodak Ltd at a weekly wage of £6.37½. A minimum weekly wage rate of £8.90 effective from 1 February 1945 was agreed upon by Simpson's trade union and an employers' association of which Kodak Ltd was not a member. Kodak Ltd carried out work for several government departments under contracts that included fair wages clauses under which Kodak Ltd agreed to pay the commonly recognised wage rates in the trade.

Simpson sued to recover the difference between the wage payments he received and the payments that he would have received if the fair wages resolution had been implemented by his employer.

The court decided that the fair wages clauses included in the contracts negotiated by Kodak with the various government departments did not entitle Simpson to recover wage rates higher than those agreed upon in his contract of employment.

3:8:1   *Terms and Conditions of Employment Act 1959 (s8)*

The provisions of s8 of this Act have been amended by the Industrial Relations Act 1971 s152 and schedule 7 part II. The following discussion of the section takes these changes into account. A written claim may be reported by a body registered as a trade union or an employers' association under the Industrial Relations Act 1971, to the Secretary of State for Employment if an employer is not observing generally accepted terms and conditions of employment in respect of an employee. The following conditions must be satisfied:

1   The terms and conditions of employment in the trade, industry or public or local authorities concerned must have been settled by an agreement or award either
(a) For general application throughout that trade or industry, or
(b) In any particular district
2   The parties to that agreement or proceedings leading to an award must have been:
(a) Organisations of employers or their representatives, and
(b) Organisations of workers, or associations of such organisations, representing a substantial number of the employees in the relevant trade or industry, whether generally or in a particular district, as the case may be, being employees of the description to which the agreement or award relates

The Secretary of State must try to settle the claim by use of appropriate machinery if necessary. If the claim is not settled the matter may be referred to the Industrial Arbitration Board. If the Board is satisfied that the claim is well founded, it may make an award requiring the employer concerned to observe the recognised terms and conditions in respect of all employees of the relevant description employed by him from time to time.

Such an award becomes effective as an implied term of the employee's contract of employment from the date specified by the Board. This date cannot be earlier than the date on which the employer was first informed of the claim giving rise to the award by the body reporting the matter to the Secretary of State. It is clear from these provisions that an award against an employer can be retrospective.

A claim may be reported under this section in respect of employees whose remuneration or minimum remuneration has been fixed by the Wages Councils Act 1959.

3:9 STATUTORY REGULATION OF WAGES

Despite the growth in the twentieth century of powerful trade unions with the ability to bargain collectively to secure better wages for their members, there are still sections of employees unprotected by a strong trade union; consequently legislation regulating wages is essential to ensure the payment of a reasonable wage. Legislation of this type is aimed at either the protection of employees in a specified industry, such as agriculture, or at a specified class of employees irrespective of the industry in which they are engaged—for example, workers protected under the Wages Councils Act 1959. About four million workers are now protected by the kind of legislation to be discussed.

The personnel manager will probably be concerned with the effect and enforcement of any wage regulation orders on workers employed by his firm.

3:9:1 *Wages councils*
There are fifty-four wages councils each of which consists of:

1   Not more than three independent persons, one of whom acts as chairman and one as deputy chairman
2   An equal number of representatives of employers and employees in the industry concerned, appointed after consultation with representative organisations

The appointments are made by the Secretary of State for Employment.

A wages council has power to submit to the Secretary of State its wages regulation proposals for fixing:

1   The wages to be paid by employers to all or any of the workers, generally, or for particular work
2   The holiday to be allowed, provided the working and holiday remuneration has been settled already for that worker. Any such proposal must also relate the length of the holiday allowed to the length of time for which the worker has been employed by the employer who is granting the holiday—for example, one day's holiday for every four weeks' employment. The times at which, and the period within which, the holiday must be taken may be stipulated. The holiday pay provisions may state the conditions upon which the pay accrues and

E*   129

becomes payable, including the provisions applicable if the employment is terminated before the time arrives for taking the paid holiday

The office of the Secretary of the wages councils (which is at 12 St James's Square, London SW1) maintains a register of all establishments it knows to be covered by wages councils. There is no obligation on employers to register but, as explained in 3:9:2, employers on the register receive copies of the councils' proposals for remuneration and holidays.

Meaning of the term "worker" (s24). For the purposes of the Wages Councils Act, a *worker* includes:

1   A manual worker
2   A clerical worker
3   A person serving under a contract of apprenticeship
4   A home worker employed under a contract for the execution
    of work, if subject to a statutory minimum remuneration

The contract of employment may be written or oral, express or implied. Persons employed casually and independent contractors are not covered (see 1:12:7, Westall Richardson Ltd v Roulson).

3:9:2   *How wages regulations are made*
Before a wages council submits its proposals to the Secretary of State, employers in the industry known to be affected must be notified. The employer must place a copy of the proposals at a place where they may be studied by workers. Both employers and workers are then in a position to make written representations, if desired, to the wages council, in the light of which the original proposals may be amended. The Secretary of State then receives a final draft and he either:

1   Makes a wages regulation order giving the proposals statutory
    force and then the wages council and persons affected are
    informed that this is the statutory minimum, or
2   Refers the proposals back to the wages council to reconsider
    in the light of his observations, after which they are returned
    to the Secretary of State

The Secretary of State cannot make an order which does not confirm the proposals of the wages council. The result can be a series of references to the wages council by the Secretary of State, followed by stubborn un-amended resubmissions by the council back to him.

3:9:3 *Effect of a wages regulation order on the employer (s12)*

If a wages regulation order is in force in relation to some particular trade or industry, and a contract of employment between an employer and a worker stipulates wages below the statutory minimum, then the statutory minimum must be paid.

If only a part of the worker's job is covered by a statutory minimum wage, then a proportionate part of that statutory minimum wage must be paid in relation to the time spent on the work so regulated.

If a contract of employment provides for the payment of holiday pay at times or subject to conditions not set out in the wages regulation order, then the times and conditions set out in the order will be applicable. If an employer fails to pay the statutory minimum wage or allow the holiday or the holiday pay as specified in the order, then he will be liable on sum-mary conviction to a fine not exceeding £20 for each offence. The employer may be ordered to pay the difference between the actual pay received by the worker and the statutory minimum due to him.

When proceedings are instituted for failure to pay the statutory minimum wage, then evidence may be admitted of other contraventions by the same employer during the two years immediately preceding the offence, provided that notice of intention to do so has been served with the sum-mons, warrant or complaint. The employer may be ordered to pay the difference between the actual pay received by the worker during the two years and the statutory minimum wage due to him.

3:9:4 *Incapacitated people (s13)*

If a worker protected by a wages regulation order is affected by infirmity or physical incapacity which renders him incapable of earning the statutory minimum wage, the wages council may issue a permit authorising employ-ment at some lower rate. The application may be made by the worker himself, the employer or a potential employer.

If the worker holds the permit when he is accepted for employment the employer must notify the wages council of the employment and the specified remuneration. Even if a permit has ceased to be valid it is treated as valid until the wages council issues a notice to the contrary.

3:9:5 *Deductions from the minimum wage (s14)*

Only the following lawful deductions may be made from the statutory minimum wage:

1 Deductions authorised by the Income Tax Acts, National Insurance (Industrial Injuries) Acts 1965 to 1971, National Insurance Acts 1965 to 1971 and other enactments authorising deductions for superannuation
2 Any deductions made at the worker's written request, either for the purpose of superannuation, for a thrift scheme or for some other purpose in which the employer has no beneficial interest (a thrift scheme means an arrangement for savings, providing money for holidays or other purposes, where the worker receives in cash sums equal to or greater than the sums deducted from his wages)
3 Deductions under the Truck Act 1896 dealing with fines, damaged goods or materials supplied (see 3 : 2 : 8)

3:9:6 *Special responsibility of the personnel manager*

The employer may delegate to his personnel manager the responsibility for ensuring that the statutory minimum wage is paid to all workers entitled to it, or at least draw the personnel manager's attention to the need to comply with the wages regulation order. If the personnel manager fails to discharge his duty properly, with the result that the employer is charged with an offence, then the employer may have the personnel manager brought before the court when the charge is heard. The employer must give information of his intention to do so and the prosecution must be given three days' notice in writing.

If the employer proves that the offence was committed as a result of the act or default of the personnel manager, then the personnel manager and not the employer may be convicted of the offence. The employer will be acquitted upon proof that he used due diligence to ensure that his personnel manager observed the statutory requirements, as by giving him appropriate instructions.

The personnel manager may be proceeded against in the first place, instead of the employer, if the commission of the offence is clearly the personnel manager's responsibility and not the employer's.

3:9:7 Wages inspectors (s19)

The Wages Inspectorate is a part of the Department of Employment; there are about 150 inspectors who enforce regulations made by the wages councils. They have the following powers:

1   Inspecting and copying any wages sheet and record of payment kept by the employer
2   Inspecting lists of outworkers, their names and addresses and payments made to them
3   Entering at a reasonable time the place of business of an employer to whom a wages regulation order applies
4   Examining any person whom they have reasonable cause to believe to be, or have been, a worker to whom a wages regulation order applies, or the employer of such person, or the employer's servant or agent carrying out the employer's business; the person examined may be required to sign a declaration of the truth of the matters that he was examined about, but he cannot be required to give any information that incriminates him
5   Institute either proceedings for an offence under the Act or civil proceedings to recover for a worker money due to him from an employer paying less than the statutory minimum wage

Every year the inspectors call on a random sample of about 7½ per cent of the half million establishments covered by the wages councils. They also investigate about 20 000 complaints by workers every year; most of these are caused by misinterpretation of the provisions for accumulated holiday pay.

The personnel manager should give an inspector every assistance. Otherwise he may be liable to a fine of £20 on summary conviction for obstructing the inspector in exercising his powers or for failing to comply with the inspector's requirements while exercising his powers.

Records to be kept. A person employing workers protected by a wages regulation order must keep and retain for three years records showing compliance with the order. Failure to do so is punishable with a fine not exceeding £20 (s17).

A person, including a personnel manager, is liable to a fine of up to £100, or imprisonment for up to three months, or both, if he:

1   Makes, causes to be made, or knowingly allows to be made a false entry of some material particular in these records, or

2   Produces or knowingly allows to be produced any wages sheet, record, list or information which he knows to be false in a material particular (s20)

It is interesting to note that in 1967 nearly 50 000 establishments were inspected and arrears of wages recovered from almost 9000 employers. Some 14 500 workers were underpaid a total of just under £182 000. The inspectors rarely have to bring cases to court: most of the underpayments they discover are caused by employers misinterpreting the wages regulation orders and by employees being ignorant of their rights. The inspectors are always happy to explain the provisions of the Act to employers.

3:9:8 How wages councils are established (s1, s2)

The Secretary of State for Employment has power to make an order establishing a wages council in one of three ways:

1   By acting on his own initiative, where adequate machinery does not exist for effective wage regulation amongst workers covered by the order

2   Where, after receiving an application from either:
  (a) A joint industrial council or other similar body representing workers and employers, or
  (b) Any organisation of workers and employers which claims that it habitually takes part in settling remuneration and conditions of employment
     he refers the application to the Commission on Industrial Relations which, after deliberation, recommends that a wages council be established

3   Where he believes that adequate machinery does not exist, or that existing machinery will cease to be reasonable in the future, so that a reasonable standard of remuneration will not be maintained, then he may refer the individual case to the Commission on Industrial Relations, which then recommends a wages council order

Reference to the CIR (s3). The Commission on Industrial Relations may consider not only the matter referred to it by the Secretary of State, but also other matters considered to be relevant, in particular, whether there are other workers closely allied with those under consideration, whose position should be dealt with as well. The Commission may decide to do one of the following:

1 Recommend the establishment of a wages council, or
2 Report that existing machinery is adequate, or alternatively that it is inadequate, together with suggestions for improvements

The Secretary of State will then give effect to any improvements he considers to be necessary.

Procedure when a wages council order is made (schedule 1). Before making a wages council order, the Secretary of State must publish a notice in *The London Gazette* which states:

1 His intention to make the order
2 The place where copies of the draft order may be obtained
3 The time (at least forty days) during which written objections may be made, stating both the grounds for objecting and the variations in the order that are desired

The Secretary of State may make the order if:

1 There are no objections
2 After considering objections, he feels that either they have been expressly dealt with by the CIR or they will be met by his own modifications to the order

Amending a wages council order. If the Secretary of State amends the draft order to embody the objections received, then the amended order must go through the same procedure as the original order, as outlined above. Alternatively, the draft order, together with any objections to be considered, may be referred to the CIR. On receiving the Commission's report, the Secretary of State may make the order on the terms of the draft or with the amendments he thinks fit.

3:9:9 *Abolition of a wages council (s4)*
The Secretary of State may abolish or vary the field of operation of a wages council, but a provision may be included establishing another wages

council to protect all or some of the workers covered by the original council. Due notice must be given of the intention to abolish or vary, and objections must be considered in the same way as when the order was first made. The abolition of a wages council is a success for autonomous bargaining. The wages councils for the cutlery, jute and paper bag industries were abolished quite recently.

Under the Industrial Relations Act 1971 the only condition to be satisfied before a wages council can be abolished will be that it is no longer necessary for the purpose of maintaining a reasonable standard of remuneration for the employees within its scope. Where possible, wages councils will be abolished if they have outlived their usefulness. It is hoped that the reform of industrial relations will promote the growth of voluntary arrangements for collective bargaining.

Abolition by application (s5). Applications for the abolition of a wages council may be made to the Secretary of State by the following bodies, on the ground that the existence of a wages council is no longer necessary to maintain a reasonable standard of remuneration for the workers it covers:

1   A joint industrial council, conciliation board or other similar body, constituted by organisations of workers and employers
2   Jointly, by organisations of workers and organisations of employers, representing substantial proportions of workers and employers
3   Any organisation of workers which represents a substantial proportion of the workers covered by the council

Consideration by the CIR (s6). When an application for abolition has been made to the Secretary of State, but he does not give effect to it, then he is obliged to refer the matter to the CIR.

He may also refer any other case where he is considering abolition or variation, but he is not compelled to make a reference.

The Commission may recommend to the Secretary of State either:

1   To abolish the wages council, or
2   To narrow the field of its operations

In either of these cases it may recommend, if expedient, the transfer of workers to another wages council.

3:9:10   *Central coordinating committees (s7)*

A central coordinating committee may be established, varied or abolished by the Secretary of State in relation to two or more wages councils, after consulting with the wages councils concerned. The committee's function is:

1   To consider whether the field of operation of the wages councils is properly divided between them, and
2   To recommend principles for the wages councils to follow when exercising their powers

3:10   WAGES IN AGRICULTURE

The Agricultural Wages Act 1948, which consolidates earlier statutory enactments, regulates wages in agriculture in a manner basically similar to regulation by the wages councils. The Act applies only to agricultural workers, but this term includes boys, girls, and women in addition to men. The definition in s17 includes:

1   Dairy farming
2   The production of any consumable produce grown for sale, consumption, or other use for the purposes of trade or business
3   The use of land for grazing, meadows or pasture land, orchard, osier land, woodland, market gardens or nursery grounds

It has been decided by the courts that the definition also covers poultry farming, and a private garden, if used for the purposes of market gardening.

3:10:1   *Composition of the Agricultural Wages Board (schedule 1)*
It is composed of the following persons, one of whom must be a woman:

1   Eight representatives of employers and eight representatives of agricultural workers
2   Not more than five independent members, appointed by the Minister of Agriculture, one being elected as chairman

Powers of the Board (s3). The Board has power:

1   To fix minimum wage rates, time rates and piecework rates
2   To fix separate rates of minimum pay for holiday periods

3   To direct the length of holiday to which agricultural workers
     are entitled
4   To attempt to secure a weekly half-holiday

Minimum rates fixed and directions as to holidays may be cancelled or
varied. The method of enforcing minimum rates and holiday periods is
the same as that discussed earlier (see 3 : 9 : 7).

In addition, the Board has statutory power to make an order defining
any benefits other than cash, such as food and non-intoxicating drink,
supplied by the employer, that may be counted as a part payment of wages.
The Board may also place a value on these benefits and limit the extent
to which non-cash benefits may be handed over in part payment of wages.
The Truck Acts do not prevent these payments in forms other than cash,
for since the Board fixes their value, this prevents any abuse by the
employer (s7).

3:10:2   Publication of a proposed order (schedule 4)

If the Board intends to make an order, in furtherance of the powers discussed, public notice of the proposals must be given, allowing fourteen days
for any objections to be lodged. The agricultural wages committee for each
county (see 3 : 10 : 3) must be informed by post. After considering any
objections, the Board may make an order in accordance with their original
proposals or modified in the light of objections. An amended order must
be republished and further objections considered. The contents must be
communicated to the wages committee and all persons concerned. If a proposal is of limited application, then it may be published and made seven
days after first giving notice of it, without following the procedure outlined above.

3:10:3   Agricultural wages committees

A committee is established for each county or combination of counties in
England and Wales. It consists of an equal number of representatives of
employers and workmen, plus two independent members and a chairman
appointed by the Minister of Agriculture (schedule 3). The committee
exercises functions as directed by the Board, including the following:

1   Granting and revoking permits for incapacitated persons,
     allowing them to be paid less than the minimum wage rates
     (s5(1)(3))
2   Granting and revoking certificates approving terms of employ-

ment of learners, where a minimum wage rate has been fixed (s6(1))

3 Approving apprenticeship agreements requiring payment of a premium (s6(5))

4 Revaluing a house occupied by a worker, where the value of the occupation forms part of the minimum wage; individual claims may be heard (s7(3))

3:11 ROAD HAULAGE WAGES

The Road Haulage Wages Act 1938 part 2 provides for the wages of workers employed by private carriers in connection with the mechanical transport of goods.

3:11:1 *Action in respect of unfair wages*

If the remuneration paid to a road haulage worker is considered to be unfair by the following people, they may ask the Secretary of State to refer the matter for settlement:

1 The worker himself

2 A trade union of which he is a member

3 A trade union which in the opinion of the Secretary of State represents a substantial number of workers employed in that industry

3:11:2 *Remuneration deemed to be fair*

Remuneration will be deemed to be fair if it is equivalent to remuneration paid:

1 Under a road haulage wages order

2 Under agreement between the employer and a trade union regulating employment in the same trade

3 For similar work to similar workers by other employers in the district, agreed upon by the employers and a trade union

4 To similar workers, under a decision of a joint industrial council or similar body

5 Under a decision of the Industrial Court (now the Industrial Arbitration Board), after a reference under the 1938 Act, to workers in the district engaged in the same trade

If an application is made to the Secretary of State in respect of wages thought to be unfair, he must refer the matter for settlement within one month to either the Industrial Arbitration Board or other machinery for settling disputes in that trade. If the Industrial Arbitration Board or other body dealing with the issue decides that the remuneration is unfair, taking into account the criteria discussed above, it will fix a statutory minimum wage, including holiday remuneration if appropriate. It may also specify the daily or weekly hours for which the worker must be employed in order to be eligible to receive the statutory minimum wage, and the number of hours employment after which overtime rates will apply.

The statutory minimum wage remains in force for three years, subject to review by the Industrial Arbitration Board after three months, at the instance of either party, and must be paid to all workers employed by the employer concerned with the reference, not only the individual worker who sought it. As between the employer and worker initiating the proceedings, the statutory remuneration is deemed to have been in force for an earlier period of up to six months, as the Board directs. Thus the worker is entitled to payment of the difference between the statutory minimum wage and the wage actually received. The method of enforcement of the statutory minimum wage is the same as that discussed above (see 3 : 9 : 7).

3 : 12 ATTACHMENT OF EARNINGS

An employer may be instructed by means of an attachment of earnings order to make deductions from an employee's earnings, where the employee has failed to meet payment of a debt or fine awarded against him by a court. The sum deducted must be sent to the court by the employer, then it is passed on to the person entitled to receive it. This is a more effective method of enforcing payment against a defaulting employee than the previously adopted sanction of sending him to prison and thereby preventing him from earning the money with which to make the payment required.

The Attachment of Earnings Act 1971 consolidates and extends the provisions of previous Acts.

3 : 12 : 1 Who is an employer for the purposes of the Act?
The relationship of employer and employee exists for the purposes of the Act in situations where one person, acting as principal (not as the employee or agent of another) pays earnings to another person. The employer may be a private individual trader, a partnership, or an incorporated body such as a club or society, a private or public company, a corporation or the Crown.

3:12:2 *What are attachable earnings?*

Earnings are defined as any sum payable to an employee:

1   As wages or salary, including any additional fees, bonus, commission or overtime pay
2   As a pension, which includes an annuity in respect of past services and periodic payments as compensation for loss of emoluments, office or employment

The following payments are not to be treated as earnings. With one exception they are not payments which the ordinary employer makes anyway, but he should be aware that these sums are to be disregarded when determining the employee's attachable earnings:

1   Sums payable by any public department of the Government of Northern Ireland or of a territory outside the United Kingdom
2   Pay or allowances payable to the debtor as a member of Her Majesty's forces
3   Pension, allowances or benefit payable under the following enactments relating to social security:
    (*a*) The National Insurance Act 1965
    (*b*) The National Insurance (Industrial Injuries) Act 1965
    (*c*) The Family Allowances Act 1965
    (*d*) The Ministry of Social Security Act 1966
    (*e*) The Industrial Injuries and Diseases (Old Cases) Act 1967
    (*f*) The Family Income Supplements Act 1970
4   Pension or allowances payable in respect of disablement or disability
5   Wages payable to a person as a seaman (but wages paid to a seaman of a fishing boat count as "earnings" under the Act)

The following deductions are permitted from earnings and the sum remaining is regarded as the "attachable earnings":

1   Income Tax (PAYE)
2   National Insurance and Health Service contributions
3   Contributions to a regular superannuation scheme

Other sums ordinarily deducted are not to be regarded when determining the attachable earnings, for example, national savings contributions.

An employer can be required by the court to make a signed statement of an employee's earnings and an offence is committed if he refuses to do so, or recklessly gives false information.

3:12:3 Protected earnings

The court allows the employee to retain a reasonable part of his earnings so that he can meet his own personal financial commitments. The sum so fixed as "protected earnings" should be taken into account before making a deduction in respect of an attachment order. Protected earnings are usually specified in the attachment order at a weekly or monthly rate.

If wages are paid at some interval other than weekly or monthly, then the employer must make a proportionate adjustment to the protected earnings figure specified in the attachment order, so that the correct sum is deducted (see examples 4 and 5).

The normal deduction

The "normal deduction" is a weekly or monthly sum specified in the attachment order, which the court regards as a reasonable payment by the employee to meet his liability as a debtor.

If the earnings are paid at an interval other than that specified in the order, the deduction must be adjusted proportionately. An attachment order operates against earnings that are paid on other days, additional to the normal pay day, as where a mid-week bonus or advance of wages is paid. In these cases it will be necessary to adjust the figure to be taken as protected earnings and the normal deduction (see examples 4 and 5). If the wage payments are reduced on the usual pay day to take the previous advance into account, the attachment order operates on the reduced earnings (see example 5).

3:12:4 How an attachment order operates

On each pay day after receipt of the attachment order the protected earnings are deducted from the attachable earnings then the normal deduction is made, and handed to the court officer at the address specified in the order. Payments may be sent through the post at the employer's risk and expense. The employer will not be liable to a penalty, however, if he fails to make a deduction on the first pay day if it falls within the week when the attachment order is first received.

Reimbursement of the employer's expenses. If he wishes, the employer may take 5p as expenses from the employee's earnings in respect of each deduction made. Where there is more than one attachment order against the same employee, 5p may be deducted as expenses in respect of each order. The employee must be informed in writing of each deduction made by way of expenses. The most convenient method of doing this is to include the relevant information as a part of the normal statement of earnings due and various deductions made, which is handed to the employee when wages are paid.

Example 1

	£
Attachable earnings	30
Less protected earnings payable to the employee	
(from which the employer may deduct 5p as expenses)	15
	15
Less normal deduction to be sent to the court	8
Balance remaining to be paid to the employee in addition to the protected earnings	7

The employee may not earn sufficient in some weeks to meet the normal deduction. Any deficit occurring in one week should not be carried forward and added to the normal deduction made in the following week.

Example 2

	£
Attachable earnings	15
Less protected earnings payable to the employee	
(from which the employer may deduct 5p as expenses)	14
	1
Less normal deduction to be sent to the court	8
Deficit	7

The employer can send £1 only to the court. On the next pay day, only £8 is deducted, not £8 plus the deficit of £7.

A further possibility is that the employee's attachable earnings may be less than his protected earnings.

Example 3

	£
Attachable earnings payable to the employee	13
Less protected earnings	14
Deficit	1

No deduction of 5p as expenses since the normal deduction of £8 is not possible. The employer must not carry forward to the next pay day the unpaid normal deduction of £8 and the balance of protected earnings of £1.

Example 4

	£
Attachable earnings (paid mid-week as a bonus)	21
Less protected earnings (5/7 of a week at £14 a week) payable to the employee (from which the employer may deduct 5p as expenses)	10
	11
Less normal deduction to be sent to the court (5/7 of a week at £7 a week)	5
Balance remaining also payable to the employee	6

	£
Attachable earnings (paid at the end of the week during which the bonus was paid)	30
Less protected earnings (2/7 of a week at £14 a week) payable to the employee (from which the employer may deduct 5p as expenses)	4
	26
Less normal deduction to be sent to the court (2/7 of a week at £7 a week)	2
Balance remaining also payable to the employee	24

Example 5   £

Attachable earnings (paid as a mid-week advance)	12
Less protected earnings (4/7 of a week at £14 a week) payable to the employee (from which the employer may deduct 5p as expenses)	8
	——
	4
Less normal deduction to be sent to the court (4/7 of a week at £7 a week)	4
	——
No Balance	
	——

Attachable earnings (payable at end of the week during which the advance was made)	£ 9
Less protected earnings (3/7 of a week at £14 a week) payable to the employee (from which the employer may deduct 5p as expenses)	6
	——
	3
Less normal deduction to be sent to the court (3/7 of a week at £7 a week)	3
	——
No Balance	
	——

Payment of earnings in advance. Earnings on a particular day may include a payment in advance to cover an impending holiday with pay—for example, two weeks' wages are paid instead of one week's wages—then the protected earnings and the normal deduction must be adjusted accordingly.

Example 6   £

Attachable earnings (2 weeks at £25 a week)	50
Less protected earnings (2 weeks at £14 a week) payable to the employee (from which the employer may deduct 5p as expenses)	28
	——
	22
Less normal deduction to be sent to the court (2 weeks at £7 a week)	14
	——
Balance remaining also payable to the employee	8
	——

An employee may receive his holiday pay after he has taken the holiday, in which case the employer should adopt the following procedure.

Example 7. 3 weeks since last receipt of pay.

	£
Attachable earnings (3 weeks at £21 a week) including holiday pay	63
Less protected earnings (3 weeks at £14 a week) payable to the employee (from which the employer may deduct 5p as expenses)	42
	21
Less normal deduction to be sent to the court (3 weeks at £7 a week)	21
	No Balance

3:12:5   *Two different types of attachment orders*

A "non-priority" order relates to the payment of a civil debt. A "priority" order is marked as such in the top right corner and relates to the payment of maintenance to wives and families and also settlement of fines.

Two or more orders may be in operation against an employee and it is important to make the required deductions in the correct sequence. If there are two orders of the same priority—that is, two non-priority orders or two priority orders—the first deduction from earnings relates to the order that was made first. If the orders are of a different priority, the priority order is taken first then the non-priority order, irrespective of the date on which they were made.

Example 8

	£
Attachable earnings	30
Less protected earnings payable to the employee (from which the employer may deduct 10p as expenses, 5p in respect of each order)	14
	16
Less normal deduction under a priority order, to be sent to the court	7
	9
Less normal deduction under a non-priority order, to be sent to the court	7
Balance remaining also payable to the employee	2

3:12:6 *Special rules applicable to priority orders only*

Unlike non-priority orders any deficit in payment of the normal deduction to the court is carried forward against future earnings until the amount specified in the order is fully met.

Example 9. Priority order		£
Attachable earnings		20
Less protected earnings payable to the employee (from which the employer may deduct 5p as expenses)		14
		6
Less normal deduction to be sent to the court		7
Deficit		1

The deficit of £1 is carried forward to the next pay day calculation.

		£
Attachable earnings		25
Less protected earnings payable to the employee (from which the employer may deduct 5p as expenses)		14
Less normal deduction to be sent to the court	£7	
Less deficit on the last pay day to be sent to the court	£1	
	—	8
Balance remaining also payable to the employee		3

In the case of priority orders any deficit in the payment of protected earnings is also carried forward to the next pay day.

Example 10. Priority order		
Attachable earnings payable to the employee; no deduction can be		£
made from earnings thus the employer cannot claim 5p for expenses		13
Protected earnings		14
Deficit		1

The deficit of £1 in protected earnings and the normal deduction of £7 are both carried forward to the next pay day.

	£
Attachable earnings	25
Less protected earnings payable to the employee (from which the employer may deduct 5p as expenses)	
(£14 plus £1 deficit carried forward from last pay day)	15
	—
Sum available to satisfy attachment order which is sent to the court	10
Less Normal deduction £7; plus £7 deficit carried forward from last pay day	14
	—
Deficit	4
	—

The deficit of £4 is carried forward to the next pay day. Deficits are carried forward until they are cleared.

3:12:7 *Variations to the attachment order*
The employer may receive a notification that the protected earnings and the normal deduction rate have been varied by the court. The new order should be operated on the first pay day after its receipt. An employer does not incur a penalty for failing to do so if the first, subsequent pay day occurs in the week during which the order is received.

If a magistrates' court exercises its power to vary the protected earnings for a period of up to four weeks, the employer will be notified accordingly. The new temporary rate should be used on the first day possible. The original protected earnings rate must be reverted to when the period of the temporary variation ends.

3:12:8 *What happens when an attachment order ceases to be effective?*
An employer must stop deductions as soon as possible on receiving instructions from the court that an attachment order has ceased or been discharged. No further deduction must be made seven days after receiving the notification. The final deduction from earnings in settlement of all sums due may be less than the normal deduction. If the employer keeps a record of the total sum to be paid by the employee and all repayments made, then he should be aware of the timing of the final deduction and the appropriate sum.

3:12:9 *An employer's responsibilities in relation to an attachment order*
The responsibility for complying with an attachment order lies with the employer, although the actual work may be carried out by an employee.

The employer commits an offence by not taking all reasonable steps to comply with an attachment order or any subsequent variation to it.

The court must be informed by letter within ten days if the attachment order is addressed to a person or body who is not the debtor's employer. The letter and the attachment order should be sent to the clerk or registrar of the court, specifying the name and address of the debtor's new employer, if this information is known. The employer commits an offence if he fails to give this information to the court or knowingly or recklessly gives false information. The same procedure should be followed if an employee leaves after the employer has been operating the attachment order for a period of time. An offence is committed for failing to do so or knowingly or recklessly giving false information.

The employer is asked to give the employee leaving his job a transfer notice which instructs him to inform the court which made the attachment order that he is leaving his present position. The employee should also be instructed to give further notice within seven days to the court of the new employer's name and address, together with a statement of earnings or anticipated earnings. The employee is liable to a penalty for failing to give notice or for giving incorrect information and the employer should warn him of this fact.

The employer commits an offence if he does not notify the court within seven days that an employee has been engaged against whom an order has been made, if the employer is aware of the fact. A statement of earnings or anticipated earnings must also be made.

INSURANCE

3:13 SOCIAL SECURITY PAYMENTS

The Department of Health and Social Security administers a wide range of welfare services whose cost is met from five sources:

1 General taxation
2 Local authority rates
3 Charges for specific services, such as prescriptions and spectacles
4 Payments by "insured persons"
5 Payments by the employers of insured persons

3:13:1 Who is insured?

Almost every person in Great Britain over school-leaving age (fifteen) and under the age of retirement (sixty for women, sixty-five for men) is an insured person. Every individual must register for insurance and obtain a National Insurance card on which social security payments are recorded. Each person is allocated a National Insurance number.

In any contribution week (midnight Sunday to midnight the following Sunday) an insured person will be in one of the following three classes, depending on the nature of his employment:

Class I. Persons gainfully employed under a contract of service or apprenticeship whether written or oral, express or implied. This class does not include people who are paid less than £4 a week (they are in Class III), but note that the provision of board and lodging is deemed to be a payment of more than £4 a week. Class I does include people who are on paid holiday. For periods of sickness, see 3 : 13 : 2.

Class II. Self-employed persons gainfully employed, but not under a contract of service. This group covers people working on their own account or working for gain, but not under an employer's control—for example, outworkers and independent contractors.

Class III. Every insured person not in Classes I or II.

The remainder of this section will deal only with people in Class I.

3:13:2 Payment of Class I contributions

If an insured person is in Class I then his employer is responsible for paying his contribution. The employer can recoup a set proportion of this contribution by deducting it from the employee's wages.

An employer is responsible for holding his employee's National Insurance card (which is the property of the Department of Health and Social Security) although the employee may demand to see it (but not more than once a month).

The main purposes of the contribution are to pay approximately 10 per cent of the costs of the National Health Service (whose facilities are available to everyone normally resident in the UK, whether insured or not) and to act as a "premium" for two insurance schemes:

1   National Insurance, which provides benefits for sickness, unemployment, maternity, widowhood, death, orphanhood, and a retirement pension; claims to these benefits may be maintained by insured persons who have paid the required

number of contributions for the claim made; the law relating to this was consolidated in the National Insurance Acts 1965–71

2   Industrial Injuries insurance, which is described in 3 : 14

Because every employed person is covered by the system for collecting National Health Service, National Insurance and Industrial Injuries contributions, it is a useful method of collecting other payments in respect of employees. So the weekly contribution includes the payment to the Redundancy Fund (this is passed to the Department of Employment which administers the fund, see 3 : 16) and the Selective Employment Tax (this tax was to be abolished when this book went to press, and will not be discussed further).

Periods of sickness. If an employee renders no services during the whole of a contribution week because of sickness, but would, if he were not sick, be in Class I, then the employment is "disregarded" for National Insurance purposes. The period of incapacity for work is normally defined by a medical certificate. Payment of sick pay for the period of incapacity does not affect the disregard. If, however, the employee is incapacitated for only part of a week but takes the rest of it off and is paid for the days when he was not incapacitated, then the week is deemed to be one of paid holiday and a Class I contribution is payable.

One of the benefits provided by the National Insurance scheme is that, during weeks of sickness, contributions are credited to the insured person —provided he has paid the required number of contributions. In cases where the contribution conditions are not met, a sick employee comes into Class III (or possibly Class II).

Industrial Injuries contributions are not payable for a week of sickness.

Opting out of the National Insurance scheme. Certain people, either because they are already covered by National Insurance or because they cannot afford the payments, may elect not to pay their share of the National Insurance contribution. The employer is, however, still liable to pay his share of the contribution (except for the low-income group) and Industrial Injuries contributions must be paid. The categories are:

1   People earning less than £468 a year
2   Widows in receipt of:
   (*a*) National Insurance widow's benefit or retirement pension
   (*b*) Widow's benefit under the Industrial Injuries scheme

3   Married women (who may, however, opt back in again at any
     time)

People over retirement age are not liable for their share of the National
Insurance contribution, although they may opt to pay it for five years
after normal retirement age.

When must the contribution be paid? The contribution for each contribution week must be paid when the wages for that week are paid. The normal
method of payment is to stick a stamp to the employee's card and cancel it
by writing or stamping the date of affixing on the face of the stamp. (Other
methods are available for employers with a large number of permanent
employees.)

   If wages are paid at intervals other than a week then the insurance
card may also be stamped for the same period. Contributions must be paid
in advance if wages are paid in advance.

Failure to pay. If an employer does not pay a contribution before the wages
for that week are paid, then he may not deduct the employee's share of
the contribution from his wages; furthermore, he cannot recover the employee's share by deducting it from future wages. An offence is committed
by an employer if:

1   He fails to pay the contribution at the correct time
2   He deducts his own share of the contribution from the
     employee's wages

An employee may sue and recover compensation from his employer if he
suffers loss of a benefit that could have been claimed under the National
Insurance scheme, but for his employer's failure to pay the required
contribution.

   An employer may be sued by the Secretary of State for Social Services
for recovery of a contribution which ought to have been paid for an employee. Unpaid contributions are recoverable from directors and other
officers of a company who are personally responsible for not making any
required payment.

3:13:3   Rate of contribution
The rates of contribution to be discussed in this section are known as "flat-
rate" contributions to distinguish them from the graduated contributions

which will be described in 3:17. The rates currently in force are set out in Schedule 1 to the National Insurance Act 1971. The rate depends on the age of the employee.

Employees under eighteen. There are different rates for:

1 Boys
2 Girls
3 Girls who are married and have opted to pay a reduced contribution

The employee's card will specify which of these three categories he or she is in.

Employees aged eighteen or over. The rate depends on:

1 Whether the employee is "contracted out" (see 3:17)
2 Whether the employee is paid more than £6 for a full working week

This gives four possibilities. For each of these there is a different rate for:

1 Men
2 Women
3 Men aged sixty-five to sixty-nine who opt not to pay the full rate and men aged seventy or more
4 Women aged sixty to sixty-four, married women and widows who opt to pay a reduced rate, and women aged sixty-five or more

The employee's card will specify which of the last four categories he or she is in.

Special circumstances where only the Industrial Injuries contribution is payable.

1 If remuneration is ordinarily £4 a week or less. (Provision of board and lodging is deemed to be a payment of more than £4 a week)
2 If employment is for not more than eight hours in a contribution week

3   If the employee normally works more than eight hours a week but is prevented from working more than four hours through illness

Unpaid apprentices. The employer must pay the apprentice's share of the contribution if the apprentice receives no remuneration in cash or kind (such as board and lodging).

3:13:4   *Employer's liability to pay contributions for student employees.* An employer must pay a Class I contribution for:

1   A student employed full-time during his vacations or part-time at weekends, whether the employment is on a permanent or temporary basis
2   A student on a sandwich course during:
  (a) Periods of paid employment with an employer who is giving him practical training, and
  (b) Periods of attendance at an educational establishment in connection with his contract of service, if some payment is made to the student (even if it is not his full wage)

3:13:5   *Persons working under the employer's general control*
An employer may be liable to pay a Class I contribution for persons under his general control and management, though they are not employed directly by him but by an intermediate employer. A factory occupier must pay contributions for persons employed on the premises under his general control and management.

3:13:6   *Employing staff through an agency*
Where staff are engaged by an employer through the medium of an agency, the agency is regarded as being the employer responsible for payment of National Insurance contributions. This provision covers nurses, office staff and office and industrial cleaners.

3:13:7   *People with several employers*
One insured person may be employed by several employers in one week, but the responsibility for stamping the insurance card lies with the employer who engaged the insured person first during that week. The different employers may reach some agreement about sharing the cost if they wish.

3:14 NATIONAL INSURANCE (INDUSTRIAL INJURIES) ACT 1965

An employee may be injured in the course of his employment without any negligence on the employer's part. In these circumstances the employee may be unable to claim damages from his employer either at common law or under a statutory provision such as the Factories Act 1961 or the Offices, Shops and Railway Premises Act 1963. The National Insurance (Industrial Injuries) Act 1965 consolidates various statutes that attempt to remedy this situation.

An insured person is entitled to compensation for physical or mental personal injuries in an accident arising "out of or in the course of" his employment, even though his ability to work is unimpaired. A benefit may be payable though earning capacity remains unaffected. An industrial disease which develops gradually is not included, unless it is one of the forty or so diseases prescribed as being within the scope of the Act.

3:14:1 *Employer's duty to investigate accidents*

Any accident to an employee must be investigated by the employer while the relevant facts are still fresh in the minds of witnesses. If a claim is to be made for the injury under the Industrial Injuries scheme, the task of the official investigating the accident is simplified. An employer should make a report of the accident and the facts as found by him if the eye witness accounts are irreconcilable with the type of injury suffered (for the record of accidents required by the Factories Act 1961 see 6:3).

An employer must give any information required by an officer of the Department of Health and Social Security concerning:

1   Any accident or alleged accident causing an employee's death for which a benefit may be payable
2   The nature and circumstance of employment of anyone suffering from or believed to have died from an industrial disease

This information must be supplied within a reasonable time after being requested.

3:14:2 *Employees for whom payment must be made*

Persons employed under a contract of service or apprenticeship in this country must be insured. This group includes 23 million out of the 25 million contributors under the Act. There are no special arrangements for sex and age difference, the number of hours worked and marital status. The following groups of persons need not be insured:

1   Self-employed persons, though working for another person under a contract for service rather than on their own account
2   Employment under a contract of service:
  (a) By one spouse of another
  (b) By a relative, where the work carried out relates to household duties
  (c) Casual employment not related to the employer's business
  (d) Children under school-leaving age in part-time employment, the group being covered by the Act without the need to pay a contribution
  (e) Seamen employed on British ships, but ordinarily resident in specified countries

The Industrial Injuries scheme is operated alongside the National Insurance scheme and most employees must be insured under both.

A contribution is payable for an insurable person who was employed or on paid holiday during all or part of a contribution week. Payment need not be made for those weeks during which the insurable person was unemployed, or incapacitated by a specific disease or bodily or mentally disabled.

3:14:3   *Benefits that may be claimed by the employee*
The actual rate of the following benefits claimable under the Act is increased periodically, usually every two years.

1   Industrial Injuries benefit for every working day lost by the insured person because of industrial injury, up to a maximum of twenty-six weeks
2   Industrial disablement benefit claimable by an insured person at the end of the Industrial Injury benefit period, where the injury leaves some lasting effect; the amount payable depends upon the degree of loss suffered
3   Industrial death benefit payable, when the insured person dies, to the widow or, exceptionally, to a dependent husband or parents

3:15 ADMINISTRATION OF THE INDUSTRIAL INJURIES AND NATIONAL INSURANCE SCHEMES BY THE DEPARTMENT OF HEALTH AND SOCIAL SECURITY

Inspectors appointed by the Secretary of State are responsible for enforcing the provisions of the National Insurance (Industrial Injuries) Act 1965. They are given power to:

1   Enter premises where persons are employed at all reasonable times
2   Question any persons on those premises
3   Inspect wages records and any other relevant records that are kept
4   Exercise such other powers as may be necessary for giving effect to the schemes, to determine whether the employer has insured all insurable persons, and whether a benefit is or was payable to any person

It is an offence to:

1   Wilfully delay or obstruct an inspector in the exercise of his powers
2   Refuse or neglect to answer a question, give information required, or produce any document when requested

The local office of the Department is responsible for the day-to-day routine administration of the schemes. Claims are scrutinised by insurance officers. There is a right of appeal where a claim has been rejected or not allowed in full to:

1   A local appeal tribunal, consisting of representatives of employees and of employers and insured persons not in Class I, under an independent chairman
2   The Chief National Insurance Commissioner, or one of his deputies, against a decision of the local appeal tribunal, at the instance of the insurance officer, the claimant or his trade union

Decisions of an insurance officer, local tribunal or the Chief National Insurance Commissioner may be reviewed by the insurance officer where:

1   There is fresh evidence
2   A decision was given in ignorance of a material fact
3   A material change in circumstances has occurred
4   The Secretary of State has reviewed a decision upon which the present case was based

3:15:1 *National Insurance matters settled by the Secretary of State*

A decision on the following matters must be made by the Secretary of State:

1   Whether the claimant has paid sufficient contributions to be able to claim a particular benefit
2   Who is entitled to any increased benefit payable
3   Under which class of insured persons does a particular person fall
4   The person to be treated as maintaining a child, or the family in which a child is to be treated as included

The High Court may determine a question of law:

1   Referred by the Secretary of State
2   On appeal against his decision

3:15:2 *"Special questions" on industrial injuries*

The insurance officer must refer "special questions" for decision to either the Secretary of State or a local medical board.

The Secretary of State determines the following issues, subject to appeal on a point of law to a judge of the High Court, unless indicated otherwise:

1   Whether a person is or was in insurable employment
2   The rate of contribution payable
3   Who must pay the employer's contribution
4   Whether exemption from payment may be claimed
5   Whether an increase in disablement benefit is payable for constant attendance, there being no appeal from a decision on this point
6   Who should receive industrial death benefit where there is more than one claimant, there being no appeal from a decision on this point

The local medical board, or a single medical practitioner if the claimant consents, determines:

1 Whether the claimant has suffered the loss of any faculty
2 If so, the degree of such loss
3 Whether it is likely to be permanent

The claimant may appeal to a medical appeal tribunal, and then on a point of law to the Chief National Insurance Commissioner, with leave of either the appeal tribunal or the Chief Commissioner.

3:16   CONTRIBUTIONS TO THE REDUNDANCY FUND

Every person who is liable to pay an employer's contribution under the National Insurance Act 1965 s3 in respect of any person over the age of eighteen is also liable to pay a Redundancy Fund contribution for the same week of 6p for men and 3p for women. An employer must make a payment in respect of his employees even though the employee belongs to a class excluded by the Act from the right to receive a redundancy payment—for example, registered dock workers.

The amount payable may be varied from time to time by an order of the Secretary of State. The National Insurance contribution and the Redundancy Fund contributions payable by an employer are treated as one combined contribution.

3:16:1   *Rebates*

A payment out of the Redundancy Fund may be made to an employer:

1 Who has made a redundancy payment to an employee
2 Who makes a payment to the Redundancy Fund for an employee disentitled to a redundancy claim, for example, registered dock workers
3 Making a payment of compensation to certain classes of public or Crown employees equivalent to a redundancy payment from superannuation funds

The Redundancy Rebates Act 1969 reduced the rebates payable to an employer in order to correct the deficit on the Redundancy Fund and encourage employers to dismiss younger rather than older employees and thereby save on the total redundancy sum to be paid. The rebate is calculated on the following principles:

1   Three quarters of a week's pay for each year of employment over forty-one
2   Half a week's pay for each year of employment over twenty-two and under forty-one
3   Quarter of a week's pay for each year of employment under twenty-two

An employer must give notice of his intention to claim a rebate to the local office of the Department of Employment:

1   Not less than fourteen days before dismissal
2   Not less than twenty-one days before the first dismissal when ten or more employees are being dismissed

If the employer fails to give the required notice without showing a reasonable cause for his failure, the amount of the rebate may be reduced by up to one tenth. A written claim for the rebate itself must be made to the local office within six months of payment by the employer.

3:17   GRADUATED CONTRIBUTIONS

3:17:1   *The basic graduated pension scheme*

National Insurance provides a flat-rate pension on retirement (£6 a week with additions for dependants when this book went to press). In an attempt to provide a pension that is related to the pensioner's level of earnings (and hence standard of living) when he was working, the graduated pension scheme was introduced in 1961. The scheme covers people who are in Class I for National Insurance and are:

1   Aged between eighteen and seventy (or sixty-five in the case of women)
2   Earning a gross pay of over £9 a week

Employers of such people pay a "graduated contribution" on their behalf of $9\frac{1}{2}$ per cent of that part of the gross pay lying between £9 and £18 a week. Most of the graduated contribution is used to pay for earnings-related pensions and part is used to finance the other social security services.

It was recognised that employers often organise their own earnings-related pension schemes. It is therefore possible for an employer to ask the

Registrar of Non-participating Employments for a certificate of non-participation (or "contracting out") for all or any defined category of his employees who are covered by a pension scheme that the Registrar considers at least as good as the State scheme.

For employees who are contracted out, no payment is made of the graduated contribution mentioned above (although payments of other graduated contributions are made—see 3 : 17 : 2). However, because part of the graduated contribution pays for the other social services, higher "flat-rate" payments are required in respect of contracted-out employees—see 3 : 13 : 3.

3 : 17 : 2 Other graduated contributions

The National Insurance Acts 1966, 1969 and 1971 introduced further earnings-related schemes from which it is not possible to contract out. The payments are 1 per cent of the gross earnings between £9 and £18 a week and 8.7 per cent of those between £18 and £42 a week. In addition to earnings-related pensions, these Acts provide for short-term (up to twenty-six weeks) earnings-related supplements to sickness and unemployment benefits.

3 : 17 : 3 Married women and widows

Although these people can opt out of the National Insurance scheme they cannot opt out of the graduated scheme, except for contracting out of the basic pension scheme.

3 : 17 : 4 Payment of graduated contributions

The employer is liable to make the contributions but can recover half the cost from the employee. The money is paid to the Collector of Taxes along with PAYE payments. The Inland Revenue Commissioners pass the money on to the DHSS.

Failure to pay is an offence.

TAX

By s204 of the Income and Corporation Taxes Act 1970, anyone paying money that (for the recipient) is income assessable to tax under Schedule E must deduct the tax payable on that money at the time it is paid, and must forward the tax to the Collector of Taxes. Income is subject to tax under Schedule E when it is "emoluments" from "any office or employment : " the system for collecting the tax is known as "pay as you earn."

3:18 PAYMENTS SUBJECT TO TAX UNDER SCHEDULE E

The term "emoluments" includes almost every receipt in money or money's worth—that is, an advantage that can be converted into money—which arises in any way from employment.

For the purpose of deducting tax, the following payments are regarded as part of an employee's gross pay:

1   Salary, wages, fees, overtime, bonus, commission and pension payments
2   Sick pay, holiday pay, but not sickness benefit from the Ministry of Social Security
3   A Christmas present, if paid in cash
4   Payment of travelling expenses between home and the usual place of employment or for time taken in travelling, but not free travel provided by the employer
5   Cash payments for meals and board
6   Lump sum payments on retirement

The following payments are excluded:

1   Payment of expenses actually incurred by the employee in carrying out his duties
2   Rent-free accommodation where the nature of the employee's duties require him to live in a certain place
3   Reasonable lodging expenses for an employee temporarily working away from home at a place other than his usual place of employment
4   Payments made instead of giving the period of notice required by the contract of employment
5   Non-transferable meal vouchers for lower paid staff, not exceeding 15p for each full working day provided they can be used only for meals. Only payments over 15p, if otherwise satisfying these conditions, are taxable

An employee's liability to pay tax will include emoluments chargeable to tax, but from which a deduction cannot be made by the employer because of the nature of the benefit. The employer must make a return to the tax office in respect of such benefits, but they are not considered to be a part of the employee's gross pay:

1   The value of national savings certificates, or gift vouchers

2   The value of meal vouchers not satisfying the requirements set out above

3   Allotment of shares in the employing company, or other company

4   Accommodation for the employee or spouse, either rent free, or at a rent below the current value, not satisfying the requirements set out above

3:18:1 *The PAYE system*

Each employee is given a code number, determined by HM Inspectors of Taxes which takes into account the individual employee's:

1   Entitlement to reliefs

2   Income from sources other than that of his main employment

3   Tax overpaid or underpaid during any previous year

The employer is notified of the coding number for each employee so that he can deduct the correct amount of tax from wages payable by reference to the code number on the tax deduction card supplied to him. Even though an employee may be challenging his coding the employer must deduct the tax in accordance with the current coding until notified of an amendment by the tax office. Tax must be deducted at the emergency rate where the employer does not have a tax deduction card for the particular employee, and in the case of certain new employees.

The system is controlled by the Income Tax (Employments) Regulations 1965.

3:18:2 *Payment in addition to payments of wages*

Tax must be deducted from additional payments, bonuses for example, that are made at different times to the payment of wages, except for small payments to employees made before a monthly or quarterly payment of salary. In this instance the whole sum, salary and additional payment, is taxed together on the next pay day.

3:18:3 *Tax liability on pensions*

Pension payments are within the scope of Schedule E taxation whether:

1   Payable to the employee as of right in respect of past services, or

2   Paid voluntarily by an employer entitled to discontinue pay-
     ment if he wishes, unless the recipient is resident outside the
     UK

3 : 18 : 4   *Fees paid by employer to employee*

Fees paid by an employer to his employee under a contract separate and
distinct from the contract of employment are assessed under Schedule E;
for example, fees paid to a member of the full-time hospital staff by the
hospital board in respect of lectures given to medical students.

3 : 19   EFFECT OF RESIDENCE

Schedule E is divided into three Cases according to the residence of the
recipient of income and where he received it.

Case I covers emoluments for the year of assessment receivable by an employee who is both resident and ordinarily resident in the UK, where the
duties of employment are not performed wholly outside the UK during the
year of assessment.

All such emoluments are assessed to tax. Foreign emoluments are excluded. These are payments to a person not domiciled in the UK in respect
of employment with a body resident outside the UK.

Duties performed in the UK which are ancillary to employment carried
out abroad are disregarded.

A short absence from the UK does not affect liability to pay tax under
Case I.

Case II covers an employee who is not resident in the UK, or if resident
not ordinarily resident in the UK. He is liable to pay tax under Schedule E
on any emoluments paid for duties carried out in the UK during the year
of assessment. There are the same provisions on foreign emoluments,
ancillary duties in the UK, and short absences from the UK as stipulated
for Case I.

Case III applies to income from employment held by a resident in the
UK (whether or not he is ordinarily resident here) which is not chargeable
under Case I or II. Tax is chargeable under Schedule E for any emolument
received in the UK :

1   Though the duties are performed overseas in the year of
     assessment
2   Whether in respect of the current year of assessment or of an
     earlier year when the employee was resident in the UK

3   Relating to the year of assessment but actually received during
       some earlier year

Emoluments are regarded as having been received in the UK:

1   If they are paid, used or enjoyed in the UK
2   If brought to the UK, whatever the manner or form of trans-
       mission
3   If the recipient's debts for money are paid by an application
       of the emoluments outside the UK, whether the money was
       lent in the UK or lent outside the UK and then remitted here

Foreign emoluments also fall within Case III.

3 : 19 : 1   *When an employee is regarded as being resident in the UK*
As a general rule an employee will be regarded as resident in the UK for
income tax purposes unless it can be proved that:

1   He is in the UK for some temporary purpose only
2   He does not intend to establish residence here
3   Within the year of assessment for tax he has stayed in the
       UK for less than six months

To refute the establishment of a residence here an employee visiting the UK
must also show that he does not fall within one of the following groups:

1   A visitor is resident in the UK for any income tax year in
       which he is here for a period or periods equal in total to six
       months
2   Habitual visitors for four or more consecutive years for sub-
       stantial periods of time each year of about three months
       become residents of the UK, although in any one year the
       period of stay does not amount to six months
3   A person living and working abroad on a temporary basis who
       maintains a home in the UK becomes resident if in any year he
       visits the UK, though the period of stay is less than six months

"Ordinarily resident" means habitual residence in a particular country.
Residence of a husband and wife are determined independently of one
another. A person may be resident in more than one country simultaneously.

3:19:2 *Tax liability where an employee is resident in Eire*

Employees resident in Eire but not resident in the UK are exempt from the payment of UK income tax. Eire tax on income from both countries must be paid. The reverse is true also: employees resident in the UK but not in Eire are exempt from the payment of Eire income tax. UK tax is payable on income from the UK and Eire.

If an employee is technically resident in both countries he must pay taxation in both countries subject to tax relief in both countries at one half of the appropriate rate of UK, or Eire tax, whichever rate is lower. Liability can be computed and settled by making one payment on application to the relevant tax office.

3:20 CASES WHERE TAX DOES NOT HAVE TO BE PAID

Where the employee's wages are normally £8 a week or under (£35 or less a month) the employer does not deduct tax unless the Inspector of Tax has given directions to the contrary by issuing a tax deduction card. When wages exceed these limits for the first time the employer must notify the local tax office immediately.

An employee may be assessed for tax directly, if he is engaged in casual employment for a period or periods of less than a week, or where the Commissioner of Inland Revenue considers deduction by reference to tax tables to be impracticable. A record of wages should be kept however, since a return may be required at the end of the tax year.

It is unnecessary to deduct tax from wages paid to students:

1 Who are engaged during vacation periods on a temporary basis
2 If a statement is signed by the student when employment begins, stating that this is the case, and
3 The employer makes a declaration on the required form supplied by the tax office

An employee with several simultaneous employments must pay tax in respect of each engagement. The tax office will allot an appropriate code number to each employer.

Where an employee performs his duties wholly abroad or is paid abroad, tax may be payable, but the responsibility for deduction does not lie with the employer. The employer should keep a record of payments. The tax office will notify the employer if he is expected to make a deduction.

3:21 PENALTIES FOR MAKING INCORRECT RETURNS

The employer must account for tax deducted from his employees' emoluments during an income tax month (sixth of one month to fifth of the next) to the collector within fourteen days after the end of that month. If the employer discovers some mistake in making a deduction he must correct it in the week or month in which he discovered the error. An under-deduction must be reported to the tax office if it is so large that it cannot be rectified in the week or month of its discovery because it exceeds the wages payable.

The employer may be liable to make good any deficiency caused by his error in making deductions unless it was done in good faith. The underpayment is recoverable from the employee if the collector so directs.

If an employer fraudulently or negligently furnishes an incorrect return he is liable to a penalty of £250, increased to £500 if fraud is established. A separate offence is committed on every occasion when an incorrect return is submitted. Proceedings must be commenced within six years of making the return.

INDUSTRIAL TRAINING

The Industrial Training Act 1964 seeks to provide industrial and commercial training for persons over the age of fifteen years, through the medium of industrial training boards set up by the Secretary of State for Employment. Before establishing a board, the Secretary of State must consult any organisations representing a substantial number of employers and employees concerned with the particular industries that will be the subject of the board's activity. In this way it is hoped that the Act may be implemented on the basis of cooperation between the government and industry.

3:22 INDUSTRIAL TRAINING BOARDS

The functions of the boards are set out in general terms, stressing the need to use existing facilities, but also, where necessary, to provide further education courses and the training needed in an industry where present facilities are inadequate. These aims are to be achieved by:

1   Providing or securing the provision of courses and other facilities including residential accommodation to train persons

employed in industry; any courses or facilities already available must be taken into account

2   Approving courses and facilities provided by other persons, for example, by further education establishments.

3   Publishing recommendations on the nature and length of training and further education needed in relation to any employment in industry which appears to require consideration. Recommendations may be made on:
  (a) The persons to give and receive the training
  (b) The standards to be attained as a result of the training
  (c) The methods of ascertaining whether those standards have been attained

4   Ascertaining whether the standards recommended by the board have been attained, and awarding certificates for reaching that standard

5   Assisting persons in finding facilities for training for employment in industry

6   Carrying on or assisting other persons to carry on research into any matter relating to training for employment in the industry

To facilitate the industrial training boards in the achievement of these objectives, the following powers have been granted to them:

1   To pay maintenance and travelling allowances to persons attending courses approved or provided by the boards

2   To make grants or loans to persons providing courses or other facilities approved by the boards

3   To pay fees to persons providing further education connected with training if provided or approved by the boards

The Secretary of State decides upon the scope of the powers and executive authority of any board set up, but there is consultation with the Central Training Council on which industries should be covered by industrial training, and how parts of industry should be grouped for these purposes. The number of employees covered by the activities of each individual training board varies considerably. The Engineering Industry Training Board covers around 3 500 000 employees, but there are a mere 48 000 employees covered by the Carpet Industry Training Board.

3 : 22 : 1   *Composition of industrial training boards*
Each board is composed of:

1   An independent chairman with industrial or commercial experience
2   A deputy chairman, if the Secretary of State thinks fit
3   An equal but unspecified number of representatives of employers and employees engaged in the particular industry with which the board is concerned
4   Persons appointed, after consultation with the Secretary of State for Employment and the Secretary of State for Education and Science, from further and technical education
5   Nominees of the Secretary of State for Employment and the Secretary of State for Education and Science and any other ministry with an interest in the meeting; these nominees cannot vote

3 : 22 : 2   *Establishment of the industrial training boards*
The first four boards were established within four months of the passing of the Industrial Training Act. A list of the boards in existence in 1971 is given below, with the date of the creation of each board in brackets:

Wool industry (1964), Jute and flax being added at a later date
Iron and steel (1964)
Construction (1964)
Engineering (1964)
Shipbuilding (1964)
Electricity supply (1965)
Gas (1965)
Water supply (1965)
Ceramics, glass and mineral products (1965)
Furniture and timber (1965)
Man-made fibres (1966)
Carpets (1966)
Knitting, lace and net (1966)
Cotton and allied textiles (1966)
Agriculture, horticulture and forestry (1966)
Road transport and vehicle repair (1966)
Hotel and catering (1966)
Air transport and travel (1967)
Petroleum (1967)

Rubber and plastics processing (1967)
Chemical and allied products (1967)
Local government
Printing and publishing (1968)
Paper and paper products (1968)
Distributive (1968)
Food, drink and tobacco (1968)
Footwear, leather and fur skin (1968)
Clothing and allied products (1969)
Hairdressing and beauty culture (1969)

3:22:3 One firm may be covered by several training boards

Where an undertaking is engaged upon a number of widely differing activities, then different sections of the same firm may be under different training boards. The firm can be attached to only one training board, however, for the purpose of levying the grant payable and determining the training duties to be discharged. The practical consequence is that an employee engaged in engineering may not be under the Engineering Training Board, but some other board. In that case the training board to which the employee is attached must ask the Engineering Training Board to provide any training necessary.

3:22:4 Employees outside the scope of the Act

Government departments are not covered by the Act, since the training available is probably equal to any training that could be provided by a training board. Other groups excluded include self-employed persons and the offices of professional consulting firms. The list of training boards established clearly shows that the nationalised industries are within the scope of the Act.

3:22:5 Central Training Council (s11)

This body advises the Secretary of State on the implementation of the Act and, if requested, on any other matter relating to industrial and commercial training. The council consists of:

1   A chairman
2   Six representatives of employers and six representatives of employees
3   Two members to be appointed after consultation with bodies carrying on the nationalised industries

4   Not more than six chairmen of industrial training boards
5   Six members to be appointed after consultation with the Secretary of State for Employment, and a further six after consultation with the Secretary of State for Education and Science

3:23   GRANTS TO INDUSTRY TO PROVIDE TRAINING

Sums received by way of levy (see 3:24) are repaid to industry as a grant through the medium of the industrial training boards. An undertaking may gain a financial benefit from these arrangements, if it is providing on average more training than other firms in the same industry. Where the grant payable exceeds the levy made on a particular establishment, a limit may be set on the excess that may be claimed. The training board determines the philosophy that fixes the amount payable by way of a grant, so that it may act as an incentive to firms which provide training. The amount is based upon the needs of the particular industry concerned. The determining factors may be:

1   The actual training costs incurred, which are then refunded, but this may lead to expenditure or training not necessarily effective

2   The amount of specific training carried out, the grant payable being determined by reference to the number and type of trainees in the firm's employment, for example management trainees or craft apprentices; here again the grant is not related to the effectiveness or quality of the training

3   The number of trainees sent on specified courses or to a particular training centre, the grant taking the form of a partial repayment of the fees incurred

4   The average standard of training in the industry, the grant being dependent upon the firm's standard by comparison with this average standard

3:23:1   How to claim a grant

If an employer wishes to claim a grant in respect of the training facilities provided, he must complete a claim form from the appropriate training board. It will be necessary to show the number of employees undergoing training. Support for the figures given must be contained in:

1   A register of trainees, that is a complete register of every person
     on the payroll receiving training and included in the return
2   A written syllabus or programme for each course of training
     provided

The documents must be available for inspection by officers of the training
board.

3:24   LEVY ON FIRMS
IN THE INDUSTRIES PROVIDED WITH TRAINING FACILITIES

Money may be raised towards meeting the costs involved in providing these
training facilities by means of a levy order made by the Secretary of State
against employers in the industry, unless they are given exemption. For
the purpose of assessing and collecting this levy, the board or any person
acting on its behalf may require employers in the industry concerned to:

1   Furnish a return and other information
2   Keep records and produce them for examination (s4)

But this information must not be used for any purpose other than the
official business of the board.

   Any person who fails to comply with these requirements is liable on
conviction to a fine not exceeding £100, increased to £200 for a second
and subsequent convictions. There are severe penalties where false information is given, whether intentionally or through neglect:

1   On summary conviction, a term of imprisonment not exceed-
     ing three months, or a fine not exceeding £100, or both
2   On conviction on indictment, a term of imprisonment not
     exceeding two years or a fine, or both

The Secretary of State has power to make substantial grants and loans to
the various training boards and with his consent the boards can borrow
money and also invest it. These powers are particularly important for a
board in the period between its establishment and the raising of levies.

3:24:1   *Amount of the levy*
Different training boards have adopted different policies regarding the
amount of the levy on firms subject to the Act. The Engineering Industry

Training Board introduced a 2½ per cent levy on the payroll of all engineering undertakings, but other boards were less ambitious and introduced a smaller levy which was increased in succeeding years. There will be a tendency for the levy to increase so that recommendations made by the boards on the extent and quality of the training that ought to be provided by an industry can be implemented.

3:24:2   Appeals against a levy assessment

An employer may appeal against his assessment for a levy to an appeal tribunal, which is given power to uphold, reduce or rescind the assessment. The only grounds for appeal are that:

1   A firm has been allocated to the wrong training board
2   The levy has been incorrectly calculated

The actual rate of the levy cannot be the subject matter of an appeal, since this has been fixed for the industry as a whole and given the Secretary of State's approval. The tribunal is presided over by a lawyer, supported by two other persons: a representative of management and a representative from the trade unions.

FOUR

Special Categories of Employees

THIS CHAPTER DEALS WITH THE STATUTORY REGULATIONS OF THE employment of particular categories of people: young persons including children, women, disabled persons, aliens and Commonwealth citizens.

Young person. This term refers to a person who has ceased to be a child—that is, a person under fifteen—but has not yet attained the age of eighteen. There are several statutes regulating the employment of young persons, all designed to prevent exploitation of a vulnerable group. The regulations differ according to age and the nature of the work. The basic law is that people under thirteen may not be employed, except in a few special cases such as by their family in agriculture and in public performances (see 4:4:1). People under fifteen must not be employed in any industrial undertaking.

To ascertain the rules about employing young people between the ages of thirteen and eighteen, it must be determined which category the workplace is in.

If it is a *factory* (the legal definition is explained in 7:1) then the Factories Act 1961 applies; the provisions of this Act are explained in 4:1.

If it is a *shop* (the definition is set out in 8:12) then the Shops Act 1950 (see 4:3) embodies the relevant legislation.

If it is an *industrial undertaking* or a *ship* then the Employment of Women, Young Persons and Children Act 1920 applies in addition to the Factories Act 1961. The provisions of the former Act are set out in 4:2.

If it is a workplace not included in the preceding categories then the employment of young persons may be regulated either by the Young Persons (Employment) Act 1938 or by local authority by-laws (see 4:4).

Women. As with young persons, the statutory regulations concerning the employment of women are designed to prevent exploitation. The basic rule that women must not be employed at night is contained in the Hours of Employment (Conventions) Act 1936 (see 4:2:3), but this is supplemented by provisions of the Factories Act 1961 (see 4:1). The Employment of Women, Young Persons and Children Act 1920 no longer applies to women.

Disabled persons. Because disabled persons are at a disadvantage in the labour market, there are statutory provisions requiring employers to include a certain number in their workforce. These are set out in Section 4:5.

Aliens and Commonwealth citizens. The regulations for people in this category are designed to protect the indigenous workforce by restricting the employment of aliens and Commonwealth citizens. The restrictions are operated by requiring work permits and controlling changes of job. The law according to the Immigration Act 1971 is given in 4:6. The definition and rights of patrials are explained.

EMPLOYING YOUNG PERSONS AND WOMEN

4:1   FACTORIES

Part 6 of the Factories Act 1961 regulates the employment of women and young persons in factories. The principal objects are to restrict their hours of work and to ensure that young persons are medically fit for the work they are doing.

Where accident, breakdown or other unforeseen emergency makes it necessary the Secretary of State may, by order, suspend, for a time, any provisions about hours and holidays to avoid serious interference with the ordinary working of a factory (s96).

4:1:1   *Fixing hours of work*
The detailed restrictions on working hours are given for each age group in the following pages. To ensure that these restrictions are observed, the Act requires a factory occupier to display a notice stating the times of starting and finishing work and of rest and meal breaks (s88). These times must, of course, comply with the provisions of the Act. It is then illegal to employ women and young persons except at the times specified in the notice, unless they are working "overtime" as permitted by the Act.

All women and young people in one factory are supposed to start and finish work and have their rest and meal breaks simultaneously, except that people aged fifteen (whose permitted hours of working are shorter than the other categories) may finish work earlier. This rather stringent condition is modified as follows:

1   Different hours can be set for "different sets of people employed on different processes"
2   Workers can be divided into different groups for using a canteen and different mealtimes can be assigned to each group (s102)

3   If the process is one which must be operated continuously
     then the meal and rest periods do not have to be taken simul-
     taneously by all workers (s102)

If a factory occupier wishes to make any change in:

1   The periods of employment
2   The intervals to be allowed for meals and rest

then he must post in the factory a notice stating his intention to do so
and also serve a similar notice on the district inspector. These notices
must specify the extent to which the proposed variations to employment
periods and intervals differ from those normally applicable. The factory
occupier must not make a change more than once in three months unless
he is given written permission to do so by the factory inspector where
there is a special reason for the variation (s88(3)).

4:1:2   *Meals and rest periods*
These must not be taken in the workroom.

4:1:3   *Sunday and holiday arrangements*
Women and young persons must not be employed
1   On a Sunday (s93)
2   On Christmas Day, Good Friday and any bank holiday, unless
     the factory occupier posts a notice throughout the factory
     three weeks before the holiday stating his intention to sub-
     stitute some other weekday (s94)

Where the Secretary of State is satisfied that the customs or exigencies
of the trade in any class of factory so require, he may, by regulation,
allow any women or young persons to take all or any of their annual
holidays on different days (s108). This is done, for example, in factories
printing newspapers.

Jewish factories (s109). A factory occupier may allow women or young
persons to work on Sunday if the factory is closed on Saturday and not
open for business on a Sunday, in cases where the occupier and employees
are both of the Jewish faith, or a member of a religion observing the
Jewish Sabbath. A partnership or company is Jewish, for this purpose, if
the majority of the partners or directors are either of the Jewish religion,
or of a religious body observing the Jewish Sabbath.

4:1:4 Short working day

The Act specifies shorter hours of work for Saturday (see below). If custom or the exigencies of trade necessitate a day other than Saturday being taken as the short working day, then the Secretary of State may substitute some other day for Saturday.

In the following sections, the provision of the Factories Act 1961 are detailed separately for the different groups of workers that it covers.

4:1:5 Persons under the age of fifteen

Persons under the age of fifteen must not be employed in a factory.

4:1:6 Persons aged fifteen

Medical examination to determine fitness for employment (s118). As a prerequisite to employment in a factory, young persons under eighteen must be:

1   Examined by the factory doctor within fourteen days of entering employment, and
2   Certified as fit for the employment to be undertaken

If the doctor needs further information or time for consideration he may issue a provisional certificate authorising employment for a maximum of twenty-one days from the date of issue. He may ask the local education committee for the school medical record and other particulars of the medical history of the young person.

When granted, a certificate is valid for twelve months, but it may be varied or revoked after a further examination before the end of that period.

The certificate may be issued subject to:

1   Conditions on the type of work that the young person may be engaged on
2   Re-examination of the young person after a specified interval

If the factory occupier does not observe the conditions imposed, an offence is committed. Any condition ceases to have effect after the young person is eighteen.

The parents of a young person may require the factory doctor to give reasons in writing where a medical certificate has been refused or revoked.

The employer must send a notice to the factory doctor not later than seven days after employing a young person who requires examination under the provisions of s118.

The factory doctor's certificate must be attached to the general register.

Inspectors may direct a young person's employment to end (s119). A factory inspector may give written notice to a factory occupier that a young person's employment must end after a stated period on the ground that a particular process is prejudicial to his health. The employment must end unless the factory doctor has examined the young person and certified that he is fit for employment in the factory after the notice has been issued.

Permitted hours of employment for persons aged fifteen (ss86, 100 and 101). The following statutory rules on hours of employment must be observed by an employer who engages persons aged fifteen to work in his factory:

1   They must not work on a Sunday
2   They must not work for more than 9 hours in any day, or 10 hours if employed on not more than five days a week
3   They must not work for more than a total of 44 hours in any week, exclusive of meal and rest intervals
4   The period of employment—that is, the overall time spent on the work premises—must not exceed 11 hours a day, or 12 hours a day if employed on not more than five days a week
5   The period of employment must not begin before 7 a.m., nor end later that 6 p.m., or 1 p.m. on Saturdays (see also 4:1:4). The Secretary of State may, by regulation or order, allow the period of employment to begin at 6 a.m. for all, or part, of the year, if required by reason of the exigencies of the trade, or for the convenience of the employees
6   There must not be continuous employment for a period over $4\frac{1}{2}$ hours, without a half-hour interval for a meal or rest. This period may be increased to 5 hours if there has been at least a ten-minute interval during those five hours

Increase in the working hours allowed (s87). The working hours of young persons under sixteen may be increased to a limit of 48 hours in a week, after representations by the employer to the Secretary of State in cases where:

1   An industry depending upon the employment of young persons would be seriously prejudiced unless they could work over 44 hours a week

2   The increase in hours is not injurious to the health of those concerned

3   Such employment will help in their training and enable them to secure permanent employment in that industry

The Secretary of State may hold an inquiry before reaching his decision.

Prohibition on cleaning machinery. A woman or young person must not clean any part of a prime mover or transmission machinery (see 6:8:1) while it is in motion (s20). Section 20 also imposes the more general condition that women and young persons must not clean any machinery if doing so would expose them to risk of injury from any moving part, either of the machine being cleaned or of adjacent machinery.

Working at dangerous machines (s21). A young person may not work at any machine prescribed by the Dangerous Machines (Training of Young Persons) Order unless he has been fully instructed about possible dangers and the precautions he must observe. He must also be under adequate supervision when working at such machinery.

4:1:7   *Persons aged sixteen and seventeen*
Employees in this group must be medically examined as a prerequisite to working in a factory, see pages 179–80. The provisions of s119 (see page 180) also apply.

Permitted hours of employment for persons aged sixteen and seventeen (ss86, 100, 101 and 105). The following statutory rules must be observed where an employer engages young persons aged sixteen or seventeen to work in his factory:

1   They must not work on a Sunday
2   They must not work for more than 9 hours in any day
3   They must not work for more than 48 hours in any week, exclusive of meal and rest intervals

4   The period of employment—that is, the overall time spent on the work premises—must not exceed 11 hours a day and it must not begin earlier than 7 a.m. nor end later than 8 p.m., or 1 p.m. on Saturday (see also 4:1:4). The Secretary of State may, by regulation or order, allow the period of employment for persons aged sixteen and seventeen to begin at 6 a.m. for all or part of the year if required by the exigencies of the trade or for the convenience of the employees

5   There must not be continuous employment for a period of over 4½ hours, without a half-hour interval for a meal or rest; this period may be increased to 5 hours if there has been at least a ten-minute interval during those five hours. Boys may work for five hours without a break if they are working with men over eighteen whose own work would be interrupted if the boys took a break

Five-day week. Where persons aged sixteen or seventeen are employed on not more than five days a week, then on any day:

1   The total number of hours worked may be extended to 10
2   The period of employment may be extended to 12 hours

The total hours of work may be extended still further for persons aged sixteen or seventeen by working overtime, either:

1   For 4½ hours on the sixth day, so long as overtime is not worked on other days, or
2   By extending the total hours worked in any day to a maximum of 10½

Overtime (s89). Overtime working in this context means working more than the number of hours otherwise permitted by the Act. It is permissible for persons aged sixteen or seventeen to work overtime where the pressure of work in the factory demands it, provided that:

1   The total number of hours worked, including overtime, does not exceed 10 a day, exclusive of meal and rest periods
2   The period of employment does not exceed 12 hours a day and does not start before 7 a.m. nor finish after 8 p.m. (9 p.m. for women) on weekdays and 1 p.m. on Saturdays

3   In any calendar year the total number of hours overtime does not exceed 100

4   It does not exceed 6 hours in any week

5   It does not occur in more than 25 weeks in a calendar year

Every fraction of an hour less than half an hour counts as half an hour, and every fraction of an hour over half an hour counts as an hour.

Before a woman or young person is employed on overtime, the details must be:

1   Given to the inspector, in writing (on an Overtime Notice, Form 21)

2   Entered in the prescribed register (Overtime Register and Report, Form 22)

3   Posted in the factory by the occupier, in accordance with the inspector's instructions (s90)

Modification of overtime working (s89). Following representations that overtime may be reduced without serious detriment to an industry, the Secretary of State for Employment may:

1   Consult with any association of employers and employees, industrial councils, wages councils or other similar bodies affected, and

2   Direct an inquiry to be held

In the light of the inquiry's findings he may reduce the permitted overtime, if he thinks fit.

The Secretary of State may also make regulations to prohibit or restrict young persons working overtime on particular processes if he is satisfied that overtime would be prejudicial to their health.

Further increases in overtime (s89). By reasons of the exigencies of the trade, the Secretary of State may, by regulation, increase the aggregate number of hours overtime employment allowed for a factory in any week, or the number of weeks in any calendar year in which overtime is allowed. Such regulations have been made for a number of industries.

Individual overtime (s89(9)). The nature of the work may require overtime by different persons on different occasions, thus making it difficult to limit overtime by reference to the factory as a whole. In such cases the

Secretary of State may, by regulation, limit overtime by reference to the individual specified, but with the following provisions:

1   The number of hours overtime worked does not exceed 50 hours in any calendar year for a young person
2   They are not employed on overtime for more than 6 hours in any week
3   They are not employed on overtime for more than 25 weeks in any calendar year

unless otherwise provided by regulation.

Shiftwork (s97, 98). Shiftwork may be undertaken by young persons of sixteen or seventeen, if authorised by the Secretary of State on application by the occupier. The number of hours worked on the shift must not exceed:

1   An average of 8 hours a day, or
2   10 hours on any day, 48 hours in a week, and 88 hours in two weeks, where authorised shiftwork is not carried out on more than five days a week

The period of employment for a shift on weekdays must be between 6 a.m. and 10 p.m. (2 p.m. on Saturdays). The Secretary of State usually grants permission for shiftwork after:

1   Consultation with employees affected by means of a secret ballot in accordance with the procedure laid down in the Shift System in Factories and Workshops (Consultation of Workpeople) Order 1936
2   Agreement to the system by the majority of employees

In the case of a new factory recently established the obligation to hold a ballot may be waived.

Permission may be revoked if the system is abused or if it has not been used for more than twelve months. An authorisation is deemed to have been revoked if it has not been used for more than two years. Factory occupiers must give written notice to the District Inspector of Factories when a shift system permitted by an authorisation is discontinued or resumed after being discontinued.

Extension of shiftwork for men in certain industries (s99). In the industries listed below it is important that work be carried on continuously day and night, consequently men over sixteen may be employed on shiftwork, outside the periods of employment set out in s97. The period of employment for any shift must:

1   End on Sunday by 6 a.m.
2   Not begin on Sunday before 10 p.m.

Young male persons over the age of sixteen may work on a Sunday shift between 6 a.m. and 10 p.m. in cases where they are employed on a system of four shifts, with turns not exceeding eight hours for each shift.

A young male worker of sixteen and over may be employed on weekdays between 6 a.m. and 10 p.m. on a system of shiftworking provided:

1   He does not work more than six turns in a week
2   He does not work between midnight and 6 a.m. on two consecutive weeks
3   At least 14 hours separate each successive turn of employment

The hours worked in one week under these provisions may exceed 48, but not 56 (or 144 in a three-week period).

The factory doctor must examine young persons:

1   Before they are employed on the shift system
2   Also at intervals not exceeding six months

Unless a young person is certified by the factory doctor as being fit for shiftwork, he must not be employed on a shift system outside his normal hours of employment.

The following industries are covered by s99:

1   Smelting of iron ore
2   Manufacture of wrought iron, steel, tinplate, paper and glass
3   The galvanising of sheet metal or wire
4   Processes in which reverberatory or regenerative furnaces, which have to be kept in operation day and night, are used in connection with the smelting of ores, metal rolling, forges or the manufacture of metal tubes or rods or other classes of work, as the Secretary of State specifies by regulation

Prohibition on cleaning machinery. The rules set out in 4:1:6 apply to persons aged sixteen or seventeen.

Working at dangerous machines. The rules set out in 4:1:6 apply to persons aged sixteen or seventeen.

4:1:8 Women aged eighteen and over

The following provisions do not apply to women with responsible managerial posts, not ordinarily involved in manual work (s95).

The rules about the employment of women in factories are, in general, the same as those for employing people aged sixteen or seventeen given in 4:1:7, including the rules about:

1   Permitted hours of employment
2   Overtime
3   Modification of overtime working; except that the possibility of prohibiting overtime working on medical grounds does not apply
4   Further increases of overtime
5   Individual overtime; but women may work 75 hours overtime in any calendar year
6   Shiftwork; except that the provisions about medical examination do not apply
7   Cleaning machinery

Seasonal and other cases of pressure of work. Where a factory is subject to seasonal or other pressures, then, in the case of women only, the Secretary of State may make regulations:

1   Increasing the hours of work and period of employment during the number of weeks specified by the regulation, not exceeding eight in any year
2   Increasing the hours of overtime in a calendar year to a maximum of 150 instead of 100

Such regulations have been made for a number of trades.

Evening work may be permitted. Permission may be granted by the district inspector to a factory occupier under the Factories (Evening Employment) Order 1950 to employ women in a factory on Monday to Friday between 5 p.m. and 10 p.m. provided they are not employed in the factory at any other time. If the period of work is for more than 4½ hours, there must be a ten-minute rest interval.

4:1:9 Employing young people as
messengers in connection with the work of a factory
Section 116 of the Factories Act covers young persons carrying out the following jobs:

1 Collecting, carrying or delivering goods and carrying messages or running errands for the purposes of a factory where the employment is wholly or mainly outside the factory
2 Employment in connection with any business carried on at a dock, wharf, quay or warehouse (other than a warehouse to which the Shops Act 1950 applies)

A young person aged fifteen may be employed in one of the above-mentioned occupations only on the following conditions:

1 Only 48 hours a week must be worked, exclusive of intervals for meals and rest
2 Employment in continuous spells must not exceed 5 hours, without a break of at least half an hour for a meal or a rest
3 A dinner break of 45 minutes must be allowed if employment covers the period between 11.30 a.m. and 2.30 p.m.
4 On one day in each week work must end at 1 p.m.
5 An interval of at least eleven consecutive hours must be allowed, including the period from 10 p.m. until 6 p.m. in every 24-hour period, between mid-day of one day and mid-day of the next
6 The occupier must keep a record of the hours worked including intervals allowed and overtime
7 They must not work on Sundays

The provisions discussed in relation to persons aged fifteen apply equally to persons aged sixteen or seventeen, with the exception that a person aged sixteen or over may work overtime in cases of seasonal pressure or emergency for not more than:

1 Six hours in any week
2 Fifty hours in a calendar year
3 Twelve consecutive weeks in a calendar year

Exemption from observance of special safeguards under s116 (s117).
Employers of young persons over sixteen may be exempted from observance of the requirements of s116, if the Secretary of State so allows, on the ground that this will maintain or increase the efficiency of industry or transport.

A general exemption regulation which applies to persons generally, or employment generally, must be made only on the application of:

1   A joint industrial council
2   A conciliation board
3   A wages council
4   Organisations jointly representing the employers and workers concerned
5   Either side of industry, following discussions with the other side

A special exemption order applies to particular persons or class of persons or to a particular employment, but it must not apply for more than a year, unless it is extended.

4:2   INDUSTRIAL UNDERTAKINGS OTHER THAN FACTORIES

This section covers the provisions of the Employment of Women, Young Persons and Children Act 1920, which covers employment in an "industrial undertaking," a term that includes:

1   Mines and quarries
2   Industries in which articles are manufactured, altered, cleaned, repaired, ornamented, broken up or demolished or in which materials are transformed, including generation, transformation or transmission of electricity or other kinds of motive power
3   Construction, repair, maintenance and demolition of buildings, railways, harbours, docks, canals, telegraphic installations, gas and electrical undertakings
4   Transport of passengers or goods by rail, road or inland waterway, but excluding transport by hand (Schedule I article 1)

4:2:1   *Persons aged fifteen*
The provisions of the 1920 Act are additional to, not in derogation of, other statutory provisions on the employment of young persons and

children. A young person aged fifteen must not work in any industrial undertaking at night unless only members of the same family work there (s1(3)). Night means a period of at least eleven consecutive hours including the interval between 10 p.m. and 5 a.m.

4:2:2 *Persons aged sixteen and seventeen*

Young persons aged sixteen or seventeen must not work in any industrial undertaking at night unless only members of the same family work there (s1(3)). Night means a period of at least eleven consecutive hours including the interval between 10 p.m. and 5 a.m. These rules do not apply where:

1   A process has to be carried on continuously day and night in relation to the manufacture of iron, steel, glass, paper, raw sugar and gold mining reduction work
2   An emergency situation arises which was unforeseeable, uncontrollable, constituting an interference with normal working and not likely to recur periodically (Schedule II articles 2, 3 and 4)

Where young persons are employed in an industrial undertaking, a register must record the date of birth, date of entry and date of leaving the employment. The register must be open to inspection at all times. Contravention of this provision may result in a £20 fine on a summary conviction (s1(4)).

4:2:3 *Women*

The provisions of the Hours of Employment (Conventions) Act 1936, which restrict the employment of women, confer protections additional to those of the Factories Act 1961 not in derogation of them.

Women, whatever their age, may not be employed at night in any industrial undertaking (s1(1)). Night means a period of at least eleven consecutive hours, including the interval between 10 p.m. and 5 a.m. An industrial undertaking bears the same meaning as that given by the Employment of Women, Young Persons and Children Act 1920, excepting the provision on transport (see above).

The general rule does not operate in the following cases:

1   To undertakings which employ only members of the same family

2   Where there has been an interruption to work which it was impossible to foresee, provided it is not of a recurring nature
3   Where materials will deteriorate rapidly
4   To women holding responsible managerial positions not ordinarily involving manual work

4:3   SHOPS

The definition of a shop is given in section 8:12.

4:3:1   *Persons under the age of fifteen*
The Children and Young Persons Acts 1933 and 1963 state that a person under fifteen must not be employed:

1   Until he is 13 years old
2   Before the end of school on a day when he is required to attend
3   Between 7 p.m. and 7 a.m.
4   For over 2 hours on a day when he must attend school or on a Sunday
5   To lift or carry heavy objects likely to cause injury (s18 1933 Act and s34 1963 Act)

A local authority is empowered to make by-laws regulating the employment of children (s18(2) 1933 Act). These by-laws may distinguish between the conditions upon which young persons may be employed by reference to:

1   Age and sex
2   Different localities, trades, occupations and circumstances

Provision may be made for the following matters:

1   Absolute prohibition of employment in any specified occupation
2   The age below which they must not be employed
3   The number of hours that may be worked
4   The times of the day when they may be employed
5   The intervals for meals and rests
6   The holidays to be allowed

Penalties for failure to observe these provisions. A fine of up to £20 on a first conviction and £50 for any subsequent conviction may be imposed upon anyone employing children in violation of:

1   The provisions of the Children and Young Persons Acts 1933 and 1963
2   The by-laws made by a local authority in pursuance of their powers (s36(1) 1963 Act)

The child employed does not commit an offence, but a parent, guardian or other person procuring the work can be convicted. An employer will not be convicted if he shows that he used all due care and diligence to avoid breaking the law.

4:3:2   *Persons aged fifteen*
A person aged fifteen may not be employed about the business of a shop for more than 44 hours in any week. A total of 48 hours may be worked during the week in which Christmas Day falls, or the week before, or the week after, but the total hours during the two weeks must not exceed 88 hours (s27 Shops Act 1950).

If employed at night an interval of eleven consecutive hours must be allowed including the hours between 10 p.m. and 6 a.m. in every 24-hour period between 12 noon of one day and 12 noon on the next day.

Persons within this group must not work for over 5 hours (or 5½ hours on a half-day) without a 20-minute break during that period of time (s20). If working between 11.30 a.m. and 2.30 p.m. they must have a break of at least 45 minutes. A break of half an hour must be allowed during the period 4 p.m. to 7 p.m. if work takes place at this time of day.

The occupier of a shop employing persons aged fifteen must keep a record of:

1   Their hours of employment and the intervals for meals and rest periods unless a notice in the prescribed form is exhibited in the shop
2   Overtime worked

In addition a notice must be exhibited stating the number of hours per week during which persons aged fifteen may be employed in accordance with the Shops Act 1950 (s32).

4:3:3 *Persons aged sixteen and seventeen*

The Shops Act 1950 states that young persons aged sixteen or seventeen must not be employed in the business of a shop for over 48 hours in any week, but overtime may be worked during periods of seasonal or exceptional pressure for:

1   6 weeks only in any year
2   A maximum of 50 hours in any year and 12 hours in any week (s24)

The occupier of the shop is liable to a fine of £10 for a contravention of these provisions.

There are exceptions to this general rule. The occupier of a shop serving meals, intoxicating liquors or refreshments to customers for consumption on the premises, may employ a young person during two consecutive weeks for:

1   60 hours in either week
2   A total of 96 hours during the two weeks (s25(1))

A notice to this effect must be posted in the shop.

The occupier of a shop selling accessories for aircraft, motor vehicles, or cycles for immediate use, may employ a young person for:

1   54 hours in any week
2   Not more than 144 hours in any period of three consecutive weeks (s26(1))

Persons aged sixteen or seventeen employed at night must be allowed an interval of eleven consecutive hours, including the hours between 10 p.m. and 6 a.m., in every 24-hour period between 12 noon on one day and 12 noon on the next day. The interval of 11 hours need not include the hours between 5–6 a.m. where a male person is employed to collect and deliver milk, bread and newspapers. The periods of rest are the same as those applicable to persons aged fifteen (see 4 : 3 : 2).

The records to be kept by the occupier of a shop are as set out in the section on persons aged fifteen (see 4 : 3 : 2).

4:4   YOUNG PERSONS IN OTHER JOBS

4:4:1 *Persons under the age of fifteen*

The rules are the same as those set out for this group of persons in relation to employment in shops (see 4 : 3 : 1). The penalties for infringing the law are also the same.

Children may be authorised to work for their parents in agricultural work, however, before the age at which employment is permissible in normal circumstances.

Restrictions on licences for performances by children under thirteen (s38 1963 Act). A licence will not be granted to allow a child under thirteen to perform in public unless:

1   The part can only be taken by a child actor of his age, or
2   It is ballet dancing as part of a ballet or opera performance, or
3   The part to be taken is wholly or mainly musical and the performance is also wholly or mainly musical or alternatively opera or ballet

When the compulsory school-leaving age is raised to sixteen these provisions will apply to children under fourteen years old.

Restriction on public performances by persons under fifteen. A person under the age of fifteen cannot rehearse or take part in those public performances stipulated below, unless a licence has been granted by the local authority in the area where the person resides. A licence is necessary for:

1   A performance for which some charge is made for admission or otherwise
2   A performance on licensed premises or the premises of a registered club
3   A broadcast performance, a recording to be broadcast, a film or public exhibition

A licence cannot be refused where the local authority is satisfied that:

1   The child is fit to take part in the performance
2   Proper provision has been made to secure his health and kind treatment
3   His education will not suffer

A licence is unnecessary in the following cases:

1   If the person has not taken part in other public performances on more than 3 days during the last 6 months

2   The performance is given by a school or by a body approved by the Home Secretary or by the local authority in the area where the performance is held. Only expenses must be payable to the performer or his representative (s37 1963 Act)

There is a right of appeal to a Magistrates' Court if a licence has been refused, revoked or varied (s39 1963 Act).

Penalties for infringement of sections 37–9 (s40 1963 Act). A fine of £100, imprisonment for three months, or both may be imposed on anyone causing or procuring a person under sixteen to take part in a performance without the necessary local authority licence, and also a parent or guardian allowing such conduct. It is a defence to show that it was believed on reasonable grounds that the person under sixteen had not taken part in other public performances on more than 3 days in the last 6 months.
    There are similar penalties for:

1   Failure to observe a condition attached to the licence
2   Knowingly or recklessly making a false statement in connection with the application for a licence

4:4:2   *Persons aged fifteen*
Local authorities do not have power to prohibit young persons aged 15 to 18 working at a specified trade (Children and Young Persons Act 1933 s19(1)(2)). By-laws may distinguish, however, between the conditions upon which young persons may be employed by reference to:

1   Age and sex
2   Different localities, trades, occupations and circumstances

Provision may be made on the following matters:

1   The number of hours that may be worked
2   The times of day at which they may be employed
3   The intervals for meals and rests
4   The holidays to be allowed

There is no power to make by-laws regulating employment that is covered by other statutory provisions such as:

1   Employment in factories, shops and offices, mines and quarries, except as a van boy, errand boy or messenger

2   Domestic service, except as a non-resident daily servant
3   Agriculture
4   On a British ship or fishing boat
5   Delivery, collection and transport of goods in the building or engineering trade, except as a van boy, errand boy or messenger

The penalties for failing to observe the provisions of any by-laws that have been made are the same as those set out for non-observance of the conditions upon which persons under the age of fifteen may work in shops (see 4 : 3 : 1)

The Young Persons (Employment) Acts 1938 and 1964. These Acts do not cover employment in agriculture, on a ship, in a factory or shop. The provisions of the Acts regulate employment, hours of work and holidays of young persons aged fifteen if engaged upon activities set out in s7 :

1   The collection and delivery of goods
2   Carrying, loading or unloading of goods incidental to collection and delivery
3   Carrying messages or running errands :
   (a) wholly or mainly outside the premises from which the business is carried on
   (b) at a residential hotel or club
   (c) at business premises where newspapers are published
   (d) at places of public entertainment and public baths
4   Reception or attendance upon guests and visitors to a residential hotel or club, places of public entertainment and public baths
5   Operation of a hoist or lift connected with mechanical power
6   Cinematograph operations
7   Receiving or dispatching goods at premises occupied for a laundry, dying or cleaning works, or other factory
8   A retail business carried on at a residential hotel or theatre
9   Some licensed premises (s1 Young Persons (Employment) Act 1964)

A person aged fifteen who is within the scope of the Act must not work over 44 hours in any week.
   A young person aged fifteen is entitled to :

1   A 30-minute break if employed continuously for more than 5 hours

2   A break for lunch of at least 45 minutes between 11.30 a.m.
and 2.30 p.m. if work takes place during those hours (s1(2))

3   Terminate his work at 1 p.m. on one day a week (s1(3))

4   Eleven consecutive hours interval, including the hours between
10 p.m. and 6 a.m. (s1(4))

5   Sundays free from employment, unless he has another day off
instead during the previous week or the week beginning with
the Sunday on which he works. This must be additional to his
half day's holiday (s1(5))

The provisions of the Act are enforceable by the local authority. Inspectors
may be appointed with the same powers and duties as a factory inspector
(s3).

Public performances by persons aged fifteen. The rules are the same as
those set out for persons under the age of fifteen, but over the age of
thirteen (see 4:4:1). The penalties for infringement of the laws are also
the same.

4:4:3   *Persons aged sixteen and seventeen*
The relevant law applicable to this group is the same as that set out:

1   For persons aged fifteen as regards the power of local authorities (see 4:4:2) and the penalties are the same as those set out
for non-observance of the conditions upon which persons
under the age of fifteen may work in shops (see 4:3:1)

2   Under the Young Persons (Employment) Act 1938, with the
following modifications as to hours of work: persons aged sixteen or seventeen within the scope of the Act must not work
over 48 hours in any week

Overtime may be worked by a young person aged sixteen or over in cases
of seasonal or special pressures or in emergencies, provided:

1   The number of hours overtime does not exceed 6 hours in
any one week and 50 hours in any year

2   The number of weeks in any year in which overtime is worked
does not exceed 12 weeks, whether or not they are consecutive weeks (s1(1))

EMPLOYING DISABLED PERSONS

A disabled person may find it difficult to secure employment in open competition with other candidates for a vacant position, consequently Parliament has granted legislative protection under the Disabled Persons (Employment) Acts 1944 and 1958.

A person is disabled if he is substantially handicapped in securing or retaining employment otherwise suited to his age, experience and qualifications by reason of:

1   Injury
2   Disease, which includes a physical or mental condition arising from imperfect development of an organ
3   Congenital deformity

4:5   REGISTER OF DISABLED PERSONS

The Secretary of State for Employment maintains a register of disabled persons. A person may become registered by applying to the Secretary of State personally or through someone like a personnel manager acting on his behalf and showing that:

1   The disablement will continue for a period of 12 months
2   He is ordinarily resident in Great Britain
3   He wishes to secure and retain employment and has a reasonable prospect of being able to do so

A person cannot be registered if:

1   He unreasonably refused to attend vocational training or industrial rehabilitation courses
2   He is of habitual bad character
3   He is of unsound mind
4   He is a whole-time hospital patient

Removal from the register. A person will be removed from the register in the following circumstances:

1   At the end of the period prescribed by the Secretary of State

2   By written application from the person registered
3   If the District Advisory Committee recommends removal when the disability justifying entry has ceased

4:5:1 *Number of disabled persons that must be employed*

An employer of twenty or more persons must engage his quota of registered disabled persons, unless he has a permit from the Secretary of State granting exemption. The employer must keep a record of disabled persons employed. The employer must not reduce his quota of registered disabled persons below the minimum number specified by:

1   Offering employment to or engaging a person who is not a registered disabled person
2   Dismissing a registered disabled person without having legal justification for terminating the employment

The Secretary of State determines the relevant quota by taking a percentage of persons employed in each particular industry. A standard percentage may be applied to those aspects of the business enterprise where it is possible to employ disabled persons, even though the work is not eminently suitable. A special percentage covers work which is specially suitable or unsuitable for disabled persons.

The employer can work out the number of registered disabled persons he must engage in the following manner:

1   By applying the standard percentage to the total number of employees within its scope: the Disabled Persons Order 1946 fixed the standard at 3 per cent
2   By applying the special percentage, if applicable, to the total number of employees within its scope. This is fixed by making an application to the local employment exchange on the form prescribed. For example, there is a special rate of 0.1 per cent for employment as master or crew of a British ship, if its owner is resident or has his principal place of business in Great Britain

Example 1. If an employer engages 565 employees and the standard percentage of 3 per cent applies to 410 of them, then 12 out of the 410 should be registered disabled persons. The calculation has produced a fraction less than one-half (12.3) and it may be ignored.

If a special percentage of, say, 4 per cent applies to the remaining 145 employees, then 6 out of that number should be registered disabled persons. The calculation has produced a fraction over one-half (5.8) and the figure must be rounded upwards to the higher whole number.

Example 2. An employer engaging 24 employees is within the scope of the Act. If the standard percentage of 3 per cent applies to his workforce, the calculation will give a fractional figure of 0.72, and being over one-half the employer is obliged to employ one registered disabled person.

4:5:2 An employer may be required
to engage only registered disabled persons

The Secretary of State may designate certain classes of employment as offering specially suitable opportunities for the employment of disabled persons, then the employer cannot engage any other type of person unless:

1   He is under a duty to reinstate an employee who is not a registered disabled person, or
2   He has a permit from the Secretary of State exempting him from employing registered disabled persons

Under the Disabled Persons (Designated Employments) Order 1946 the following employments have been designated:

1   Passenger electric lift attendant, other than those installed in a ship
2   Car park attendant (excluding a garage or part of a garage used for the purpose of protecting cars and their contents) and issuing tickets and collecting fees from users of the car park

4:5:3 Penalties for non-observance of the statutory requirements

An employer commits an offence punishable with a £100 fine or three months imprisonment or both if:

1   He fails to employ his quota of registered disabled persons, or,
2   He dismisses such persons from his employment without legal justification, provided a District Advisory Committee has investigated the dismissal and the employer has been given the opportunity to make representations. The Committee must also report to the Secretary of State

All prosecutions require the consent of the Secretary of State.

EMPLOYING ALIENS AND COMMONWEALTH CITIZENS

The Immigration Act 1971 and Immigration Rules of Practice introduce a comprehensive set of rules governing the right of admission to the UK of aliens and Commonwealth citizens and formulate the control to be exercised over them while they remain here.

4:6 CITIZENSHIP

In the United Kingdom there are the following classes of persons:

Citizens of the UK and Colonies. These are persons who are nationals of the UK, Channel Islands, Isle of Man and all the Colonies and they also have the status of British Subjects. Citizenship is acquired by birth in the UK or the Colonies or by descent from a father who is himself a citizen, irrespective of the child's place of birth. Registration is dealt with below.

Citizens of independent Commonwealth countries, who also have the status of British subjects. Legislation granting independence to former Colonial territories provides for the retention of UK nationality if a person does not take the nationality of the new, independent state. Asians in Kenya have not acquired local nationality but retained their status as citizens of the UK and Colonies.

A commonwealth citizen or a citizen of Eire may be registered as a citizen of the UK and Colonies if:

1   He is of full age and capacity
2   He is of good character
3   He has sufficient knowledge of the English or Welsh language
4   He has been ordinarily resident here for the five years preceding his application for registration or engaged on one of the employments listed in 5 below
5   He intends to reside in the UK or a colony or alternatively to enter or continue in the following types of employment:
   (a) Crown service under Her Majesty's government in the UK
   (b) Service under an international organisation of which Her Majesty's government is a member

(c) Service in the employment of a society, company or body of persons established in the UK

A registered citizen becomes a patrial and cannot be deported.

Aliens are nationals of foreign states who are neither British subjects nor citizens of Eire. An alien may become a citizen of the UK and Colonies by naturalisation at the Home Secretary's discretion, if the following conditions are satisfied:

1   Residence here during the year preceding the application or employment in Crown service
2   For four of the seven years preceding the year of residence, he has either resided in the UK or a colony, or been in Crown service
3   He is of good character, with a sufficient knowledge of the English language
4   Intention to reside in the UK or a colony, or to work in Crown service or with an international organisation of which the UK government is a member

A naturalised citizen becomes a patrial and cannot be deported.

Irish citizens are placed in a special category. The British Nationality Act 1948 provided that henceforth citizens of Eire were not to be British subjects merely by virtue of being citizens of Eire, nor would birth in Eire create the status of British subject in the future. It is expressly provided, however, that citizens of Eire are not aliens and the Representation of the People Act 1949 gave them the right to vote on the same terms as British subjects, but they can be deported.

An Irish citizen may be a registered citizen of the UK and Colonies in the same way as a Commonwealth citizen, then he cannot be deported.

Citizens of Eire are not subject to any control on entry into the UK. It is expressly provided that a person shall not require leave to enter to the UK if he arrives here from the Republic of Ireland, the Channel Islands or the Isle of Man.

4:7 PATRIALS

The Immigration Act 1971 introduces the completely new concepts of patrials and non-patrials, which has been superimposed on the existing classification into citizens, aliens and Irish citizens.

Patrials have a "right of abode" in the UK. They are not subject to immigration control and may be admitted from abroad to take up employment without having a work permit. Patrials cannot be deported.

A patrial is defined as a citizen of the UK and Colonies by reason of:

1 Birth, adoption, naturalisation or registration
2 Being born or legally adopted by a parent with citizenship at the time of birth or adoption
3 Being settled in the UK and also ordinarily resident there for the last five years or more

The term "patrial" also includes:

1 A citizen of a Commonwealth country born to or legally adopted by a parent with citizenship of the UK and Colonies at the time of the birth or adoption
2 The wife of a citizen of the UK and Colonies or the wife of a Commonwealth citizen, provided that she is a Commonwealth citizen herself

Patrials may be registered as citizens of the UK and Colonies:

1 If of full age and capacity, and
2 If during the five years preceding application the applicant has been ordinarily resident in the UK or engaged on:
   (a) Crown service under Her Majesty's government in the UK
   (b) Service under an international organisation of which Her Majesty's government is a member
   (c) Service in the employment of a society, company or body of persons established in the UK

Holders of UK passports who are not patrials will continue to need special vouchers before being admitted for settlement. Work permits will be issued on the same conditions as those imposed on other Commonwealth citizens. Asians living in East Africa fall within this group.

4:7:1 *Non-patrial Commonwealth citizens already settled in the UK*
A non-patrial, his wife and children who had already settled in the UK before the Immigration Act 1971 became effective, has leave to enter and remain there. Such persons may be offered employment without a work permit. Approval of the Department of Employment is not required before changing employment.

Persons falling within this category may apply for registration as citizens of the UK and Colonies: if, at the date of the application, they have been ordinarily resident in the UK for the last five years (or if ordinarily resident for over five years it includes the period since the Immigration Act 1971 became effective) without being subject to a restriction under an immigration law on the period of stay allowed.

4:8 DEPORTATION

The Home Secretary may deport a Commonwealth citizen, an Irish citizen or an alien, if they are not patrials, in the following circumstances:

1   If the time-limit imposed on the leave to stay has expired or if the conditions attached to leave to enter the country have not been observed: for example, if there has not been registration with the police as required. These provisions do not apply to a person who was a Commonwealth citizen or citizen of the Irish Republic when the Immigration Act 1971 came into force, provided he has been resident in the UK for the five years preceding the deportation decision

2   If the Home Secretary deems deportation to be conducive to the public good, a power exercised against persons engaging in undesirable political activities. This provision does not apply to a person who was a Commonwealth citizen or citizen of the Irish Republic when the Immigration Act 1971 came into force if either:
    (a) He has been ordinarily resident in the UK since that time, or
    (b) Ordinarily resident in the UK for the last five years preceding the deportation order

3   If they are dependents of a person deported and will be a charge on public funds unless deported, provided that not more than eight weeks have elapsed since the person upon whom they depend was deported. "Dependants" are the wife or wives, and children under 18 of a man being deported and

children under 18 of a woman being deported. A legally adopted child is regarded only as the child of the adoptor. A child not legally adopted may be treated as a child of the adoptor but not necessarily. An illegitimate child is regarded as the child of its mother. A dependant cannot be deported if he is a Commonwealth citizen or a citizen of the Irish Republic when the Immigration Act 1971 came into force, provided he has been resident in the UK for the five years preceding the deportation decision

4   If after attaining the age of seventeen, a person is convicted of an offence punishable with imprisonment where the court recommends deportation. This provision does not cover a person who was a Commonwealth citizen or citizen of the Irish Republic when the Immigration Act 1971 came into force, if at the time of conviction he had been ordinarily resident in the UK for the preceding five years

4:9 ENGAGING STAFF
AT PRESENT LIVING OUTSIDE THE UK

The Home Secretary has power under the Immigration Act 1971 to lay before Parliament rules of practice, to be followed by immigration officials in the administration of the Act, to regulate entry into the UK of non-patrials requiring permission to enter. It is anticipated that these rules will closely follow the draft rules already published which will now be discussed.

4:9:1 *Securing a work permit*

Commonwealth citizens and aliens who are non-patrials wishing to come to the UK to work must be in possession of a work permit. Irish citizens will continue to be admitted to take up employment without a work permit. The same rule applies to persons entering from the Channel Islands and the Isle of Man.

A permit will be granted in the first instance for a fixed, initial period of twelve months. It is the prospective employer's responsibility to secure the work permit from the Department of Employment before the prospective employee's arrival here. The wife and children of the employee will be admitted on the same conditions as the employee himself.

In the past, permits have been granted where it could be shown that jobs of persons already employed here would not be jeopardised or the standard of wages reduced by the engagement of foreign or Commonwealth labour at lower rates of pay. There is trade union opposition in some trades to the granting of permits to aliens.

A person granted limited leave to enter and remain in the UK may have to register with the police.

4:9:2   Extending an employee's period of stay

Any application to the Department of Employment by the employee requesting an extension of stay should be accompanied by a letter from his employer stating that he is willing to continue the applicant's employment. The request may be granted if it is appropriate in the light of the following relevant circumstances:

1   Whether the applicant has observed the time-limit and conditions imposed when he was admitted to the UK
2   Whether his character, conduct and associations make it undesirable to continue his stay
3   Whether he is a danger to the national security
4   Whether it will be impossible to return him to another country if he is allowed to remain here
5   Whether he has been convicted for an offence that does not warrant deportation

An extension of stay may be denied even though the applicant appears to have observed all the requirements of good conduct implicit in these considerations.

The applicant should also apply for an extension of stay for his wife and children. The Department of Employment will not extend the stay of an unskilled seasonal worker beyond 31 October in any year.

4:9:3   Removal of the time-limit on an employee's period of stay

A person admitted initially for a twelve-month period of employment, who has remained for four years in approved employment, may have the time-limit on his stay removed, unless there are relevant circumstances which make his continued presence inadvisable, such as those set out in 4:9:1. If the time-limit on the stay is removed, employment may be changed at will and registration with the police is no longer required.

A non-patrial, whether an alien or Commonwealth citizen, will be guilty of an offence punishable with a fine of up to £200, or imprisonment for up to six months, or both if he remains in the UK beyond the time stipulated, or fails to observe a condition of his leave, such as seeking employment when he is supposed to be a tourist or visitor. Further, a fine of £400 or six months' imprisonment or both may be incurred by anyone knowingly harbouring a person acting in this manner. An employer offering work to a non-patrial without a work permit may commit this offence if the term "knowingly harbouring" is deemed to cover his conduct where it is obvious that the conditions of stay imposed on the applicant are being violated.

4:9:4 Students
Doctors, dentists and nurses admitted as postgraduate students may take up full-time employment associated with their studies without a work permit.

Students admitted for a course of study cannot stay on in full-time employment, though vacation employment between periods of study is permissible.

A maximum stay of twelve months will be granted to foreign nationals engaged in work that cannot be considered as proper full-time employment, taken to help them improve their knowledge of English and widen their business or industrial experience.

4:9:5 Commonwealth citizens admitted as trainees
The Department of Employment may issue a permit allowing a Commonwealth citizen to enter the UK to train on the job in some profession or employment. The period of stay allowed will be twelve months or the period of training, whichever is the shorter. A condition will be imposed restricting the trainee to the approved employment. An extension of stay may be granted if the training is still being continued.

4:9:6 Admission for a working holiday
A Commonwealth citizen employed in the UK while on holiday will not be allowed to take employment indefinitely. There is a twelve-month limit on young people admitted on an extended working holiday, subject to an extension of stay to a maximum period of three years.

4:9:7 Visitors
People admitted as visitors are usually allowed to stay for a period of six months. The immigration officer may have imposed a condition prohibiting employment which will not be withdrawn unless the Department of

Employment is prepared to approve the proposed employment. In such cases an extension of stay may be granted.

4:9:8 *Marriage of a non-patrial and admission of his fiancée*

An employee lawfully resident in the UK without any time-limit on his stay may seek admission of a woman who does not reside in the UK so that he may marry her. The woman will be admitted for three months so that the marriage may take place, but this time-limit will be removed after the marriage has occurred. If she marries a man with limited leave to stay, her leave to stay should be varied to coincide with her husband's period of stay.

If the marriage does not take place within the three-month period, an extension of stay will be granted only if there is a good reason for the delay or satisfactory evidence that the marriage will take place in the near future.

FIVE

Liability under Common Law for Injured Employees

In THE FOLLOWING FOUR CHAPTERS THE EMPLOYER'S LIABILITY FOR injuries to his employee in the course of employment will be considered. It is important to bear in mind that there are two categories of liability. An employer has both common law and statutory duties.

The common law duties binding the employer will be considered first. A breach of these duties will render him liable in damages to the employee in a civil law action. They are of general application and their scope is wide, but the employer may take the benefit, where applicable, of the various defences that are open to him to negative or reduce his liability. For example, the employee may have consented to running the risk of harm (see 5 : 10) or by his own negligence contributed to the cause of the accident (see 7 : 3 : 8).

It is not simply a question of liability for injury to an employee suffered on the employer's premises. An employer may also be responsible for injuries to the employee of an independent contractor who has been engaged to complete a given task on the employer's premises for his benefit. Further, the employer may have to pay damages for accidents to his own employees caused by the defective state of the premises of a third party, at which the employee is working for the employer's benefit.

Although the common law protects an employee who is injured in the course of his employment by imposing a required standard of care on the employer, these principles of liability are inadequate in a highly industrialised environment where there is serious risk of harm, unless stringent precautionary measures are taken. The common law protection is related to the standard of care to be expected from a reasonable employer and the standard changes as industrial conditions and methods change. These common law duties are expressed in broad generalisations, making it difficult to determine how the established principles will apply in a novel situation. It is difficult for the employer to ascertain the precise nature of any safety precautions that he is expected to take in furtherance of these duties, nor do they impose a comprehensive system for the protection of the employee's health and welfare. The common law compensates the employee only if the employer is at fault in exposing him to a risk that he should not be expected to take in those particular circumstances. This issue is determined after an accident has occurred, but the real need may lie in the provision of a set of regulations to prevent such accidents in the first place.

The Factories Act 1961 and the Offices, Shops and Railway Premises Act 1963 are intended to cover areas and problems that the common law cannot possibly cope with. The detailed requirements of the Acts on safety, health and welfare aim to prevent industrial accidents, and clearly indicate to the employer the precise scope of his responsibilities on such issues.

The statutory duties owed to an employee will be discussed in Chapters 6, 7 and 8. These duties apply to premises within the statutory definition of a factory or alternatively, an office, shop or railway premises, thus at the outset their scope is limited to specific groups of employees. Once within the statutory protection, however, the employee is covered by numerous detailed provisions ensuring an effective safeguard for his welfare. The statutes establish civil and criminal liability against the employer who is in breach of their provisions.

The rules of common law and statute are complementary. In any action a claim for damages may be made under both heads, but damages will not be awarded twice for the same injury, if the employer has violated both the common law and statutory rules. If a claim fails under one head it may succeed under another (see Nolan v Dental Manufacturing Co Ltd 7 : 3 : 7).

Other premises covered by legislation. Although most statutory duties owed by employer to employee are those under the Factories Act or the Offices, Shops and Railway Premises Act, a few employers will have obligations under the Mines and Quarries Act 1954 or the Agriculture (Safety, Health and Welfare Provisions) Act 1956.

For the purposes of the Mines and Quarries Act, a mine is defined as an excavation or system of excavations made for the purpose of, or in connection with, the getting, wholly or substantially by means involving the employment of persons below ground, of minerals (whether in their natural state or in solution or suspension) or products of minerals.

A quarry is defined as an excavation or system of excavations made for the purpose of, or in connection with, the getting of minerals (whether in their natural state or in solution or suspension) or products of minerals, being neither a mine nor merely a well or bore-hole or a well or bore-hole combined.

The term "minerals" as used in these definitions includes stone, slate, clay, gravel, sand and other natural deposits other than peat. Thus the Act will extend to such things as sand-pits and chalk-pits, which many firms may operate as ancillary operations to their main business.

The Agriculture (Safety, Health and Welfare Provisions) Act applies to all places where persons are employed in agriculture, here defined as including dairy-farming, the production of any consumable product which is grown for sale or for consumption or other use for the purpose of trade or business or of any other undertaking, and the use of land as grazing, meadow or pasture land or orchard or osier land or woodland or for market gardens or nursery grounds. The Act itself lays down few provisions; its main purpose is to enable the Minister to make special regulations. Codes of regulations under the Act include those for tractors, threshers and balers and other machinery, safety of workplaces, and ladders.

Workers engaged in spraying fruit trees or other crops are protected by the Agriculture (Poisonous Substances) Act 1952 and this now extends to "soil application operations" where the poisonous substance is applied direct to the soil instead of being sprayed onto the crops.

5:1 EMPLOYER'S LIABILITY FOR HIS NEGLIGENT ACTS

A prudent employer must not expose his employees to unnecessary risks arising from the conduct of his business. When determining the precise scope of the employer's common law liability in damages for injury to an employee caused by the failure to establish a safe system of work, it is necessary to discuss the various constituent elements of that system. These differing elements cover the physical conditions in which employees must work, it being essential that the work premises and machinery installed should be safe for use by employees. The employer's duty is more extensive, however, for any safety precautions provided must be properly supervised and, within limits, effectively enforced. Further, the effectiveness of any safety measures must not be nullified by the actions of incompetent employees whose personal qualities make them unsuitable for carrying out the work assigned to them. The selection of competent employees may be a task for the personnel manager, consequently he must be careful not to choose persons whose inability to conduct themselves in the manner required will cause harm to fellow employees and impose legal liability on the employer.

The cases to be discussed in this chapter will indicate to the personnel manager the most common type of situation where the employer will be deemed to be at fault and in some instances the precautionary, remedial action that can be taken to avoid liability. Since each case turns on its own facts it is sometimes difficult to appreciate why one employee is awarded damages, while another fails to establish his claim; nonetheless there is a theme that is common to all such cases. Liability in this context is based upon negligence, that is the infliction of injury on the employee because of the employer's failure to take that degree of care required by law in the individual circumstances. It must be remembered that an employer's moral responsibility to safeguard the health and well-being of his employees is not equivalent to his liability at common law. "Acts or omissions which any moral code would censure cannot in a practical world be treated so as to give a right to every person injured to demand relief." (Lord Atkin)

If the employer is to be held liable in damages for harm caused by a negligent act, the employee who has suffered injury must establish the existence of a duty on the employer to take care and a failure to discharge that duty.

5:2 WHAT IS MEANT BY A DUTY OF CARE?

The employer must take reasonable care to avoid committing any act, or failing to take any precaution, which he can reasonably foresee as being the likely or probable cause of injury to his employees. He is not expected to foresee the mere possibility of some injury. Employees are a class of person so directly affected by the employer's acts or omissions that they ought to be in his contemplation as a group of persons who will suffer from his wrongful acts. The numerous cases on duty of care cannot be reduced to a few simple rules, though general guiding principles have emerged. Different industries will carry differing degrees of risk of injury to employees working there, and standards of safety and precautionary measures will vary accordingly.

5:2:1 Acts that constitute a breach of an employer's duty of care

If the employer wishes to escape liability for his acts causing injury to the employee, his conduct must be judged by the standard of care that is expected from the ordinary reasonable man acting in the same situation as the employer. If he fails to achieve that standard he will be liable in damages. The standards of the reasonable man vary with the circumstances, but it must not be assumed that they are low standards of care. The more dangerous the situation in which an employee has to work, the greater the standard that would be expected from the reasonable man and, in turn, from the employer directly responsible. "Negligence is the omission to do something which a reasonable man, guided by those considerations which ordinarily regulate the conduct of human affairs would do, or doing something which a prudent and reasonable man would not do" (Baron Alderson). The reasonably prudent man would not allow injury to be sustained by an employee if he could reasonably foresee that an accident could be the direct result of his conduct. The employer must achieve the same standard to avoid liability for negligence in respect of his actions causing loss or injury to an employee. "The standard of foresight is in one sense an impersonal test. It eliminates the personal equation and is independent of the idiosyncrasies of the particular person whose conduct is in question." (Lord McMillan)

5:2:2 Factors to consider when determining
the degree of care to be expected from an employer

The following factors may be considered in an attempt to determine whether the employer has shown that degree of care for his employees' safety and welfare that ought to be expected, bearing in mind the circumstances surrounding the particular case in issue. The precautions that an employer must take against causing harm to his employees are closely related to the seriousness of the risk of injury involved in the work undertaken. If there is an obvious danger of injury being suffered, then exceptional precautions must be taken.

Bell v Arnott & Harrison Ltd (1967, Court of Appeal)

Bell, a toolmaker, was injured by an electric hand-drill when a loose screw came away from the drill, thereby releasing a brush inside which was alive with electricity. The drill vibrated considerably while being used. Bell sued his employer for damages for the personal injuries suffered.

The court decided that with equipment of this type the employer was obliged to make regular checks to ascertain whether it could be used with safety. By reason of his failure to provide a safe system of working the defendant employer was guilty of negligence and liable in damages to the injured employee.

An employer does not have to adjust the methods of work on his business premises to guard against any peculiar infirmities or susceptibilities of which he is ignorant.

On the other hand, if an employee suffers from a physical defect which makes it dangerous for him to work under conditions that are regarded as acceptable and safe by other employees, then he must be given preferential treatment, otherwise the employer fails to provide a safe system of work.

Paris v Stepney Borough Council (1951, House of Lords)

Paris worked for the defendant council on the maintenance of vehicles. The council knew that Paris had lost the sight of one eye, but they failed to take any special precautions to prevent injury to his good eye. He could have been provided with goggles even though these were not supplied to other mechanics. While working under a bus, a chip of metal flew into Paris's good eye and made him totally blind. The court decided that the council had failed to discharge the special duty of care owed to Paris by reason of his physical defect. The obligation to provide a safe system of working required the provision of goggles.

Even if the employer knows of his employees' peculiarities, his duty is only to take reasonable care in the circumstances to ensure protection, it is not an absolute duty to guard against all possible risks.

Withers v Perry Chain Co Ltd (1961, Court of Appeal)

An employee was forced to stop work after five years on the same job when she contracted dermatitis, caused by the grease with which she came into contact in the course of her job. At her own request she was given an alternative job which was the driest available for her, but there was some contact with grease and she contracted dermatitis again on three separate occasions. On returning to work after each illness she asked to be given the same job again. She claimed damages from her employers for negligence, in giving her a job knowing that she might contract a disease as a direct consequence.

The court decided that the employers were not liable. They were not under a duty to dismiss or refuse employment to an employee wishing to do a job because it involved slight health risks, provided that the employer did not impliedly warrant that the job was safe, or conceal inherent dangers in carrying out a particular task.

When circumstances necessitate the taking of an exceptional risk, the employer is protected against liability if injury is sustained by an employee.

Watt v Hertfordshire County Council (1954, Court of Appeal)

A jack, which was insecurely fixed to a lorry, slipped and injured Watt, a fireman who was travelling in the vehicle. The lorry was not equipped to carry a jack of this type, but it was urgently required at the scene of an accident to free a woman trapped in wreckage. A suitable vehicle able to carry the jack with safety was not available at the time.

The court decided that the defendants were not liable to Watt in damages for the injuries he sustained. It was not negligent to use the lorry though unsuitable for that particular purpose and drive it at speed, since a fireman is expected to take much greater risks than those countenanced in other employments.

5:3 PROVISION OF COMPETENT STAFF

An employer must not engage or continue the engagement of an incompetent employee, for if that employee causes injury to a fellow employee the employer will be liable in damages.

Hudson v Ridge Manufacturing Co Ltd (1957)

Hudson fractured a wrist at work because of a jest by Chadwick, a fellow employee. The defendant employers knew that Chadwick often behaved in a stupid manner, but they had only reprimanded him for such conduct.

The court decided that the employers were liable in damages for a breach of their common law duty to engage only competent employees, because they failed to stop Chadwick's conduct or dismiss him when he continued to misbehave.

An employer will be liable for an employee's negligent act in the course of his employment which causes injury to a fellow employee. Any attempt to exclude or limit the employer's liability in this respect by a term in the contract of employment or apprenticeship or any collateral contract will be void (Law Reform (Personal Injuries) Act 1948 s1(3)).

Smith v British European Airways Corporation (1951)

It was a condition of Smith's employment as a flight steward with BEA that he should be a member of the Airways Corporations' pension scheme, which provided that the defendant corporation and its employees were not liable to Smith or his dependants for any negligent acts. Smith was killed in a collision between a BEA plane and an RAF plane, which was caused by the combined negligence of the pilots of both planes. His widow sued for damages under the Fatal Accidents Acts 1846–1908.

The court decided that the clause in the pension scheme excluding the employer's liability for injuries caused to Smith by the negligent act of his fellow employee was collateral to Smith's contract of employment and void. The widow was entitled to damages.

5:4 PROVISION OF SAFE AND SUITABLE MACHINERY

The employer has an obligation to provide proper machinery and appliances and this duty cannot be delegated to other employees in order to negative the employer's personal liability. Even if a defect in the machinery is latent and not obvious on a reasonable examination, either when first acquired or during use, the employer may be liable for injury caused by that machinery under the Employers' Liability (Defective Equipment) Act 1969.

Where an employee is injured in the course of his employment because of a defect in equipment provided by his employer, which is attributable to the fault of a third party such as the maker or supplier, then the employer is also liable for negligence under this Act, irrespective of any other liability imposed on him by common law or statute. The law relating to contributory negligence is unaffected, and any damages recoverable from the employer may be reduced if the employee injured was also at fault. If the employer is held liable in damages, he may in turn bring an action in tort for negligence by claiming damages against the supplier or maker of the defective equipment. Any attempt by the employer to exclude or limit his liability under the Act is void. For the purposes of the Act:

1   *Employee* means a person who is employed by another person under a contract of service or aprenticeship
2   *Equipment* includes any plant and machinery, vehicle, aircraft and clothing
3   *Fault* means negligence, breach of statutory duty or other act or omission, which gives rise to liability in tort
4   *Personal injury* includes loss of life, any impairment of a person's physical or mental condition, and any disease

These provisions are binding on the Crown.

Compensation must be paid to an employee who is injured because of his employer's failure to provide safe plant and machinery. This general duty has many different aspects.

The employer may be liable for failing to provide the type of plant, machinery or equipment required by the employee for completion of the **task entrusted to him.**

Lovell v Blundells and Crompton & Co Ltd (1944)

Lovell was injured while using unsafe planking to reach boiler tubes that he had been instructed to overhaul. The defendant employer had not provided Lovell with any equipment to enable him to carry out the repair work properly.

The court decided that the employer was liable in damages to Lovell for the injuries he sustained since there was negligence in failing to supply the equipment required for the task in hand.

If the correct equipment is provided it must be readily available for use, otherwise the employer fails to discharge his common law duty.

Machray v Stewarts & Lloyds Ltd (1964)

Machray, an experienced rigger, was injured while attempting to complete an urgent task. He did not use the proper, recognised equipment for the job since it was not readily available, although the defendant employer did own such equipment. Machray claimed damages for his injuries, alleging negligence by his employer in failing to provide proper plant. The defendant alleged that Machray had been guilty of contributory negligence on the ground that an experienced rigger should not have used make-shift equipment.

The court decided that Machray was not guilty of contributory negligence. He was "adopting a course of conduct not for the sake of saving himself trouble, but in order to get on with his employer's business . . . he has been prevented from doing the work in the way in which he would have preferred to do it by the employer's breach in not providing him with proper tackle." (Mr Justice McNair)

If plant and machinery in need of repair has become dangerous it must not be used. The employer should make alternative arrangements until essential repairs can be carried out.

An employer is not required to remove obsolete equipment and install the most modern plant or adopt the latest improvements. He does not act negligently if his equipment is not as safe as that generally used by other employers, but he will be expected to incorporate devices that greatly increase standards of safety for his employees.

Complex equipment should be fully checked by an expert before being used for the first time to determine whether it may be operated with safety, and even the most experienced employee should not be entrusted with this task. Plant and machinery must be checked, serviced and over-hauled periodically at whatever interval of time is necessary for equipment of the particular type in use, to ensure that it is in good working order and safe to use. The employer will be liable in damages for injuries to an employee if he fails to remedy a defect in equipment of which he is aware (see 5 : 10 : 1, Baker v James Brothers & Sons Ltd).

In many cases the employer should record in writing any complaints by employees about equipment in use. Employees must be instructed and encouraged to report any defects in plant and machinery as soon as they become apparent.

Franklin v Edmonton Corporation (1965)

Drivers of the defendant corporation's lorries were instructed to make a written complaint detailing any defects in their vehicles. In practice, verbal complaints were made in a haphazard, unorganised manner. Franklin made two verbal complaints about a slipping handbrake, but they were ignored. He claimed damages from his employer for injuries suffered as a result of the defect.

The court decided that the Corporation was liable for failing to main-tain the vehicle in good working order. The system of reporting and rectifying defects in vehicles was ineffective.

This case demonstrates the importance of ensuring that a system for reporting defects is really working. It must be easy for the employee to use and it must bring effective remedial action.

5 : 4 : 1 *Employers must ensure that proper working appliances are used*
The employer must not only supply safe and proper working appliances but must also check them periodically to ensure that they are maintained in proper condition and are used.

Monaghan v W H Rhodes & Sons (1920, Court of Appeal)

Monaghan, a dock labourer, was injured while unloading a ship. Per-manent iron ladders were provided by the defendant employers, but because they were blocked by fellow employees Monaghan had to use a rope ladder instead. The employers had warned the foreman of the danger involved in using the rope ladder which they considered to be unsafe. Monaghan sued for damages for personal injuries sustained.

The court decided that the employers were liable since, having knowledge of all the relevant facts, they were in breach of their common law duty to maintain in use the proper appliances required for the work undertaken by their employee.

The employer's duty to provide safe equipment covers all acts which are reasonably incidental to the employee's daily work.

Davidson v Handley Page Ltd (1945, Court of Appeal)

Davidson sustained injury by falling on a duckboard that had become slippery and dangerous to walk on by reason of suds spilling from a row of vats overhead. At the time of the accident she was on her way to a tap in order to wash a tea cup for her own use. Davidson sued for damages for the injury suffered.

The court decided that she was entitled to her claim since the employer had failed in his common law duty to use reasonable skill and care in the provision of safe appliances. In this instance the employee's actions were normally and reasonably incidental to her work.

5:4:2 *Employer's liability when he delegates his duties to an employee*
The employer remains liable for any failure to provide a safe system of working, even though he delegates his responsibilities to an employee whom he reasonably believes to be competent.

Wilsons & Clyde Coal Co Ltd v English (1938, House of Lords)

A miner sued his employers for damages in respect of personal injuries caused by their failure to provide a reasonably safe system of work while men were being raised to the surface. The owners of the mine were prevented by the Coal Mines Act 1911 from interfering in the matter, which lay in the control of qualified mine managers, appointed for this specific purpose.

The court decided that the employers were liable. Although the employers were obliged by law to rely on the advice of delegates with specialised knowledge, this did not relieve them of their personal responsibility.

It is difficult to imagine a situation in which an employer would have a stronger defence in a case concerned with delegation of his responsibility to others. On the other hand, if a safe system of work has been provided and an employee reasonably believed to be competent has been appointed to supervise that system, the employer is not generally liable for injury to an employee, if caused by the incompetence of the supervisor.

An employee cannot claim damages for injuries sustained consequent upon his failure to use the proper equipment made available, provided he was sufficiently experienced to be able to choose the correct equipment on his own initiative without explicit instructions from his employer.

Johnson v Croggan & Co Ltd and Another (1954)

Johnson was employed by Croggan & Co as a steel erector. He was instructed to erect a steel roof on the premises of the second defendant and obtain all the necessary equipment, including ladders, from the main contractors, Paddy and Company. Johnson disobeyed these instructions and borrowed the second defendant's ladders which were normally used for fruit-picking. The top rung of one of these ladders snapped and Johnson was injured. He claimed damages from the second defendants for the injuries he sustained.

The court decided that the second defendants had not acted negligently or in breach of their common law duty to provide proper plant and equipment. They merely gave permission for the ladders to be used without making any representations about their suitability for the job in hand. Johnson alone was to blame for selecting the unsuitable equipment.

5:5 SUPERVISION OF SAFETY PRECAUTIONS

Although the employer is under a duty to provide a safe system of work with adequate safety precautions, he is not necessarily liable for injuries to employees if, for example, they refuse to take advantage of the protections offered which an experienced employee should realise to be vital to his safety.

Qualcast (Wolverhampton) Ltd v Haynes (1959, House of Lords)

Haynes, aged thirty-eight, who had been a moulder for the whole of his working life, was splashed by molten metal which caused injury to his feet. He was not wearing protective spats, which were available on request free of charge, though he appreciated the risks of injury by not using them. The employers did not order, advise or bring any pressures to bear on their employees to make or encourage them to use protective clothing.

The court decided that the employers had provided a safe system of work and also safe and proper plant and equipment. Reasonable care had been taken to provide for the employee's safety, though the wearing of protective clothing was not made obligatory.

Where there is serious risk to an employee's safety, the employer should insist on the use of any safety devices that are provided. The extent of the supervision required from the employer in fulfilment of his duty of care varies according to the degree of risk involved in any given work. The employer's duty also varies with the experience of the employee involved. The individual circumstances of each case must be carefully examined and previous decisions, based upon the peculiar facts exclusive to their own case, are not to be considered as binding precedents. If an employer displays a notice warning employees of the dangers involved in not using protective devices supplied, he is not under a duty to ascertain whether employees affected are literate; he may assume that they can read. Warnings should be written in the appropriate language if immigrant workers are employed.

To protect himself fully against the risk of liability at common law, the employer should insist on the use of protective devices and also warn his employees of the dangers of refusing to cooperate.

Crookall v Vickers-Armstrong Ltd (1955)

Crookall contracted silicosis while working in a foundry in which siliceous sand was used. The defendant employer provided protective masks for employees to wear, but few used them despite the manager's efforts to persuade them otherwise.

The court decided that the defendants were in breach of their common law duty to take all reasonable precautions to reduce the risk of harm to their employees. Employees should have been warned of the danger to their health by not wearing a mask, and there should have been effective supervision to ensure that masks were used.

5:5:1 *Employer's duty to give instruction on safety precautions*
It does not constitute a safe system of work for the employer merely to

provide his employees with a copy of the relevant statutory rules to be observed when completing a given task. He must also provide practical instruction.

Barcock v Brighton Corporation (1949)

Barcock assisted a superintendent who did not follow the proper statutory instructions laid down for making electrical tests, on the ground that the work would never be completed if some risks were not taken. Eventually Barcock was allowed to make these tests without supervision, on being appointed an authorised person for the purposes of the statute. A copy of the regulations that Barcock was bound by law to follow was handed to him by the employers, but without further advice or training. He was injured by an explosion while making a test in the illegal manner usually practised by the superintendent.

The court decided that Barcock acted in breach of the statutory duty by carrying out tests in an illegal manner, but the employers were liable in damages for a breach of their common law duty of care by not providing a safe system of work. It was not enough to direct an employee to study the necessary regulations after allowing them to be ignored over a period of time.

5:6 WORKING PREMISES MUST BE SAFE

The employer is not absolutely responsible for ensuring that his working premises are safe; he is only expected to take reasonable care to make them safe for employees using them in the ordinary and customary manner. The degree of care he is expected to show must bear some relation to the risks involved.

Latimer v AEC Ltd (1953, House of Lords)

The defendant's factory floor became flooded after an exceptionally heavy rain fall. The flood water mixed with oil in the factory, leaving an oily film on the floor when the flood water subsided. Sawdust and sand were spread on the floor to make it safe for use, but supplies were short and some areas remained untreated. The plaintiff slipped on one of these untreated patches and was injured.

The court decided that the defendants had done what was reasonable in the circumstances and consequently they were not liable. They were not obliged to close down the factory and send employees home until the premises could be made absolutely safe, because of the remote possibility of injury to an employee.

5:6:1 Employer's responsibility
for the defaults of an independent contractor

The employer cannot evade responsibility for making his working premises safe by delegating particular aspects of his duties to an independent contractor. It is not a defence for the employer to show that, because of the skilled nature of the work delegated, he was unable to check it on completion to determine whether it had been properly executed.

Paine v Colne Valley
Electricity Supply Co Ltd and British Insulated Cables Ltd (1938)

The first defendants were supplied with a transformer kiosk by an independent contractor, the second defendants. The kiosk was faultily constructed and an employee of the first defendant was killed while working inside it. The employee's executrix sued for breach of statutory and common law duty.

The court decided that the first defendants were liable for a breach of their common law duty to provide a safe place in which to work, and it was not a good defence to prove that the cause of the accident was a fault on the part of the independent contractors.

In a similar situation arising today the employer would probably be liable under the Employer's Liability (Defective Equipment) Act 1969, as well as at common law.

5:6:2 Employer's liability towards an independent contractor

An employer is not under any liability at common law towards an independent contractor for injuries caused because working conditions on the employer's premises are unsafe, but there may be liability under the Factories Act 1961 (see 6:12:1).

Herbert v Harold Shaw Ltd (1959, Court of Appeal)

Herbert fell and sustained injuries while fixing asbestos roofing sheets to the steel framework of a shed. He claimed damages from the defendants for negligence at common law. Although Herbert had worked for the defendant company continuously for several years, the indications were that he was an independent contractor since:

1   He engaged and paid an assistant to help him, then charged the assistant's wages to the defendants
2   He was himself paid sometimes at an hourly rate and on other occasions by piecework
3   He paid his own National Insurance stamp as a self-employed person
4   He was assessed under Schedule D for tax purposes, on the assumption that he was carrying on his own business

The court decided that the defendants were not liable at common law for negligence, since Herbert was an independent contractor. While working on the roof Herbert made his own arrangements for borrowing ladders and any necessary boards that he might require. The contract between the parties to this case was an ordinary contract between independent contractors and no question of employer and employee arose.

5:6:3   *Protection of the employee's clothing*
The provision of a safe system of working is intended to secure the personal safety of the employees working under that system, but the employer's responsibilities in this respect do not extend to safeguarding an employee's clothing.

Edwards v West Hertfordshire
Group Hospital Management Committee (1957, Court of Appeal)

Edwards, a house physician, was obliged under his contract of employment to live in and pay for accommodation in a hostel adjoining the hospital where he worked. He was given a key to his room, but under hostel rules this had to be left in the lock. Some of Edwards' clothing was stolen from his room.

The court decided that at common law an employer does not owe a duty to his employee to take reasonable care to protect their property.

It should be noted, however, that liability may be established under the Factories Act 1961 (see 6:21:3) or the Offices, Shops and Railway Premises Act 1963 (see 8:1:8) in the appropriate circumstances.

If the employee's clothing is damaged as a result of the employer's negligence, it was suggested in the case of Deyong v Shenburn (1946, Court of Appeal) that the employer may be liable. In my opinion damage to clothing caused by the failure to provide a safe system of work should be the employer's responsibility.

5:7 SAFE SYSTEM OF WORK
ON THE PREMISES OF THIRD PARTIES

The employer's duty to provide a safe place of work for his employees extends only to premises under his control. He is not obliged to inspect the premises of a third party to determine whether it is reasonably safe for his employees to work there before sending them on a given task. It may be assumed that the premises are safe unless notice has been given of a defect likely to cause danger, in which case an employer may be liable if he fails to visit the premises concerned to see for himself whether they are safe.

Cilia v H M James & Son (1954)

A plumber's mate entered the loft of a private house at which he was working, to investigate the overflow from the water tanks. He was electrocuted by a defective electrical conduit. The deceased's mother claimed damages from the employers for an alleged breach of their common law duty to provide reasonably safe working premises.

The court decided that the employers were not liable. They were under no duty to make premises outside their control which they did not occupy reasonably safe.

If an employer knows of a danger on the premises of a third party at which his employees work, he must either give them an adequate and effective warning or take whatever steps are appropriate to avoid subjecting them to unnecessary risks.

Although an employer does not owe a duty to his employees to guarantee the safety of the premises occupied by another person, he must provide a safe system of work suitable for those premises.

General Cleaning Contractors v Christmas (1953, House of Lords)

Christmas, an experienced window cleaner employed by General Cleaning Contractors, fell and was injured when a sash closed on his fingers while he was cleaning a window from a sill at the Caledonian Club. Safety belts were made available by the employer, but it was impracticable to use one on this occasion because there were no hooks to which the belt could have been attached.

The court decided that the employers were in breach of their duty to take reasonable care to lay down a reasonably safe system of work and were liable in damages to their employee. The employer could have:

1   Provided wedges to prevent sashes closing and directed their employees to test sashes for looseness, or
2   Instructed employees to do their cleaning from a ladder instead of from the window sill, or
3   Asked the occupier to allow hooks to be inserted in the brick-work so that safety belts could be attached.

A window cleaning firm is not obliged to inspect the premises of its customers before directing their employees to work there, but they must be taken to know that window sashes move unexpectedly and make allowances accordingly in the practice to be observed by employees.

Where dangers exist on the premises of third parties that are obvious and apparent to a skilled employee, an employer need not give repeated warnings about those dangers.

Wilson v Tyneside Window Cleaning Co (1958, Court of Appeal)

Wilson was injured while cleaning a window when the handle came away in his hand, thus causing him to fall. He knew that the window was defective and had been generally instructed by his employers to leave uncleaned any window at any building if cleaning was unusually difficult or unsafe.

The court decided that the defendants had taken reasonable care not to expose Wilson to unnecessary risks; consequently, they were not liable for damages in respect of his injuries. Wilson was an experienced window cleaner and the dangerous condition of the window was known to him. The issuing or repetition of warnings would be likely to do more harm than good.

Even if the employee fails to establish liability against his own employer it may be possible to sue the occupier of the defective premises under:

1   The Occupiers' Liability Act 1956, which establishes a common law duty of care owed by an occupier of premises

to lawful visitors, such as employees of an independent contractor (see 10 : 2)

2   The statutory provisions of the Factories Act 1961 or the Offices, Shops and Railway Premises Act 1963 (see 6 : 12 and 7 : 3)

5 : 8 EMPLOYER'S LIABILITY FOR FATAL ACCIDENTS AT WORK

The provisions of the Fatal Accidents Acts 1846–1959 are of general application, but they also affect the employer–employee relationship.

The employee's death may be caused by some wrongful act for which the employer is responsible. He may then be sued for damages by the deceased's dependants, provided the deceased employee would have had a right of action against his employer if he had survived. If the employer would have had an effective defence against the claims of the deceased if he had lived, he may still rely upon that defence if he is sued by the employee's dependants.

If it is the employer's negligence that gives rise to the alleged wrong-doing, it must be shown that a duty of care was owed by the employer to the deceased employee at the time when the accident occurred. Any damages recoverable will be reduced to reflect any contributory negligence on the employee's part.

5 : 8 : 1 *Who is entitled to sue and when*
A claim must be brought within three years of the employee's death, by his executor or administrator or by the dependant for whose benefit the personal representative would have sued :

1   If he had been appointed, or
2   Where he has been appointed, but has neglected to sue for a period of six months

Dependants include the wife, husband, children (including adopted children), grandchildren, brother, sister, parent, grandparent, uncle or aunt and their issue. An illegitimate child is regarded as the child of the mother and the reputed father (if any). Relatives of the deceased's spouse are treated in the same way as the deceased's own relatives: thus a brother-in-law is treated as a brother. Relationship may be traced through step-relatives. The dependants share the damages awarded as the court deems to be appropriate.

A claim may be maintained by a child en ventra sa mere (in the womb of the mother), but not by:

1   A woman separated from her husband if neither maintained by him nor taking proceedings to recover maintenance
2   A husband separated from his wife
3   A relative who is already provided for financially

5:8:2   How much must the employer pay?

The dependants may recover damages for the actual or potential pecuniary loss that has been suffered as a result of the employee's death, but not for grief or injured feelings. It is not necessary that the deceased should have been making a financial contribution to the support of the person claiming damages at the time when death occurred, though this is often the case, provided the claimant had a reasonable expectation of receiving some monetary benefit if the deceased had continued to live and earn money.

Taff Vale Railway Co v Jenkins (1913, House of Lords)

Two months before completion of her apprenticeship as a dressmaker, a sixteen-year-old girl was killed in a railway accident caused by the negligence of the railway company's employees.

The court decided that since the girl was expected to earn a substantial wage at an early age, her parents, who brought the action, were entitled to compensation for loss of a reasonable expectation of pecuniary advantage.

The principle in this case is also applicable where the employer's negligence is the cause of his employee's death.

A claim may be made for the cost of providing services to replace those rendered free of charge by the deceased; for example, when a husband has to employ a housekeeper after his wife's death.

The amount of wages being earned by the deceased is taken as the starting point, less a sum to cover his own personal and living expenses. The figure arrived at is then turned into a lump sum, by reference to the likely working life of the deceased, if he had lived. The lump sum so determined may be reduced to take into account a number of uncertainties, such as remarriage of a dependent widow. The death of a male employee may result in a monetary gain for his dependants, who then become entitled to a pension, but any insurance money, benefit, pension or gratuity, which has been, will, or may be paid as a result of the death is not to be taken into account (Fatal Accidents Act 1959 s2(2)).

Damages may be awarded for funeral expenses actually incurred by the dependants, for whose benefit the action is brought. The cost of employing a housekeeper must be taken into consideration if the deceased employee was a woman managing a home for her dependants.

5:8:3 *Further claims in respect of the same death*

If the deceased employee had lived and suffered merely injury, as the result of his employer's negligence, he could have sued his employer for pain and suffering, and loss of expectation of life and amenities of life, in addition to loss of earnings. A claim in respect of these matters can be maintained by the executor for the benefit of the deceased's estate under the Law Reform (Miscellaneous Provisions) Act 1934, in addition to and separate from the claim by the dependants under the Fatal Accidents Acts. The reason for allowing the claim is that the dependants may not be the recipients of any benefit under the deceased's will or on his intestacy. Since any damages awarded under the Law Reform (Miscellaneous Provisions) Act will belong to the deceased's estate, that benefit will not necessarily be conferred on the dependants, hence their right to claim under the Fatal Accidents Acts.

If the dependants do benefit under the deceased's will or on his intestacy, damages awarded under the Law Reform (Miscellaneous Provisions) Act, which are considered to be a financial gain consequent upon the employee's death, must be accounted for when awarding damages under the Fatal Accidents Acts. Damages under these two Acts are intended to provide only the actual compensation needed by the dependants to offset any financial loss suffered when their breadwinner dies.

Time within which to bring an action. An action under the Law Reform (Miscellaneous Provisions) Act must be brought within three years from the date when the cause of action first arose, that is, from the time when the injury causing death was first sustained. This rule can result in an injustice, if the employee is unaware that he has suffered any injury until after the expiration of the three-year period. Some industrial diseases, such as pneumoconiosis, are slow to be detected and may not be sufficiently recognisable before the end of the three-year limitation period. In some cases it is difficult to relate an injury to the cause giving rise to it.

The Limitation Act 1963 allows an action for personal injury to be brought, though three years have already expired from the time when the cause of action first arose, provided the claimant was unable to sue earlier because he was unaware of certain material facts of a decisive character, for example, that he had sustained an injury. An action must be brought, however, within twelve months after discovering these material facts. These rules cover claims under the Law Reform (Miscellaneous Provisions) Act and the Fatal Accidents Acts, where the injury causes the employee's death. The twelve-month period runs from the time when either:

1　The deceased employee knew or ought to have known of his injury, though it occurred over three years previously, or

2　From the date of his death, if he could not have discovered the existence of the fatal injury, which occurred more than three years previously

5:9　EXTENT OF THE EMPLOYER'S LIABILITY IN DAMAGES FOR INJURY CAUSED TO HIS EMPLOYEE

If an employee successfully sues his employer for damages in respect of injury suffered consequent upon a breach of the common law or statutory duty of care, then the damages recoverable are based upon the actual loss suffered by the employee. Money will be awarded as compensation for the wrongful act and all its natural and direct consequences, including a claim under the following heads:

1　Loss of earnings through inability to carry on with his employment

2　Loss of earnings up until the date of the hearing

3　Medical and similar expenses, even though National Health Service facilities available have not been used

4　Compensation for pain, suffering and mental anxiety

5　Loss of a limb

6　Loss of amenities

7　Loss of expectation of life

5:9:1　*Reducing the damages where the injured party remains unconscious*

It is possible to assess objectively the damages payable under heads 4–7. But there is also a subjective assessment, in that an employee rendered unconscious by the accident may suffer less pain than if he remained conscious. Damages awarded for pain and suffering will be reduced accordingly to reflect this element. The same reasoning applies to mental anxiety.

The House of Lords have refused, however, to apply this subjective element to recovery of damages for loss of amenity (West & Son Ltd v Shephard (1963)). The injured party's unconscious state following the accident does not eliminate the actuality of his deprivation of the amenities of life that would have been open to him but for the accident.

Where damages are awarded for physical injury and consequent loss of amenity, it is immaterial that the injured party will not live to enjoy the money personally, as where he is likely to remain unconscious during the rest of his life and is unaware of his present physical condition. The injured party is free to use the damages awarded in whatever manner he wishes; they must not be withheld if he does not have any personal use for the money, as where he is already amply provided for or is too ill to enjoy using it. A claim may be validly maintained when once the loss has been quantified.

5:9:2 Extent of the damages for loss of expectation of life
Loss of expectation of life may be assessed objectively, but in the case of Benham v Gambling (1941, House of Lords) it was stated that any award of damages must be moderate. In that case, however, the party killed was a young child, and from an objective point of view he was not conscious of his loss of expectation of life. If an employee is injured, then consideration must be given to the subjective element of the distress that will be caused to an adult surviving an accident, where he must face up to the likelihood of a shorter life span than that originally contemplated. In such cases the damages awarded should be higher than the sum given to a child.

5:9:3 Loss of earnings is related to loss of expectation of life
If an employee claims for loss of earnings and also for loss of expectation of life, any damages awarded for loss of earnings are related to the period left to the employee after receiving his injuries, though this now falls short of the period during which he expected to be employed before the accident.

5:9:4 Deductions to be made from the damages awarded
Any benefit accruing to the employee as a result of his accident, which comes to him as a result of his own thrift, must not be deducted from the sum awarded against the employer as damages.

Judd v The Board of Governors of the
Hammersmith, West London & St Mark's Hospitals (1960)

Judd was obliged to retire from his employment with the Hammersmith
Borough Council before the time originally anticipated, because of injuries
received as a result of negligent driving by an employee of the defendants.
Judd received a pension of £300 a year on retirement from the Council's
superannuation fund, to which he had made compulsory contributions.

The court decided that this sum must be ignored in assessing damages
payable in respect of Judd's future loss of earnings.

On the other hand, any obligatory benefit payable by the employer or
the State consequent upon the accident will be deducted: for example,
pension payments payable by the employer to which the employee has
not made any contribution. An injured employee is entitled only to the
loss of the contents of his pay packet. Thus National Insurance contributions which would have been deducted from any wages earned must be
taken into account when assessing damages recoverable for loss of earnings. Unemployment benefits will be deducted, since the employee may
claim these sums as of right, but not supplementary benefits, which are
discretionary and too collateral and remote to be considered.

Where a benefit is obtainable by the employee for his industrial injuries
under the National Insurance Acts, during the five years commencing at
the date of his cause of action, then one-half of this sum must be deducted
from any damages awarded for loss of earnings.

Further deductions must be made for income tax that the employee
would have paid on his salary if it had been earned (see 13:5:8). The
same principles apply to an award of damages for injuries that prevent
the employee from working.

5:10 DEFENCE OF VOLENTI NON FIT
INJURIA MAY BE AVAILABLE TO THE EMPLOYER

The employer may plead volenti non fit injuria as a defence to an action
for breach of his common law duties. The phrase means that harm is not
done to any person who consents to it, and in the context of the employer
and employee relationship it means that the employee may consent to
taking the risk of infliction upon him of accidental damage. The employer,
as defendant, must prove as a question of fact that the plaintiff employee
agreed voluntarily to accept the risk that resulted in injury to his person.
An employee is not to be considered as willing to undertake this risk

unless he is in a position to choose freely. Freedom of choice connotes full knowledge of the risk undertaken, and absence from the employee's mind of any pressure fettering his decision. If the employee is required to use dangerous plant or machinery, he must agree expressly or by implication to undertake personal responsibility for the risks involved and relieve his employer of any consequent liability.

Lord Justice Scott said in the Court of Appeal decision in Bowater *v* Rowley Regis Borough Council (1944): "Without purporting to lay down any rule of universal application, I venture to doubt whether the maxim can very often apply in circumstances of injury to a servant by the negligence of a master."

5:10:1 *Knowledge by the employee of the risk involved may not relieve the employer from liability*

An employee does not impliedly consent to the taking of a risk merely because he is aware of the risk involved; it is only evidence that he may have consented.

Baker *v* James Brothers & Sons (1921)

Baker, a traveller, was supplied with a car by his employers, the gear box of which was defective. Despite his continual complaints the employers did not take any steps to remedy this mechanical fault. Eventually Baker was injured while attempting to start the engine.

The court decided that Baker was entitled to damages. He was not guilty of contributory negligence in respect of the accident, for although he knew of the dangerous state of the vehicle and continually used the car, his repeated complaints showed that he did not consent to taking the risks involved.

Employment may of necessity carry with it the risk of injury to the employee, in consequence of which a higher wage may be paid by the employer as compensation. For example, a test pilot obviously undertakes some risk, but he receives a higher salary in return. In such circumstances the maxim, volenti non fit injuria, is available to the employer, if the employee is injured as the result of an accident where the risk of harm lies with him. The employer will be responsible, however, if his negligence creates a risk not usually present in employment that is dangerous in itself.

In cases where the employment is not in itself dangerous, then the defence of volenti non fit injuria will not usually apply.

Smith v Baker & Sons (1891, House of Lords)

Smith worked in a quarry where it was customary to move large blocks of stone by swinging a crane over the heads of the employees. Whenever possible, Smith moved away to avoid being injured by falling stone, but despite complaints from the employees, a warning was not given before the crane was operated. Smith was injured by a falling stone from a load that had been negligently strapped.

The court decided that Smith was entitled to damages for his injuries. He was aware of the risk, but there was no evidence that he had voluntarily consented to it.

An employee may act in breach of a statutory duty, thereby injuring a fellow employee. If the injured party tries to make his employer vicariously liable for the wrongs of the employee at fault, the employer may plead volenti non fit injuria as a defence, if two conditions are satisfied :

1   The injured employee must be shown to have consented to running the risk of injury
2   The employer must not have committed a breach of any statutory duty cast upon him

Imperial Chemical Industries Ltd v Shatwell (1964, House of Lords)

George and James Shatwell were qualified shotfirers employed by ICI Ltd. They were injured in an explosion during a shotfiring test, because they failed to take cover in a shelter. They knew that failure to take cover was contrary to the employer's instructions and to a duty imposed upon them personally by statutory regulations. Both men fully appreciated the risk of injury. George sued his employers claiming that they were vicariously liable for James's conduct, though admitting that he and his brother were equally responsible for the accident.

The court decided that each brother was responsible for the injury that he suffered personally. George's wrongs against James were the same as James's wrongs against George. A defence of volenti non fit injuria was available to the employers in answer to a claim by an employee of vicarious liability. The employers had not committed a breach of any statutory duty imposed upon them, nor were they guilty of negligence, having carefully explained the risk of injury unless essential safety precautions were observed and protective devices used.

This decision has been criticised, however it was followed in Bolt v Wm Moss & Sons (1966) and the judge in O'Reilly v National Rail & Tramway Appliances Ltd (1966) would have applied it if necessary.

The defence of volenti non fit injuria is not available to an employer who is personally in breach of a statutory duty imposed upon him: for example, where he has failed in his duty to fence dangerous machinery under the Factories Act 1961. It is clearly against public policy to allow private agreements between employer and employee to nullify such protections imposed by statute.

5:11 EMPLOYEE'S OWN NEGLIGENCE MAY HAVE BEEN A CONTRIBUTORY CAUSE OF THE ACCIDENT

Where an employer is in breach of his common law duty, as outlined above, he may seek to reduce the damages payable to an employee who is injured in consequence of that breach, by establishing that the employee was at fault also. This defence is fully discussed in 7:3:8.

5:12 EMPLOYERS' LIABILITY (COMPULSORY INSURANCE) ACT 1969

Although an employee may sue his employer and be awarded damages as compensation for the injuries he has suffered, in some cases the employer may be insolvent and unable to make payment. To guard against this contingency the Employers' Liability (Compulsory Insurance) Act 1969 will require all employers to insure against this particular risk. The Act will be effective from 1 January 1972.

The provisions of the Act are as follows. Every employer must insure against liability for bodily injury or disease sustained by an employee in the course of his employment. Regulations will prescribe the amount of the insurance to be taken out, and if the employer fails to do so he commits an offence punishable with a fine up to £200. An offence is also committed by a director, manager, secretary or other officer of a corporation who consents to or connives at, or facilitates violation of the Act's provisions.

The employer must (from 1 January 1973) display copies of the contract of insurance for the information of his employees, and produce a copy when demanded by an inspector authorised to make such a request. Failure to comply with these requirements may result in an employer being fined up to £50.

An employee is defined for the purposes of the Act as an individual working under a contract of service or apprenticeship, whether by way of manual labour, clerical work or otherwise. The contract may be express or implied, and either oral or in writing. The following employments are excepted:

1   Where the employee is a relative of the employer—that is, a spouse, parent, step-parent, grandparent, child, stepchild, grandchild, brother, sister, half-sister and half-brother
2   Employees not ordinarily resident in Great Britain
3   Employment with a nationalised industry, undertaking owned or controlled by the State and local authorities
4   Employment outside Great Britain

SIX

Safety, Health
and Welfare in Factories

THE LAST CHAPTER DISCUSSED THE EMPLOYER'S COMMON LAW DUTY to his employee to make provision for his safety. These requirements do not specify how the employee is to be protected against the risk of injury when working in a factory, nor do they adequately define where responsibility lies if an employee is injured.

Various statutes, which were consolidated in the Factories Act 1961, have defined the minimum requirements for safe working in factories. Most people know what a factory is although defining it for legal purposes is a lengthy and complex job; the full definition is given in the next chapter. The main problem, for legislators, is the enormous variety of industrial processes that are carried on in factories. An Act of Parliament cannot possibly include precise rules covering every one of these processes: what the Factories Act does is to lay down general principles and allow the Secretary of State for Employment to make rules for specific industries, which are given in statutory instruments that have the full force of Acts of Parliament although they are not subject to the lengthy procedures of parliamentary debate.

Many statutory instruments applying to factories have been made over the last seventy years. It would be impossible to attempt to describe them in this book: their application is enforced by the Factory Inspectorate (see 6:1) and the manager who is given responsibility for safety in a factory will normally work with the local inspector to solve the problems of his own particular workplace. It should be noted, however, that the Electricity Regulations are of almost universal application since they apply to every factory where electricity is used. A factory occupier should be familiar with the detailed provisions of these regulations.

This chapter and the next deal with the general principles of the employer's statutory duty to safeguard his workforce: they also show how the courts interpret the statutes when accidents do occur and the factory occupier is sued for damages.

The duties imposed on the factory occupier by the Factories Act 1961 are numerous and technical. In cases of dispute the court must decide upon the meaning, scope and practical application of these statutory provisions. As a preliminary issue it is important to determine whether the wording of the statute can be deemed to cover the situation that has occurred, thereby permitting an injured party to sue the person responsible. On purely moral grounds two different claims may each merit a remedy in damages but this is not the deciding factor. One claim may be within some statutory protection while another is outside it. For example, the duty to adequately fence dangerous machinery under s14 does not cover machinery produced in the factory, but only machinery forming part of the manufacturing process carried out there. The injured employee in Parvin v Morton Machine Co Ltd (see 6:8:5) was unsuccessful in his claim for damages, but the injured employee in John Summers & Sons Ltd v Frost (see 6:8:2) recovered compensation.

The Act imposes criminal liability and payment of a fine for infringement of its provisions. When criminal liability is in issue the court will adopt a narrow, restrictive interpretation of any statutory duties imposed which effectively favour the person prosecuted, usually the factory occupier. The same legislative provisions may also provide an injured employee with a civil law remedy in damages if relevant statutory duties are not observed. And as regards safety precautions, the courts favour the employee's claim when determining liability, if such an interpretation is permitted by the wording of the statute.

Whether an employee will succeed in his action for damages depends upon a number of varied factors, a selection of which may be significant in any given case. These matters will be dealt with more fully in the various discussions on the Act, but a brief summary may be useful as a preliminary guide to the problems surrounding the establishing of liability at civil law. At the same time it is possible to see the kind of argument that an employer may raise as an effective defence to negative any civil liability alleged by his employee.

A civil action is possible if the following requirements are satisfied by the claimant against the factory occupier, where, to take just one example, an employee claims damages for injury caused by the factory occupier's failure to securely fence dangerous machinery, as required by s14(1) (see 6:8:2). The claimant must prove that:

1   The statutory provisions properly interpreted intended to give him a right of action; for example, the machinery causing personal injury must be capable of being considered dangerous and the claimant must be the type of person intended to be given protection

2   The statutory provision must have been ignored by the party being sued (usually the factory occupier) where, for example, dangerous machinery has been insecurely fenced

3   The employee must have suffered that kind of harm which the statute intended to prevent, for example, personal injuries or death

4   The harm must have been caused not by any extraneous

factor, but by the breach of the statutory duty, that is contact
with dangerous machinery through inadequate fencing

If the claimant successfully satisfies these requirements the court then
considers the nature of the factory occupier's liability. Many of the statutory safeguards impose an absolute liability, particularly those concerned
with fencing dangerous machinery. In such cases of strict liability it is
not a defence for the factory occupier to show that he acted without negligence and took reasonable care to observe the statutory requirements. The
severity of this liability may be reduced, however, if the occupier can show
that the accident was not the reasonably foreseeable result of his failure
to take more effective precautions, but a remote contingency that could
not be anticipated.

Other duties such as the obligation to keep floors, passages and stairs
safe are not absolute. In this and other similar instances where qualifying
phrases like "as far as is reasonably practicable" are incorporated into the
relevant section of the Act, then it is a good defence for the employer
to show that he has taken all reasonable care and acted as a reasonable
man would act in the particular circumstances of the case (see 6:12:3).

ADMINISTERING THE
PROVISIONS OF THE FACTORIES ACT 1961

6:1 FACTORY INSPECTORATE

Enforcement of the Factories Act and the regulations made under it is,
with a few exceptions, the responsibility of HM Factory Inspectorate, part
of the Department of Employment. Britain is divided into thirteen divisions, each under a superintending inspector, and each division is split
into districts. The factory occupier will normally work with the district
inspector whose address is in local directories.

Factory inspectors have wide powers (see 6:1:1) and the Factories Act
imposes heavy penalties for failure to comply with its provisions: the
inspectorate, however, prefers to work in cooperation with factory occupiers and cases are brought to court only if an occupier is recalcitrant or
a serious accident has been caused.

6 : 1 : 1 *Powers of factory inspectors*

An inspector appointed by the Secretary of State has the following powers under s146 and s147:

1.   To enter, inspect and examine any factory at all reasonable times by day or night, where there is reasonable cause to believe that any person is employed there

2.   To enter by day any place which he has reasonable cause to believe to be a factory where explosive or highly inflammable materials are stored or used

3.   To take a police officer with him, if there is reasonable cause to expect any serious obstruction in the execution of his duty

4.   To inspect, examine and copy any register, certificate, notice or document kept in compliance with the Act

5.   To examine and inquire whether the provisions in the Factories Act and other enactments relating to public health are being complied with

6.   To require any person in the factory to give information about the identity of the occupier

7.   To require every person in the factory where necessary to:
   (a) Be examined on fulfilment of any statutory duty imposed by the Act
   (b) Sign a declaration of the truth of the matters on which he is examined, though no one need give any answer that will incriminate him

8.   To carry out medical examinations necessary to the fulfilment of duties under the Act, provided the inspector is a fully registered medical practitioner

9.   To exercise such other powers as may be necessary for carrying the Act into effect

10.   To require the factory occupier, his agent and servants to allow entry, inspection, examination, inquiry, and taking of samples so that the inspector's powers under the Act may be exercised in relation to that factory

11.   To enter, inspect and examine at all reasonable times by day or night any warehouse, if he has reasonable cause to believe that a young person is employed there; there are similar powers exercisable in the daytime only, if he has reasonable cause to believe that a young person (that is, under eighteen) was employed there within the last two months

A person who obstructs an inspector in the execution of his powers is guilty of an offence and liable to a fine not exceeding £20. The factory occupier also commits an offence.

An officer of the fire brigade has the same powers of entry and inspection as an inspector, if written authorisation is given by an inspector, for the purpose of reporting on any matter within the inspector's duties relating to fire (s148).

6:2 FACTORY DOCTORS (s151)

The chief inspector, or superintending inspector for a division, may appoint a sufficient number of fully registered medical practitioners as factory doctors. The factory occupier pays the doctor's fees relating to:

1 Any examination or certification respecting the fitness of a young person for factory employment
2 Medical supervision of persons employed

The factory doctor has power to:

1 Inspect the general register of the factory at all reasonable times
2 Make such special inquiry and examination of employed persons as the Secretary of State may direct

An annual report must be submitted to the Secretary of State dealing with examinations made and other duties performed in pursuance of the Act, including reporting accidents and the examination of young persons. If a factory doctor is not appointed, the medical officer of health for the administrative local area will act instead.

6:3 GENERAL REGISTER (s140)

A general register must be kept in every factory or other place approved by the district inspector, containing particulars of:

1 The young persons employed in the factory
2 The washing, white or colour washing, painting or varnishing of the factory
3 Every accident and case of industrial disease occurring in the factory of which notice must be sent to the inspector

4   Every exception to the requirements of the Act of which the factory occupier avails himself

5   All reports and particulars to be entered in or attached to the general register as required by any other provisions of the Act, for example, ss22–25 dealing with hoists and lifts (see (6:13:1)

The certificate of the fire authority, relating to means of escape in case of fire, must be attached to the general register.

The general register, other registers and records required by the Act must be available for inspection by any inspector or factory doctor for at least two years or any other period prescribed (s141).

6:4   NOTICES TO BE SENT TO THE FACTORY INSPECTOR

Notice of occupation of a factory and use of mechanical power (s137). At least one month before a person begins to occupy or use any premises as a factory, he must serve a written notice on the district inspector. This is on a prescribed form, copies of which can be obtained from HM Stationery Office. At least one month before the date on which mechanical power is first used in a factory, the occupier shall serve on the district inspector a written notice stating the nature of the mechanical power. If the district inspector gives written permission a person may:

1   Occupy or use premises as a factory
2   Use mechanical power in a factory

for the first time less than one month after the notice required has been served.

Occupation of a factory may begin:

1   Less than one month after notice has been served, or
2   Before serving the notice

if it is taken over from another person without changing the nature of the work, provided notice is served as soon as practicable and within one month of taking over.

Any person failing to comply with the provisions of this section is guilty of an offence, and if convicted may be fined up to £40 for the first day of non-compliance with the requirements, and £10 for each subsequent day.

Periodical returns of persons employed (s142). The factory occupier must send to the chief inspector, at intervals of not less than one year, a correct return specifying:

1   The number of persons employed in the factory
2   The particulars prescribed by the Secretary of State in relation to:
  (*a*) The hours of employment of women and young persons
  (*b*) The age, sex and occupation of all persons employed

A form for this purpose is sent automatically to every factory occupier.

6:5   CHECKLIST OF NOTICES TO BE POSTED

In the following list of statutory notices which have to be displayed, where relevant, references are made to the sections of the Factories Act in which the requirement appears. An asterisk against an item indicates that the notice displayed has to be in a prescribed form, copies of which can be obtained from HM Stationery Office.

1   *Prescribed abstract of the Factories Act (s138)
2   *Prescribed abstract (or a copy) of any statutory regulations made under the Factories Act and applicable to the premises (s139)
3   *Notice in each factory workroom showing the maximum number of persons permitted to work in that room, unless the factory inspector exercises his power to exempt a factory from this requirement
4   Notice showing the name of person in charge of the first-aid box for the workroom or office
5   Notice showing the addresses of the inspector of factories for the district and the superintending inspector for the division, and the name and address of the appointed factory doctor (space for this information to be inserted is provided on the prescribed abstract of the Act)
6   Notice showing the hours of work, times of meal breaks etc, for women and persons under eighteen (s88, 90, 94 and 115)

7   Notice specifying the clock, if any, by which the period of employment of women and young persons is regulated (s138)

8   *Cautionary placards required to be displayed under regulations for certain special processes, for example chromium plating

9   Placards showing the recommended treatment for electric shock if electricity is used at voltages above 125 volts a.c. or 250 volts d.c.

10   Notice in sanitary conveniences used by persons handling food, requesting them to wash their hands (this is a requirement of the Food Hygiene Regulations 1960)

11   Notice showing the piecework rates payable for certain prescribed operations (s135 and orders made under the Act)

It is an offence for any person to deface or pull down a notice displayed under the Acts.

6:6 PROCEDURE FOR MAKING SPECIAL REGULATIONS AND ORDERS

The Secretary of State for Employment has overall responsibility for the administration of the Factories Act 1961. He has power to make any special regulations and orders authorised by the Act itself, with the object of making the statute as effective and complete as possible.

The procedure set out in the 4th schedule to the Act for making regulations is as follows:

1   Notice of any proposed special regulation must be published either in *The London Gazette* or by any other convenient means for informing those affected

2   Written objections may be made, stating the change desired and the reasons for the change, within the time allowed, which must be at least twenty-one days

3   If the regulation is amended in the light of objections, it is published again and further objections may be lodged. In the absence of objections, the regulation becomes a statutory instrument with the force of law

A public inquiry must be held if a general objection is made after publication of the draft regulation, whether it is the original or the amended draft. Objectors may appear in person or be legally represented and witnesses may be examined on oath. The term *general objection* means an objection by any one of the following:

1   A majority of factory occupiers affected
2   An occupier or occupiers employing a majority of the employees affected
3   Persons representing the majority of the employees affected

A general objection may also be lodged by persons in the above groups where special conditions existing in the factories affected make the regulations unnecessary or inappropriate.

A regulation must be laid before Parliament and within forty days either House may pass a resolution annulling it.

SAFETY IN FACTORIES

6:7   ACCIDENTS AND INDUSTRIAL DISEASES

The word *accident* is used in its popular and ordinary sense. It means an unlooked-for mishap or an event not expected or designed. To constitute an accident the cause must be referrable to a particular time and place.

A disease that develops as a result of industrial conditions over a period of time cannot, in law, be the consequence of an accident, unless it is so prescribed by regulations. Factory employees are, however, protected by the Factories Act from harm suffered as the result of an industrial disease.

6:7:1   *Notification of accidents (s80)*
Written notice of an accident in a factory must be sent to the district inspector where it:

1   Causes loss of life to an employee
2   Disables him for more than three days from earning full wages at his normal work

The notification must be on a prescribed form, copies of which are available from HM Stationery Office. The factory occupier must inform the district inspector of the death of a person disabled by an accident already reported to him, as soon as the occupier becomes aware of it. If the factory occupier is not the employer of the person killed or injured, then the employer must report the accident to the occupier immediately, otherwise he is guilty of an offence punishable with a fine of up to £10.

Certain accidents, defined in the Dangerous Occurrences Regulations 1947, although they do not cause death or injury, must also be reported to the district inspector.

6:7:2 Notification of industrial diseases (s82)

When an employee is believed to have contracted an industrial disease such as lead, phosphorus, arsenical or mecurial poisoning, or other diseases specified by the Secretary of State by regulation as a result of working in any factory, then:

1   A medical practitioner called in to visit him must notify the chief inspector
2   The factory occupier must give written notice to the district inspector and the factory doctor

The notification to the inspector must be on a prescribed form, copies of which are available from HM Stationery Office.

6:7:3 Investigation of accidents and cases of disease (s84)

The Secretary of State may direct a formal investigation into the causes and circumstances of any accident or case of disease contracted, or suspected of having been contracted, in a factory, by appointing a competent person and an assessor with legal or special knowledge.

The investigation sits as an open court. It has the powers of a magistrates' court trying informations for offences under the Act, and also the following additional powers:

1   To enter and inspect any place or building necessary for the purposes of the investigation
2   To require attendance of all persons, as the court thinks fit, for examination
3   To require the production of books, papers and documents considered to be important
4   To administer the oath and require any person examined to sign a declaration of the truth of statements made during his examination

The court must make a report to the Secretary of State stating the causes and circumstances of the accident or disease, adding any observations it thinks fit.

6:7:4 Factory doctor's duty to investigate and report death and injury (s85)

The factory doctor must investigate and report on cases of death or injury:

1   Caused by exposure in a factory to fumes or other noxious substances, or because of other special causes specified by the Secretary of State as requiring investigation
2   Referred to him by the district inspector in pursuance of instructions from the Secretary of State

There is a similar duty in any case of disease of which he receives notice under the Act.

6:8   DUTY TO FENCE MACHINERY

The purpose of sections 14–16 of the Factories Act is to provide a system of work which is as safe as it possibly can be, by means of fencing machinery. Machinery must be fenced if it comes within the specific, detailed provisions of s12, but s14 is more significant in that it imposes a more general duty to fence every dangerous part of any machine. If an employee wishes to sue for non-compliance with this general duty, it is for the court to determine the exact scope of s14, and decide whether the omission or fault causing the injury is within its purview. Cases like Eaves v Morris Motors Ltd (see 6:8:3) show that not every injury sustained in connection with dangerous machinery is covered under s14. The provisions of s15 and s16 relax the stringent requirements on fencing while the machinery is being examined, lubricated or adjusted, but only when such maintenance work can only be done if the machinery is unfenced and in motion—and then only if the operation is carried out by a specially appointed machinery attendant (see 6:10 and 6:10:1).

6:8:1   Duty to fence specified machinery

It is required in s12 that the following machinery shall be securely fenced whether it appears to be dangerous or not:

1   Every flywheel connected to any prime mover and every moving part of any prime mover, whether the flywheel or prime mover is situated in an engine house or not

2   The head and tail race of every water wheel and of every water turbine

3   Every part of electric generators, motors and rotary coverters, and every flywheel directly connected to them, but there is no statutory duty to fence if it is in such a position or of such a construction as to be as safe to every person employed or working on the premises as if it were securely fenced

A "prime mover" is defined in s176 as "every engine, motor or other appliance which provides mechanical energy derived from steam, water, wind, electricity, the combustion of fuel or other source."

Transmission machinery is defined in s176 as any device by which the motion of a prime mover is transmitted to or received by any machine or appliance. It is required by s13 that:

1   Every part of the transmission machinery shall be securely fenced, unless it is in such a position or of such a construction as to be as safe to every person employed or working on the premises as it would be if securely fenced

2   Efficient devices must be provided which will promptly cut off power to the transmission machinery in emergencies

3   Driving belts must not rest upon a revolving shaft when not in use

4   Efficient striking gear or mechanical appliances must be provided, maintained and used to move driving belts to and from fast and loose pulleys forming part of the transmission machinery; such mechanical appliances must be constructed, placed and maintained in such a way as to prevent the belt from creeping back on to the fast pulley

The Secretary of State may exempt an employer from compliance with these duties, with the exception of the first, if compliance is unnecessary or impracticable.

6:8:2   *All dangerous machinery must be fenced*
It is provided in s14(1) that every dangerous part of any machinery, other than prime movers and transmission machinery, shall be securely fenced, unless it is in such a position or of such construction as to be as safe to every person employed or working on the premises as it would be if securely fenced.

If the safety of a dangerous part of any machinery cannot be secured by a fixed guard, because of the way in which it operates, then an automatic device may be provided which prevents the operator from coming into contact with that part of the machinery (s14(2)).

It is a defence for an employer contravening s14 to show that he used some protective device, which was equally as effective as the one required by statute (s14(4)).

The occupier's duty to fence imposed by ss12–14 is a strict or absolute liability. Any duty imposed upon him by the Act must be complied with, and it is not possible to escape liability by showing that reasonable care was taken to prevent any violation of the statutory obligation or that there was no intention to fail to carry out the duty imposed. The next case shows that the duty to fence under s14 is absolute: if a machine can only be used without proper fencing then it must not be used at all. The duty is not qualified by a phrase such as "so far as is reasonably practicable."

John Summers & Sons Ltd *v* Frost (1955, House of Lords)

Frost was injured, while grinding a metal bar, when his thumb came into contact with a power-driven machine. The upper part of the machine was guarded, but a gap of 180mm was left to allow grinding to take place. He claimed damages from his employer for a breach of s14(1) of the Factories Act.

The court decided that s14 imposed an absolute duty on the employers to fence dangerous machinery securely and it was not a good defence to show that it would be mechanically impossible to comply with the statute and still allow the machinery to be used commercially. The duty imposed must be observed, though in effect the machine cannot be used as a working unit. The employers were in breach of their statutory duty and Frost was entitled to damages.

The imposition of such strict liability on the employer seems to lead to an absurd conclusion, but s76 allows the Secretary of State to introduce special regulations to modify the employer's duty to fence dangerous machinery. For example, the Woodworking Machinery Regulations, the Power Press Regulations, the Horizontal Milling Machine Regulations and the Abrasive Wheels Regulations lay down standards of safety to replace the requirements under s14 which could not be carried out in practice.

Automatic Woodturning Co Ltd v Stringer (1957, House of Lords)

Stringer was injured when her hand was caught in a power-driven circular saw, while she was using a push stick to remove offcuts of wood. She claimed damages from her employer for the injuries sustained.

The court decided that the general duty to fence dangerous machinery imposed by s14 had been modified by the Woodworking Regulations. These regulations had been observed by the employer in respect of the only dangerous part of the machinery, consequently liability could not be established by the employee.

6:8:3 Abnormal movement by a machine

The duty to fence is confined to creating a protection in respect of the normal operation of the machine, but not a protection against unusual movements.

Eaves v Morris Motors Ltd (1961, Court of Appeal)

Eaves injured his finger in a milling machine that made an unusual movement. He saw what was happening and quickly withdrew his finger, but was injured on an irregularity in the bolt that was being milled in the machine. Eaves claimed damages against his employers for a breach of their statutory duty under s14(1).

The court decided that the unusual movement of the machine did not make it dangerous, thus there was no duty on the employer to fence it, and the claim for damages failed.

6:8:4 Insertion of materials may make a machine dangerous

There is a duty to fence a machine where it becomes dangerous on the insertion into it of materials for processing.

Midland & Low Moor Iron & Steel Co Ltd v Cross (1965, House of Lords)

To operate a machine which straightened iron bars, the workman had to feed the bar into the machine between two sets of grooved wheels, at a speed of about 20in/s. The workman was distracted for a few seconds and his hand was carried along by the moving bar and nipped between the bar and the first of the wheels. A factory inspector preferred information against the occupiers of the factory for contravening s14(1).

The court decided that if a machine becomes undoubtedly dangerous while being operated in a normal way as a result of the insertion of materials, then it follows that the machine is dangerous within the meaning of s14(1) and must be fenced. The accident was reasonably foreseeable (see 6:9) and the case was remitted to the justices with a direction to convict.

6:8:5 No duty to fence machinery made in the factory
The duty to fence dangerous machinery imposed by s14(1) covers machinery used in the factory, but it does not extend to any machinery made in the factory.

Parvin v Morton Machine Co Ltd (1952, House of Lords)

The defendant company manufactured machinery known as dough brakes. A fitter had removed the guard on one of them to allow Parvin, a seventeen-year-old apprentice fitter, to clean it as instructed. Parvin claimed damages from his employers for a breach of statutory duty under s14(1) after suffering serious injuries in the process of cleaning.

The court decided that the duty to fence under s14(1) did not extend to machinery produced in the factory which did not form part of the manufacturing process carried out there. Parvin was not entitled to damages.

6:8:6 Injury caused by ejection of fragments from dangerous machinery
Section 14 requires machinery to be fenced so as to prevent workmen from coming into contact with those parts of the machinery that move. An employer is not under a statutory duty to protect workmen from injury likely to be sustained from fragments flying from the machinery itself or from the material being processed in the machinery. The employee will probably be able to bring an action against his employer for breach of the common law duty of care, however, where such occurences are frequent.

6:8:7 No duty to fence while dangerous machinery is being erected
A statutory duty to fence does not exist in the period during which machinery is being erected for subsequent use in the factory, though it may be dangerous when completed and require fencing. There is a duty to fence any part of a dangerous machine that has been completely erected if it has become an independent machine in its own right.

Irwin v White, Tomkins & Courage Ltd (1964, House of Lords)

Irwin was fatally injured while testing a sack hoist during the course of installation of machinery in his employer's mill. The machinery had not been completely installed at the time of the accident, but the sack hoist itself was complete, ready for use and operating at its normal speed. His widow brought an action for damages for breach of the statutory duty to keep a dangerous part of the machinery securely fenced.

The court decided that there cannot be a dangerous part of any machinery until there exists machinery which has been installed as part of the equipment of the factory. There is no statutory obligation to fence while a machine is being erected. At that stage the employee can rely only on his employer's common law obligations. Here the hoist was an independent machine in its own right, having been erected and completed before the accident. It was not securely fenced by the employers as required by s15(1) Factories Act (Northern Ireland) 1938 (corresponding to s14 in the Factories Act 1961) and the defendants were liable in damages.

6:9 FENCING MACHINERY: RESTRICTING THE EMPLOYER'S LIABILITY WHERE THE HARM CAUSED WAS NOT FORESEEABLE

It has been shown that the factory occupier's duty to fence machinery in accordance with the provisions of ss12–14 imposes an absolute or strict liability on him. This liability cannot be evaded by showing that reasonable care was taken to prevent an infringement of the statutory obligations or that there was no intention to avoid the duties imposed. But the concept of foreseeability considerably reduces the strictness of the statutory duty, as illustrated by the next case which deals with the precise meaning of the word "dangerous" in s14(1).

Close v Steel Co of Wales (1962, House of Lords)

Close was injured when the bit of an electric drill shattered and a fragment hit him in the eye. It was not unusual for fragments to shatter, but they were usually light and harmless; this was the first serious accident to happen in this manner. Close sued his employers for damages for a breach of s14(1), alleging that the bit was dangerous and required fencing.

The court decided that "no one had ever known an accident to an eye before and the chances of grave injury were 'extremely remote' . . . in the ordinary course of human affairs, danger could not reasonably be anticipated from the use of the drill unfenced. It cannot therefore be classed as dangerous" (Lord Denning). In the absence of a duty to fence under s14 the employers were not liable in damages to the injured employee.

6:9:1 Protection must be provided against an employee's carelessness

Fencing may be deemed inadequate if it does not provide effective protection against accidents, even though an employee has acted carelessly while using the machinery.

Smith v Chesterfield & District Co-operative Society Ltd (1953, Court of Appeal)

A puff pastry machine comprised a pair of rollers fitted with a guard, reaching to within 75mm of the table top on which they rested. The gap between the guard and the table allowed dough 75mm thick to be fed into the machine. Smith, a sixteen-year-old girl, acting contrary to instructions, placed her hand under the guard and was injured. She sued her employers for damages alleging that the machine was not properly fenced as required by s14.

The court decided that Smith was entitled to damages, though they were reduced to 40 per cent of the total sum awarded because of her contributory negligence. Although Smith's actions were wrongful, they could have been reasonably foreseen by the employers; consequently, the machine was not securely fenced within the requirements of the Act.

6:9:2 Employee's unreasonable acts need not be guarded against

Machinery is securely fenced if it would effectively prevent an employee being injured in the course of his work, provided he acts in the way in which he is reasonably expected to act.

Burns v Joseph Terry & Sons Ltd (1950, Court of Appeal)

Burns, a seventeen-year-old boy, was employed to clear away beans left lying around the factory. In order to reach beans that had spilled on a shelf, he placed a ladder against a revolving shaft, situated above a machine protected from the front by a 4ft fence. The ladder moved sideways and while grabbing for support the boy's hand was crushed between a pulley wheel and a pinion. Burns claimed damages from his employers for a breach of s13, in not securely fencing transmission machinery.

The court decided that the employers were not liable in damages to the injured employee, since the machine was properly fenced against reasonably foreseeable damage. The factory inspector had seen this fencing many times and an accident had not occurred over the past twenty years, during which the machine was in use.

6:9:3 *Employer's liability for inadequately fenced machinery*
An employer is liable to an employee who is injured by inadequately fenced dangerous machinery, though at the time of the accident the employee was not engaged on his employer's business.

Uddin v Associated Portland Cement (1965, Court of Appeal)

Uddin worked in a cement packing factory. During working hours he stalked a pigeon into a part of the factory where he was not authorised to enter and in the process he was caught up in the machinery.

The court decided that the employer was liable to Uddin for damages on the ground that dangerous machinery had not been properly fenced under s14(1), though the amount of the damages was reduced by 80 per cent to take into account Uddin's contributory negligence.

A person is within the protection of the Factories Act, if at the time of the accident he is:

1   Working on the employer's premises, or
2   Engaged in employment on those premises during working hours, though not carrying out his usual duties, as in the above case

If it is shown that machinery is dangerous and needs fencing, the employer is potentially liable to all employees who suffer from the failure to fence properly, though the conduct of the employee which results in an accident is stupid and negligent.

The employer is not liable for breach of a statutory duty if an employee is injured while acting completely outside the scope of his employment at the time of the breach (see 7 : 3 : 5).

6:10   WHEN MACHINERY NEED NOT BE FENCED

Machinery that must normally be fenced, under ss14 or 16 need not be fenced during:

1   The examination, lubrication or adjustment of machinery in
     motion, where unavoidable (s15(1)(a))

2   Lubrication, mounting or shipping of belts in transmission
     machinery, where stopping the machinery would seriously
     interfere with the carrying on of the process (s15(1)(b))

provided (s15(2)) that these operations are carried out by a male person over
eighteen years old, in accordance with the Operations at Unfenced
Machinery Regulations.

6:10:1   Construction and maintenance of fencing

It is required by s16 that all fencing and other safeguards provided by the
occupier in accordance with the requirements of the Act must be of substantial construction. Fencing must be kept in position while the machinery
is in motion or use, unless it is absolutely necessary to expose it for
examination, lubrication or adjustment, and then only if the operation is
carried out by a properly instructed machinery attendant appointed under
the Operations at Unfenced Machinery Regulations.

The section uses the terms "in motion" and "in use." A machine will
be in use if it is running normally and doing the work it was intended to
do. A machine may be in use without being in motion, if, for example,
it has stopped for a short time while the operator takes a break. Alternatively, a machine may be in motion at its usual speed without being in
use for its normal purpose where, for example, a machine is being prepared for normal working (see 6:10:3). In both cases s16 applies and, if
dangerous, the machinery must be fenced.

6:10:2   Manual operation of a machine not protected by s16

Where machinery is operated by hand it is not "in motion or in use" for
the purposes of s16; consequently there is no duty to fence.

Richard Thomas & Baldwin Ltd v Cummings (1955, House of Lords)

Cummings, a fitter, was adjusting part of a machine driven by belts passing
over pulleys. It was dangerous machinery for which fencing was required
under s13 and s14. The power had been cut off and the guards for the
belts and pulleys taken away. Cummings pulled one of the belts manually
and trapped his hand. He sued his employers for breach of their statutory
duty under s16.

The court decided that s16 does not prohibit the removal of fencing when this is necessary to effect repairs. The words "in motion or in use" do not refer to movement of machinery by hand. The employers were not liable for damages. "Using the phrase in its ordinary sense, I do not think that one would naturally say of a man moving parts of a machine round to a required position that he had set the machine or its parts in motion. The phrase 'in motion' appears to me to be more apt to describe a continuing state of motion lasting, or intended to last, for an appreciable time." (Lord Reid)

This decision should be applied with some caution and should not be extended, for two reasons:

1   It is a departure from the literal meaning of the words "in motion"
2   It diminishes the statutory protection conferred on the employee

The method of starting the machinery is often significant. Part of a machine may be moving without its being considered to be in motion, as where it is being moved slowly by hand, as in the above case, or slowly inched over by use of an inching button.

Knight v Leamington Spa Courier Ltd (1961, Court of Appeal)

Knight removed a guard so that he could clean the revolving rollers of a printing press. To facilitate the cleaning process he pressed an inching button to make the rollers move under power at a very slow speed of five rev/min. Knight was injured when his hand was drawn into the rollers. He claimed damages from his employer for failing to fence the rollers while they were in motion or use.

The court decided that the rollers were not in motion or use when the accident occurred; thus there was no duty to fence. The machine was not being used for its ordinary commercial purpose of printing. It was a slack period during which the machine was not being used at all and Knight was taking advantage of this fact to clean it. The employers were not liable for damages.

Mitchell v W S Westin Ltd (1965, Court of Appeal)

Mitchell, an experienced turner employed by the defendant company, removed the protective fencing from a machine that was not working properly so that he could make the necessary adjustment. He rotated the machine by quickly switching it on and off, and sustained injury when his finger was caught in the machine. Mitchell sued his employers for damages, alleging that they had failed to discharge their statutory duties imposed by what are now ss14 and 16 of the 1961 Act.

The court decided that the machine was only moving intermittently when the accident occurred, and was moving in a manner that was entirely different to the way it moved when it was operating normally. The machine was not in motion within the meaning of s16 and the employers were not in breach of their statutory duty to fence imposed by s14.

6:10:3 *Importance of the speed and character of a movement*
The effect of the next decision has been to modify the approach in the three cases discussed in 6:10:2 and give greater protection to the employee.

When determining whether a moving machine is to be considered as in motion for the purposes of s16, the speed and character of the movement are the important factors, rather than the purpose for which the machine is being moved at the relevant time. When these factors have been taken into account, it is a question of fact and degree in any situation whether the machinery is "in motion." This approach reduces a decision in any given situation to a question of fact, as the next case illustrates.

Stanbrook v Waterlow & Sons Ltd (1964, Court of Appeal)

Stanbrook was employed by the defendant company as a printing machine operator. To prepare the machine for printing he had to remove the guard, put pieces of paper round the cylinder and smooth them with his hand. Only a little could be smoothed at a time, and so the cylinder had to rotate slowly so that the smoothing operation could be completed. Rotation was controlled solely by an electric motor which drove the machine when it was printing normally. The motor started up very quickly when switched on and therefore, when preparing the machine, it had to be switched on and off very rapidly so that the cylinder did not rotate too quickly. Stanbrook failed to do this and his hand was drawn into the machine. He sued his employers for damages for a breach of s14(1) and s16.

The court decided that, although the movement of the machine was not intended to last for more than a moment of time, the machine was in motion for the purposes of s16, and therefore required fencing. The employers were in breach of this duty and liable to Stanbrook. "There is, I think, a broad distinction between a thing which is 'being moved' slowly and a thing which is 'in motion' at a fast speed. Accepting for present purposes that a thing which is being moved slowly is not in motion, I am of the opinion that the cylinder going at the very high pace here was in motion." (Lord Denning)

The object of the Factories Act is to protect workmen from dangerous machinery while it is running at the usual speed, even though it is not being used for its normal purpose at the time of the accident.

Horne v Lec Refrigeration Ltd (1965)

Horne, a toolsetter, was using an electric drill inside an electrically operated press while the press was not in use. To do this it was necessary to remove a fence. Horne was familiar with the safety procedure, which required all switches to be turned off and the key to be removed from the safety key switch, but he failed to follow these procedures. The cable of the drill caught the switch of the press and turned on the machine. Horne was killed when his head was crushed by the press. His widow brought an action against her deceased husband's employer for breach of the statutory duty imposed by s16, alleging that at a time when the press was "in motion and in use" it was not securely fenced, contrary to s14.

The court decided that the machinery was dangerous within s14 and there was a duty to fence it. The fence should have remained in position, for although the machine was not in use for its ordinary commercial purpose, it was in motion. Though switched on accidently the machine was moving in the same manner and place, at the same speed and the same extent as when working normally. It was stated, however, that "The sole cause of the breach was the deceased's conscious disregard of the prescribed safety procedure which he knew and understood. There was no breach of statutory duty when he unbolted the guard covering the press so that he might adjust the mould. The machine was not then in motion or in use. The breach of statutory duty occurred only when he caused the machine to be set in motion as a result of his own disregard of instructions" (Mr Justice Cantley). The employers were not liable for damages.

6:11 CONSTRUCTION AND SALE OF MACHINERY

With machines intended to be driven by mechanical power:

1   Every set screw, bolt or key on any revolving shaft, spindle, wheel or pinion must be so sunk, cased or guarded as to prevent danger
2   All spurs and toothed or friction gearing, not requiring frequent adjustment while in motion, must be situated in a safe position or completely encased (s17)

It is an offence for the employer to use machinery in a factory which does not comply with s17(1). In addition, the person selling or hiring the machine will be liable to a fine not exceeding £200. If the machinery originated abroad, an agent in the UK will be liable if the principal cannot be prosecuted (s17(2)).

Biddle v Truvox Engineering Co Ltd (1951)

Biddle, a workman, was injured by a machine containing toothed or friction gearing which was not completely encased in accordance with s17(1). He sued the occupier of the factory for damages, and the occupier joined the manufacturer of the machine as a third party to the action, claiming contribution towards the damages on the ground that the workman's injury was caused by a breach of the manufacturer's duty under s17(2) not to sell the machine with the parts not encased.

The court decided that the duty owed by the employer, to compensate his employee in a civil action for damages for any injury suffered by reason of the employer's failure to comply with s17(1), did not extend to the manufacturer of the machine that caused the employee's injury. The manufacturer was liable to pay the statutory fine, but not a contribution towards the damages awarded against the employer as a result of a civil action brought by the employee.

The situation in the last case is now covered by the Employers' Liability (Defective Equipment) Act 1969 under which an action can be brought against a manufacturer of equipment for damages paid to an employee injured by it (see 5:4).

6:12 SAFETY AND
SUITABILITY OF THE PLACE OF EMPLOYMENT

Every place of employment must be made and kept safe for employees and independent contractors working there, so far as is reasonably practicable. It is for the occupier to prove that it was impossible for him to establish and maintain a safe place of work, rather than for the employee or independent contractor to show the possible, practicable steps that the occupier might have taken (s29).

Liability under s29 will be established where a failure to provide proper equipment results in the employee falling and injuring himself for in these circumstances his place of employment is not safe.

Ross v Associated Portland Cement
Manufacturers Ltd (1964, House of Lords)

Ross, a steel erector, was instructed to repair a wire safety net situated 22ft above the ground. It was an unusual task for a steel erector and Ross did not receive proper instructions on how to undertake the repair work or proper equipment to work with. The netting collapsed when Ross placed a ladder against it, causing him to fall to his death.

The court decided that the employers were liable for damages to the deceased's widow for a breach of what is now s29(1) of the Factories Act 1961. The employer had not provided proper equipment, in consequence of which Ross's place of work had not been kept safe. The deceased's decision to use the ladder was reached on the basis that more suitable equipment was not available. "The failure of the respondents to take any steps to see that proper equipment was available contributed a great deal to the accident. Ross's working place was the place where he was working, near the top of the ladder, and there is nothing to show that it was not reasonably practicable for the respondents to provide the equipment which the expert says ought to have been used—a movable platform." (Lord Reid)

Damages were reduced by one third to take into account the deceased's contributory negligence. He should not have been satisfied with the use of makeshift equipment and was negligent in using a ladder that was clearly dangerous.

6:12:1   *Access to a place of employment must be kept safe*
The occupier is under a duty to provide and maintain a safe means of access to every place at which employees and independent contractors are required to work (s29).

Callaghan v Fred Kidd & Son (Engineers) Ltd (1944, Court of Appeal)

Callaghan fell over some iron bars lying on the floor, and he came into contact with a revolving grindstone. He claimed damages from his employers for the injuries he suffered, claiming a breach of the statutory duty embodied in what is now s29 of the Factories Act 1961.

The court decided that he was entitled to succeed on the ground that safe means of access must be provided at all times. An employer is obliged to make and enforce a regulation which prevents obstacles from being placed in such a manner as to render access to a working place unsafe.

An employer occupying a factory is liable under s29 for failure to provide safe access to a place of work, if his employees are injured while using an access provided by an independent contractor working for the occupier.

Hosking v De Havilland Aircraft Co Ltd (1949)

The defendants employed an independent contractor to carry out building work on land adjoining a factory in their occupation. The contractors placed a plank across a trench in the ground which was used by their own workmen, but also by employees of the defendant company as a means of reaching their place of work. Hosking, one of these employees, was injured when the plank broke while he was crossing the trench and he sued for damages alleging a breach of what is now s29(1).

The court decided that the employers were liable in damages, since they had failed to maintain a safe means of access for their employees, so far as it was reasonably practicable for them to do so. Even though the plank was placed in position by contractors, employees of the defendant company were intended to make use of it. The amount paid in damages was recovered from the contractors under an express indemnity given by them, which entitled De Havillands to reclaim any losses they suffered because of the contractors' defaults.

Although the occupier's duty imposed by s29 is owed to independent contractors and their employees working at the factory as well as the occupier's own employees, the occupier may pass the burden of his civil and criminal liability to the independent contractor if he is the person responsible for any accident caused.

Whitby v Burt, Boulton & Hayward Ltd and Another (1947)

The first defendants, occupiers of a factory, engaged independent contractors, the second defendants, to repair damage to the factory. The occupiers authorised the contractors to take down and use corrugated iron sheets, which were nailed to defective timber beneath a glass skylight in the factory roof. Whitby was injured when the timbers collapsed and he fell some 20ft to the ground.

The court decided that the factory occupiers were liable in damages to Whitby for a breach of what is now s29 of the Factories Act 1961. The means of access to Whitby's place of work, that is, the iron sheets and the nails fastening them to the timber, was not as safe as was reasonably practicable. The factory occupier is responsible for compliance with the requirements of s29, even though the operation in question is being completed by an independent contractor. The factory occupier may claim an indemnity from the independent contractor under the Law Reform (Married Women and Tortfeasors) Act 1935, if the accident was caused by a fault attributable to the independent contractor rather than the occupiers. In this case, a full indemnity was granted. The occupier may try to avoid criminal liability by using s161 (see 7 : 2 : 6).

6 : 12 : 2   *Safety precautions where a person works above the ground*

Any person, whether an employee or independent contractor, working at a height of over 6ft 6in (1.98m) above the ground must be provided with a secure foothold (and a secure handhold, where necessary) so far is reasonably practicable; or else be protected against falls by fencing or other suitable means. If such precautions are not taken, the place of work will not be considered safe (s29(2)).

Wigley v British Vinegars Ltd (1964, House of Lords)

The widow of an experienced window cleaner claimed damages against British Vinegars Ltd for an alleged breach of what is now s29(2) of the Factories Act 1961. Her husband, an independent contractor, had fallen to his death from a 30ft ladder, while working on the company's premises, because of a failure to provide any safety belts or hooks, or any means of fastening the swinging window on which the deceased was working. The ladder itself was not defective, nor had it moved or caused the deceased to fall.

The court decided that the section in question applied to an independent contractor, like the deceased, as well as to employees of the company. The words "any person" in s29(1) and (2) covered persons whose duty it was to work for the purposes of the factory; consequently the deceased was within the protection of the section. However, the widow's claim failed for other reasons.

6:12:3 Floors, passages and stairs must be kept safe

All floors, steps, stairs, passages and gangways must be of sound construction and properly maintained. They must also be kept free from any obstruction or substance likely to cause persons to slip, but only so far as is reasonably practicable: the duty here is not absolute (s28). The standard of care to be expected from the reasonable, prudent man must be adopted by the party responsible for observance of the requirements of the section.

Jenkins v Allied Iron Founders Ltd (1969, House of Lords)

In the moulding shop of the respondent's factory it was the practice to empty moulding boxes and pile the castings into heaps. When the castings were rapped out, surplus metal ("gates") which had been poured into the moulding box either fell off or were knocked off. Cleaners cleared away the gates when the pile of castings had been removed. Jenkins was injured by a fall, caused by catching his heel in a gate embedded in several inches of sand on the factory floor. He sued for damages for a breach of s28(1) of the Factories Act 1961.

The court decided that the factory occupiers were not liable in damages for a breach of their statutory duty, even though the gates were an obstruction within the meaning of s28. An "obstruction" is something on the floor that has no business to be there, which is a source of risk to persons ordinarily using the floor. On the whole evidence, however, it was established that it was not reasonably practicable to keep the floor clear during the process of moving the castings, having regard to the expense and delay of a preventive system and the improbability of such an accident or serious injury. The only way in which it was suggested that the gate in question could have been detected and removed before the accident was to post a man with a rake who, as soon as each casting was removed from the heap, would go over the sand on which it rested to see that there was no obstruction.

It is also provided in s28 that every staircase must have a substantial handrail. Where the staircase has an open side the handrail must be placed on that side. Two handrails must be provided if the staircase:

1   Has two open sides
2   Is specially liable to cause accidents, because of either the nature of its construction or the condition of its surface

The open side must also be guarded by a lower rail or other suitable device.

Openings in floors must be securely fenced, as far as is reasonably practicable. All ladders must be soundly constructed and properly maintained.

6:12:4   Humid factories (s68)
A humid factory is one in which atmospheric humidity is artificially produced by steaming or other means, in connection with any textile process. The factory occupier must give written notice to the district inspector before artificial humidity is first used, and there are special provisions to protect employees working in such conditions.

6:12:5   Restriction on the use of underground rooms (s69)
An underground room is one where at least half of the height from the floor to the ceiling is below the surface of the adjoining street. The district inspector may certify that an underground room is unsuitable for work on account of construction, height, light, ventilation or hygiene, or because the fire escape is inadequate. The room can then be used only for storage or for any other purpose which the Secretary of State allows by order. Notice of intention to use an underground room must be given to the district inspector on a prescribed form obtainable from HM Stationery Office.

6:12:6   Closing down unsafe working premises (s54, s55)
Where, on a complaint by a factory inspector, a magistrates' court is satisfied that either:

1   Any part of the ways, works, machinery or plant in a factory is in such a condition or so constructed that it cannot be used without risk of bodily injury, or
2   A process of work is carried on, so as to cause risk of bodily injury

then the court may prohibit its use altogether, or until it is repaired, altered or the danger is removed.

The court may make an interim order prohibiting use altogether, or allowing use but subject to stated conditions, until the complaint can be heard by the court.

The court may prohibit the use of a factory, or part of it including new premises to be used as a factory, if satisfied that they are in such condition that any process of work cannot be carried out with due regard to the safety, health and welfare of employees. The prohibition may last indefinitely, or until steps have been taken to remove the source of dissatisfaction.

6:13 SAFETY PRECAUTIONS RELATING TO HOISTS AND LIFTS, DANGEROUS SUBSTANCES, FUMES AND INFLAMMABLE SUBSTANCES

The safety precautions relating to the matters listed have been grouped together under this heading, since the statutory provisions to be observed are set out in detail. If applicable in any factory over which a manager has responsibility, it is important that he is aware of the duties and obligations that he may be expected to discharge, such as regular examination of hoists and lifts and breathing apparatus.

6:13:1 *Safety precautions relating to equipment used in the factory (ss22–7)*

All hoists, lifts and cranes must be well constructed mechanically, of sound material and adequate strength, and properly maintained. It is not enough to show that the hoist or lift was of sound material when first installed; it must remain so throughout the whole period during which it is in operation. The statutory obligations are absolute. Thus it is a breach of duty to allow a latent (non-obvious) defect to exist in a hoist or lift, though it existed at the time of installation and could not have been discovered at any later time. There is a breach of the duty to "properly maintain" if a failure in the mechanism occurs, even though all reasonable care has been taken to maintain a suitable hoist or lift in efficient working order and a good state of repair.

Whitehead v James Stott & Co (1949, Court of Appeal)

Whitehead was injured while using a hoist when the cage fell and the winding gear dropped on him. He claimed damages for the injuries suffered and alleged that the defendant company were in breach of their statutory duty in failing to provide a hoist of good mechanical construction, contrary to what is now s22 of the 1961 Act.

The court decided that there was a latent (non-obvious) defect in the winding gear, which had probably been present since the time of its installation some years earlier. However, the statutory duty was absolute, and the defendants were liable despite their ignorance of the existence of the defect and their consequent inability to correct it.

The House of Lords affirmed this strict interpretation of s22 in Galashiels Gas Co Ltd v O'Donnell (1949). They also indicated that it is not a good defence for the employer to show that experts have examined the mechanism and failed to detect any defect that could have caused the accident.

A competent person must examine:

1   Every hoist or lift at least once every six months
2   Every crane at least once every fourteen months

A signed report of the result of each examination must be entered or attached to the general register, within twenty-eight days of that examination. Where a hoist or lift is found to be unsafe after examination, necessary repairs must be carried out immediately, or within a specified time depending upon the nature of the defect. The inspector for the district must receive a copy of the report, within twenty-eight days of the examination.

The hoistway or liftway must be protected by a substantial enclosure, fitted with gates which cannot be opened unless the cage is at the landing. The cage must be capable of moving only when the gate is closed. These requirements prevent anyone from falling down the hoistway or liftway or coming into contact with moving parts. Hoists and hoistways, lifts and liftways must be constructed so as to prevent any person or goods carried from being trapped. The maximum working load that may be carried must be clearly stated (s22 and s27). Chains, ropes and lifting gear must be:

1   Of good construction, sound material and adequate strength, free from obvious defects and not used for any load exceeding the safe working load
2   Examined by a competent person every six months
3   Examined, tested and the safe working load certified by a competent person before being used for the first time (except a fibre rope)

These details must be entered in a table in the store where the equipment is kept, with the safe working load prominently displayed on that table (s26). This requirement does not apply to lifting tackle which is itself clearly marked with the safe working load.

6:13:2 Protection from dangerous substances (s18)

Every fixed vessel, structure, sump or pit containing scalding, corrosive or poisonous liquid, the edge of which is less than 3ft (0.91m) above the ground, or which has a platform from which a person might fall into it, must be securely covered, or fenced to at least 3ft above the ground or platform.

If covering or fencing is not possible, because of the nature of the work, all practicable steps must be taken to prevent persons falling in, and any ladder or stair placed above, across or inside must be at least 18in (0.46m) wide and securely fenced to a height of 3ft.

6:13:3 Safety precautions to
prevent harm from dangerous fumes (s30)

Where work in a factory must be done inside any chamber, tank, vat, pit, pipe, flue or other similar confined space in which dangerous fumes are likely to be present, with the risk that persons might be overcome, the following safety precautions must be taken:

1   In the absence of some other adequate means of exit, a manhole must be provided:
   (a) At least 18in (0.46m) long and 16in (0.41m) wide if rectangular
   (b) At least 18in (0.46m) in diameter if circular
   (c) For mobile plant, the manhole must be at least 16in (0.41m) long and 14in (0.36m) wide if rectanglar, and 16in (0.41m) in diameter if circular
2   A person must not enter or remain in the confined space unless he is:
   (a) Wearing suitable breathing apparatus
   (b) Authorised to enter by a responsible person
   (c) Wearing a belt with a rope securely attached, if practicable, with a person keeping watch outside holding the other end of the rope and capable of pulling him out of the space
3   If a responsible person has certified that it is safe to enter the confined space without breathing apparatus, then these provi-

sions do not apply, but a confined space must not be certified as safe unless:

(a) Effective steps have been taken to prevent the entry of dangerous fumes

(b) Sludge or other deposits liable to give off dangerous fumes have been removed

(c) The space has been adequately ventilated and tested for dangerous fumes and has an adequate supply of air for respiration

4 Breathing apparatus, reviving apparatus, belts and ropes must be readily available, maintained and examined monthly, and a report on the examination, signed by the person making it, must be available for inspection; a sufficient number of persons employed must be trained in the use of the apparatus

In addition to the above requirements a person must not enter a confined space in which the proportion of oxygen in the air is substantially reduced unless:

1 He is wearing suitable breathing apparatus, or

2 The space is adequately ventilated and a responsible person has tested and certified it as safe for entry without breathing apparatus

Work must not be permitted in any boiler, furnace or flue until it has been made sufficiently safe by ventilation or otherwise.

6:13:4 *Safety precautions*
in relation to explosive or inflammable substances (s31)
Where any grinding, sieving or other process causes dust that is liable to explode on ignition, all practicable steps must be taken to prevent an explosion, by:

1 Enclosure of the plant used in the process

2 Removal or prevention of accumulation of any dust that may escape in spite of the enclosure

3 Exclusion or effective enclosure of possible sources of ignition

If the plant is not constructed to withstand the pressure of any such explosion, steps must be taken to restrict the spread and effects of the explosion by the provision of effective appliances such as chokes, baffles and vents.

6:14 SAFETY PRECAUTIONS IN CASE OF FIRE

6:14:1 *Safety requirements*
relating to the structural condition of the premises (s48)

The following fire precautions must be taken, unless the Chief Inspector allows a dispensation subject to any specified conditions set out in a local fire authority's certificate:

1   While any person is in the factory, either for employment or meals, all doors giving a means of exit must be unlocked and capable of being opened from the inside

2   All doors providing a means of exit for employees must open outwards unless they are sliding doors

3   Every hoistway and liftway in a building constructed after the end of June 1938 must be completely encased with fire-resisting materials; all doors to the hoist or lift must be fitted with fire-resisting materials

4   In case of fire, all means of escape by window, door or other means of exit, other than those in ordinary use, must be distinctively and conspicuously marked

5   The contents of any room in which persons are employed must be arranged to leave a free passageway of escape in case of fire for the persons employed in that room

6:14:2 *Fire instruction for employees (s49)*

Effective steps must be taken to ensure that all persons employed are familiar with the means of escape and the routine to be observed if there is a fire, in cases where a factory has:

1   More than twenty persons employed above the first floor or more than twenty feet above the ground level

2   Explosive or highly inflammable materials stored in it where persons are employed

6:14:3 *Statutory provisions concerning fire fighting (s51, s52)*

Adequate means for fighting fire must be readily available and properly maintained in every factory unless the Secretary of State has granted exemption. He may also make regulations:

1   Specifying the means for notifying the fire brigade when a fire occurs

2   Requiring employees to be familiar with fire appliances

3   Making a person liable for a contravention of these provi-
     sions in place of or in addition to the occupier

The fire warning system must be tested or examined every three months
or when required by the inspector. The result of the test, and the need to
rectify any defect discovered, must be entered in the general register
(see 6:3).

6:14:4   *Factory must be certified by the fire authority (ss40-3)*
The following safety precautions apply to all factories:

1   In which twenty persons or more are employed

2   Completed before 30 July 1937, in which more than ten people
     are employed in the same building above the first floor, or
     more than 20 ft (6.10m) above ground level

3   Constructed or converted to a factory after 30 July 1937, in
     which more than ten people are employed in the same build-
     ing on any floor above the ground floor

4   In or under which explosive or highly inflammable materials
     are stored or used (s45)

Effective means must be provided and maintained for giving warning in
case of fire; the warning must be clearly audible throughout the building
and must be able to be operated without exposing any person to undue
risk.

Premises must not be used as a factory unless a certificate from the local
fire authority (the county council or county borough council) states that
adequate means of escape are provided in case of fire. A certificate may
not be granted unless alterations are made to the premises within a given
time. If the occupier uses premises as a factory without a certificate having
been issued he is liable to a heavy fine, unless he has applied for a certificate and is waiting for it to be granted.

The certificate, a copy of which must be attached to the general register,
must state in detail:

1   The means of escape provided, which must be properly main-
     tained and kept free of obstruction

2   The maximum number of persons employed or to be employed
     (s40)

The fire authority may examine the factory periodically to determine whether changed conditions have rendered the existing means of escape inadequate. The occupier must give written notice of his intention to the fire authority if, after the granting of a certificate, it is proposed:

1   To make any material extension or structural alteration
2   To increase materially the number of persons employed
3   To begin to store, or increase materially the storage of, inflammable or explosive materials

If the changes make the existing means of escape inadequate, the fire authority may require the occupier to make any necessary alterations within a specified time.

An inspector may give written notice to the fire authority that, in his opinion, an escape from a fire exit is in a dangerous condition. The fire authority must examine the factory and require the occupier to make any necessary alterations within the period stated in the notice. The fire authority will amend the original certificate or issue a new one when the changes have been made and send a copy to the inspector. If the changes are not made the certificate may be cancelled forthwith and the inspector informed (s41).

The inspector may make a complaint to the magistrates' court if the factory, a part of it, or a particular process is so dangerous that remedial steps ought to be taken immediately. The court may prohibit further work at the place where the danger exists until necessary changes have been made. If, within one month, the fire authority fails to act upon the inspector's written notice informing the authority of the dangerous state of a factory, then the inspector may take the steps that the authority should have taken (s42).

An occupier aggrieved at the decisions that have been taken by the inspector or fire authority by use of the powers conferred by s40 and s41 may appeal to a court of summary jurisdiction within twenty-one days. Until the appeal has been determined an offence is not committed if the occupier is without a certificate (s43).

HEALTH AND WELFARE IN FACTORIES

The occupier must observe the requirements set out below for the protection of his employees' health. Any breach of the obligations imposed is a criminal offence, and in addition, a civil action for damages may be maintained by the employee who is injured by the non-observance of the statutory duties (see 7:2 and 7:3). In general, it is the factory inspector who ensures that the health and welfare provisions of the Act are complied with. However, the provisions relating to sanitary conveniences are enforced by the local borough or district council. In factories where no mechanical power is used, the local council is also responsible for enforcing ss1–7 of the Act.

6:15 CLEANLINESS

Every factory must be kept in a clean state, free from effluvia arising from any drain, sanitary convenience, or nuisance (s1). In addition to this over-riding general requirement, and without prejudice to it, the following specific obligations are imposed, unless exempted by order from the Department of Employment:

1   Accumulations of dirt and refuse are to be removed daily from floors and benches of workrooms, staircases and passages
2   The floors of workrooms are to be cleaned at least once a week by washing or, if effective, by sweeping or other means

Where mechanical power is used, or ten or more persons are employed, all interior walls, ceilings, sides and tops of passages and staircases must be:

1   Washed at least once every fourteen months, with hot water and soap or other effective detergent, if they have a smooth impervious surface
2   Repainted or revarnished every seven years, if so required, and washed at least once every fourteen months with hot water and soap or other effective detergent
3   Whitewashed or colourwashed every fourteen months in other cases

The provisions of s1 are amplified in the Factories (Cleanliness of Walls and Ceilings) Regulations 1960.

6:15:1 *Drainage of floors (s6)*
Where any process is carried on whereby the floor becomes so wet that the water can be removed by drainage, then effective drainage must be provided and maintained.

6:16   OVERCROWDING (s2)

A factory must not be so overcrowded that there is a risk of injury to the health of the employees. Each employee must have a minimum space of 400ft³ (11.3m³). Space over 14ft (4.27m) from the floor must not be taken in consideration when calculating the space available. With this obligation in mind, a notice must be posted in every workroom, stating the number of persons who may be employed there, unless the district inspector otherwise allows.

Where explosives are manufactured or handled, the Chief Inspector may by certificate make whatever special provisions he thinks fit, if the obligations imposed by s2 are inappropriate or unnecessary.

6:17   HEATING, LIGHTING AND VENTILATION

6:17:1   Temperature (s3)

Provision must be made for securing and maintaining a reasonable temperature, by a method that does not involve injurious or offensive fumes escaping into the air. What is a reasonable temperature depends upon the surrounding circumstances, but in workrooms where the work is done in a sitting position, without requiring serious physical effort, a temperature of less than 16°C (60°F) after the first hour is not reasonable while work is going on. At least one thermometer must be placed in a suitable position in each workroom.

The determination of a reasonable temperature must be decided on the facts of each individual case, but the following factors will be relevant:

1   The type of work done
2   The time of year
3   The prevailing weather conditions, whether exceptionally hot or cold
4   The type of heating system used, the movement of air, the ventilation system, and the radiation and convection of heat

6:17:2   Lighting (s5)

Effective provision must be made for securing and maintaining sufficient and suitable lighting, whether natural or artificial, in every part of a factory in which persons are working or passing.

All glazed windows and skylights used for the lighting of workrooms must be kept clean on the inside and outside, so far as is practicable. Windows and skylights may be whitewashed or shaded to prevent heat or glare. Lighting must comply with the standards of the Factories (Standard of Lighting) Regulations 1941.

Lane v Gloucester Engineering Co Ltd (1967, Court of Appeal)

Lane, a welder, employed by the defendant company in their workshop, habitually arrived for work twenty minutes early. Being the first to arrive, he switched on the tungsten lights, the switch for which was situated near his work position. On the day of the accident he crossed the workshop to switch on the fluorescent lighting instead, and sustained injuries by tripping over an obstacle in his path. He sued his employer for damages for a breach of s5.

The court decided that even if there was a breach of duty under s5, Lane himself was fully responsible for the accident. It was unnecessary for him to venture into the working area without switching on the tungsten lights which were situated quite close to him as he entered the factory.

6:17:3 Ventilation (s4)

Effective and suitable provision must be made for securing and maintaining adequate ventilation by means of circulating fresh air in each workroom. All fumes, dust and other impurities generated within the factory by reason of the work being carried on that may be injurious to health, must be rendered harmless so far as is practicable. The Secretary of State may, by regulation, prescribe a standard of adequate ventilation for any factory or part of it.

6:17:4 Removal of dust and fumes (s63)

All practicable measures must be taken to:

1   Protect employees against inhalation of:
   (a) Dust, fumes and other impurities likely to be injurious, or
   (b) Any substantial quantity of dust of any kind
2   Prevent their accumulating in any workroom

If practicable, exhaust appliances must be provided as near as possible to the point of origin of the dust or fumes, to prevent them from entering the air of the workroom.

Stationary internal combustion engines must not be used, unless the exhaust gases are conducted into the open air and the engine is partitioned off from the workroom to prevent fumes from entering it, except when being tested.

Use of the words "all practicable measures" in s63 does not impose an absolute duty.

Richards v Highway Iron Founders (West Bromwich) Ltd
(1955, Court of Appeal)

Richards, a moulder employed by the defendant company, contracted silicosis as a direct result of inhaling dust created by removing sand from castings. He claimed damages from his employers for a breach of what is now s63 of the 1961 Act.

The court decided that, in 1949 when Richards became ill, it was not realised that inhaling dust from this type of industrial process could cause silicosis. The employers had not violated their statutory duties under s63, since they were unaware of the danger to an employee's health arising from the dust, which was invisible. It was not realistic to expect the employer to require protective masks to be worn.

The factory occupier must take those precautions which are reasonable, having regard to the present state of scientific knowledge, concerning the dangers that exist in certain factory conditions. Provision of protective clothing coupled with advice to employees to use it, is not a sufficient discharge of the duty imposed by s63 (see 5 : 5, Crookall v Vickers-Armstrong Ltd).

In any workroom where there is :

1 Lead, arsenic or other poisonous substances giving rise to dust or fumes
2 A process giving rise to siliceous or asbestos dust, as prescribed by regulation by the Secretary of State

then an employee is not permitted to :

1 Eat or drink there, and meals must be taken in a suitable place which the employer is required to provide
2 Remain there during meal or rest times, with the exception of intervals allowed during continuous employment (s64)

Nicholson and Others
v Atlas Steel Foundry & Engineering Co Ltd (1957, House of Lords)

Nicholson was employed in a factory where there was a great deal of dust containing siliceous particles. He died of pneumoconiosis, and his employers admitted that they were in breach of *s*4, since the only ventilation in the workroom came from the doors. They denied, however, that there was any connection between their breach of duty and Nicholson's death. His widow claimed damages for a breach of *s*4.

The court decided that the failure to ventilate properly had exposed Nicholson to a greater degree of risk than would have been the case if the duty imposed under *s*4 had been observed. Pneumoconiosis was a progressive disease and on a balance of probabilities the presence of the siliceous particles had materially contributed to Nicholson's condition. The employers were liable in damages for a breach of *s*4.

Section 4 applies only to cases where the fumes are generated within the factory by reason of the work being carried on.

Brophy *v* J C Bradfield & Co Ltd (1955, Court of Appeal)

Brophy opened the door of a furnace in order to warm himself, but died from carbon monoxide poisoning. He was not acting in the course of his employment when he entered the boiler room, where the furnace was situated.

The court decided that the defendant employers were not liable in damages to the deceased's widow for a breach of *s*4, since the boiler room was not a workroom of the factory and the poisonous gas was not generated in the course of any process or work carried on in the factory. The furnace and boiler had worked without accident for twenty years and, but for interference such as occurred here, it would have continued to work safely.

6:18 SANITARY CONVENIENCES (*s*7)

Sufficient and suitable sanitary conveniences must be provided, maintained, kept clean and effectively lit for the benefit of persons employed in the factory. There must be separate accommodation for persons of either sex, where members of both sexes are employed or are to be employed.

The scale and standard of sanitary conveniences is laid down in the

Sanitary Accommodation Regulations 1938. The general scale is one convenience for every twenty-five workers (men and women being counted separately).

6:19   MEDICAL SUPERVISION (s11)

The Secretary of State may require medical supervision in any factory or class or description of factory in which there is a risk of injury to the health of persons employed there because of:

1   The type of work carried out, which he believes to have caused illness in the past
2   The introduction of new processes or new substances
3   The employment or intended employment of young persons
4   The material that is being brought to the factory for use or handling
5   The changed conditions of work

6:20   PROTECTION OF EYES (s65)

Suitable goggles or effective screens must be provided by the factory occupier to protect the eyes of his employees, where they are engaged in a process specified by the Protection of Eyes Regulations as involving special risk of injury from fragments ejected in the course of that process. The occupier's duty does not extend to employees of independent contractors working in the factory. It is necessary to:

1   Place the goggles so that they are easily accessible by the employee about to use them, or
2   Give clear directions as to where they are stored

The statutory duty is not discharged if goggles, which employees are not in the habit of using, are stored away so that employees are unaware of their location.

The obligation to provide suitable goggles is absolute, but the section does not impose an absolute obligation that the goggles provided shall ensure protection.

K

Daniels v The Ford Motor Co Ltd (1955, Court of Appeal)

In discharge of their statutory duty under what is now s65 of the Factories Act 1961, the defendant employers provided goggles of a type well adapted to the process at which Daniels worked, but they had a tendency to mist over while being worn. Daniels was injured in his right eye by a fragment of metal after removing the goggles in order to clear away the mist that had formed. He sued his employers for damages for a breach of statutory duty.

The court decided that the employee was not entitled to recover damages. The statutory obligation was to provide suitable goggles to protect the wearer's eyes, but this could not be interpreted as meaning that there was an absolute obligation to protect the wearer's eyes. An employer is not guilty of a criminal offence or in breach of a statutory duty if he provides the best adapted goggles available.

6:21 GENERAL STATUTORY PROVISIONS RELATING TO THE WELFARE OF EMPLOYEES

The general provisions concerning welfare in ss57–61 may be varied by the Secretary of State by special regulations. Further, he may make regulations additional to, in substitution for, or by way of variation of the provisions in ss57–61 where required by :

1   The conditions and circumstances of employment
2   The nature of the processes carried on

As with the statutory provisions relating to health discussed above, if the employer is in breach of the obligations imposed, a criminal and a civil action may be brought against him (see 7 : 2 and 7 : 3).

6:21:1   Drinking-water supply (s57)

An adequate supply of wholesome drinking water from the public main or other source approved in writing by the district council must be provided and maintained at suitable points, accessible to all persons. If the water is not laid on, it must be contained in suitable vessels and renewed daily. All practicable steps must be taken to keep both the water and the vessels free from contamination. The district inspector may direct that the supply be clearly marked as "drinking water." Cups or other vessels and facilities for rinsing them must be provided, unless the water is supplied by an upward jet.

6:21:2 *Washing facilities (s58)*

Washing facilities must be provided and maintained in accordance with the following requirements:

1   Soap and clean towels (or other suitable means of cleaning and drying) must be available
2   Clean running hot and cold or warm water must be available
3   The facilities must be conveniently accessible, and in a clean and orderly condition

The Secretary of State, by regulation, may make some different provisions or grant exemption, where compliance is either difficult or unnecessary because of the existence of alternative arrangements.

It was held in Reid *v* The Westerfield Paper Co Ltd (1957, Court of Appeal) that damages could be recovered for a breach of what is now s58, by showing that failure to provide washing facilities required by statute had resulted in the claimant contracting dermatitis.

6:21:3 *Accommodation for clothing (s59)*

Adequate and suitable accommodation for an employee's clothing not worn during working hours must be provided. Reasonably practicable arrangements must be made for drying an employee's clothing.

McCarthy *v* Daily Mirror Newspapers Ltd (1949, Court of Appeal)

McCarthy, a printer's assistant employed in a factory by the defendant company, was provided with a peg on which to hang his outdoor clothing during working hours. He sued his employers for damages for a breach of what is now s59 of the Factories Act 1961 when his clothing was stolen from the peg.

The court decided that the section does not place an absolute obligation on the employers to keep employees' clothing safe, but the risk of theft was an element to be considered in deciding whether the accommodation provided was suitable. The case was remitted to the county court judge for further consideration of this point. What is suitable may depend on the number of employees or the access which employees from other departments have to different departments in the building. It is essentially a question of fact to be dealt with in a common-sense way by taking a broad view of all the circumstances.

6:21:4 Sitting facilities (s60)

Suitable facilities must be provided for employees having reasonable opportunities for sitting down during the course of their employment, without detriment to their work. A seat of suitable design must be provided for an employee who carries out a substantial proportion of his work sitting down, with a foot-rest to support his feet, if needed.

6:21:5 Lifting excessive weights (s72)

A person must not be employed to lift, carry or move any load so heavy that it is likely to cause injury to him. The Secretary of State may make special regulations on this matter.

6:21:6 First aid (s61)

A first-aid box or cupboard, containing first-aid appliances only, must be provided and maintained in a readily accessible position. The minimum contents are prescribed in the First Aid Boxes in Factories Order 1959.

An additional box is required for every additional 150 employees, or fraction of that number. A responsible person must be in charge of the first-aid box:

1   Always readily available during working hours
2   Whose name is displayed in every workroom

If there are more than fifty employees, the person in charge of the first-aid box must be either:

1   A registered or enrolled assistant nurse (defined by the Nurses Act 1957 and the Nurses (Scotland) Act 1951), or
2   A holder of a certificate in first aid issued within the last three years, or otherwise recognised as being qualified in first-aid treatment, by a training organisation (such as the St John Ambulance Association)

Where an ambulance room is provided to ensure the immediate treatment of all injuries, the chief inspector may grant exemption from the first-aid requirements.

SEVEN

Liability Under the Factories Act

THE POSITION AT COMMON LAW REGARDING LIABILITY IS STRAIGHT-forward since the duty to take care clearly rests on the employer, but with statutory liability under the Factories Act 1961 the person responsible is usually the occupier of the factory or in a few cases the owner (see 7:1, 7:2:1, 7:2:6, 7:2:8, 7:2:9, 7:3). In many cases the factory occupier is also the employer, but to use this term instead of factory occupier in discussions on the Act would be a misrepresentation of the true position.

The statutory duties are intended to protect employees under a contract of service, but the individual section of the Act in question must be interpreted to determine whether any other class is covered, such as an independent contractor (see 6:12:2). Any person claiming that the duty imposed by the section has been violated and injury thereby caused, must prove that he is within the class of persons that the section intended to protect.

7:1   IMPORTANCE OF DETERMINING
WHETHER WORK PREMISES ARE A "FACTORY"

If an employee has been injured at work, he may sue his employer and allege a breach of the statutory duty imposed under the Factories Act 1961, in addition to a claim at common law. The Act requires an employer to take safety precautions for the protection of his employees, but only where the work premises constitute a "factory" in law. Consequently it is vital to determine whether work premises are within the definition.

7:1:1   *What is a "factory" for the purposes of the Act?*
A factory is defined by s175(1) as any premises or precincts in which persons are employed in manual labour for the purpose of:

1   Making any article or part of any article, a process whereby "form value" is added to an article
2   Altering, repairing, ornamenting, finishing, cleaning, washing, breaking up or demolishing any article
3   The confinement of animals awaiting slaughter
4   Adapting for sale any article, whereby its original state is altered, which judicial interpretation has held to include:
  (a) Arrangement of flowers into a wreath
  (b) Compression of paper into bales
  (c) Aeration and bottling of beer

(d) Packaging of chocolates into boxes

(e) Separation of the saleable from the unsaleable part of a city's refuse

The courts have held that the following are not covered by the Act:

(a) Cooling or bottling of milk

(b) A pumping station where water is put under pressure

(c) Testing and certifying of cables and anchors

The work must be carried out on the premises concerned:

1   By way of trade, or

2   For the purpose of gain

and the employer must have a right of access or control.

7:1:2   Meaning of "manual labour"

There are a number of phrases and terms in s175(1) that require closer examination and explanation. The definition of a factory must be satisfied in all respects before the Act applies. Work premises will be within the definition of a factory, provided the purpose for which the place is used is substantially the employment of persons in manual labour, but not otherwise. For example, where a porter is employed in a chemist's shop to carry out manual work, the shop does not become a factory for the purposes of the Act. Where work with the hands is the main activity it is manual labour, even though the degree of physical energy and strength expended is not considerable, as in sitting down to pack sweets into boxes for retail sale. A back room behind a shop may be a factory, though only one person is engaged in manual labour, provided the labour is the main purpose for which the room is used.

J & F Stone Lighting & Radio Ltd v Haygarth (1966, House of Lords)

The company as occupier of a shop and workroom was charged with offences against the Factories Act 1961, upon information preferred by Haygarth, a factory inspector, in that it did not keep an abstract of the Act posted at the principal entrance of the factory, and did not provide a readily accessible first-aid box. It was contended that the premises were not a factory within s175(1) and that consequently the employers were not bound by its provisions. An electrical business was carried on in the shop and in the workroom an engineer repaired radio and television sets, a task requiring some degree of skill and care.

The court decided that a person working for most of his time with his hands is employed in manual labour, even though technical knowledge is also essential. To limit the operation of the Act to unskilled manual labour, to the exclusion of skilled manual labour, would prevent the protections embodied in the Factories Act from operating in places where its application is most appropriate. The employer was responsible for non-compliance with the provisions of the Act.

7 : 1 : 3   *Explanation of the phrase*
"by way of trade or for the purposes of gain"
The two phrases must be taken separately and they represent two distinct purposes. *Trade* is not confined to the sale of goods; it includes the provision of services for payment, and so a repair works for public transport vehicles may be a factory. Premises in a residential area were held to have been converted into a factory when used by a consulting engineer for tests on materials used in building construction. The financial gain from these activities was indirect, taking the form of fees paid by builders seeking the engineer's advice (Hendon Corporation v Stanger (1948, Court of Appeal)).

Premises occupied for building and engineering operations undertaken by the Crown or by a public or municipal authority in the course of providing a public service, are within the Act, though the work is not carried out by way of trade or for the purposes of gain, as it is in a commercial undertaking. It would be illogical to exclude this area of activity, even though it is not strictly within the terminology of s175(1). Workshops in prisons, hospitals, or technical colleges are outside the scope of the Act. Consequently there is not a statutory duty to fence dangerous machinery there.

7 : 1 : 4   *Are other work premises*
within the precincts of a factory part of the factory?
A place sited within the factory precincts is not a part of that factory if it is used solely for a purpose different to the processes carried on in the factory (s175(6)). Examples include:

1   The residence of some official employed at the factory
2   Office buildings in the factory

3   A canteen used by administrative staff only, within the factory premises

However, a canteen within factory precincts forms part of the factory if used to feed and entertain factory employees, this being a purpose incidental to the processes of manufacture carried on in the factory (Luttman v Imperial Chemical Industries Ltd (1955)).

An area separate and distinct from the factory may be considered as a separate factory if, in the circumstances of the case, it is within the definition of a factory.

To determine whether an area within the precincts of a factory is to be considered as part of that factory, it is necessary to compare the processes being carried out in the two separate places.

Walsh v Allweather Mechanical Grouting Co Ltd (1959, Court of Appeal)

Walsh, an employee of a firm of contractors, sustained an eye injury while breaking up and re-laying concrete on an apron adjoining a hangar in an airfield. He claimed damages from the defendant company, as occupiers of the factory, for a breach of the Protection of Eyes Regulations 1938, made under s49 of the Factories Act 1937, which required goggles to be supplied to persons working in a factory.

The court decided that the hangar was a factory, since aircraft were assembled and tested there. The apron was not part of that factory, since it was being used at the time of the accident for a process different from that carried on in the hangar. The court rejected the claim that the apron was a separate factory on its own. Thus Walsh's claim failed.

Thurogood v Van Den Berghs & Jergens Ltd (1951, Court of Appeal)

Thurogood was injured while testing a fan in a separate building within the precincts of the defendants' factory. The building was used for maintenance work on plant and equipment from the factory. He claimed damages from the defendants for a breach of the statutory duty imposed by s14(1) of the Factories Act for failing to fence dangerous machinery securely.

The court decided that the maintenance workshop was used for the processes carried on in the factory. Consequently the fan was a piece of machinery that required fencing. The defendants were liable to the plaintiff for damages for the injury caused by failure to fence the fan properly.

The administrative offices attached to a factory may form part of the factory, if the processes carried out in the offices do not differ from those carried out in the factory itself.

Powley v Bristol Siddeley Engines Ltd (1965)

Powley was employed by the defendants at premises most of which comprised a factory producing aircraft engines, but there was also an administration block within the precincts housing technical staff. While walking through the courtyard of the administration block, in the course of his employment, Powley fell on some ice and was injured. He sued his employers for a breach of the Factories Act 1961 s28(1), which provides that all steps shall be kept free, so far as is reasonably practicable, from any substance likely to cause persons to slip.

The court decided that the processes carried out in the administration block where aircraft engines were designed and developed were incidental to the making of the engines. Consequently the administration block was a part of the factory and s175(6) was inapplicable. The defendant company was in breach of the statutory duty imposed by s28, but Powley was personally responsible for the accident to the extent of 50 per cent.

7:1:5 *Extension of the definition of a "factory"*
The definition of a factory in s175(1) is extended by s175(2) which states that certain premises are to be deemed factories for the purposes of the Act, even though they may not be covered by s175(1). A list of these premises follows, which has been given in full mainly for the purpose of reference:

1   Any yard or dry dock in which ships or vessels are constructed, reconstructed, repaired, refitted, finished or broken up
2   Any premises in which the business of sorting any articles is carried on as a preliminary to work carried on in any factory
3   Any premises in which the business of washing or filling bottles or containers or packing articles is carried on incidentally to the purposes of any factory
4   Any premises in which the business of hooking, plaiting or packing of yarn or cloth is carried on
5   Any laundry carried on as ancillary to another business
6   Any premises in which the construction, reconstruction or

repair of locomotives, vehicles or other plant for use for transport purposes is carried on as ancillary to a transport undertaking or other industrial or commercial undertaking

7   Any premises in which printing is carried on by way of trade or for purposes of gain or incidentally to another business so carried on

8   Any premises in which the making, adaptation, or repair of dresses, scenery, or properties is carried on incidentally to the production, by way of trade or for purposes of gain, of cinematograph films or theatrical performances

9   Any premises in which the business of making or mending nets is carried on incidentally to the fishing industry

10   Any premises in which mechanical power is used in connection with the making or repair of articles of wood or metal incidentally to any business carried on by way of trade or for purposes of gain

11   Any premises in which the production of cinematograph films is carried on by way of trade or for purposes of gain; but the employment at any such premises of theatrical performers, within the meaning of the Theatrical Employers Registration Act 1925, and of attendants on such theatrical performers shall not be deemed to be employment in a factory

12   Any premises in which articles are made or prepared incidentally to the carrying on of building operations or works of enginering construction, not being premises in which such operations or works are being carried on

13   Any premises used for the storage of gas in a gasholder having a storage capacity of not less than 5000ft^3

7:2   CRIMINAL LIABILITY FOR OFFENCES UNDER THE ACT

The factory occupier is the person most likely to be criminally liable for infringement of the various provisions of the Act. He may escape liability by showing that some other person is responsible, such as the owner of a tenement factory. Some attention has been given to the liability of the employee himself, since the duties imposed upon him to act in a responsible manner are expressed in general terms and will be applicable in a multitude of circumstances. Further, the employee's offence may be relied upon by the employer to negative his own civil law liability for damages, if he is sued by an employee whose injuries have been caused by his own folly. The person hiring out or selling machinery may be liable to a fine for infringement of the provisions of s17 (see 6:11).

7:2:1 Liability of the factory occupier

The duties and liabilities imposed by the Act usually fall upon the factory occupier, and if he fails to discharge them he may be criminally liable (s155(1)). The word "occupier" is not defined in the Act, but it has been interpreted judicially as meaning "the person who runs the factory, regulates and controls the work that is done there." This person is usually the employer. In relation to the duties imposed by the Act, several persons may be occupiers, for different purposes, of the same premises.

7:2:2 Liability of the owner or hirer of machinery (s163)

The factory occupier may use machinery moved by mechanical power, but the machinery may be owned by or hired by some other person. The owner or hirer is regarded as the factory occupier in respect of any offence, whether criminal or civil, committed under the Act against one of his own employees.

Whalley v Briggs Motor Bodies Ltd (1954)

Whalley, an employee of T A Hanson, a firm of contractors, was working in a factory occupied by the defendant company. He injured his eyes while breaking up concrete with a pneumatic pick, which was either the property of, or hired by, the independent contractors. Neither his employers nor the factory occupiers had provided any goggles as protection. Whalley sued the defendants, as factory occupiers, for damages, alleging a breach of the statutory duty imposed by s49 of the Protection of Eyes Regulations 1938.

The court decided that Whalley was employed by Hanson as far as the pneumatic pick was concerned, since it was either owned by or hired to him. Hanson was deemed to be the occupier of the defendants' factory in respect of any offence arising out of the use of the pick, by virtue of the provisions of what is now s163 of the Factories Act 1961. Consequently the defendants were not liable.

7:2:3 Liability of the factory employee

The employee upon whom a duty is expressly imposed by the Factories Act is guilty of an offence if he fails to carry out that duty. In such cases the factory occupier will not be liable, unless it is proved that he failed to take all reasonable steps to prevent contravention of the statutory duty (s155(2)). One of the most important duties expressly imposed on factory employees is embodied in s143(1), which provides that they must not wilfully interfere with or misuse any appliance or other thing provided in pursuance of the Act, for securing the health, safety or welfare of employees in the factory. Section 143 covers intentional interference or misuse, in the sense of perverse meddling with an appliance. By relying on s155(2) the occupier can avoid being held solely responsible for a wrong committed by an employee, for which that employee is liable, under s143, for the penalties specified in s156 (see 7 : 2 : 12).

Wright v Ford Motor Co Ltd (1966)

A gate set in one side of a 4ft high fence was forced open by an employee who could not be identified. The fence guarded a machine with a nip, which was dangerous within the meaning of s14(1) of the Factories Act. Normally the machine would not work unless the gate was locked, nor could it be started while the gate was open. Reilly, an employee, went inside on finding the gate open on the assumption that the machine would not start, but he caught his foot in the nip. Information was laid against the employers by Wright, a factory inspector, for contravention of s14(1) in failing properly to fence dangerous machinery.

The court decided that the combined effect of s143(1) and s155(2) provided the Ford Motor Co Ltd with a defence to any offence that they had committed under s14(1). A factory occupier is not liable for contravention of an obligation imposed on an employee under s143(1). The person criminally liable for a breach of that section was the unidentified person who opened the gate.

7:2:4 *Employee's duty to use any appliance provided (s143(1))*
When the employer provides an appliance for securing the health or safety of his employees, then under s143(1) the employee is obliged to use it. The obligation imposed on the employee is absolute, and if he fails to use any appliance provided, he will be in breach of the section. The employee is not liable for failing to use an appliance if the employer has not instructed him how to use it correctly.

Norris v Syndi Manufacturing Co (1952, Court of Appeal)

Norris, a tool setter employed by the defendant company, lost the top joints of three fingers while testing a power press from which the guard had been removed. The machine was inadvertently started during the testing. The defendants had acquiesced in Norris carrying out his work without the guard, but he had never been told not to use it. He had been instructed to replace it after testing and before operation. Norris sued his employers for damages for a breach of what is now s14 and s16 of the Factories Act 1961, for failure to provide a safe system of work. The employers alleged that Norris acted in breach of his duty under what is now s143(1), and this fact was used by them as a defence to an action for damages at civil law.

The court decided that Norris was in breach of s143(1). Thus the damages awarded to him against his employers must be reduced by one fifth. The words of that section imposed an absolute duty on the employee to use the guard provided, and the employee was not excused from observance of his duty because the employer had acquiesced in the work being carried out without the guard.

If the employer encourages his employee not to use a guard provided, the employer's responsibility is increased and the employee's responsibility is lessened. But the employee's responsibility is not altogether removed. If under the Act the guard must be used, the employee must use it whatever the view of the employer, unless the employer forbids its use altogether.

7:2:5 Employees must not
endanger themselves or other employees (s143(2))
There is a further duty imposed on factory employees not to do anything wilfully and without reasonable cause that is likely to endanger themselves or others. For an offence to be committed under this provision, the employee must be guilty of negligence in not foreseeing that his actions will cause harm to himself and others.

Ginty v Belmont Building Supplies Ltd (1959)

Ginty, an employee of the defendant company, was stripping asbestos from a factory roof when he fell and was injured. Duckboards were provided and placed against a wall where Ginty could see them, but he did not use them. Ginty sued his employers for damages, alleging a breach of what is now s29 of the Factories Act, in that they had failed, as far as was practicable, to provide him with a safe place of work with a secure foothold and handhold, while he was working at a height of over 6ft 6in.

The court decided that it was the employer's obligation to provide the duckboards but both employer and employee were obliged to ensure that they were used, and they both failed to carry out that duty. The employee contravened what is now s143(1), but he was in breach of s143(2) also, since he acted wilfully in disobeying instructions, and without reasonable cause by stepping on to the roof without using a duckboard. Ginty had acted in a manner that was likely to endanger his safety and in those circumstances it was impossible to impose any liability on the employer. The employee's wrongful conduct was used by the employer as a defence to a civil law claim for damages.

Even if the immediate and direct cause of the accident is the employee's wrongful act, he may not be the only person responsible for the accident so caused. It must be determined whether the employer was a contributory cause by acting contrary to statute in a manner which went beyond the employee's wrongful act, as by:

1 Failing to give proper instructions on the use of appliances provided
2 Employing inexperienced workers
3 Acquiescing in the wrongful acts of his employees

7:2:6 *Special defence available to the factory occupier under s161(1)*
If, despite the provisions of s155(2) casting liability on an employee in the circumstances set out in s143, the factory occupier is prosecuted for an offence under the Act, then he may use s161(1) as a protection.

This section provides that a factory occupier charged with an offence under the Act may be relieved of liability by:

1 Bringing the actual offender before the courts, that is, the employee or other person
2 Proving that:
  (a) He used all due diligence to enforce compliance with the Act, and
  (b) The offence was committed without his consent, connivance or wilful default

7:2:7 *Liability imposed on the owner of a tenement factory (s121)*
A tenement factory is defined by s176(1) as any premises where mechanical power from any prime mover, within the curtilage of the premises, is

distributed for use in manufacturing processes to different parts of the same premises occupied by different persons, so that those parts constitute, in law, separate factories.

The owner of a tenement factory, whether or not he is the occupier, is responsible for contravention of the following provisions of the Act:

1   Cleanliness, space, temperature, ventilation, lighting, drainage of floors and sanitary conveniences (see 6 : 15–18)
2   The general provisions regarding welfare (see 6 : 21)
3   Provision and maintenance of fencing and safety appliances; the construction, maintenance, testing and examination of machinery or plant; the construction and maintenance of floors, passages and stairs (see 6 : 8–12)
4   The removal of dust and fumes (see 6 : 17 : 4)
5   The notification and investigation of accidents and industrial diseases (see 6 : 7)
6   Notices fixing the hours of employment for women and young persons (see 4 : 1 : 1)
7   The posting of abstracts and notices (see 6 : 5)

The owner is not responsible for any contravention of those provisions arising from the use of any fencing, appliances, machinery or plant where the matter is outside his control. In such cases the occupier is the person responsible.

A magistrates' court may order the occupier to allow the owner to carry out any work, test or examination required under the Act where the occupier is preventing fulfilment of those duties (s120, schedule 2 para 7).

7 : 2 : 8   *Liability where part*
of a building is let as a separate factory (s122)
Where part of a building is let by the owner to another person as a separate factory (not being a tenement factory) then in general the occupier of that separate factory must comply with the requirements of the Act. There are exceptions to this general principle; thus the owner is liable for any contravention of the provisions relating to:

1   Sanitary conveniences, where they are used in common by several tenants
2   Hoists and lifts, in so far as the provisions relate to matters within his control

Where machinery or plant belongs to or is supplied to the occupier, he is liable for any contravention of the provisions of the Act relating to use of chains, ropes and lifting tackle, cranes and other lifting machines, steam receivers, steam containers and air receivers. In other cases the owner is liable unless the contravention is outside his control.

7:2:9 *Liability for the rest of a building*
when only a part is let as a separate factory (s122)
Part of a building may be let off as a separate factory without being part of a tenement factory. The owner of the building is responsible for compliance with the Act in respect of the following matters in any part of the building used for the purposes of a separate factory but not included in it:

1   Cleanliness and lighting
2   Prime movers, transmission machinery, hoists, and lifts
3   The construction and maintenance of, and keeping free from obstruction and slippery substances, all floors, passages and stairs
4   Cranes and lifting machines, chains, ropes and lifting tackle
5   Steam boilers and steam receivers, steam containers and air receivers

7:2:10   *Liability of a director,*
manager, secretary or other company officer (s155(5))
Where an offence under the Act, committed by a company, is proved to have been committed with the consent or connivance of, or facilitated by, a director, manager, secretary or other officer of the company, the officer is liable in addition to the company and may be punished accordingly.

7:2:11   *Liability of an agent, servant or worker (s160(1))*
An agent, servant or worker or other person is guilty of an offence and liable to a fine for an act or default for which he was personally responsible as if he were the occupier, owner or other person normally responsible for contravention of the provisions of the Act.

7:2:12   *Sanctions imposed*
for contravention of the provisions of the Act (ss155–7)
Where a person is found guilty of committing an offence under the Factories Act, the penalty is usually stipulated in the particular section that

has been contravened. In the absence of an express penalty he will be liable
to:

1   A fine not exceeding £15 if he is an employee; in other cases
     a fine not exceeding £60
2   A maximum fine of £15 for every day upon which the contra-
     vention continues after conviction
3   If the offence is likely to cause death or bodily injury, and
     where an express penalty is not provided for, s156(1)(2)
     stipulates a fine:
(a) Not exceeding £75 in the case of an employee
(b) Not exceeding £300 for other persons

The occupier or owner may be ordered to take steps to remedy the situation, instead of or in addition to a fine. There is also a maximum fine of
£10 for each day during which the situation is not remedied after the
time stipulated in the court order (s157).

7:3 ESTABLISHING CIVIL LIABILITY AGAINST A FACTORY OCCUPIER FOR A BREACH OF HIS STATUTORY DUTIES

Although the Factories Act sets out the duties of a factory occupier in
great detail, the question of civil liability is not dealt with, and it is necessary to determine whether such liability can be implied from the terms of
the statute.

It is clearly established that breach of the statutory provisions relating
to the safety of employees does give rise to an actionable right and the
cases discussed in Chapter 6 illustrate this point.

"Where a statute provides for the performance by certain persons of a
particular duty and someone, belonging to a class of persons for whose
benefit and protection the statute imposes the duty, is injured by failure
to perform it . . . an action by the person so injured will lie against the
person who has failed to perform the duty" (Lord Justice Vaughan
Williams). The employer is also civilly liable for a breach of s17 to the
employee injured, to the exclusion of the party selling or hiring out the
machines. The preponderance of legal authority is strongly in favour of
allowing a civil action against the employer for non-observance of the
health provisions in part 1 of the Act (see 6:15–6:19). In the case of
Nicholson and Others v Atlas Steel Foundry & Engineering Co Ltd
(see 6:17:4) the House of Lords seemed to assume that a civil remedy

was available to the widow and children of a deceased employee, and they confined their attention to other issues. This case also shows that a civil action for damages may be maintained, whether physical injury or an industrial disease is caused by the breach of a statutory duty.

A civil action by the employee for violation of the welfare provisions in part 3 of the Act (see 6:21) may be inappropriate in many cases, since it will not be easy to show any personal loss or injury, where, for example, there is a breach of s57 dealing with the supply of drinking water. On the other hand, some of the provisions in part 3 are concerned essentially with health and safety. Consequently a civil action for damages may be maintained (see 6:21:3, McCarthy v Daily Mirror Newspapers Ltd).

It has been shown in the last section that a factory occupier may escape civil liability in damages by establishing that some other party is at fault, such as an owner or the person hiring machinery or the employee himself (see 7:2:2 and 7:2:5).

7:3:1 Persons to whom the occupier is liable
Where the section imposing a duty on the occupier states that it is owed to "any person," those two words cannot be of entirely general application. A policeman who enters the factory in pursuit of a wrongdoer, or a fireman who enters to put out a fire, is not covered by the section although he is a "person" who is also "working" at the factory. The true distinction is between those who are at work for the purposes of the factory and those who are not.

Hartley v Mayoh & Co (1954, Court of Appeal)

A fireman, called to a fire at a factory occupied by the defendant firm, was electrocuted because of the unlawful transposition of switches. His widow sued the defendant firm for damages for a breach of the statutory duty, set out in regulations made under s60(1) of the Factories Act 1937, which refers to the protection of "persons employed."

The court decided that the words "persons employed" did not sufficiently extend the ambit of the Act to cover a fireman who comes to the premises to fight a fire, whether called by the occupier or anyone else. Consequently the widow's claim failed.

7:3:2 Injury must have been
caused by non-compliance with a statutory duty
The employee's injury must be of the kind that could have been prevented

by taking the precautions imposed by statute. If injury occurs despite the observance of all precautions required by statute, then a civil claim for damages cannot be maintained.

Carroll v Andrew Barclay & Sons Ltd (1948, House of Lords)

While operating a lathe, Carroll was injured when a revolving belt broke and lashed out over a 5ft high protective fence. It was not unusual for a belt to break, but it had never caused injury to anyone outside the protective fencing. Carroll sued for damages, alleging a breach of s13, which requires every part of the transmission machinery to be securely fenced.

The court decided that the obligation to fence securely under s13 is not breached if there is an accidental breakdown which makes part of the machinery fly out and cause injury. All machinery is potentially dangerous if it breaks up. The Act does not protect employees against dangers of that kind, but only against dangers that exist while the machine is in operation. The claim for damages failed.

7:3:3 *Civil liability for reasonably foreseeable injuries*

There is liability at civil law even though the employee's injury is not of the type that the statutory provisions are designed to prevent, provided the injury was the reasonably foreseeable result of the factory occupier's non-compliance with the provisions of the Act. The duty to fence dangerous machinery imposed by s14(1) was not intended to protect an employee from injury while engaged in an act of extreme folly, such as stalking a pigeon into a part of the factory which the employee is not authorised to enter, as in Uddin v Associated Portland Cement (see 6:9:3). Nonetheless, the injured employee was entitled to damages for the injury suffered as a result of leaning over the dangerous machinery to reach the pigeon, since it was reasonably foreseeable that someone would act in this way at some point in time, whatever his motive for so doing might be.

7:3:4 *Burden of proving a*
statutory duty and its breach lies on the employee

An employee claiming damages for his injuries must prove that:

1   A statutory duty was owed to him by the person being sued, usually his employer, and
2   His injuries were caused by a breach of that duty

The employee must show that on the balance of probabilities the breach of duty materially contributed to his injury. The employee need not show exactly how the injury occurred; it suffices if his explanation of the events is the more likely version of the truth. The employer's obligations are well summarised by Lord Justice Willmer: "Employers are not insurers; they are under a duty . . . to take certain measures to protect their workmen, but a workman who seeks to recover must prove his case. The workman in the present case has not proved how the accident occurred. The court has to speculate and this is not sufficient."

In exceptional cases, however, the employee is entitled to damages if he establishes a breach of duty by the employer which resulted in the accident, even though there is considerable uncertainty as to the precise manner in which the accident occurred.

Allen v Aeroplane & Motor Aluminium Castings Ltd (1965, Court of Appeal)

Allen's finger was injured in the nip of dangerous machinery. The accident would not have occurred if the machinery had been securely fenced as required by s14(1) but it was not entirely clear how the accident happened.

The court decided that the defendant employers were liable in damages to the plaintiff. "It is often said that a plaintiff who cannot give an acceptable version of the accident which befell him or her really cannot ask the court to start to find where liability lies. But this is an exceptional case; it is one where the facts show clearly that there was a breach of duty, and they show equally clearly that it was because of that breach, because of the dangerous nip, that this accident occurred." (Lord Justice Sellars)

If an employee is seeking to prove that his injury was caused by the employer's breach of statutory duty, the issue may turn upon the employer's failure to provide a protective device.

McWilliams v Arrol & Co Ltd (1962, House of Lords)

A steel erector was killed by a fall at a shipbuilding yard. His widow claimed damages from the occupiers of the working premises for a breach of what is now s29 of the Factories Act, for failing to provide a safe place of employment (see 6:12). It was alleged that the deceased should have been provided with a safety belt.

The court decided that to establish her claim the widow must prove that the occupiers were in breach of a statutory duty to provide a safety belt which would have been used by the deceased thereby preventing the accident. The court did not accept that the deceased would have used a safety belt even if one had been available, consequently his death was not caused by the occupiers breach of statutory duty.

7:3:5 Injury to an employee acting outside the scope of his employment
The employer is not vicariously liable for breach of a statutory duty if the employee injured was acting outside the scope of his employment at the time of the breach.

Napieralski v Curtis (Contractors) Ltd (1959)

Napieralski, a joiner employed by the defendants, operated a circular saw which was not securely fenced as required by s14(1). After clocking off one evening, he was injured by the saw while voluntarily helping another employee to make a table for his own personal use. The employer allowed employees to engage in private activities on his premises after working hours. Napieralski sued his employers for damages in respect of his injury, alleging a breach of the statutory duty imposed by s14.

The court decided that the defendant employers did not owe a duty to Napieralski under s14, since at the time of the accident he was not working on the premises under a contract of service as required by the section.

7:3:6 Injury to an employee failing to carry out his duties
The employer is not liable in damages to an employee who is injured through failure to carry out a duty delegated to him, the performance of which will ensure his own safety.

Vincent v Southern Railway Co (1927, House of Lords)

Vincent and an assistant were instructed by the defendant employers to repair some signalling apparatus. While working on the railway track Vincent and the assistant, who acted as a look-out for oncoming trains, stepped on to the adjacent track to avoid an oncoming train. Both men were killed by a train running along the track upon which they were standing for safety.

The court decided that the foreman's widow was not entitled to damages from the railway company for a breach of the statutory duty imposed by rule 9 of the Prevention of Accidents Rules 1902. The employers had not omitted to discharge their statutory duty of providing a look-out while work was in progress on a railway track in use. Death was caused by the negligence of the two employees working on the line or Vincent's failure properly to instruct his assistant on the duties of a look-out.

7:3:7 Carelessness by the employee may preclude a claim for damages

It is open to the employer to show that, even if he had fulfilled his statutory duty by taking the safety precautions required, they would not have been observed by the employee, and that consequently the real cause of the accident was the employee's carelessness and not the employer's breach of statutory duty.

Nolan v Dental Manufacturing Co Ltd (1958)

Nolan, a tool setter, sued his employer for damages for a breach of statutory duty after being injured by a chip that flew off a carborundum wheel on which he was sharpening his tools.

The court decided that the defendant employer was not liable, for even if goggles had been provided, as required by the Protection of Eyes Regulations 1938 and what is now s65 of the Factories Act 1961, there was no evidence that they would have been used by Nolan. It would have required strict orders and supervision to ensure that goggles were used in the factory when tools were sharpened.

The defendant employers were in breach of their common law duty not to expose Nolan to unnecessary risk, since they had failed to provide goggles and give strict orders to ensure their use, backed by supervision to make their orders effective.

7:3:8 Defence of contributory negligence

Where an employer is in breach of either his statutory or common law duty, he may seek to reduce the damages payable to an employee who is injured in consequence of that breach, by establishing that the employee was also at fault (see 6:9:1, Smith v Chesterfield & District Co-operative Society Ltd). The Law Reform (Contributory Negligence) Act 1945 provides that, where an employee suffers personal injury or loss of life as a result partly of his own fault and partly of his employer's fault, a claim for damages by the employee or his representatives shall not be defeated, but the damages recoverable from the employer shall be reduced as the court thinks just and equitable, to reflect the employee's share of responsibility for the damage. "Fault" is defined by s4 as covering any negligence, breach of statutory duty or other act or omission giving rise to tortious liability.

When the employee fails to exercise care. Failure by the employer to discharge the statutory duty of care imposed upon him, for example, to guard dangerous machinery, does not prevent him from pleading that his employee was guilty of contributory negligence, if the accident could have been avoided by the injured employee using the ordinary degree of care to be expected in the circumstances.

Cakebread v Hopping Bros (Whetstone) Ltd (1947, Court of Appeal)

Statutory regulations required that a guard on a circular saw should be so positioned that work might be carried out with the minimum amount of risk. Cakebread, a skilled and experienced woodworker, objected to this positioning of the guard, on the ground that it impeded his view of work he was doing. After adjusting the guard he sustained an injury while using the saw. He sued his employers for damages.

The court decided that the defendant employers were in continuing breach of their statutory duty, since, to the knowledge of their foreman, the guard had not been placed in the best position possible to prevent injury to an employee using it. The damages were apportioned equally between the parties, however, since Cakebread had not exercised that degree of care for his own safety to be expected from a prudent employee with his knowledge of the dangers involved.

The employer may be held liable for not providing the proper equipment to complete the task in hand, with the result that an employee is injured. Damages may be reduced, however, to reflect the employee's contributory negligence, if he should have expressed his dissatisfaction with inadequate equipment and refused to use it (see 6:12, Ross v Associated Portland Cement Manufacturers Ltd).

Instructing employees on the use of safety devices. A recent House of Lords decision suggests that while it may not be necessary for an employer relying on the defence of contributory negligence to show that he has instructed a craftsman on how to avoid obvious dangers connected with his work, as in Cakebread's case, nonetheless instruction should be given on the need to observe statutory regulations where the danger is not apparent.

Boyle v Kodak Ltd (1969, House of Lords)

Boyle claimed damages for injuries sustained while climbing a ladder which was resting on a rail running round the top of a 30ft high tank. He was attempting to lash the ladder at the top, so that he could then use it to paint the top of the tank. Building regulations imposed a statutory duty on the employer to lash the ladder in such circumstances. A staircase running around the outside of the tank could have been used by Boyle in order to lash the ladder, without causing any risk of personal injury, but he had not been instructed so to act.

The court decided that damages should be apportioned equally between employer and employee. The employer was in breach of his absolute duty under the regulations since the ladder being used by Boyle was not lashed. There was a safe method of doing this by using the staircase, but Boyle had not been instructed to use it. Thus the employer had not done everything reasonably possible to ensure compliance with the statutory regulations. Boyle was also in breach of his absolute statutory duty in not using the available staircase on his own initiative.

In similar circumstances arising in the future, if an employer wishes to rely on the defence of contributory negligence his position will be strengthened considerably if he can establish that the employee deliberately failed to observe statutory duties of which he was made aware.

There are some cases where the damage caused is solely the responsibility of the employee. The employer may then claim 100 per cent contributory negligence (see 6:10:3, Horne v Lec Refrigeration Ltd, and 7:2:5, Ginty v Belmont Building Supplies Ltd).

EIGHT

Safety, Health and Welfare in Shops and Offices

HEALTH, SAFETY AND WELFARE IN SHOPS AND OFFICES ARE GOVERNED
by the provisions of a number of statutes, principally the Offices, Shops
and Railway Premises Act 1963, which sets out detailed provisions basically
similar to those found in the Factories Act 1961. References to the Secretary of State in this chapter may be taken to mean the Secretary of State
for Employment.

8:1 PROVISIONS FOR HEALTH AND WELFARE
(OFFICES, SHOPS AND RAILWAY PREMISES ACT 1963)

These provisions are basically similar to those in the Factories Act 1961,
but there are some differences and for clarity and completeness a summary
of the relevant sections has been given.

8:1:1 *Cleanliness (s4)*

Shops and office premises and all furniture, furnishings and fittings in such
premises must be kept in a clean state. No dirt or refuse must accumulate
in places where employees work, or in places passed by employees in the
course of their work. Floors and steps must be cleaned at least once a week
by washing, sweeping (if effective and suitable) or some other method.
Additional regulations may be made by the Secretary of State for premises
covered by the Act.

8:1:2 *Overcrowding (s5)*

A room in which work is being carried out must not be so overcrowded
as to cause risk of injury to the health of persons working there. In determining whether a room is overcrowded, consideration will be given to the
following matters, among others:

1   The number of persons who may be expected to be working
     in the room at any time
2   The space occupied by furniture, furnishings and fittings,
     machinery, plant, equipment and appliances

The minimum amount of space per person is 40ft^2 or 400ft^3, but this
provision does not apply to a room which members of the public are
invited to enter, and those parts of a shop that are used for selling goods
to members of the public are excluded.

8:1:3 *Temperature (s6)*
The provisions of s6 correspond to s3 of the Factories Act 1961 (see
6:17:1). The provisions of s6 do not apply to an office or shop to which
members of the public resort, where it is not reasonably practicable to
maintain a reasonable temperature, or where to do so would cause goods
kept there to deteriorate.

8:1:4 *Ventilation (s7)*
Effective and suitable provision must be made for securing and maintaining the ventilation of every room where persons work, by the circulation
of adequate supplies of fresh air or artificially purified air.

The Secretary of State may by regulation prescribe for premises to
which the Act applies a standard of adequate ventilation which must be
conformed with.

8:1:5 *Eating facilities (s15)*
Suitable and sufficient facilities for eating meals must be provided for
employees who choose or who are obliged to eat meals on the premises. If
they go outside for their meals, there is no obligation to provide facilities.

8:1:6 *Lighting; sanitary conveniences; washing facilities*
The provisions of the Offices, Shops and Railway Premises Act 1963 in
respect of lighting (s8), sanitary conveniences (s9) and washing facilities
(s10) are substantially the same as the corresponding provisions in the
Factories Act 1961 and are dealt with respectively in 6:17:2, 6:18 and
6:21:2.

8:1:7 *Drinking water (s11)*
An adequate supply of wholesome drinking water must be provided and
maintained at suitable places conveniently accessible to employees. If it
is not piped it must be contained in suitable vessels and renewed at least
once daily. All practicable steps must be taken to prevent the water and
the vessels containing it from being contaminated. If water is not supplied
by a jet, drinking vessels must be provided which:

1   Can be discarded after use, the supply of such vessels to be
     renewed when necessary, or
2   Can be rinsed in clean water, if they cannot be discarded
     after use

8:1:8 Accommodation for clothing (s12)

Suitable and sufficient provision must be made to allow employees to hang up, or otherwise accommodate, clothing not worn during working hours. Reasonably practicable arrangements must be made for the drying of such clothing.

There are similar provisions regarding special clothing worn by employees during working hours which they do not take home.

8:1:9 Sitting facilities (s13, s14)

Where employees have, in the course of their work, a reasonable opportunity for sitting without detriment to that work, suitable sitting facilities must be provided in conveniently accessible places. This provision covers shop premises to which customers are invited, and at least one seat for every three employees must be provided (s13).

Where all or the substantial part of an employee's work can be done while sitting, each employee must be provided with a seat suitable for him, and a foot-rest if he cannot do without one.

8:2 PROVISIONS FOR SAFETY

Many of the provisions securing safety in the 1963 Act are similar to those in the Factories Act 1961. The regulations relating to floors, passages and stairs in s16 are substantially the same as the provisions of s28 of the Factories Act 1961 (see 6:12:3). As regards the fencing of exposed parts of machinery, the provisions of s17(1) and (2) correspond to s14(1) and (2) of the Factories Act 1961 (see 6:8:2). Section 17(3) corresponds to s15(1)(a) (see 6:10). Section 17(4) corresponds to s16 (see 6:10:1–3). Section 17(5) corresponds to s15(2) (see 6:10). Section 18 provides that a young person under the age of eighteen shall not clean any machinery, if he is exposed to risk of injury from a moving part or adjacent machinery.

J H Dewhurst Ltd v Coventry Corporation (1969)

A bacon slicer in the back room of a butcher's shop was used by the manager and another employee, a boy aged sixteen. The bacon was sliced by a cutting blade that rotated when a handle was turned manually. When the machine was cleaned the guard protecting the blade had to be removed. The blade could be cleaned while in position without being removed, by exposing one half of the cutting blade for cleaning, then turning the handle to expose the other half for cleaning. While cleaning the machine in the manager's absence, the boy cut off the tip of a finger.

An information was preferred against the employers, alleging contravention of s18(1) of the Offices, Shops and Railway Premises Act 1963.

The court decided that the bacon slicer was "a moving part of machinery" and the sixteen-year-old boy cleaning the blade was exposed to injury contrary to s18. The occupier of the premises was guilty of an offence, unless he could show that the accident could not have been prevented by taking reasonable care, and could not have been reasonably foreseen.

Section 67 provides that the occupier has a good defence to a charge of contravening a provision of the 1963 Act, if he can prove that he used all due diligence to secure compliance with the provision. In this case, active steps had been taken by notices and periodic visits of inspectors to focus the attention of employees on the requirements of s18, but the occupier should have realised that the method of cleaning involved use of the machine handle while the employee's hand was in close proximity to the blade. In those circumstances there was a failure to exercise the due diligence required by s67 and the defence failed.

8:2:1 Training and supervision
of persons working at dangerous machines (s19)
An employee must not work at a machine prescribed by order of the Secretary of State as being of a dangerous character, unless:

1   He has been fully instructed about its dangers and the precautions to be observed
2   He is either:
   (a) Sufficiently trained in working at the machine, or
   (b) Adequately supervised by a person with knowledge and experience

This section corresponds to s21 of the Factories Act 1961, but it is not limited in its operation to the training and supervision of young persons.

8:2:2 Regulations for securing health and safety
The Secretary of State may make special regulations for protecting persons against risk of injury to body or health:

1   By using any machinery, plant, equipment, appliance or substance (s20)
2   Arising from noise or vibrations, where it may adversely affect their welfare (s21)

8:2:3 *Penalising an employee's dangerous acts (s27)*
This section is the counterpart to s143 of the Factories Act 1961, which makes employees indulging in dangerous conduct guilty of an offence. An employee working on premises covered by the Act is guilty of an offence if:

1   He wilfully and without reasonable cause does anything likely to endanger the health and safety of other employees
2   He wilfully interferes with, wilfully misuses, or without reasonable excuse removes, any equipment, appliance, facilities or other thing provided in pursuance of the 1963 Act

8:2:4 *Putting an end to dangerous conditions and practices (s22)*
If a magistrates' court is satisfied that:

1   Any part of the premises covered by the Act is in such a condition or so constructed that it cannot be used without risk of bodily injury or injury to health
2   Machinery or equipment used or operations and processes carried out constitute a similar risk

then further use may be prohibited for an unlimited period or until the risk has been eliminated. Interim orders may be made pending the hearing of the case, if the occupier of the premises has been given:

1   Three days' notice of the intention to make an application
2   An opportunity to be heard

Complaints under this section may be brought by the body or person charged with enforcing the provisions of the Act in respect of the premises in question (see 8:9).

8:2:5 *Prohibition of heavy work (s23)*
This section corresponds with s72 of the Factories Act 1961 (see 6:21:5).

8:3 PROVISION OF FIRST-AID FACILITIES (s24)

A readily accessible first-aid box must be provided, containing only first-aid requisites and appliances, as prescribed by the Secretary of State. Where the number of employees on the premises exceeds 50, an additional first-aid box is required for each additional group of 150 or any fraction of that number. A responsible person must be in charge of the box and the same person must not be in charge of more than one box.

8:3:1 *Where more than one box is provided*
If two or more first-aid boxes are required then:

1   One of the persons in charge must be:
  (a) Trained in first aid (see 6:21:6)
  (b) Always available during working hours
2   A notice must be displayed, easily seen and read by employees giving:
  (a) The name of the person in charge of first-aid box and his availability during working hours
  (b) The name of persons in charge of and trained in first aid, where there is more than one, and their availability

These provisions relating to first-aid facilities do not apply where a first-aid room is maintained for immediate treatment of persons suffering bodily injury or becoming ill.

8:4 SAFETY PRECAUTIONS IN CASE OF FIRE
All premises covered by the Act must provide employees with such means of escape in case of fire as may reasonably be required, this being dependent upon the number of persons expected to be:

1   Working on the premises at the time
2   Resorting to the premises though not employees, for example, lawful visitors to an office or customers in a shop (s28)

8:4:1 *Certification of premises (s29)*
Unless there is a fire certificate in force, it is unlawful on premises to which the act applies, for:

1   More than twenty persons to be employed at any one time in any premises
2   More than ten persons to be employed elsewhere than on the ground floor
3   Any person to be employed on premises where explosives or

highly inflammable materials prescribed by the Secretary of State are stored or used

A certificate will be issued only if the fire authority is satisfied with the provision of the means of escape.

In determining whether a fire certificate is required, employees in different employment on the same premises must be aggregated together. It is the responsibility of the employer, as occupier, to apply for the certificate, except where one building is let to different occupiers, in which case the owner of the building is responsible.

If an application in the proper form has been made by the occupier, the premises may be used until the fire authority gives its decision. A certificate may be granted on condition that specified alterations are made by the applicant within a specified time; if a certificate is not issued within the time specified, and no extension of time granted, then a certificate has been refused. The fire certificate must be kept on the premises while it is in force.

A penalty of £200 will be incurred by either occupier or owner, as appropriate, if he uses his establishment for working in breach of these conditions.

8:4:2 *Maintenance of a means of escape in case of fire (s30)*
All means of escape specified in a fire certificate must be properly maintained and kept free from obstruction. The fire authority may inspect the premises at any time to see if conditions on the premises have changed. Written notice must be given to the fire authority if the occupier proposes to:

1   Extend his premises
2   Materially increase the number of employees
3   Store explosive or highly inflammable materials prescribed by regulations

In the light of an inspection, the fire authority may require the occupier to make alterations as specified, and failure to comply may result in:

1   A cancellation of the fire certificate by the fire authority, whether or not proceedings are brought
2   The occupier being charged with an offence, with the certificate being cancelled on conviction

8:4:3   *Right of appeal on certification and maintenance (s31)*
The occupier or owner may appeal to a magistrates' court where:

1   A certificate or amendment to a certificate is refused
2   A certificate is cancelled
3   Alterations are required (there is a right of appeal against the period allowed)
4   There is a prohibition on the use of premises until alterations are made

The appeal must be made within twenty-one days of the refusal, cancellation or prohibition, as the case may be. The court may make whatever order it thinks fit, which is then binding. Until determination of the appeal, it is not unlawful to employ persons to work on the premises concerned.

8:4:4   *Prohibition of employment*
on premises without proper facilities (s32)
Where a fire authority is satisfied that conditions of escape in case of fire are so dangerous that employees should not be employed there at all, or not in connection with a particular process, until the risk is eliminated, then a complaint may be made to the magistrates' court and the court may make an order accordingly.

8:4:5   *Safety provisions relating to doors (s33)*
While any employees are working or taking meals on the premises, all doors must be capable of being opened immediately. The contents of every room must be arranged in such a manner as to leave a free passage, allowing an employee to have access to a means of escape. Every exit providing a means of escape, other than the ordinary exit, must be conspicuously marked on a notice, and the lettering used must be of adequate size.

8:4:6   *Provision and maintenance of fire alarms (s34)*
At all premises obliged to obtain a fire certificate, an effective system of giving warning in case of fire must be maintained, without exposing the operator of the system to undue risk. The fire alarm must be tested or examined every three months, or more frequently if required. The Secretary of State may prescribe the nature of the test or examination to be carried out.

8:4:7   *Fire instruction for employees (s36)*
Effective steps must be taken by the occupier to familiarise employees with the means of escape from fire, their use and the routine to be followed when fire breaks out. Since employees are required to be familiar with the use of the means of escape provided, any procedure falling short of an actual fire drill, such as reading out the rules to be followed or handing a copy to the employee to read, will probably be insufficient.

8:4:8   *Provision of fire-fighting equipment (s38)*
The occupier is obliged to:

1   Provide appropriate fire-fighting appliances
2   Maintain them properly
3   Place them in positions where they will be available for use whenever they are required

8:4:9   *Special regulations*
made by the Secretary of State (ss35, 37 and 38)
The Secretary of State may make special regulations in relation to:

1   The means of escape to be provided in case of fire
2   Steps necessary to reduce the risk of the outbreak or spread of fire
3   The internal construction of premises and the materials to be used
4   The means and testing of fire-fighting equipment

8:4:10   *Enforcement of fire precautions*
For office and shop premises the fire authority is the county borough council or county council. The factory inspector is the appropriate person to enforce these provisions in relation to those premises listed in 8:9.

8:5   WHERE ONE BUILDING IS
OCCUPIED BY SEVERAL DIFFERENT EMPLOYERS (s42, s43)

Sections 42 and 43 deal with the problems raised by buildings that are owned by one person but occupied by various employers. Certain parts of the building will be used by all the different occupiers and their employees, for example, corridors, staircases, entrance halls and some sanitary conveniences. Compliance with the requirements of the Act relating to matters of cleanliness, lighting, floor, stairs, steps, passages and gangways of common parts of the building is the responsibility of the owner. Contravention of the rules governing sanitary conveniences and washing facilities are also the owner's responsibility, where they are provided for use jointly by employees working on the premises and other persons also. The owner is the party responsible for seeking a fire certificate.

8:6 EXEMPTION FROM THE
OBSERVANCE OF SOME STATUTORY REQUIREMENTS (s45)

The Secretary of State has power to exempt, unconditionally or subject to conditions, with or without a time limit:

1   Premises or rooms of any class from the statutory requirements on overcrowding and temperature
2   Premises of any class from the statutory requirements on sanitary conveniences and washing facilities

where in his opinion it would be unreasonable to require compliance.

Before making any regulation the Secretary of State must first consult with organisations representing employers and employees concerned, or other organisations of persons with an apparent interest.

An individual employer may seek these exemptions from the local authority or the factory inspector with power to enforce the provisions of the Act (s46).

8:7 NOTIFICATION OF ACCIDENTS (s48)

Where an accident occurs in any shop or office premises, whereby an employee is either killed or disabled from working for over three days, then written notice of the accident must be sent at once by the occupier to the local authority. A second notice must be sent, if death occurs after giving notice of disablement. If the occupier is not the employer of the employee killed or disabled, then the employer must notify the occupier immediately, otherwise he is liable to a fine of up to £10.

8:8 NOTIFICATION THAT
PERSONS ARE BEING EMPLOYED (s49)

Before an employer first begins to employ anyone to work in any office or shop, he must send to the local authority two copies of a notice stating that persons will be employed together with any other information prescribed by the Secretary of State.

8:9 ENFORCEMENT OF THE PROVISIONS OF THE ACT (s52)

It is the duty of every local authority to appoint inspectors for the purpose of enforcing the provisions of the Act, with the exception of those concerned with fire precautions. It is the duty of factory inspectors to enforce the provisions of the Act as it affects:

1 County council premises
2 Local authority premises
3 County council or local authority premises for the administration of justice
4 School premises
5 Probation committee premises
6 Police authority premises
7 Atomic energy authority premises
8 Premises in, but not part of, a factory
9 Railway premises
10 Offices used in connection with:
  (a) Building operations or works of engineering construction
  (b) Electrical stations
  (c) Docks, quays and certain warehouses
  (d) Railway undertakers
  (e) Fuel storage premises owned by railway undertakers

The powers of inspectors of local authorities and factory inspectors carrying out functions under the 1963 Act are similar to the powers given to factory inspectors under the Factories Act 1961 (see 6:1:1).

8:10 OFFENCES, PENALTIES AND LEGAL PROCEEDINGS (ss63–72)

The occupier of office or shop premises is liable for a contravention of the provisions of the Act. The term "occupier" is not defined, but it probably bears the same meaning as that given to it in relation to factory legislation (see 7:2:1). Some other person may be made liable as well as the occupier. For example, an employee may be prosecuted under s27 for any dangerous act that he commits, but the occupier may be liable as well under s17 for failing to provide adequate safety precautions. The occupier may be relieved of liability where the Act clearly stipulates that some other person is responsible, for example the owner under s42 and s43 (see 8:5).

A person guilty of an offence under the Act for which an express penalty is not provided is liable to a fine:

1   Not exceeding £60
2   £15 for each day during which the contravention continues after conviction
3   £300, where the court is satisfied that the contravention was likely to cause death or serious bodily harm to any person (s64)

Where the offence has been committed by a corporate body with consent, connivance or neglect by any director, manager, secretary or other similar company officer, then that person is guilty of an offence and may be fined as well as the company. This section is particularly significant to the personnel manager, who must avoid being party to any contravention of the statutory requirements (s65). It is a defence, however, for a person charged with contravention of the Act under s65, to prove that he used all due diligence to secure compliance with that provision (s67) (see 8:2, J H Dewhurst Ltd v Coventry Corporation).

A fine not exceeding £100 or imprisonment for up to three months, or both, is provided by s68 for any person:

1   Forging documents, such as a fire certificate or an instrument granting exemption from the provisions of a regulation made under the Act
2   Making a false statement to procure a fire certificate or instrument of exemption
3   Wilfully making a false entry in a register, book, notice or other document required by the Act to be kept, served or given

8:11 CIVIL LIABILITY FOR INJURIES CAUSED BY NON-COMPLIANCE WITH STATUTORY PROVISIONS

The occupier of an office or shop is liable to employees for any injury caused by non-observance of the duties imposed by the 1963 Act, in the same way as the factory occupier is liable for a breach of the duties set out in the Factories Act 1961 (see 7:3).

8:12 DEFINITION OF A SHOP (SHOPS ACT 1950 s74)

The present law on shops is contained in the following statutes:

1   Shops Act 1950, consolidating earlier legislation dealing with employment in shops and regulation of opening hours
2   Offices, Shops and Railway Premises Act 1963, which covers health, welfare and safety
3   Shops (Early Closing Days) Act 1965, a minor amending Act

A shop is defined by s74 of the Shops Act 1950 as premises where any retail trade or business is carried on. The following types of premises do not constitute a shop:

1   A blacksmith's shop
2   A booth where the playing of games of chance by the public results in the awarding of a prize to the winner
3   A stall in an open market used twice a week, consisting of a board on trestles
4   A mobile van equipped as a shop
5   Premises used for the purpose of selling services elsewhere

In contrast, the following have been held to be within the definition of a shop:
1   A temporary bookstall, consisting of a board on trestles at a railway station
2   Premises at which only repairs are carried out
3   The part of a hotel where non-residents are served with meals
4   A garage where petrol and motor accessories are sold and repairs carried out

The definition of a shop is extended by s1(3) of the Offices, Shops and Railway Premises Act 1963 to include:

1   A building or part of a building which is not a shop, where the principal use is carrying on a retail trade or business
2   A building or part of a building occupied by a wholesale dealer or merchant, where goods are kept for sale wholesale, excluding a warehouse belonging to the owners, trustees or conservators of a dock, wharf or quay

3   A building or part of a building which the public may use for delivering goods for repair or carrying out repairs themselves

4   Any premises occupied for the purpose of storing fuel for the trade or business of selling solid fuel, excluding colliery or dock storage premises

5   Premises maintained in conjunction with a shop, to sell or supply employees with food or drink for immediate consumption, whether or not the premises are part of a shop; for example, a staff canteen would be shop premises, though situated somewhere away from the shop premises, and the canteen and canteen staff would be covered by the health, welfare and safety provisions in ss4–48 of the 1963 Act (s1(5))

Not only must the premises be capable of being considered as a shop, but a retail trade or business must be carried on there, before they can be a shop within the meaning of the Act. A retail seller is a person dealing with consumers, but a wholesale shop is included, if occupied by a wholesale dealer or merchant who keeps his goods there to sell wholesale to a customer who comes to the premises.

The expression "retail trade or business" includes by virtue of s74(1) of the 1950 Act:

1   The business of a barber or hairdresser
2   The sale of refreshments or intoxicating liquors
3   The business of lending books or periodicals for gain
4   Retail sales by auction

But it specifically excludes the sale of programmes, catalogues and other similar sales at theatres and places of amusement.

It was never the intention of the legislature to limit the meaning of the word "trade" to the business of buying and selling.

8:13   WHO IS A SHOP ASSISTANT? (SHOPS ACT 1950 s74)

A shop assistant is any person wholly or mainly employed in a shop in connection with:

1   The serving of customers
2   The receipt or orders
3   The dispatch of goods

The courts have held that the persons carrying out the functions listed below are shop assistants for the purposes of the Act:

1 A kitchen maid, though she has no contact with the customers being served in the restaurant, but merely facilitates the service rendered
2 Hotel kitchen workers preparing food for consumption by residents and non-residents
3 A waiter serving non-residents in a hotel
4 A potman employed in a public house to wash glasses, clean cutlery and generally keep the premises clean

The Act does not apply to a young person employed:

1 In a residential hotel
2 As a shop assistant for less than twenty-five hours in a week (s18)

8:14 DEFINITION OF AN OFFICE
(OFFICES, SHOPS AND RAILWAY PREMISES ACT 1963 s1)

For the purposes of the Act, the term "office premises" means a building or part of a building solely or principally used as an office or for office purposes. The term "office purposes" includes:

1 The purposes of administration
2 Handling money
3 Telephone and telegraph operating
4 Clerical work which covers writing, book-keeping, sorting papers, filing, typing, duplicating, machine calculating, drawing and the editorial preparation of matter for publication

Premises form part of the office premises where they are occupied:

1 Together with office premises
2 To further the activities carried on in the office premises, for example, storage rooms and rooms used by staff such as dining rooms

Premises are considered to be an office if maintained in conjunction with an office to sell or supply employees with food or drink for immediate consumption, whether or not those premises form part of the office (s1(5)). For example, a staff dining room located some distance from the main office premises is an office.

8:15 SHOPS AND OFFICES
OUTSIDE THE PURVIEW OF THE 1963 ACT

The provisions of the Act do not extend to premises:

1   Where the only employees are immediate relations of the employer, that is, a spouse, parent, grandparent, children, grandchildren, brother or sister (s2)
2   Occupied by persons who work at home by arrangement with their employer (s2)
3   Where the average weekly work period does not exceed twenty-one actual working hours, not including meal times and other breaks (s3)
4   Occupied on a temporary basis only, for fulfilment of a purpose to be completed within six months if the premises consist of movable structure, or within six weeks in other cases (s86)

NINE

Employers' Liability for Employees' Wrongs to Others

A TORT IS A CIVIL WRONG CAUSING HARM TO ANOTHER PERSON, entitling that person to sue for damages. Where a tortious act of this type is committed, liability arises even though there is no contractual relationship between the claimant and the party being sued. A person who performs a tortious act is called a *tortfeasor*.

If an employee causes injury to a third party (for example, personal injury caused to a member of the general public by negligent driving) by his tortious, fraudulent or criminal act then the injured party may bring an action against both the employee responsible, as the actual tortfeasor, and also against the employer, if in the circumstances he is thought to be *vicariously liable* for his employee's act. The injured party may prefer to sue the employer, since he is more likely to be able to pay any award of damages made. The employer's responsibility for a wrong that he did not commit personally is justifiable on the following grounds:

1 He is in a position to control the actions of his employee
2 He derives the profit from his employee's work, so he should also bear the losses caused by the employee's wrongful acts
3 He should choose only persons as employees who will discharge their duty with care; if they are not careful this is the fault of the employer, who must then pay damages to the party injured

The employer can reclaim any payments made to the third party from the employee at fault if he can satisfy any claim established (see 9:3). To protect himself against the consequences of vicarious liability, it is usual for an employer to take out appropriate comprehensive insurance. Nonetheless it is obvious that claims of this type cannot be sustained with any degree of frequency.

If the personnel manager is responsible for engaging staff, the need to choose persons who will discharge their duties with care is readily apparent from a study of the cases discussed below.

9:1 ESTABLISHING VICARIOUS LIABILITY

To establish vicarious liability, the party making the claim must prove:

1 That the relationship of employer and employee existed under a contract of service, as opposed to a contract for the services of an independent contractor (see 1:12), and

2   That the employee committed the wrongful act in the course of his employment

It is difficult to determine whether the employee's tortious acts are within the scope of his employment and the cases on this point often appear to be contradictory. It is impossible to frame any general principle that will give the employer an easy answer on the question of liability, if he is threatened with legal proceedings by a third party who has been injured by his employee's actions. The cases discussed below are indications of the way in which the court approaches this problem.

The doctrine of vicarious liability is not used if the employer expressly authorised the action that caused injury: in such a case, the employer is liable because he issued a wrongful instruction.

9:1:1   *How can the employer avoid liability for his employee's wrongs?*
To this question there is not an easy and straightforward answer. The object of this chapter is to indicate when and why the employer will be liable in the multifarious circumstances that may arise. It is clear that on general principles he will not be liable if:

1   The employer has excluded liability by means of an exemption clause or notice that is effective for this purpose (see 9:8 and 9:1:4)
2   The employee's acts are unconnected with the duties he is employed to discharge though the facts may suggest a superficial connection (see 9:1:2, 9:1:6, 9:1:7)

The employer cannot evade liability in the following cases:

1   By expressly forbidding commission of the wrongful actions which when committed will injure third parties (see 9:1:3)
2   Where the employee carries out in an improper manner those duties that he is employed to perform (see 9:1:5 and 9:1:7)

The precise extent of the monetary payments for which the employer is held liable will be indicated where possible, though the figures given must be interpreted according to the date of the decision so that the fall in the value of money over the years may be taken into account. This will illustrate the serious nature of a successful claim against an employer, especially if he cannot claim reimbursement, for some reason in the particular circumstances, from the employee actually responsible or an insurance company.

It must be appreciated that many of the decisions referred to were based upon the peculiar facts of that particular case and it is not easy to reconcile the cases one with another unless this factor is considered.

9 : 1 : 2   Employee's acts outside the scope of his employment

The employer is not responsible for his employee's acts if they are independent of and distinct from his employment, as when he either:

1   Does something entirely alien to the job he is employed to do,
     or
2   Stops working to indulge in an act for his own personal convenience

Beard v London General Omnibus Co (1900, Court of Appeal)

Beard was injured in a collision caused by the negligence of a bus conductor in turning round a bus for the return journey in the temporary absence of the driver. He sued the conductor's employer for damages.

The court decided that such conduct had nothing to do with the proper duties of a conductor; thus the employer was not liable in respect of the collision caused.

The employer is not liable even if he has given his employee permission to indulge in a personal act that causes the injury, where the act in question is outside the scope of the employment.

Crook v Derbyshire Stone Ltd (1956)

A driver employed by the defendants was allowed to stop for refreshments during a journey. He parked the lorry opposite a café and while crossing the road he collided with Crook, a motor cyclist, who sustained injuries. Crook sued the driver's employers for damages.

The court decided that taking refreshment was not part of the driver's duties, and so the employer was not liable. The employee was "a stranger to his [employer] from the moment when he left the lorry . . . until he returned to the lorry and resumed his journey." (Mr Justice Pilcher)

9 : 1 : 3   *Express prohibition by the*
employer of acts committed by the employee

If the employee is carrying out those tasks that he is employed to do, it is no defence for the employer to show that he had expressly forbidden the act in question. If this defence were possible, an employer could frequently evade liability in tort by giving restrictive instructions to his employee.

Limpus v London General Omnibus Co (1862)

The defendant company expressly instructed their drivers not to race with buses run by rival companies, in an attempt to be first at a bus stop to pick up all passengers waiting there. Limpus sued for damages in respect of injuries he suffered when these instructions were disobeyed by one of the defendant company's drivers.

The court decided that the defendant's were liable, since the driver was doing what he was employed to do, namely driving a bus. It was immaterial that the employers had expressly forbidden their employees to race. The plaintiff was awarded damages of £35.

This decision was followed in the next case.

London County Council
v Cattermoles (Garages) Ltd (1953, Court of Appeal)

Preston, a garage hand employed by the defendant company, was authorised to move parked vehicles from one part of the garage to another when this was necessary, but he was expressly forbidden to drive them. He drove a van on to the public highway to make way for other vehicles wishing to use the petrol pumps. His negligent driving caused a collision with a vehicle belonging to the London County Council, who now claimed damages from Preston's employers for the loss sustained.

The court decided that the employers were liable, since Preston was acting within the scope of his employment, even though he acted wrongfully and in an unauthorised manner. Driving the van on to the highway was necessarily incidental to his work and the fact that he had been forbidden to drive vehicles did not affect the employer's liability. The plaintiff was awarded damages of £23.

Here the employee was not only indulging in a forbidden act, but also embarking upon something entirely different; driving a van rather than merely pushing it. This decision seems to carry Limpus v London General

Omnibus Co one stage further, for in that case the employee was author-ised to drive and the forbidden act of racing at an excessive speed was concerned only with the manner of driving.

The test seems to be whether the employee's act, though expressly for-bidden by his employer, is a wrongful method of performing acts of the type that he is authorised to carry out; if so, the employer is liable for resultant harm to third parties. In both of the above cases the employee was authorised to do the act in question, that is, drive a bus and move cars around the garage respectively, but these acts were performed in a wrong-ful manner, as in the next case.

Ilkiw v Samuels (1963, Court of Appeal)

A driver employed by the defendants, acting against his employer's orders, allowed an incompetent stranger to drive his lorry, thereby injuring Ilkiw. The employers were sued by Ilkiw in respect of the injuries he received.

The court decided that the driver remained in charge of the lorry even though the stranger was sitting at the controls. The employers were liable to Ilkiw for £2077 in damages for their employee's negligence, since the vehicle was being used, albeit improperly and against orders, in the course of their business. Ilkiw's injuries were the result of the driver's disobeying express instructions, but this factor was not necessarily material in deter-mining whether the driver was acting within the course of his employ-ment in allowing another party to take control of the vehicle.

9:1:4 Where an employee offers
lifts in the employer's vehicle to a stranger

If a stranger is given a lift in the employer's vehicle by his employee, the employer will not wish to be held liable in damages for any injury sustained by that stranger, where it is caused by the employee's negligent driving. In order to negative his liability the next case suggests that the employer should:

1   Expressly forbid his employees to offer lifts, and
2   Prominently display a notice to this effect in the cabin of the vehicle

Twine v Bean's Express Ltd (1946)

A driver employed by the defendants gave a lift to a hitch-hiker, though this was forbidden by his employers and a notice to this effect was displayed on the dashboard. As a result of negligent driving the passenger was killed and his widow sued the driver's employers for damages.

The court decided that the employers were not liable to the passenger's widow, since their driver was acting outside the scope of his employment when he offered a lift. The passenger was a trespasser in the vehicle; thus a duty of care was not owed to him by the defendants.

A similar decision was reached in the case before the Court of Appeal of Conway v Wimpey (George) & Co Ltd (1951). Lord Justice Asquith declared, "Was the driver, in giving a lift to the deceased acting within the scope of his employment? The answer is clearly, No! He was doing something which he had no right whatever to do, and qua the deceased man was as much on a frolic of his own as if he had been driving somewhere on some amusement of his own, quite unauthorised by his employer."

Giving a lift to a stranger was not a wrongful method of performing an act that the driver was authorised to perform, but the performance of an act which he was not employed to perform. It is difficult to accept this reasoning and these two cases cannot easily be reconciled with the three decisions in 9:1:3. It is an inescapable fact that the passenger was injured while the employee was driving the vehicle in the course of his employment, since driving was the job he was employed to do.

If the passenger given a lift is a fellow employee, rather than an outsider, and if both the driver and a superior employee have given permission, then the employer is liable for any injury suffered by the passenger. The important difference in this situation is that the superior employee, and probably the driver as well, have at least ostensible authority to permit fellow employees into the vehicle for a lift.

9:1:5 *Improper performance of acts an employee is employed to perform*
The employer is liable for the employee's tort, if it is within the scope of his employment, even though it is an improper way of performing the act in question.

Century Insurance Co
v Northern Ireland Road Transport Board (1942, House of Lords)

A driver delivering petrol to a garage lit a cigarette, then threw away the lighted match; the resultant explosion caused considerable damage to the garage. The Transport Board, as the driver's employers, claimed reimbursement from the insurance company of the amount of the garage owner's claim of £1001.

The court decided that the respondent employers were liable for the negligent way in which the driver carried out his job. The act of lighting a cigarette was for the driver's own convenience and in itself harmless, but it was still within the scope of his employment. It could not, however, be regarded in abstraction from the circumstances, being a negligent method of conducting his work. The employers were liable for the employee's wrongs and consequently they could make a claim against the insurance company. Unlike Crook v Derbyshire Stone Ltd (see 9:1:2), the employee's personal act was committed simultaneously with performance of his duties to his employer.

9:1:6 Employer's liability if an employee uses the firm's car

If an employer allows his vehicle to be used by an employee for his own personal business, then any injury caused to a third party by the employee's tortious acts while driving that vehicle is not the employer's responsibility. The employee is not in this instance acting within the course of his employment.

Britt v Galmoye and Neville (1928)

Galmoye lent his car to his employee, Neville, so that he could take his friend, Britt, to the theatre after completing his work for the day. Britt was injured because of Neville's negligent driving and he sued both Neville and Neville's employer for damages.

The court decided that Galmoye was not vicariously liable for his employee's negligent driving, since Neville was not using the vehicle in the course of his employment. The journey did not benefit Galmoye and he could not be regarded as having control over the vehicle.

The employee may take a journey in the course of his employment, but then deviate from the direct route most appropriate. It is then a question of degree as to how far the deviation could be considered to be a separate unauthorised journey, such that the employer is not vicariously liable for wrongs committed during that deviation. Although not called upon to decide the point, Chief Justice Cockburn commented in Storey v Ashton (1869): "I am very far from saying that, if the [employee] when going on his [employer's] business took a somewhat longer road, that, owing to this deviation, he would cease to be in the employment of the [employer] so as to divest the latter of all liability; it is a question of degree as to how far the deviation could be considered a separate journey."

If a journey is unauthorised, its character is not changed if during that journey the employee performs some act benefiting his employer, as shown by the next case.

Rayner v Mitchell (1877)

A brewer's driver used his employer's van for a private journey, but on the way back he collected some empty beer barrels on behalf of his employer. He then injured the plaintiff in an accident. The plaintiff sued the driver's employer for damages.

The court decided that the employer was not liable for the injury.

An employer is still liable for an employee's torts committed in the course of employment when the employee uses his own property in execution of his duties instead of using his employer's property as ordered. In McKean v Raynor Bros Ltd (1942) an employee was deemed to be acting in the course of his employment when he delivered a message by using his own car instead of the firm's lorry as instructed.

9:1:7 Employer's liability when an employee assaults a third party

In cases of emergency an employee has an implied authority to protect his employer's property if it is in danger and carry out any necessary act even though it be different in kind from the acts he is expressly authorised to perform. The employer is liable for any wrongs so committed, even if the employee's acts tend to be excessive.

Poland v John Parr & Sons (1927, Court of Appeal)

A carter, while off duty, saw boys apparently robbing his employer's wagon. To prevent this imagined theft he struck one of the boys, who fell under the wagon and received injuries resulting in the loss of a leg. The injured boy sued the carter's employers for damages in respect of the injury sustained.

The court decided that the employers were liable for the injuries caused to the boy by reason of their employee's actions. Damages were assessed at £500.

If the employee assaults someone while over-zealously carrying out his duties, the employer is liable in damages to the person assaulted, even though the acts complained of have been excessive, provided they are directly concerned with obligations imposed on the employee.

Bayley v Manchester, Sheffield & Lincolnshire Railway Co (1873)

A porter in the employment of the defendant company mistakenly believed that Bayley, a passenger, was in the wrong train. Bayley sustained injuries when he was ejected by the porter from the train as it was moving away from the platform. The porter had been instructed to ensure that passengers travelled on the correct trains.

The court decided that the employers were liable in damages to Bayley for their employee's tortious act, since, although wrongful, it was committed in the course of his employment. The porter had been given a discretion as to how he should perform his duties and the employer could not escape liability when he exercised the discretion improperly, provided that his acts were not so excessive that he stepped outside the scope of his employment.

The employer is not liable, however, if the employee is acting for his own personal benefit and doing something he is not employed to do; if for example, he assaults a third party from motives of personal vengeance rather than in the over-zealous performance of his duties.

Warren v Henley's Ltd (1948)

A pump attendant, employed by the defendants, thought that Warren was about to drive away without paying for the petrol supplied to him. After an argument Warren threatened to report the attendant to his employers, whereupon the attendant assaulted Warren.

The court decided that the defendants were not vicariously liable, since the assault was an act of personal vengeance, not committed by the attendant in the course of his employment or within the class of acts that he was employed to do.

9:2 EMPLOYER'S CIVIL LAW
LIABILITY FOR CRIMINAL ACTS BY HIS EMPLOYEE

An employer is liable at civil law for injury suffered by a third person because of his employee's criminal conduct in the course of employment.

Morris v C W Martin & Sons Ltd (1965, Court of Appeal)

The plaintiff sent her mink stole to a furrier to be cleaned. With the plaintiff's permission, the furrier handed it to the defendants who were cleaning specialists. The article was stolen by one of their employees. The owner of the mink stole sued the cleaners for damages, alleging that they were responsible for the loss of the fur.

The court decided that the defendants were vicariously liable either in conversion or negligence for the value of the stolen article, which was assessed at £200. Conversion is the wrong of intentionally handling goods in a manner inconsistent with the rights of the person having either actual possession or entitlement to possession, whether or not that person is also the owner.

This decision covers only cases where the party sued is a bailee for reward and the employee responsible for the wrong is entrusted with the goods in question. Thus a theft by an employee not employed to do anything in relation to the goods bailed is entirely outside the scope of his employment and his employer cannot be made liable.

A bailee is a person to whom possession, but not ownership, of goods is entrusted by the owner, with some given purpose in mind such as repair or cleaning of the goods. If the bailment benefits both bailor and bailee, as when the bailee receives payment or other reward, then the bailee is responsible for loss or damage to the goods if he fails to protect them in the same way as the ordinary prudent man protects his own property.

An employer is vicariously liable for the fraudulent acts of his employee in the course of employment, even if they are committed for the benefit of the employee and not the employer.

Lloyd v Grace, Smith & Co (1912, House of Lords)

At the instance of Sandles, a managing clerk employed by a firm of solicitors, Lloyd, an elderly lady, signed papers believing that this would enable her property to be sold. In fact the documents were conveyances to Sandles, who then sold the property and absconded with the proceeds. Lloyd sued the solicitors to recover the money that she had lost.

The court decided that the firm was liable to pay £450 damages for Sandles' fraud, since by advising Lloyd he was fulfilling the job he was employed to carry out.

9:3 WHEN MUST THE EMPLOYEE
PAY FOR THE DAMAGE HE HAS CAUSED?

The injured party may sue the employer only or the employee only, but he can if he wishes bring an action against both of them jointly. If, in these circumstances, judgement is given in favour of the injured party, then:

1　The full amount of the damages awarded may be entered against both employer and employee, and

2　Execution for the whole amount (or any part thereof) may be levied against either employer or employee, provided not more than the total amount awarded is recovered

If the injured party successfully sues one joint tortfeasor only (the employee) this does not bar a later action against the other tortfeasor (the employer). A second action is useful if the first judgement cannot be satisfied because of lack of funds (Law Reform (Married Women and Joint Tortfeasors) Act 1935 s6(1)(a)). The total amount recovered must not exceed the total amount awarded in the first action.

By virtue of s6(1)(c) of the above Act, if the injured party recovers the full amount awarded from the employer, then he may claim a *contribution* from the employee in a separate action, so that the employer wholly or partially recoups the loss suffered. The employer could join the employee as a co-defendant to avoid the necessity of a separate action later.

The contribution of each tortfeasor is a matter of discretion for the court. It must be a just and equitable sum having regard to the extent of the responsibility for the damage caused.

9:3:1　*Indemnification under the contract of employment*
If the injured third party has successfully sued the employer in tort for damages, then the employee responsible for the tort may be in breach of his contract of employment. Consequently the damages paid over by the employer may be recoverable from the employee. It has been stated that since the employer has this remedy for damages for breach of the contract of employment, it should be used instead of the tortious remedy of contribution discussed above.

When accepting employment, an employee expressly or impliedly professes possession of the skill and care necessary for the performance of his work. The nature of the employment determines the extent of the skill and care required.

337

Lister v Romford Ice & Cold Storage Co Ltd (1957, House of Lords)

Lister, a skilled lorry driver, carelessly backed his lorry, causing injury to a fellow employee who then recovered damages from his employer by virtue of the doctrine of vicarious liability. The employer's insurers paid the damages and they sued Lister in the company's name for a full indemnification on the ground that they were entitled to recover all sums paid by the employer to the injured party.

The claim succeeded on the ground that Lister was in breach of an implied term of his contract of employment to perform his duties with the requisite degree of skill and care. The insurers were entitled to recover the damages of £1600 they paid to the injured party on behalf of the employer.

The employer cannot recover damages from his employee for breach of a contractual duty of care, if the employee is employed to do work different from the type of work he professes an ability to do. Nonetheless, damages may be recovered by way of a contribution under the Law Reform (Married Women and Joint Tortfeasors) Act 1935 s6(1)(c), where the employee's negligence causes the accident and consequent loss.

Harvey v R G O'Dell Ltd (1958)

The defendants employed a man named Galway as a storekeeper. As a concession to his employers, Galway used his own motor cycle for their business and on one such occasion he was killed and his passenger Harvey, a fellow employee, was injured. Harvey sued his employers, alleging that they were vicariously liable for Galway's negligence.

The court decided that the defendant employers were vicariously liable to Harvey for Galway's negligent conduct, since the journey was within the scope of Galway's employment. Damages were assessed at £1598. On the other hand, there was no implied duty in Galway's contract of employment to take reasonable care when driving and to indemnify his employers when he failed to do so, since he was not employed as a driver. Galway was liable, however, to indemnify his employers fully for their losses occasioned by his tortious acts, by virtue of s6(1)(c) of the Law Reform (Married Women and Joint Tortfeasors) Act 1935.

9:4 EMPLOYER'S LIABILITY FOR
THE ACTS OF AN INDEPENDENT CONTRACTOR

An employer often engages an independent contractor to complete a given project. One of the many problems resulting from the actions of the independent contractor's employees is to determine who is liable for the faults of those employees, whether it is the independent contractor as the immediate superior or the employer engaging the independent contractor. As a general rule an employer is not liable for the torts committed by employees of an independent contractor, subject to the important exceptions noted below.

Reedie v London & North Western Railway Co (1849)

The defendants were given power by statute to build a railway, but the work was executed on their behalf by independent contractors. The plaintiff's husband was killed by a stone that fell from a bridge in the course of construction. The accident was caused by the negligent act of an employee of the independent contractors.

The court decided that the defendants were not liable for the loss of life so caused, since the wrongdoer's act was the vicarious legal responsibility of the independent contractors employing him.

9:4:1 Tort that is authorised or ratified

The tort committed by the independent contractor may have been authorised or later ratified by the employer, thereby making him liable in respect of it.

Pickard v Smith (1861)

Pickard fell down an open shute to a cellar on a station platform and sustained injuries. The cover of the shute had been removed by an employee of a coal merchant, and then left unguarded. The cellar was occupied by Smith, who had contracted with the coal merchant for the delivery of the coal. Pickard sued Smith for damages for the injuries he sustained.

The court decided that Smith was liable for the negligent act of the independent contractor's employee. The wrongful act of leaving the coal shute open was Smith's though he performed it through the agency of the coal merchant.

9:4:2   Requiring an unlawful act to be performed
The employer is liable for consequent damage, if he employs an independent contractor to perform an unlawful act.

Ellis v Sheffield Gas Consumers Co (1853)

Acting without any legal authority, the defendant company employed an independent contractor to commit what amounted to a public nuisance, by digging up the street for the purpose of laying pipes. Ellis fell over a heap of rubble left lying in the street during the progress of the work. He sued the defendant company for damages for the injuries he sustained.

The court decided that the defendant company was liable for damages in respect of the injury to Ellis, having authorised the commission of the unlawful act.

9:4:3   Necessary information not communicated
The employer is personally liable if he does not give the independent contractor all the information necessary to complete properly the task undertaken.

Robinson v Beaconsfield Rural Council (1911, Court of Appeal)

The council, exercising their statutory authority, employed an independent contractor to cleanse pools in their district.

The court decided that the council was responsible for the nuisance caused when the independent contractor deposited filth from the pools on Robinson's land, since they had failed to give instructions about its disposal. The council were not discharged from their duty by casting it on the contractor.

9:4:4   Statutory duties cannot be delegated
If the employer is under a statutory duty to fulfil a task in a given manner, he cannot transmit responsibility for its completion to an independent contractor.

Hole v Sittingbourne & Sheerness Railway Co (1861)

The railway company had statutory power to build a bridge provided that navigation on the river was not unduly affected. Navigation was seriously impaired because of a defect in the bridge's construction, the fault of the independent contractors employed by the railway company to construct it. Hole sued for the loss caused to him because of the delay to navigation.

The court decided that the railway company was liable in damages, being unable to avoid its statutory responsibilities by employing another party to complete the work.

9 : 4 : 5 Delegation of dangerous work

Where the work delegated to the independent contractor is of a dangerous nature, the employer may be liable for damage caused if he fails to take adequate safety precautions.

Honeywill & Stein Ltd v Larkin Bros Ltd (1934, Court of Appeal)

A cinema owner allowed the plaintiffs to photograph the interior of the cinema. The plaintiffs engaged Larkin Bros to take the photographs but while they were using a magnesium flare the theatre curtains caught fire, causing considerable damage.

The court decided that the plaintiffs had employed the photographers as independent contractors to do certain work, which caused harm to the cinema owner, a third party; consequently the plaintiffs were liable for that harm. They had authorised work of a hazardous nature, but having settled the theatre owner's claim the plaintiffs could claim an indemnity from the photographers.

9 : 4 : 6 Interference with the use of the highway

Where the employer personally interferes with the work of his independent contractor, he is liable for damages for harm caused by such interference. For example, an employer may promise to remove an obstruction on the highway, created by his independent contractor but then fail to do so causing injury to a person using the highway.

Even if he does not interfere with the work of the independent contractor, the employer will be liable for his acts if they create a danger on or near the public highway.

Holliday v National Telephone Co (1899, Court of Appeal)

Holliday sued for injury caused by an explosion on the public highway which resulted from the negligence of an independent contractor employed by the defendant company. The injury was caused by the use of a defective blow-lamp.

The court decided that the defendants were liable in damages to Holliday since they were under a duty to take care that persons acting on their behalf should not negligently cause injury to members of the public using the highway.

Finally, where the employer coordinates the work of several sub-contractors, he must provide a safe system of work. Thus he is liable for injuries suffered by the employees of those subcontractors if such injuries could have been foreseen.

As the case of Honeywill & Stein Ltd v Larkin Bros Ltd shows, if the employer satisfies the claims of a third party for the torts of an independent contractor, he will usually be able to claim an indemnity from the contractor responsible (see also 1 : 12 : 8).

The employer himself will be regarded as having acted negligently if he employs an independent contractor without ensuring that he is competent to execute the work. Any harm that results from the acts of the independent contractor will be the responsibility of the employer.

9:5 EMPLOYER'S CRIMINAL LIABILITY FOR HIS EMPLOYEE'S ACTS

If the employer authorises his employee to do a criminal act, then the employer will be guilty of aiding and abetting any crime so committed. The main concern of this section is with criminal liability under a statutory provision. At common law, the general rule is that an employer is not criminally responsible for his employee's unauthorised acts, except for a public nuisance created on the employer's property, or on the highway or some other public place.

R. v Medley (1834)

Refuse was discharged by a gas company into the river, killing fish and polluting the water.

The court decided that though ignorant of their employees' acts causing this public nuisance, the directors of the company were responsible.

The object of a prosecution in these circumstances is not to punish the employer, but prevent continuance of the public nuisance.

9:5:1 A guilty mind is usually a prerequisite for criminal liability

Many statutory enactments require people to do or refrain from doing some stated act and failure to observe the law may result in criminal prosecution. Under the Trade Descriptions Act 1968 for example, it is an offence for any person to:

1   Apply a false trade description to any goods
2   Supply, or offer to supply, any goods to which a false trade description has been applied

"Trade description" is widely defined to cover indications of quantity, size, composition, fitness for a stated purpose, strength, performance and previous ownership. Thus it is an offence to incorrectly describe a car offered for sale as having had "one previous owner only." The person allegedly infringing these provisions of the Act may be liable though he did not have a guilty intention.

The general rule is that a person is not guilty of a violation of the criminal law unless his mind is guilty (mens rea) at the time of committing the offence. When interpreting a statutory provision creating a criminal offence, the courts assume that a guilty mind is a constituent element of the offence and it is therefore a good defence to show that a guilty mind was not present. There are variations from one enactment to another as to the nature and degree of the guilty mind. In theft (see 10:5:1) it is necessary to prove dishonesty, intention to appropriate the property allegedly stolen, and also an intention permanently to deprive the owner of it. Gross negligence sometimes evidences a guilty mind, while in other instances only slight negligence is required—for example, driving without due care contrary to s3 of the Road Traffic Act 1960. Use of the word "knowingly" in a statutory provision signifies that guilty knowledge of the circumstances surrounding commission of the crime is expressly required before a person has a guilty mind. In such cases an employer is liable only if he *knows* of his employee's wrongful act.

James & Son Limited v Smee (1954)

The appellant company sent out an employee in charge of a lorry and trailer, but after making a delivery a brake cable was not reconnected, thus causing a breach of the Motor Vehicles (Construction and Use) Regulations 1951, which provides that a trailer drawn behind a lorry must have an efficient braking system.

The court decided that the company could not be convicted of permitting the use of the vehicle contrary to statute, since to permit involves knowledge and the employer was unaware of the employee's wrongful acts.

343

9 : 5 : 2   *Absolute (or strict) liability under statute*

A statutory provision or regulation may impose an absolute duty on an employer, in which case he is liable for non-compliance with the duty imposed even though he did not have a guilty mind. It is not a good defence to show that general conduct of the business has been delegated to employees, with careful supervision of staff to ensure performance of the statutory duties and to prevent a wrongful act from being committed.

Sopp v Long (1969)

Long, secretary of British Transport Hotels Limited, was the licensee of a railway refreshment room. He had delegated his authority and duty to supervise such establishments to a general manager, who in turn delegated responsibility to a district manager and finally to the manageress of the particular refreshment room in question. Long had given instructions to ensure compliance with the law. Sopp, a chief inspector of Weights and Measures preferred informations against Long under the Weights and Measures Act 1963 s24 for causing to be delivered to a purchaser, whisky of a lesser quantity than that purported to be sold.

The court decided that Long had committed the offence even though he did not know that a short measure was being delivered and had not given prior authority for commission of the act in question. In law only a licensee can sell and, being absent from the premises, Long sold through his employee, the barmaid. For every sale she made, Long "caused" the thing sold to be delivered to the buyer, whether it was a proper sale or delivery of a short measure.

If the employer has not delegated the general conduct of his business to the employee, then the employer is not liable for an infringement of statutory provisions where the employee exceeds the authority conferred on him in the course of his employment.

Barker v Levison (1951)

Levison, manager of a block of flats, authorised his employee, Parkins, to lease a flat to a prospective tenant, if he was deemed to be suitable. Parkins demanded a £100 premium from the prospective tenant, as a condition of the grant of a lease. Levison was charged with an offence against the Landlord and Tenant (Rent Control) Act 1949.

The court decided that Levison had not authorised his employee to negotiate the terms of the lease, but only determine the suitability of the tenant. Being unaware of the demand for a premium by Parkins, Levison was not responsible, but he might have been liable if general management of the flats had been delegated to Parkins.

Absolute criminal liability of a corporate entity. If a natural person may be held vicariously liable for the crimes committed by his employees, then a limited company may also be liable.

Mousell Brothers Limited v
London and Northwestern Railway Company (1917)

Mousell Brothers Limited were successfully prosecuted under ss98–9 of the Railway Clauses Consolidation Act 1845 for giving a false account of goods delivered for carriage with intent to avoid payment of tolls. The false account had been given by a manager employed by Mousell Brothers Limited.

The court decided that it was a case where, on an interpretation of the words of the statute, an employer could be held criminally liable for his employee's acts. It was immaterial that the employer was a limited company. If a guilty mind is not necessary to make an employer liable, then a limited company is in exactly the same legal position as any other employer.

9:5:3 *Determining whether a particular statute imposes absolute liability*
Some guiding principles have been established to assist the courts in determining whether a statute imposes absolute liability on persons infringing its provisions. If the imposition of absolute liability will ensure enforcement of the statute as a warning to others, then any violation of its provisions may result in a conviction though the wrongdoer does not have a guilty mind.

The court also tries to discover whether there are precautions that the employer might have taken directly or indirectly to ensure observance of the statute by employees under his control, whether by way of supervision, inspection, or improvement of business methods.

In the twentieth century state control of an individual's freedom of action has increased considerably, restraints being imposed in many instances so that society as a whole may benefit. Judges have been more willing than their predecessors to impose criminal liability on an employer without an accompanying guilty mind, though the wrongful act is

M

essentially that of his employee. Statutory offences imposing absolute liability on an employer are basically new forms of public nuisance rather than crimes which carry moral disapproval when committed.

More recently, however, there have been two important decisions by the House of Lords, which have mitigated the hardship to an employer from the imposition of absolute liability. In Sweet v Parsley (1969) Lord Reid said that:

1   In the absence of a clear indication, there is a presumption that Parliament did not intend to make criminals of persons committing acts for which they are not to blame
2   In a statute, some sections may require a guilty mind as a prerequisite to criminal liability, but if other sections do not give any precise indications on this point it must not be assumed that an absolute offence has been created. In such instances it is necessary to go outside the wording of the Act and examine all relevant circumstances in order to ascertain Parliament's intention

In the second of these decisions the House of Lords protected an employer from absolute criminal liability under the Trade Descriptions Act 1968, by favourably interpreting the words of a statutory defence provided by the Act itself.

Tesco Supermarkets Limited v Nattrass (1971, House of Lords)

At one of its several hundred supermarkets, Tesco Limited continued to display a large advertisement, giving details of a special offer, after it had terminated. The advertisement stated that "Radiant" soap powder was being sold at 2s 11d instead of 3s 11d, the usual price. An information was preferred against the company for indicating that goods were offered at a price below that at which in fact they were offered for sale, contrary to s11(2) of the Trade Descriptions Act 1968. The offence resulted from a failure by Clements, a store manager, to implement company policy by checking the work of his subordinate staff and correcting their errors. He should have removed the advertisement or continued to offer the soap powder at the reduced price.

The House of Lords decided that Tesco Limited could rely on s24(1) of the 1968 Act as a defence to the charge. Commission of the offence was caused by the act or default of the store manager, himself a subordinate employee. The employers had taken all reasonable precautions and exercised all due diligence to avoid commission of the offence, either personally, or by employees under their control.

The owner of a large-scale business organisation, whether a natural person or a limited company cannot personally supervise all his employees' activities which may lead to an offence. It is sufficient if, as in this case, an effective system is devised and implemented to prevent offences being committed, with managerial staff supervising the work of subordinate employees. This is not a delegation of the duty to exercise due diligence, but performance of that duty. A limited company fails to exercise due diligence where the acts are those of a director or senior manager in actual control of the company's operations, identifiable with the controlling mind and will of the company. Clements was only one of several hundred store managers and he could not be identified with the company.

9:5:4 How to determine the extent of an employer's liability

The employer will wish to determine whether he is absolutely liable under a statutory provision for his employee's acts, or liable only if he, the employer, is personally at fault. It is necessary, therefore, to examine the wording of each statute separately, having regard to such matters as:

1   The object of the statute
2   The words used
3   The nature of the duty laid down
4   The person upon whom it is imposed
5   The person by whom it will be ordinarily performed
6   The person upon whom the penalty is imposed

The employer's position regarding statutory liability for crimes committed by his employees may give him some cause for concern. The employer is advised to ascertain how far he is directly affected by statutory enactments (including statutory instruments), and if possible to determine the exact nature of his liability, whether it is absolute or otherwise, but neither of these tasks is easy. If the employer complies with the requirements set out by the statute and takes care to ensure that his employees also observe the statutory rules, then he has done everything possible to safeguard his position. Despite these precautions, if the statutory duty imposed is absolute, the employer may still be liable for his employee's wrongful acts, though they are unauthorised or expressly forbidden, unless they fall outside the scope of his employment altogether.

It is impossible to attempt a classification of statutes which impose absolute liability on the employer as opposed to those which do not. In the first place, the business of one individual employer will be regulated by an entirely different group of statutory provisions to the undertaking of another employer discharging a different function. Second, the judicial construction of a given expression in one statute does not necessarily assist in the construction of similar wording in another statute, where circumstances surrounding application of the law demand a wider or narrower interpretation. Everything depends upon the actual words used by the legislature and the individual facts of the case in issue.

9:6 EMPLOYER'S DUTY TO INDEMNIFY HIS EMPLOYEE

An employer is obliged to indemnify his employee against any loss suffered or caused by authorising him to undertake any lawful act. It is often a third party that is injured by the tortious act, in consequence of which he sues the employee responsible for damages. The employee may also claim an indemnity where the act authorised by the employer is illegal, provided the employee is unaware of this fact.

Gregory v Ford (1951)

Gregory sustained injuries from a lorry driven by an employee in the course of his employment and he sued the employers who owned the lorry, and also the employee for damages. The employee believed that the lorry was insured against third party risks, but this was not the case. The court was asked to make the employer indemnify the employee for any damages payable by him to Gregory.

The court decided that where an employee is employed to drive his employer's vehicle there is an implied term in the contract of employment that the employee must not be required to do an unlawful act. The employer must observe any statutory provisions applicable. In this case there was an implied term in the contract of employment that the employer would take out the required insurance and that the employee would be indemnified by the insurers for any damage caused while driving the vehicle. The employee was entitled to an indemnity from his employer.

The employer is frequently liable to third parties for loss suffered by them as a result of the actions of an employee. If the third party elects to sue and recovers damages from the employee personally, as the actual wrongdoer, it does not follow that the employer must indemnify the employee in every case: for example, where the employee's acts are:

1   Outside the scope of the employee's authority or employment
2   Known to be in breach of duty or contrary to public policy
3   Within the scope of the employee's employment, but carried out negligently
4   Tortiously or criminally wrong to the knowledge of the reasonable man

In Lister v Romford Ice & Cold Storage Co Ltd (see 9:3:1), the employee, whose negligent driving injured a fellow employee, could not have claimed an indemnity from his employer for any damages that he might have been held liable to pay if sued by the injured party. Here the employee's loss would have been the result of his own wrongful act, not attributable to the execution of the orders of his employer or to the duties owed to him. Viscount Simonds said in the course of judgement in the Lister case, "Is it certain that, if the imaginary driver had said to his employer 'of course you will indemnify me against any damage that I may do however gross my negligence,' the employer would have said 'yes, of course!'? For myself I cannot answer confidently that he would have said so or ought to have said so."

9:7 EMPLOYER'S LIABILITY FOR INJURY INDIRECTLY INFLICTED BY HIS EMPLOYEE'S ACTS

If the activities of employees cause injury to a third party who is not on the employer's premises at the time of the accident, then the employer may be liable in a tortious action for damages in respect of the injury so caused, even though it is indirect.

Lord Atkin said in the famous House of Lords decision in Donaghue v Stevenson (1932), "You must take reasonable care to avoid acts or omissions which you can reasonably foresee would be likely to injure your neighbour." Neighbours are those persons "who are so closely and directly affected by my act that I ought reasonably to have them in contemplation as being so affected when I am directing my mind to the acts or omissions which are called in question." In applying this principle, the employer will be liable to a stranger who suffers injury as a result of the employee's negligent breach of duty, if the employer (if he thought about it) could reasonably foresee that the breach of duty was likely to cause injury to someone.

Baker v T E Hopkins & Son Ltd (1959, Court of Appeal)

The defendant company of builders and contractors undertook to clear a well of water. A platform was erected 29ft down the well to support a petrol driven pump. Two workmen were lowered into the well and were overcome by dangerous fumes produced by the petrol engine. Baker, a doctor, went down the well to try to rescue the men, though he had been warned not to do so. He was overcome by fumes and while being hauled out, the rope attached to his body caught on a pipe in the wall. He died shortly after being brought to the surface.

The court decided that Dr Baker's widow was entitled to damages from the defendant company because of the negligence that caused her husband's death. It was a natural and proper consequence of the defendant company's negligence towards the two workmen that someone would attempt to rescue them, and the defendant company, in failing to foresee that possibility, was in breach of its duty to the doctor.

The company could not rely on a defence of volenti non fit injuria (see 5 : 10). Lord Justice Morris dismissed that possibility in these words: "If [a person] actuated by an impulsive desire to save life, acts bravely and promptly and subjugates any timorous over-concern for his own well-being or comfort, I cannot think that it would be either rational or seemly to say that he freely and voluntarily agreed to incur the risks of the situation which had been created by [another's] negligence."

A third party may be injured while assisting an employee, although there was no real danger to be averted and the third party freely consented to running the risk of incurring some injury. In this type of situation, the employer is not liable in damages to compensate the third party for the injuries he has suffered.

Cutler v United Dairies (London) Ltd (1933, Court of Appeal)

A horse, drawing a milk cart owned by United Dairies, bolted down the road where it had been left and ran into a meadow. The driver of the cart, an employee of United Dairies, ran after the horse and shouted for help. Cutler came to the driver's assistance and sustained injuries by being thrown from the horse. The horse was unfit for work and the employers were negligent in allowing it on the road.

The court decided that the defendants were not liable to Cutler in damages for the injuries he sustained. Cutler had voluntarily undertaken the risk of injury (volenti non fit injuria). There was no immediately apparent danger of injury to anyone.

9:8 HOW CAN THE EMPLOYER EXCLUDE HIS LIABILITY FOR HIS EMPLOYEE'S WRONGFUL ACTS?

The employer may wish to relieve himself of any liability that he may incur to third parties for the tortious, fraudulent or criminal wrongs of his employees and thereby save the time, trouble and expense involved in defending an action for damage caused. The third party suffering the loss is then limited to an action against the actual wrongdoer. It is clear from many of the cases discussed in this chapter that the employer cannot warn the third party before the occurrence of the event giving rise to liability that he will not accept liability in such circumstances, since the employer does not have reason to suspect that any harm will be inflicted. The facts of Beard *v* London General Omnibus Co in 9:1:2 illustrate this contention.

In some situations the employer is well aware that his employees are likely to cause personal or proprietary loss to third parties and in effect the employer becomes an insurer in respect of the harm suffered. The profit made by the employer from his business may be insufficient to support claims of this type, consequently it is vital for him to totally exclude or severely limit his liability by an effective exemption clause.

In a typical situation the employer may contract with customers to supply a service, for example, transporting a car by ferry, cleaning clothes, or garaging a car. Damage may be caused to the goods in question by the negligence of an employee and the employer should negative his vicarious liability for such wrongs by inserting an exemption clause in the contract. The effectiveness of this device depends upon two vital considerations.

First, the clause must be drafted in terms that will exclude liability of the kind that has actually arisen on the facts of the individual case in question. On this matter it is advisable to take professional advice since individual requirements will vary considerably. The drafting of a comprehensive exclusion clause will require skill, ingenuity and a knowledge of relevant decided cases appropriate to the particular circumstances applicable. If there is any doubt as to the meaning and scope of an exclusion clause, the ambiguity will be resolved by an interpretation contrary to the interests of the employer who inserted it into the contract and now wishes to rely on its protection.

Secondly, the existence of the clause must be brought to the attention of the person who is to be bound by its provisions. Here the employer must take care to lay down an effective procedure for notification, and ensure that this is followed by instructing employees to draw the customer's attention to the existence of the clause. Failure to take these precautions will usually render totally ineffective the protection given by the exemption clause.

9 : 8 : 1 Embodying an exemption clause
in a document signed by the party to be bound

If a contractual document is signed by the customer when the contract is concluded, then he is bound by any exemption clause embodied in it. The signature is regarded as acceptance of all terms in the agreement. This proposition remains true even if the customer has not read the document, for by adding his signature to the contract he is fixed with constructive notice of its contents even if he does not have actual notice. If an employee is asked to explain the meaning of an exemption clause he must not misrepresent the true position by giving an inaccurate assessment of its effect, for then the protection of the clause is lost.

Curtis v Chemical Cleaning & Dyeing Co Ltd (1951, Court of Appeal)

Mrs Curtis took a white satin wedding dress to the defendants for cleaning. She signed a document which included a clause excluding the company's liability for any damage to the garment however it might be caused while in the defendant's custody. Before she signed, Mrs Curtis was told by an employee of the company that the document excluded liability for damage to beads and sequins. Mrs Curtis then signed the document without reading it. The dress was stained in some unexplained manner, presumably through the negligence of an employee.

The court decided that the defendant company was liable in damages to Mrs Curtis for the loss caused. The employee's innocent misrepresentation as to the true meaning and scope of the exemption clause had the effect of excluding it from the contract between the parties.

9 : 8 : 2 Legal position when the exclusion
clause is not embodied in a signed agreement

In those cases where a contractual document is not signed, an exemption clause is only incorporated into a contract if reasonable steps have been taken by the employer to bring it to the customer's notice. It is not necessary to show that the clause has actually been brought to the customer's attention. Additionally, there must be a clearly worded statement or other indication on the face of the document drawing the customer's attention to the existence of the exemption clause. A clause will not be binding if it is made illegible by a date stamp, buried among advertising matter, or contained in a document that has been folded in such a way as to conceal the relevant clause.

Richardson, Spence & Co v Rowntree (1894, House of Lords)

Miss Rowntree was handed a ticket on paying the fare for a voyage on one of the plaintiff company's steamers. The ticket contained a clause excluding liability for any loss or injury on the voyage in excess of $100. The ticket was folded in such a manner that the exemption clause could not be read except by opening it out. Miss Rowntree claimed damages in excess of $100 for losses sustained and the company relied on the clause limiting their liability.

The court decided that Miss Rowntree knew that there was writing on the ticket but was unaware that it included an exemption clause. The company had not done what was reasonably sufficient to give her adequate notice of it. The exemption clause was not binding and Miss Rowntree was entitled to recover damages to the full extent of the damage suffered.

The company should have instructed its employees to carefully draw the customer's attention to the existence of the clause and preferably explain its precise meaning as well. It is safer to include a clause intended to relieve an employer of considerable monetary liability in a contractual document which requires the customer's signature, coupled with an explanation of its effect.

9:8:3 Tickets may be only receipts and not contractual documents
It is not advisable to rely on an exemption clause which is written on the back of a ticket handed over at the conclusion of the contract. The danger here is that the ticket is likely to be regarded in law as a receipt for payment, rather than as a document which forms an integral part of the contract evidencing its terms and possibly including an exemption clause. Tickets handed over:

1   On entry to cinemas, sports stadiums, zoos and pleasure gardens
2   After boarding public transport vehicles
3   When booking a seat for a future theatre performance or future conveyance of passengers or goods

are often small insignificant documents which a reasonable man would regard as evidencing payment for the service or facilities provided and nothing else. A large, conspicuous and clearly worded notice should be displayed setting out the terms of the exclusion clause in easily understood language:

1   At the entrance to the area to which admission is given
2   At the point of entry to public transport vehicles
3   At the place where the contract for future services is concluded, usually some type of booking office

Employees should be instructed to direct a customer's attention to the notice.

It should be noted that the Road Traffic Act 1960 (s151) and the Transport Act 1962 (s43(7)) prevent bodies responsible for the conveyance of passengers on public service vehicles and British Railways from excluding liability for causing death or bodily injury to passengers in respect of transport services offered to the public. Damage to a passenger's luggage caused by the negligence of driver, conductor or other employee is not covered and to exclude liability an exemption clause is required.

9:8:4   Employee's wrongful conduct may
negative protection given to an employer by an exemption clause

An employer cannot rely on an exemption clause the existence of which is unknown to the customer. Nor can reliance be placed upon an exemption clause embodied in a contractual document of which the customer does have notice, if the contract is performed in an entirely different way to that contemplated by employer and customer because of an employee's wrongful, unauthorised intervention.

Mendelssohn v Normand Ltd (1969, Court of Appeal)

Mendelssohn parked his car at a garage owned by Normand Ltd. An employee, who acted as an attendant, told Mendelssohn that garage rules required the car to remain unlocked and the keys to be left in the ignition so that the car could be moved. This was untrue, the rules required a car to be locked and Mendelssohn had always done this on the previous occasions when he had used the garage. Mendelssohn explained that a suitcase on the back seat contained valuables and the attendant promised to lock the car after moving it. A ticket was handed over by the attendant to Mendelssohn on which was printed a clause excluding the employer's responsibility for any loss of a car's contents. At the reception desk there was a similar disclaimer of liability for goods lost while entrusted with Normand Ltd, but Mendelssohn had never read this notice. When Mendelssohn went to collect his car it was still unlocked, the keys were in the ignition and the valuables had been stolen, presumably by the attendant, who was never seen again. An action for damages was successfully brought by Mendelssohn to reclaim the value of the stolen property.

The court decided that the exemption clause printed on the back of the ticket handed to Mendelssohn was repugnant to the attendant's promise to protect the valuables, implicit in his assurance that the car would be locked after moving it. It was within the attendant's ostensible authority to make such a promise which would take priority over the printed condition. The exemption clause could not be relied on by the employer since the contract had been performed in an entirely different way to that anticipated. Exclusion of liability for loss of a car's contents was based upon the difficulty of access to a locked vehicle. Nor could reliance be placed on the similar exclusion clause displayed at the reception desk. The notice had not been brought to Mendelssohn's attention in such a way that he must be taken to have known of it and agreed to be bound by it.

9:8:5 Communication of an exclusion
clause after the contract is concluded is ineffective

The customer may be able to prove that the document or notice containing the exemption clause was given to him or brought to his attention only after completion of the contract with the employer. Here the communication is too late in time for the clause to be an effective part of the contract. A belated notice is valueless. For example, if a guest agrees to stay at an hotel the contract may be concluded at the reception desk. The proprietor wishing to exclude liability for the negligent acts of his employees cannot communicate his intentions by a notice in the guest's room, for by that time all terms of the contract have been settled.

In such cases, however, the employer may be able to establish the existence of previous dealings with the same customer during which time a similar contractual document was handed over, or a conspicuous notice was displayed, giving actual or constructive notice of the exemption clause's existence. Although the communication was belated and ineffective on that occasion, it may bind the customer in his subsequent dealings with the same employer. If, in the above example, the guest returns to the hotel for a second visit, he will be bound by the exemption clauses conspicuously displayed in his room on the previous visit. He now has constructive notice of the exemption clause even if he did not read it on the previous occasion.

The employee will not usually be a party to his employer's contracts excluding liability for a customer's personal or proprietary loss; consequently he remains personally liable to the party injured as the result of his conduct.

Adler *v* Dickson (1954, Court of Appeal)

The plaintiff took a Mediterranean cruise on a boat belonging to a shipping company. She was issued with a sailing ticket which contained an exemption clause negativing the company's liability for their employees' negligent acts causing personal injury to passengers on the cruise. The plaintiff alleged that she was injured as a result of the negligent conduct of the company's employees.

The court decided that the shipping company were protected by the exclusion clause. On the other hand, employees of the company were not parties to the contract nor were they entitled to its benefits, consequently they could be sued for damages as the parties occasioning the injuries. Even if the exclusion clause had contained words purporting to exclude the liability of the employees they could not have relied on that clause since they were not parties to the contract in which it was contained. Only a party to a contract can take advantage of any benefit it purports to confer on him.

9:8:6 *Use of the exemption clause in other circumstances*
An employer may use an exemption clause to exclude his liability for injury caused to lawful visitors on his premises by displaying a notice to this effect. This point is discussed in 10:2:1.

TEN

Employers' Rights and Liabilities in Respect of Property and Premises

THIS CHAPTER IS MAINLY CONCERNED WITH THE PRACTICAL STEPS THAT an employer may take to protect his property and premises, including property found on his premises, against the undesirable activities of employees and outsiders, including trespassers. A number of diverse topics will be covered and some attention given to the employer's duties as well as his rights as an occupier of premises, as against persons using them, where such persons are not employees protected by legislative enactments, such as the Factories Act 1961 and the Offices, Shops and Railway Premises Act 1963.

The problems connected with theft, arrest and search are interrelated and should be regarded as different aspects of one major problem, namely, how to deal with the dishonest employee. This may necessitate the determination and pursuit of a settled policy when thefts are detected. The law on arrest and search is complex and it is easy for the employer himself to commit a legal wrong, unless he carefully analyses the situation that has arisen and acts strictly in accordance with his legal rights.

10:1 WHO IS ENTITLED TO LOST PROPERTY FOUND ON THE EMPLOYER'S PREMISES?

Any lost property found on the employer's premises belongs to and may be claimed by the true owner of that property. The true owner may be an employee or some other person visiting the premises. By displaying an effective notice it may be possible to trace the owner and return the property.

10:1:1 *Claim by the owner of the premises*
If, after the notice has been displayed for about four to six weeks, the owner does not come forward, the property may be claimed by the owner of the premises where it was found, if it was attached to the premises in some way, for example, embedded in the ground or lodged between the brickwork. The person who actually finds the property may be an employee, but the employer is entitled to claim it.

South Staffordshire Water Co v Sharman (1896)

Sharman, a labourer employed by the plaintiffs to clean out a pool, claimed two gold rings that he found there in the course of his work.

The court decided that the employers were entitled to the rings since they owned the pool, exercised practical control over it, and had the right to prevent any person from coming on to the land where the pool was sited.

If the employer is merely the lessee of his business premises, the property found may be claimed by the lessor who owns the freehold of the premises, though in practice a claim of this nature will probably be confined to cases where the property found is very valuable.

Elwes v Brigg Gas Co (1886)

The defendant gas company took a ninety-nine year lease of certain land for the purpose of erecting a gas holder. While excavating the site they found a prehistoric boat, 6ft below the surface, in a good state of preservation.

The court decided that the plaintiff, as lessor of the property, was entitled to the boat. He had a better claim than the lessees, though they were the finders.

A clause in the lease may expressly provide that valuable items found belong to the lessor, often an important right where excavations are to precede the erection of a new building.

London Corporation v Appleyard (1963)

The corporation owned the freehold of a site which they leased to Yorkwin Investments. One of the clauses in that lease provided that articles of value found on any part of the site were the property of the corporation. Two workmen engaged on the site found an old safe containing banknotes to the value of £5728 in the cellar of a demolished building.

The court decided that since the owner of the notes could not be traced, the corporation was entitled to them. Yorkwin Investments being in possession of the site had a better title than the workmen who found them, but the corporation's claim under the lease prevailed against any claim by the lessees.

10:1:2 Claim by the finder

If the lost property is simply lying around and not attached to the premises in any manner, then if the finder happens to be someone other than an employee, he may retain the property, since he has a better claim than the owner of the premises.

Bridges v Hawkesworth (1851)

Bridges, a traveller for a firm, entered Hawkesworth's shop on business and found banknotes to the value of £55 on the floor. He handed the money to the shopkeeper so that it could be returned to the owner, but after three years the owner could not be found.

The court decided that the property in the money belonged to the finder; consequently the shopkeeper was obliged to hand the notes over to Bridges.

10:1:3 *Theft by the finder*

The finder of the property may know who the owner is or believe that it is possible to discover him by taking reasonable steps, such as reporting the matter to an official, like a personnel manager, and asking him to display a notice. If the finder appropriates the property found with the intention of permanently depriving the owner, he will be guilty of theft (Theft Act 1968 s2(1)) formerly called larceny by finding.

Where the finder does not believe that the owner of the property can be found by taking reasonable steps, then it is not theft if the finder appropriates the property while under that belief. An example would be a cleaner who finds a dust-coated coin lodged behind a filing cabinet that is rarely moved. There is an important qualification to add here. If the finder later becomes aware of the owner's identity but decides to appropriate or dispose of the property found, with the intention of permanently depriving the true owner, then the finder is guilty of theft.

10:2 EMPLOYER'S DUTY TO NON-EMPLOYEES TO KEEP HIS PREMISES SAFE

The employer, as an occupier of premises, owes a duty to lawful visitors to take such care as is necessary, in the circumstances of the case, to make the premises reasonably safe for the purpose for which they are used by those visitors (Occupiers' Liability Act 1957 s2). If the premises are unsafe and the visitor is injured, he may sue the occupier for damages in tort for negligence. The term "visitor" covers persons invited or permitted to use the premises by the employer, for example, salesmen, representatives and persons being interviewed for a job. A person has an implied permission to enter the premises to transact business which he believes will interest the employer, though he is not invited or even expected in some cases. An example would be a representative for a firm trying to establish a business relationship with the employer.

10 : 2 : 1   *How the employer can escape liability*

The occupier does not incur liability to a visitor in respect of any injury caused by the defective state of the premises, if the visitor has willingly accepted that risk. Any damages awarded against an occupier in respect of a lawful visitor's injuries will be apportioned accordingly if the visitor has contributed to his injuries by his own negligence (see 7 : 3 : 8). If the occupier knows that a danger exists on his premises, he may warn visitors accordingly by written notice or a verbal communication. If the visitor is then injured because the warning is not heeded, the occupier may be absolved from liability. The warning must be sufficiently effective to protect from any harm a visitor who takes reasonable care for his own safety.

The employer may go even further and by displaying a notice clearly state that he completely excludes his liabilities as occupier of the premises for any duty of care imposed on him to lawful visitors under the Occupiers' Liability Act 1957. The notice must be clear, precise and conspicuously displayed, since it will not exclude liability if the person injured did not read it or have the opportunity of reading it. Where damage is caused to a visitor by a danger of which he has been warned by the occupier, that warning by itself does not absolve the occupier from liability. unless in all the circumstances it was enough to enable the visitor to be reasonably safe (s2(4)).

Ashdown v Samuel Williams & Sons Ltd (1957, Court of Appeal)

Mrs Ashdown, a lawful visitor on the defendant's property, claimed damages in respect of personal injuries which were caused by the defendant's employees negligently shunting trucks along a railway line. The defendants had posted notices warning lawful visitors that they entered the property at their own risk, and excluding any claim for injury against the defendants however caused. Reasonable steps had been taken to bring these exemption clauses to Mrs Ashdown's notice.

The court decided that the defendants were not liable, on the ground that an occupier can limit or totally exclude liability for his own or his employees' negligent acts by an appropriately drafted exemption clause brought to the notice of the persons affected. In fact the plaintiff had read only part of the notice, but she had the opportunity of reading all of it, and consequently she was bound by its terms.

The occupier may escape liability by delegating work on the premises to an independent contractor, reasonably believed to be competent, and then examining the work done to make sure that it has been completed properly—in so far as the occupier is competent to do this. For example, the employer may engage an electrician to install an overhead light fitting. If a lawful visitor receives injuries when the fitting collapses, caused by the faulty workmanship of the contractor, then the employer is not vicariously liable, if he has examined the work and found nothing apparently wrong with it. The lawful visitor must sue the contractor who was responsible.

Hazeldine v Daw & Son Ltd (1941, Court of Appeal)

In this case an employer was sued for damages by a lawful visitor to his premises in respect of personal injuries caused while using a lift that had been negligently repaired by an independent contractor. Lord Justice Scott stated that: "Having no technical skill [the employer] cannot rely on his own judgement, and the duty of care towards his [lawful visitors] requires him to obtain and follow good technical advice. If he did not do so, he would indeed be guilty of negligence. To hold him responsible for the misdeeds of his independent contractor would be to make him insure the safety of his lift."

The employer will be liable for the negligence of an independent contractor if the premises are left in a condition that is obviously dangerous.

Woodward v Mayor of Hastings (1945, Court of Appeal)

A pupil was injured by a fall at school, caused by slipping on an icy step. A cleaner had negligently left the step in this dangerous condition and the defendant was sued for damages as the employer responsible.

The court decided that even if the cleaner was an independent contractor the defendant was liable for the injury sustained by the pupil. The employer could have easily appreciated the existence of a danger without exercising any technical knowledge. "The craft of the charwoman may have its mysteries, but this is no esoteric quality in the nature of the work which the cleaning of a snow-covered step demands." (Lord Justice Du Parcq)

10:2:2 *Liability to an independent contractor*
An independent contractor working for an employer may sue for any injuries sustained in the course of his work, and use the duty of care

imposed by the Occupier's Liability Act 1957 to establish liability. The employer may, where appropriate, rely on the defence of contributory negligence or consent to running the risk of harm (volenti non fit injuria, see 5 : 10).

Bunker v Charles Brand & Son Ltd (1969)

Bunker, a foreman employed by a firm of constructional engineers, was hired out to the defendant company to work on the construction of a tunnel. A machine for digging tunnels was also hired out. Bunker was engaged by the defendants to modify the digging machine, during a week-end when it was not in use. He sustained injuries by walking on rollers that moved, thereby causing him to fall, but the accident might have been prevented if he had held on to a nearby girder. Bunker sued for damages under s2 of the Occupiers' Liability Act 1957.

The court decided that the rollers were a hazard and a danger on the work premises when the machine was out of commission for a substantial period. Bunker was the defendants' visitor within the meaning of s2 of the 1957 Act. The defendants were occupiers of the tunnel, the machine and the rollers, through the medium of their responsible officials working on the site. The plaintiff had full knowledge of the risk involved in walking over the rollers. Section 2(5) states that the common duty of care does not impose on an occupier any obligation to a visitor in respect of risks which he willingly accepts as his own (volenti non fit injuria).

It must be remembered, however, that "knowledge of the danger . . . is not to be treated without more evidence as absolving the occupier from liability unless in all the circumstances it was enough to enable the visitor to be reasonably safe" (Mr Justice O'Connor). The defendants should have placed planks beside the rollers or lashed planks on top of the rollers to give a secure foothold. They were in breach of the common law duty of care owed to Bunker under the 1957 Act. Bunker was guilty of 50 per cent contributory negligence in not using the girder as a handhold. He recovered only half of his damages.

10:2:3   Occupier's liability for children who are lawful visitors
Section 2(3)(a) of the Occupiers' Liability Act 1957 provides that "an occupier must be prepared for children to be less careful than adults." Although children do not constitute a special group for legal purposes, nonetheless they may be tempted to play with objects capable of inflicting injury, machinery for example, which an adult would carefully avoid

coming into contact with. In exercising his duty of care, the occupier is expected to take into account the likelihood that children with access to the premises, will interfere with potentially dangerous objects.

Holdman v Hamlyn (1943, Court of Appeal)

Holdman, a boy aged ten, was a lawful visitor on farm premises. The defendant's employee was in charge of the premises and while his back was turned for a moment the boy climbed on to a threshing machine. His foot was drawn into an aperture in the machine with the result that his leg had to be amputated. The boy sued the employer as occupier of the premises for monetary compensation in respect of his injuries.

The court decided that the plaintiff was entitled to damages amounting to £2000. Although the boy was reasonably intelligent he did not know or appreciate the dangerous nature of the machine. It was the employee's failure to supervise the boy's movements that resulted in him climbing on to the threshing machine which constituted a dangerous allurement. "A defendant who has lured an invitee into a forbidden area cannot thereafter treat him as a trespasser." (Lord Justice du Parcq)

An occupier is not liable for injury to a child if this is caused by interference with an object that cannot be regarded as a trap or allurement. What amounts in law to a trap or allurement must be decided on the facts of each individual case. If a child is injured while playing on a heap of stones the occupier is not liable for two reasons. Firstly a heap of stones cannot be regarded as being inherently dangerous and secondly it is not unusual to use land for the purpose of depositing stones.

10:2:4 Occupier's duty to very young children

Most things constitute a potential danger for very young children, but if they enter business premises a condition may be implicitly imposed that they must be accompanied by a responsible person. In determining the extent of an occupier's obligation to make his premises safe for very young children who may be lawful visitors, it is necessary to consider the kind of precaution that prudent parents could be expected to take for safeguarding their children's welfare. "It is [the parents'] duty to see that such children are not allowed to wander about by themselves, or at least to satisfy themselves that the places to which they do allow their children to go unaccompanied are safe for them to go to. It would not be socially desirable if parents were able to shift the burden of looking after their children from their own shoulders to those of persons who happen to have accessible bits of land" (Mr Justice Devlin). Usually an occupier will have discharged his duty of care to very young children if he makes his premises reasonably safe for them when accompanied by that type of guardian whom the occupier might expect to be in charge.

Phipps v Rochester Corporation (1955)

A five-year-old boy and his seven-year-old sister walked across a large open space which was being developed by the defendants as a housing estate. The children frequently played there without any attempt by the defendant corporation to exclude them. In the middle of this open space the defendant's employees had dug a long deep trench. An adult would have realised that the trench constituted an obvious danger and the girl avoided it by walking round the end, but the boy fell into the trench and broke his leg. An action by the boy to recover damages for his injuries caused by the dangerous state of the land did not succeed.

The court decided that the boy was a lawful visitor, but a prudent parent would not have allowed two small children to wander alone on an open space without first determining whether it was a safe area for them to play in. If the parents had examined the space they would have realised the danger of their children falling into the trench and forbidden them to go there until it was filled in. The defendant corporation was not in breach of the duty of care owed to lawful visitors.

10:3 DEALING WITH TRESPASSERS

There are a number of occasions when unauthorised persons may trespass on the employer's premises. A lawful visitor becomes a trespasser if he refuses to leave the premises when requested to do so, or uses the premises for a purpose other than the one contemplated by the occupier, or strays into a part of the building where he has not been authorised to enter.

If an employee is instantly dismissed without notice, following an unpleasant scene, he may be asked to leave immediately. An employer is not obliged to continue the employment of a person he no longer wishes to employ or even allow him to remain on the premises. If the employee refuses to leave he becomes a trespasser and may be forcibly removed.

The duty of care owed to a trespasser is much lower than that owed to the lawful visitor. The general rule is that a trespasser enters at his own risk and the occupier's only duty to him is not to deliberately or recklessly inflict damage if the trespasser is known to be present, or if it is reasonable to expect his presence to have been known. A trespasser cannot complain if he is injured because of the state of the premises upon which he trespasses, if for example he slips on a patch of oil or a wet surface, since he must take the property as he finds it. The court's attitude to trespassers is well illustrated in the next case.

Robert Addie & Sons (Collieries) Ltd v Dumbreck (1929, House of Lords)

A four-year-old boy died as a result of being crushed in the terminal wheel of a colliery haulage system operated by employees of the defendant company. Children were in the habit of playing in the field where the wheel was situated and despite warnings to keep away by employees they continued to use the area as a playground. When the accident occurred the wheel could not be seen by the employees who set it in motion.

The court decided that the defendants were not liable in damages for the child's death. "Towards the trespasser the occupier has no duty to take reasonable care for his protection or even to protect him from concealed danger. The trespasser comes on to the premises at his own risk. An occupier is in such a case liable only where . . . [there is] some act done with the deliberate intention of doing harm to the trespasser, or at least some act done with reckless disregard of the trespasser." (Lord Hailsham)

An almost identical factual situation arose in Excelsior Wire Rope Co Ltd v Callan (1930, House of Lords), but there the employers were held liable in respect of the injury caused. The reason for the differing decisions is that in the later case the employee giving the signal to start the wheel was standing a mere twenty yards away, and if he had turned round before giving the signal to start he would have seen the children by the wheel. This failure to check that it was safe to start the mechanism was regarded as a reckless disregard for the presence of a trespasser.

The employer who is tired of the activities of habitual trespassers cannot set traps for them and if they are used the trespasser may sue for any injury he suffers as a result. Trespassers may be discouraged from entering by the use of reasonable deterrents, like spikes or broken glass cemented into the top of a wall, and a trespasser injured by these devices cannot sue the occupier.

10:3:1 *Use of force to remove a trespasser*

If a person trespasses upon the employer's premises without using any force, as by merely entering without permission, then he must be asked to leave peaceably and force in removing him is not justified at this stage. A trespasser refusing a request to leave or entering forcibly may be removed by force and any resistance to removal constitutes assault and battery. To determine what is "reasonable" force it is necessary to examine the circumstances of the individual case.

Trespass is a tort and the employer may sue the trespasser for damages, without having to prove that he has suffered any actual damage. If the trespasser has not caused any real harm, the employer will recover only nominal damages to compensate him for the interference to his right to possession; consequently in these cases it is not worth suing. Since the essence of trespass to land is the interference with possession, the appropriate person to sue is the present possessor, whether or not he is owner as well. An employer leasing his business premises from another person is entitled to proceed against trespassers.

An action in damages is a useless remedy against a persistent trespasser, but in these circumstances an injunction is available to restrain the offender.

10:3:2 *Legal position where children trespass on land*

The duty owed by an occupier to a child trespasser is exactly the same as the duty owed to an adult trespasser.

Herrington v British Railways Board (1971, Court of Appeal)

A six-year-old boy playing in a meadow stepped over a broken fence and was electrocuted while crossing railway tracks on adjoining land. He sued the defendants as occupiers of the premises for damages in respect of injuries suffered. The local stationmaster knew that children had been trespassing on the land and although he had told the police, steps were not taken to inspect or repair the fence.

The court decided that the British Railways Board was guilty of reckless disregard for the boy's safety. The Board knew that children had been seen on the line and that trespassing was probably facilitated by a broken fence. The fence should have been repaired to protect child trespassers from the hidden and mortal danger of the electrified railway line. An occupier's carelessness in relation to trespassers can be so gross as to constitute a reckless disregard for their safety.

If the occupier is aware that children habitually trespass on his property he must take reasonable measures to deter them by effectively fencing the property, promptly repairing the fence when broken by children to make an entrance, and if possible, by instructing employees to warn children off. If such steps are not taken the children will become lawful visitors to whom a much higher duty of care is owed. Where this happens the occupier may be held liable for injury sustained by the child if caused by the dangerous state of the premises or interference with some object that constitutes an allurement to children.

Cooke v Midland Great Western Railway of Ireland (1909, House of Lords)

On land close to a public road the defendant kept an unlocked turntable which constituted a dangerous allurement to children. A four year old boy was seriously injured while playing on the turntable with other children. Company employees realised that trespassing children frequently acted in this way. A warning notice was habitually ignored. In any case the notice was an ineffectual warning as regards children since it was unintelligible to them. There was easy access to the land through a well-worn gap in the fence surrounding the property, although the company was obliged by statute to maintain the fence in good repair.

The court decided that the defendant occupiers were liable in damages for injuries to the child caused by playing on the turntable. The boy was not a trespasser on the land or the turntable but, by acquiesence of the defendant's employees, a lawful visitor.

10:3:3 Precautions that an occupier may take

Where land may be used by children as a playground or by adults as a short cut, the employer as occupier of the property should take effective precautions to remove any possibility of a successful action in damages for injuries sustained by those persons while using the premises. The cases discussed suggest that:

1 The total area of the land should be fenced and repaired immediately if broken, and if this is not feasible, then any dangerous part of the land should be fenced or cordoned off

2 A simply worded notice should prohibit entry on to the land, but this is not effective as a protection against claims by young children who cannot read and understand the notice

3 Persons entering without permission must be excluded and warned not to act in this way in the future

4   Before using machinery on the land it is advisable to make
     sure that trespassers are not in the vicinity and likely to be
     injured by the machine when in motion

If these precautions are taken then any child or adult entering without
permission will be a trespasser, not a lawful visitor to whom a higher duty
of care is owed.

10:4   SECRET PROFITS AND BRIBES

An employee is under a duty to render full and proper accounts to his
employer. If, with a fraudulent intent, the employee fails to do so, the
employer is justified in dismissing him without notice. If the employee has
made a secret profit by an improper use of his position without the employer's permission, then the profit must be accounted for to the employer.
In order to recover the secret profit the employer need not show that he
has suffered any damage as a result of his employee's conduct.

Reading v Attorney General (1951, House of Lords)

Reading, an army sergeant stationed in Cairo, secured £20 000 by wearing
his uniform while transporting illicit spirits, thereby avoiding police
inspection. He was arrested and convicted for conduct prejudicial to
good order and military discipline. Following release after conviction,
Reading tried to recover the money which had been impounded by the
Crown.

   The court decided that there was an implied term in Reading's contract
of employment that he should account to his employer for all money
received in respect of his employment. A member of Her Majesty's forces
is not accurately described as a servant under a contract of service, but
he owes to the Crown a duty as fully fiduciary as the duty of an employee
to his employer. As a result, all profits gained by the use or abuse of his
military status may be claimed for the benefit of the Crown. The principles
emerging from this case apply equally to the relationship of employer and
employee.

10:4:1   *Bribery of an employee*

Bribes are a special type of secret profit, being a payment which the
employee and the third party know to be improper, made with the intention of keeping it secret from the employer.

An employee may be entrusted with the negotiation of contract for the purchase of goods or services on the employer's behalf. A person wishing to secure the contractual right to supply the goods or services may bribe the employee to accept his offer on the employer's behalf. The bribe may take the form of a lump sum payment or a percentage of the monetary value of all business transacted with his employer. On discovering these improper arrangements the employer may :

1   Dismiss the employee without notice
2   Recover the bribe from the employee
3   Repudiate the contract made with the third party
4   Sue both employee and third party for damages for any loss caused by contracting with the third party, without deducting the amount of the bribe already recovered from the employee

Salford Corporation v Lever (1891, Court of Appeal)

Salford Corporation invited tenders for the supply of coal. Lever promised an employee of the plaintiff corporation a payment of one shilling for every ton of coal supplied to the corporation, if Lever's tender to supply coal was accepted. In order to recoup the amount of the bribe, Lever quoted one shilling per ton higher in his tender than would have been necessary if the bribe had not been made.

The court decided that the corporation could recover damages from Lever at the rate of one shilling for every ton of coal purchased under the contract of supply. They could also recover from their employee the one shilling per ton he received by way of bribe.

10:4:2   *Where bribery of an employee is a criminal offence*
If an employee tries to secure a personal advantage from another person, in return for doing some act connected with the employer's business, a criminal offence is committed where the act in question is done corruptly. The person who offers or pays the bribe also commits a criminal offence. The actual wording of the Prevention of Corruption Act 1906 is somewhat technical, but the following summary gives a full account of the scope of this offence when it is committed by an employee in connection with the duties imposed upon him by the contract of employment. It is a criminal offence to offer, agree to give, or give an employee a bribe, which is defined as any gift, money or other valuable consideration as an inducement to:

1   Do or forbear from doing, anything in relation to his employer's business, or
2   Show favour or disfavour to any person in relation to his employer's business

It is also a criminal offence for an employee to accept or attempt to obtain a bribe. The punishment that may be inflicted upon the giver or receiver of the bribe are the same, being either:

1   Imprisonment for two years and/or a fine of £500 on indictment, or
2   Imprisonment for four months and/or a fine of £50 on summary conviction

It is only necessary to show that a bribe was received as an inducement to show favour, not that favour was actually shown. If the recipient did not do the thing he was bribed to do, that is no reason for acquitting him on a charge of taking a bribe. If the recipient informs the authorities, this will usually negative corruption on his part (R v Carr (1957)).

10:4:3   *Special provisions governing*
bribery of an officer of local or public bodies
It is a criminal offence, punishable with two years' imprisonment and/or a fine, if a member or officer of any local or public body receives a reward for doing or not doing some act connected with the work of the body for whom he works. It is also an offence, carrying the same punishment, to offer a reward in these circumstances. If the offer relates to a contract with any government department or public body, then the term of imprisonment is a maximum of seven years under the Prevention of Corruption Act 1916. Further, contrary to the general rule, corruption is presumed if it is established that a gift has been given, offered or requested. The offender giving or receiving the bribe is subject to the following liabilities as well:

1   To pay to the body concerned the amount of the bribe or any part thereof as stipulated by the court
2   To suffer disqualification for seven years from election or appointment to any public office
3   To forfeit any such office held at the time of conviction
4   To forfeit any rights or claims to compensation or pension, at

the court's discretion, in the case of an officer or employee of a public body

5 On conviction for this offence a second time, to suffer a perpetual disqualification from holding public office and five years' disqualification from voting at parliamentary and local elections (Public Bodies Corrupt Practices Act 1889 s1 and s2)

In a criminal action in 1971, Sporle, a former chairman of a local authority housing committee, was sentenced to four years' imprisonment on charges of corruption involving council housing contracts. He was barred from acting as a councillor for five years. Sporle accepted considerable sums of money from four different concerns who were interested in obtaining contracts from the local authority to build houses. Day, a construction engineer, was imprisoned for twelve months for corruptly offering Sporle £500 to promote the interest of John Laing Construction Ltd, in a £6½ million building contract.

Judge Clarke stated, "You represent local government on the one hand and commercial business on the other, between which there is a bond and contracts involving many millions of pounds. It is essential that the trustees of ratepayers' money should be honest and above suspicion. When corruption is found drastic means are necessary to stop it. People who play for high stakes must pay the consequences."

10:5 WHEN IS AN EMPLOYEE GUILTY OF THEFT?

The Theft Act 1968 introduced many important changes in the law relating to stealing and allied offences, such as embezzlement and fraudulent conversion. Those sections of the Act that are important to the personnel manager having to deal with dishonest employees will now be discussed. The most important factor is to know whether the conduct of the employee amounts to a crime. The employer may not wish to prosecute, even if it seems likely that the employee is guilty, unless it is necessary to give a warning to other members of the staff where theft is becoming a serious problem. In many cases it may be preferable summarily to dismiss the employee in question, for a serious breach of his contract of employment.

10:5:1 Legal definition of theft

An employee will be guilty of theft if he appropriates property belonging to his employer with the dishonest intention of permanently depriving his employer of it (s7). The offence is punishable with imprisonment for up to ten years. If the employee takes the property (which may be money) from his employer, he is guilty of theft, provided that he intends from the outset to deprive his employer permanently or forms this intention at some later time after taking it away. If the employee intends to use the property and then return it he is not guilty of theft, since he lacks the intention to deprive his employer of it permanently.

Distinction between ownership and possession. It is important in this context to appreciate clearly the legal significance of a number of terms that are used somewhat loosely by the layman. Ownership is the right of exclusive enjoyment of property, the greatest right that a person can have over property. Though one person may own goods he does not necessarily have possession of them. If the owner (O) hires the goods to another person (P) then O remains the owner, but P has the right to possession during the period of hire. P may allow a friend C to use the goods, then C has physical control over them, but C is not entitled to possession or ownership. Theft is a violation of ownership or the right to possession.

An employee will be guilty of theft if, on being given custody of his employer's goods, he dishonestly appropriates them with the intention of permanently depriving the employer of those goods, whether the employer is the owner or merely entitled to possession. This covers the crime formerly known as embezzlement where the employee misappropriates money in his control on the employer's behalf.

What is meant by the term "appropriation." The employee appropriates his employer's property by asserting the rights which belong to an owner against the goods in question. This includes cases where he receives the property innocently without stealing it, but at a later stage asserts the right to keep it.

If an employee is ordered to collect goods which his employer has purchased, then the employee has legal possession when the goods are handed to him. If he dishonestly appropriates them with the intention of permanently depriving his employer, then the employee is guilty of theft, since the employer is the owner.

Section 5(3) of the Act covers the special situation where the employee is guilty of dishonest appropriation of property but at the same time has a proprietary right to the property taken, a situation falling outside the scope of s7 discussed above. For example, Evans, an employee, may receive cheques payable to himself on account of his employer which he is expected to pay into his employer's bank account. If Evans cashes the cheques and retains the money he is guilty of theft. Here the employee has received property on his employer's behalf and he is obliged to retain and deal with that property (or its proceeds) in a particular way; consequently the property is regarded as belonging to the employer.

10:5:2 *Retaining an over-payment of wages*
If the employee receives the full amount of his weekly wage, say £20, having received already say £5 in advance, then he is under an obligation to restore the £5 overpaid. The employee is guilty of theft if he appropriates the £5 on realising the employer's mistake (s5(4)). The employer may have been deceived by his employee into thinking that the full sum of £20 was due, as where the employee falsely states to the manager of the wages department that the £5 advance has been repaid. In that case the employee is guilty of theft under s5(4), but he is also guilty of obtaining money by deception contrary to s15, which is also punishable by imprisonment for up to ten years.

10:6 SEARCHING EMPLOYEES TO FIND EVIDENCE OF THEFT

If an employer suspects that thefts are being committed by certain members of his staff, he may wish to search their person and belongings, such as handbags and brief cases, to ascertain the truth or falsity of his belief. This is an odious task and the legal position is fraught with difficulties for anyone, including the personnel manager, entrusted with the supervision or execution of the search. It is advisable to ask the permission of the employee concerned before embarking on the search. If this is granted then the subsequent search will not result in undesirable legal consequences. If the employee refuses co-operation, the search must not be made, for to act against the employee's wishes in this way amounts to committing assault and battery if the search does not result in the discovery of any stolen property. The wronged employee could then sue his employer and the person carrying out the search for substantial damages for an affront to his personal dignity (see 10:7:3).

10:7 POWERS OF ARREST (CRIMINAL LAW ACT 1967 s2)

The offences under the Theft Act discussed above are "arrestable" offences, because the possible punishment involved is imprisonment for five years or longer—though a lighter sentence may be imposed after conviction according to the circumstances of the particular case. An arrest for theft may be effected by a private individual, such as the employer or his personnel manager, or by a constable. The arrest of an employee is a deprivation of his personal liberty. Such action must be justified by some lawful authority, otherwise it is a tortious wrong called false imprisonment for which damages may be claimed by the person wrongfully arrested. After arrest the suspect must be taken to a police station so that he may be questioned and, if necessary, charged with committing theft. If arrest is effected by a private individual the police should be called immediately to supervise further proceedings.

10:7:1 *When the personnel manager may arrest an employee*
First, a private individual may arrest without warrant any person who is in the act of committing a theft, where, for example, the thief is caught red-handed. Secondly, an arrest may be made by a private individual where he has reasonable cause to suspect someone to be in the act of committing an arrestable offence. Here the person suspected must be engaged on an act which the person arresting believes with reasonable cause to be a theft, even though it later transpires that a theft was not being committed. For example, if the personnel manager apprehends an employee or other person leaving his employer's place of business carrying money or goods which he believes with reasonable cause to have been stolen, then he is justified in effecting an arrest, though the act in question turns out to be quite innocent. Finally, where an arrestable offence such as theft has actually been committed, any person may arrest without warrant a person suspected, with reasonable cause, of being guilty of that offence. The overriding requirement here is that a theft must have been committed by someone; only then can the arrest be effected. But if the wrong person is arrested it is necessary for the person making the arrest to show reasonable cause for his believing that he was apprehending the thief.

In every case, the employee must be told why he is being arrested, but simple non-technical language suffices. Reasons need not be given where it is obvious why the arrest is being made, as where the employee is caught in the act, or if he runs away or starts a brawl, thus making any explanation impossible.

10:7:2 *Arrest by a police officer*
Where a constable has reasonable cause to suspect that an arrestable offence:

1   Has been committed
2   Is being committed
3   Is about to be committed

he may arrest without warrant anyone whom he has reasonable cause to suspect of being guilty. The constable's powers have been set out in full since a careful analysis of the wording will show that his powers are wider than those of the ordinary individual. A constable is justified in arresting an employee for theft on a reasonable suspicion, even though it is established later that an offence has not been committed at all, for example, where property believed to be stolen is later found to have been mislaid. The ordinary individual is justified in arresting an employee for theft on a reasonable suspicion only if an offence has been committed by someone, though not necessarily the person arrested.

Unless the employer or personnel manager feels certain that he is able to justify the arrest of an employee or an outsider for stealing the employer's property by reference to one of the rules enumerated in respect of arrest by the ordinary individual, then in suspicious circumstances it is advisable to call the police and allow a constable to arrest by use of his more extensive powers. The next case clearly illustrates the dangers for the ordinary individual in effecting an arrest.

Walters v W H Smith & Sons Ltd (1914)

The defendant booksellers suspected Walters of stealing books from their counters at King's Cross station. Eventually an employee of the defendants challenged Walters while he had one of their books in his possession. Walters, having been acquitted on a charge of theft brought by the defendants, sued them for damages in a civil law action for false arrest.

The court decided that the arrest without warrant by the employee was unlawful. Consequently the defendants were liable in damages to Walters for false arrest, by way of an action in tort for false imprisonment.

An arrestable offence had not been committed in the presence of the employee, there was no reasonable cause to suspect that Walters was in the act of stealing, and although there was reasonable cause for suspecting Walters to have committed theft, it transpired that a theft had not been committed, by Walters or anyone else. The three heads under which the employee could arrest failed to protect him in the circumstances of the case. It is important to appreciate that a constable arresting in these circumstances would not have made a false arrest, since he would have had reasonable cause to suspect that an arrestable offence had been committed and reasonable cause to suspect Walters of being guilty of that theft.

10:7:3 *Search after arrest*

Though the point is not clearly decided, a constable is probably entitled to search a person whom he lawfully arrests and to detain property found in his possession, if it will be material evidence in any prosecution brought. This is an added reason for calling on the police to deal with suspected thefts. Not only do they have the necessary powers of arrest and search, but the responsibility for a mistake is placed on their shoulders. The employer is not liable for false imprisonment if he gives the relevant information to a constable, who then effects the arrest by acting on his own initiative.

One more word of caution should be added. If the employer actually directs a police officer to arrest an employee, where there is no lawful justification for so acting, the constable becomes the employer's agent and then the employer is liable in damages for false arrest, just as if he had effected the arrest himself.

10:8 CAN AN EMPLOYEE GUILTY OF THEFT EFFECT RESTITUTION?

In cases of theft by an employee of his employer's money or goods, the employer or his personnel manager may wish to keep the whole matter under his control, without police intervention. If the employee is dismissed without notice, this may in itself be a sufficient warning to other employees that a serious view is taken of such conduct. In some cases, however, large sums of money or very valuable property may be involved, and then the employer's main concern is restoration of the property taken. If the money has been spent, or the goods sold and the proceeds dissipated, the chances of recovery may be remote, but if the property is still under the employee's control the employer may make an agreement not to prosecute for theft if restoration is made.

Until recently any such compromise of criminal proceedings was illegal, but the law on this point was radically altered in 1967 by s5(1) of the Criminal Law Act 1967, the effects of which will now be discussed.

Where an employee has committed an arrestable offence, such as theft, and the employer has knowledge which might be of assistance in securing the prosecution or conviction of the employee, then if the employer either accepts or agrees to accept any consideration, usually money, for not disclosing that information he is guilty of an offence. There is one vital qualification to this rule. Where the employee has stolen his employer's money or goods, then the employer may accept any consideration from the employee, usually payment or restoration of the stolen property, to make good the loss or injury caused by the theft. Consequently an agreement between employer and employee to compromise a prosecution for theft from the employer is both legal and enforceable. Failure by the employer to report the theft to the police is not a crime.

It is open to the employer to prosecute for theft where he cannot get complete or partial restitution of his property from the employee or simply if he prefers this course of action to a compromise of proceedings. If the employee is convicted of theft, the employer may pursue a civil law remedy to try and recover his losses, if the employee's resources make it worth while bringing an action.

10:9 WHEN AN EMPLOYEE'S UNAUTHORISED USE OF HIS EMPLOYER'S VEHICLE AMOUNTS TO THEFT

An employee is guilty of an offence punishable by imprisonment for up to three years if, without his employer's consent, he:

1   Takes his employer's vehicle for his own or someone else's use, or
2   Drives or rides in that vehicle, where it has been taken by another person, without having the employer's consent (Theft Act 1968 s12)

An offence is not committed if the employee deviates from the route authorised by his employer, while driving his employer's vehicle in the course of employment.

Mowe v Perraton (1952)

Perraton, a van driver, on finishing his day's work, without his employer's consent drove the van to his house and loaded a radiogram on it with the intention of taking it to the house of a relative. This act was contrary to his instructions, which were to take the van to a specified garage on completing the day's work.

The court decided that the driver was in lawful possession of the van before he took it for the unauthorised purpose. Consequently, he was not guilty of the offence with which he was charged of taking and driving away a motor vehicle without the owner's consent.

If an employee uses the employer's vehicle without his permission for private purposes outside working hours, an offence is committed under s12 of the Theft Act 1968.

R v Wibberley (1966, Court of Appeal Criminal Division)

Wibberley, a truck driver, was required to return the vehicle to his employer's yard at the end of his day's work. Instead he parked the truck outside his house for two hours while he had dinner and watched television. He then drove the truck away and used it for his own purposes. Wibberley was charged with taking and driving away a motor vehicle without the owner's consent.

The court decided that there was a distinction between deviation from employment during working hours, when the driver was still intending to carry out his instructions to drive the vehicle to its garage, and taking the vehicle after working hours, following an interval of time, when the driver did not intend to drive it back to the appropriate garage. The employee had custody of the truck when it was outside his house, but driving it away afterwards for his own purposes was in law a theft.

In Mowe v Perraton, the driver had not completed his tour of duty with the vehicle when he drove it away for his own purposes. He still had to take the van to the garage and it was his intention to drive the van there after delivering the radiogram. His day's work had not been completed when he drove it away.

The facts in R v Wibberley show that the employee's work had been completed for about two hours before he used the truck for his own purposes, and he did not intend to return it to the employer's garage that night. The employer did not object if the truck was left outside an employee's house all night but there was no authority for its use by the employee for his private purposes before the next day's work began.

10:10 LIABILITY IMPOSED UPON AN EMPLOYER AS OCCUPIER OF LAND FOR DAMAGE TO ADJOINING PROPERTY

If an employer as occupier of land acquires and keeps there anything likely to cause damage if it escapes, then he is liable for all the direct consequences of allowing the escape, even though it was not caused by his negligent conduct. This is one of the most important instances of strict or absolute liability, whereby an employer may be held legally responsible for accidental harm in the absence of negligent conduct or wrongful intent. This form of tortious liability was expounded in the next case, which gives one of the most important pronouncements concerning occupation of property ever made by the courts.

Rylands v Fletcher (1868, House of Lords)

The defendants constructed a reservoir on their land for use in conjunction with a mill. When the reservoir was filled, water flowed through disused mine shafts on the defendant's land of which he had no knowledge. Considerable damage was caused to the plaintiff's mine by flooding and he sued the defendant to recover his losses.

The court decided that the defendant was liable in damages for harm caused to the property adjoining his own even though he had not acted negligently, "The rule of law is, that the person who for his own purposes brings on to his land and keeps there anything likely to do mischief if it escapes, must keep it at his peril, and if he does not do so, is prima facie answerable for all the damage which is the natural consequence of its escape." (Mr Justice Blackburn)

An action may also be maintained for personal injuries inflicted by the escape in addition to any claim for damage to property.

The following have been judicially held as likely to do mischief if they escape: chemicals, water, sewage, fire from chimney stacks, gas, electricity, explosives, a heap of waste that may cause a landslide, and caravan dwellers fouling adjoining land and property.

10:10:1 *Non-natural user of land*

The imposition of liability under Rylands v Fletcher depends upon the presence of several vital elements. The occupier's use of his property must be non-natural, for example, constructing a reservoir or accumulating gas in pipes in large quantities. It must also be established that the occupier was actively responsible for the presence on his property of the thing causing the damage. There is no liability for water that escapes onto a neighbour's land if it has accumulated by a natural process on the property of the occupier now being sued. Further, the damage suffered by the adjoining occupier must be the natural consequence of the escape from the plaintiff's property.

North Western Utilities
v London Guarantee & Accident Co Ltd (1936, Privy Council)

North Western Utilities carried gas at high pressure under the streets of a city. Gas escaped and destroyed a hotel building which was insured by the London Guarantee & Accident Co. The insurance company claimed from North Western Utilities the losses incurred by making payment on an insurance policy to the hotel owners. The damage was caused by the activities of a third party, who fractured the gas main while laying a storm sewer.

The court decided that North Western Utilities were liable for the damages claimed, since the operations of the third party responsible were open and conspicuous, consequently the possibility of an accident should have been foreseen and guarded against. It was negligent to leave the matter to chance.

It is natural to have the ordinarily accepted utilities on property, like gas, electricity and water, together with necessary attachments such as wiring to ensure a proper supply.

Collingwood v Home & Colonial Stores Ltd (1936, Court of Appeal)

Collingwood's shop was damaged by fire which began on premises occupied by the defendant company. It was impossible to determine the exact cause of the fire, but it was thought to be partly attributable to faulty electrical wiring.

The court decided that Collingwood could not claim compensation for the losses he suffered from the defendant company, since the fire began accidentally and was not connected with a non-natural user of the premises.

10:10:2 Damage to the property of another person

It is a second requirement for liability under the rule in Rylands v Fletcher that there must be damage beyond the limits of the defendant's land caused by something originating on the defendant's land, such as the fire in the above case. There must be an escape from a place over which the defendant occupier has control to a place outside his occupation or control.

Read v J Lyons & Co Ltd (1947, House of Lords)

Read, an inspector for the Ministry of Supply, was injured by an explosion at a munitions factory while carrying out her duties. Although it was neither alleged nor proved that the respondents were negligent, it was claimed that the manufacturer of dangerous highly explosive shells was absolutely liable to anyone injured by the explosion while lawfully on the premises.

The court decided that damages were not recoverable by Read in respect of the injuries suffered, since the vital element of "escape" to establish liability under the rule in Rylands v Fletcher was absent.

10:10:3 *Various defences available to the occupier when sued*

The employer is not liable in damages if the loss is occasioned by the peculiar sensitivity of the plaintiff's property, rather than by the escape of something likely to cause harm from the employer's property.

Eastern & South African Telegraph Co Ltd
v Capetown Tramways Corporation Ltd (1902, Privy Council)

Electricity escaped from the uninsulated return rails of a tram-car system belonging to Capetown Tramways. This interfered with the transmission of messages on a submarine cable belonging to the appellant company. An action for damages was brought to recover compensation for the interruption and the cost of installing protective devices to prevent any recurrence of the interference.

The court decided that the claim must fail. A person cannot increase the legal liabilities of the adjoining occupier by using his own premises to carry on a special business which requires peculiarly sensitive apparatus being brought on to the land.

10:10:4 *Decisive factor may have been an act of God*

An act of God causes "circumstances which no human foresight can provide against, and of which human prudence is not bound to recognise the possibility, and which when they do occur, therefore, are calamities which do not involve the obligation of paying for the consequences that may result from them." (Lord Westbury)

Nichols v Marsland (1876, Court of Appeal)

Marsland dammed up a natural stream to form three artificial lakes on his land. After an exceptionally heavy rainstorm far worse than anything in living memory the dam, which was well constructed and maintained, gave way and the water caused damage on the adjoining property belonging to Nichols.

The court decided that Marsland was not liable in damages to Nichols for the harm suffered. The flooding was an act of God, which could not have been anticipated and guarded against.

This decision has been criticised on the ground that a heavy rainfall is not an act of God, nonetheless the defence will operate in appropriate circumstances, for example, cloudbursts, tornadoes, earthquakes and lightning.

10:10:5 Stranger's action may be the real cause of damage inflicted

An employer will escape liability if he can establish that damage to the adjoining owner's property was caused by a third party whose actions the employer was powerless to control, provided reasonable care has been taken to avoid external interference with any installation that may result in harm.

Rickards v Lothian (1913, Privy Council)

On the top floor of a block of offices an unknown person maliciously blocked the waste pipe of a wash basin and turned the tap on. Flooding on the floor below caused damage to Lothian's stock. He sued his landlord, Rickards, for the losses incurred.

The court decided that Rickards was not liable in damages. The loss was caused by the stranger's action which Rickards could neither control nor reasonably prevent. It was a natural use of the building to provide a reasonable and proper supply of water. If the employer could have taken reasonable steps to prevent the damage then he would not have been able to avoid liability (see North Western Utilities v London Guarantee & Accident Co Ltd, 10:10:1).

The employer is not entitled to the protection of this defence if the wrongful acts are committed not by a stranger but by his employees, agents or independent contractors working for his benefit, since their actions are under his general control and direction.

H & H Emanuel Ltd v Greater London Council and another (1970)

The Greater London Council employed a demolition contractor to remove a building from land within the council's occupation. The contractor lit a fire to burn rubbish and the sparks set alight buildings, transport and stock belonging to H & H Emanuel Ltd, a company of furniture manufacturers. The council and the contractors were sued by the company for damages as compensation for the losses incurred.

The court decided that the escaping sparks from the council's property almost certainly caused the fire. The council were not vicariously liable for this negligent act however, since the demolition experts were independent contractors and not council employees (see 9 : 4).

On the other hand the council was absolutely liable under the rule in Rylands v Fletcher for allowing the fire to escape and cause damage. They were in occupation of the premises during demolition and could have instructed the independent contractor not to light a fire at all or keep it under stricter control. An independent contractor could not be regarded as a "stranger" to his employer for the purposes of the defence under discussion.

10 : 10 : 6 *Injured party may have*
consented to the risk of damage being inflicted
Different floors of business premises are often occupied by several parties and the installation and supply of amenities like electricity, gas and water are essential to both landlord and tenant. The employer as landlord is not liable for damage caused by the escape of gas or water provided he has not acted negligently or failed to service the installations properly to ensure that they are in proper working order. Conversely if the employer is a tenant he cannot sue his landlord in these circumstances.

It is the element of common benefit to all occupiers derived from the use of these amenities that provides the landlord with a defence.

Kiddle v City Business Properties Ltd (1942)

Kiddle leased a shop in an arcade from the defendant company. Accumulations of rubbish in a pipe carrying water to a sewer caused an overflow from the roof of the arcade into Kiddle's shop. A term of the lease provided that the landlord should ensure the free passage of running water from adjoining land or buildings. Satisfactory arrangements had been made by the defendant company for periodic inspection and cleaning of the pipes. Kiddles sued to recover compensation for damage to his stock.

The court decided that a lessee of a portion of premises must take them as he finds them. It could not be proved that the defendant company had

N*

385

acted negligently in discharging their duties as landlord and they were not liable to Kiddle for the losses he had sustained.

10:10:7 *Statutory authority for non-natural user of property*

A statute may compel an authority to provide a service such as water supply. A clause in the statute may stipulate that the authority is liable for any nuisance caused in performance of these obligations. Nonetheless the authority is not liable for wrongs committed in performance of their statutory duties where the wrong was not caused by a negligent act.

Green v Chelsea Waterworks Co (1894, Court of Appeal)

The defendant company was authorised by statute to lay a water main. Green's premises were flooded when the water main burst, but this was not attributable to any negligence by the defendants. Green sued the Chelsea Waterworks Co for the losses he sustained because of the flooding.

The court decided that the defendant company was not liable to compensate Green. They were obliged by statute to lay mains and maintain a continuous supply of water. It was inevitable that damage would result from bursts that were bound to occur from time to time. If the defendant company had not acted negligently in allowing the main to burst, they were implicitly exempted by statute from liability to those who suffered from consequential flooding.

In other instances the statutory authority may be permissive rather than compulsory. In the absence of a statutory clause imposing liability for nuisance, the authority exercising the statutory powers is not responsible for non-negligent acts that cause damage. If there is a statutory clause imposing responsibility for nuisance there is liability for all wrongs, though committed without negligence.

Charing Cross Electricity Supply Co
v Hydraulic Power Co (1914, Court of Appeal)

A hydraulic main belonging to the Hydraulic Power Co burst and caused damage to the plaintiff's electric cables. There was statutory authority to lay the main, but no statutory exemption from liability for nuisance caused in the course of providing the service. It could not be shown that the burst main was the result of the defendant's negligent conduct. The Charing Cross Electricity Supply Co sued the defendants to recover damages for the injury caused.

The court decided that the defendants were liable for nuisance in accordance with the principle in Rylands v Fletcher. The defendants "are not incorporated as waterworks supply companies with an obligation to supply water to the public, but they are given powers of taking water and of laying mains without being under an obligation to keep their mains charged with water at high pressure, or at all. This serves at once to distinguish the class of cases of which Green v Chelsea Waterworks was an illustration." (Lord Sumner)

ELEVEN

Industrial Relations

THIS CHAPTER IS DEVOTED TO A DISCUSSION OF THE INDUSTRIAL Relations Act 1971 and other legislation governing industrial relations. Unless otherwise stated all references are to the 1971 Act, the general purpose of which is to promote good industrial relations by means of:

1   Collective bargaining
2   Peaceful settlement of disputes by negotiation, conciliation or arbitration
3   Free association of employees into trade unions and of employers into employers' associations
4   Protection for workers against unfair industrial practices by employers and trade unions and their officials (s1(1))

To further these purposes s2(2) requires the Secretary of State for Employment to prepare a code of practice within one year, to deal with such matters as the extent to which employers must disclose information about their business affairs to trade unions and employees so that collective bargaining can be effective (see 11 : 17). The draft code already published has been severely criticised by employees' representatives as being paternalistic and not relevant to the real problems in issue between employers and employees. It is likely that many changes will be incorporated in the code in its final form and for this reason it will not be discussed further. All references to the Secretary of State in this chapter are to the Secretary of State for Employment.

The Act sets out those standards to which industrial conduct must conform, methods being provided by which differences between opposing sides in a dispute may be resolved. It is vital to provide the machinery for strengthening negotiation and consultation. Strikes are an important facet of poor industrial relations, often caused by furthering sectional interest at the expense of the community's needs. In the realm of employment, however, there are many other ways in which a breakdown in human relationships may manifest itself.

The philosophy of the Act is to establish a legal framework by providing a clear statutory enunciation of a party's fundamental rights in the hope that it will lead to an improvement in relationships not only between unions and management, but also between unions and their members. It is hoped that the principles set out, which embody the concept of personal liberty and freedom of choice, will establish guidelines which the parties concerned will follow without recourse to pressure.

More specifically the Act regulates:

1 An employee's freedom to join or refrain from joining a trade union (see 11 : 10)
2 Setting up an agency shop, or a closed shop (see 11 : 11 and 11 : 12)
3 An employee's protection against unfair dismissal (see 11 : 13)
4 Collective agreements, which are to be legally binding (see 11 : 14)
5 Recognition of a trade union as having bargaining rights (see (11 : 16)
6 Remedial action to be taken where a procedure agreement, regulating relations between an employer and a trade union, is either non-existent or defective (see 11 : 15)
7 The employer's duty to disclose to a trade union with which he negotiates, information about the state of his business, in order to make collective bargaining more realistic (see 11 : 17)
8 Conditions to be satisfied before an organisation of workers is recognised as being a trade union in law, following registration (see 11 : 6 and 11 : 7)
9 Immunity from legal action for a trade union, its officials and unregistered bodies in respect of actions taken in contemplation or furtherance of an industrial dispute (see 11 : 19 and 11 : 20)
10 Declaration of a cooling-off period where a strike will cause a national emergency, so that negotiations may continue (see 11 : 18)
11 Complaints against trade unions and employers' associations where their activities constitute an unfair industrial practice as defined by the Act (see 11 : 9)

11:1 METHODS AVAILABLE TO THE SECRETARY OF STATE FOR SETTLING INDUSTRIAL DISPUTES

The Secretary of State will retain powers granted by Acts other than the Industrial Relations Act 1971, where he is attempting to settle an industrial dispute.

11:1:1 *The use of conciliation (Conciliation Act 1896)*
Where an industrial dispute of "difference" exists or is apprehended between employers and employees, then the Secretary of State may:

1   Inquire into the causes and circumstances of the dispute, the body undertaking this task usually being known as a Committee of Investigation

2   Arrange for the parties to meet to settle differences, under the chairmanship of a person selected by the Secretary of State or mutually agreed upon

3   On application by either employers or employees interested, not necessarily both, appoint a conciliator or board of conciliation, after taking into account the adequacy of any existing means of conciliation. The conciliator will attempt to bring the two sides together for discussions that will produce an acceptable settlement, then report to the Secretary of State. A copy of any settlement reached must be signed by the parties and delivered to the Secretary of State

4   Appoint an arbitrator on the application of both parties to the dispute, the most serious of the four alternatives that may be taken under the Act. Any award made is committed to writing, the intention throughout being that the award should be accepted as binding

The Act encourages the use of voluntary conciliation boards that may exist in any trade or district. These boards may apply to the Secretary of State for registration if they wish to do so.

The powers under this Act cover not only industrial disputes but also "differences," and in the absence of any clear definition of this term, the use of conciliation in the sphere of industrial strife appears to be very wide in scope.

11:1:2 *Setting up a*
Court of Inquiry under the Industrial Courts Act 1919
The Secretary of State may on his own initiative, without the consent of the parties to the dispute, set up a Court of Inquiry, to examine issues concerning an existing or apprehended trade dispute referred to it, and then make a report for submission to Parliament.

The court is comprised of a chairman, together with such other persons as the Secretary of State thinks fit, or alternatively it may consist of one person only, appointed by the Secretary of State.

Such an inquiry will only be resorted to after all other attempts at conciliation and arbitration have failed, where it is vitally important to the public interest that some attempt be made to find an acceptable solution.

There is power to require anyone with knowledge of the matter in hand to give evidence on oath. Any information given during the inquiry regarding a trade union, individual, firm or company, which would not have been available except as the result of that inquiry, must not be included in the report, unless the person or body concerned gives consent. The report of the inquiry does not have any legal force, but any suggestions made in it for resolving the dispute may be adopted nonetheless.

11:1:3 Referring a dispute to arbitration
(Conciliation Act 1896, Industrial Courts Act 1919)
The Secretary of State may, if he thinks fit, refer an existing or apprehended trade dispute to arbitration provided:

1 Both sides to the dispute agree
2 Settlement cannot be reached by agreed conciliation or arbitration machinery within the industry itself

The dispute may be dealt with by:

1 The Industrial Arbitration Board
2 A board of arbitrators, representing both sides, under an independent chairman, with the Secretary of State regulating procedure. Legal representation is allowed, if adequate notice is given to the board, so that the opposing side may be informed and given the opportunity of requesting representation as well
3 One or more arbitrators, as appointed, who may sit with assessors. The arbitrator makes the procedural rules

Any award made by the board or single arbitrator is not made public, the contents of the award are only for the use of parties involved. Unlike arbitration by a Court of Inquiry, even an obvious error in the award cannot be amended when once it has been made, but the Secretary of State can ask that an award be interpreted by the arbitrator, if this is necessary, and if both parties consent.

11:2 ADMINISTRATIVE AND JUDICIAL MACHINERY

A number of new bodies have been established to adjudicate upon industrial matters referred to them under various sections of the Act. These new organs of control will be discussed first, to give a general impression of the nature of their work and the powers granted to them to enable work to be carried out. These bodies are responsible for enforcing the sanctions and penalties provided for an infringement of any right conferred by the Act.

11:2:1   The National Industrial Relations Court

This is a newly constituted court, referred to as the Industrial Court, set up by s99 of the Act, with the following composition:

1   Judges of the High Court and Court of Appeal
2   At least one judge from the Court of Session in Scotland
3   Other members with special knowledge or experience of industrial relations
4   A president, appointed by the Lord Chancellor from amongst the judges already nominated

The exact nature and extent of the court's powers will emerge from a discussion of the various provisions of the Act in the succeeding sections of this chapter.

The Industrial Court may be given power under s114 to hear certain appeals on points of law from decisions of industrial tribunals dealing with matters arising under:

1   The Contracts of Employment Act 1963
2   The Redundancy Payments Act 1965
3   The Equal Pay Act 1970
4   A complaint under the Industrial Relations Act itself
5   An award of damages for breach of a contract of employment, but excluding any breach causing personal injury or death

Proceedings in tort in other courts must be stayed and the Industrial Court will have jurisdiction where the proceedings relate to acts or threatened acts which constitute:

1   A breach of duty imposed by the Industrial Relations Act (s131)
2   An unfair industrial practice as defined by various sections of the Act. For example, it is an unfair industrial practice for a trade union or its officials to take part in a strike in an attempt to induce an employer to interfere with his employee's right to join or refrain from joining a trade union (s33)

11:2:2 *Sanctions that may be imposed by the*
Industrial Court against persons committing unfair industrial practices
Any person, including an employee, may present a complaint to the
Industrial Court, if he has suffered loss as a result of an unfair industrial
practice committed by another person including a trade union or employers' association. If the Court finds that the complaint is well founded,
it may grant one or more of the following remedies, if it would be just
and equitable (s101):

1   An order determining the rights of the opposing parties
2   Monetary compensation, payable by the party committing the
     wrong unless he is an official of a trade union or employers'
     association acting within the scope of his authority as an offi-
     cial (although this remedy is available against the organisation
     concerned)
3   An order restraining the wrongdoer's activities, except in the
     case of a complaint against a Minister of the Crown or a
     government department, or one against an official of a trade
     union or employers' association acting within the scope of his
     authority as an official (although this remedy is available
     against the union or employers' association involved)

Where the complaint to the Industrial Court refers to a threat, such as a
threat to organise a strike, lock-out, or other irregular industrial action,
instead of issuing an order to restrain the wrongdoer's activities the Court
may make an order directing him (s105(3)):

1   To discontinue any threat that is being made
2   Not to take any action that has been threatened

The provisions of s101 do not apply to unfair industrial practices by an
employer in connection with:

1   The provisions of s5 which deals with an employee's right to
     join or refrain from joining a trade union or
2   The provisions of s22 dealing with unfair dismissal

These two cases are covered by s106. A complaint may be presented
against an employer by the employee involved to an industrial tribunal
where proceedings are less formal and more suited to dealing with such
matters than the Industrial Court.

11:2:3 Procedural rules applicable to the Court (Schedule 3)
The Industrial Court:

1   May sit at any time and in any place in Great Britain, whether as a single court or in two or more divisions concurrently
2   Must try to avoid formality in its proceedings where practicable
3   Must determine all the material facts by such means as the production of documents and the administration of interrogatories—that is, questions posed by one party which the other party must truthfully answer
4   May require persons to attend to give evidence and produce documents and commit persons to prison for contempt of court
5   May sit privately to hear evidence concerning national security, confidential matters set out in s158 (see 11:17:2) and information communicated to the registrar or a conciliation officer while investigating a complaint, unless the individual concerned gives permission

Anyone may appear in person, or be represented if he so wishes, by counsel, a solicitor, a representative of a trade union or employers' association, or any other person.

The Industrial Court cannot order the payment of costs or expenses of any party to proceedings, except where, in the Court's opinion:

1   The proceedings were unnecessary, improper or vexatious
2   There has been unreasonable delay or other unreasonable conduct in bringing or conducting the proceedings

Legal aid will be available in appropriate cases. Any amount of compensation may be recoverable by execution, as if it were a judgement by the High Court.

The decision of the Industrial Court on a question of fact will be final, but on a question of law there may be an appeal to the Court of Appeal.

11:2:4 Industrial tribunals
Tribunals established under s12 of the Industrial Training Act 1964 will be given further powers by the 1971 Act, which will be dealt with in discussions on the various sections of the Act. Statutory instruments may

be made to confer power to award damages for breach of a contract of employment excluding any breach causing personal injury or death (s113). The practical and informal approach of these tribunals may be better suited to the settlement of questions of employment than a court of law. A tribunal consists of a legally qualified chairman, with two other members.

The Secretary of State is given power by Schedule 6 to make regulations on the following matters,

1   Requiring persons to attend to give evidence and produce documents for inspection
2   Authorising the administration of oaths to witnesses
3   Prescribing procedure on any appeal, reference or complaint
4   Provisions for enabling a review of any decisions made or a revocation or variation of any orders and awards made
5   Determining who may represent the parties to the proceedings
6   Appointment of assessors, where statutory provisions provide for their appointment
7   Awarding and taxing of costs and expenses and enforcing their payment
8   Authorising private sitting for hearing evidence concerning national security and confidential information (see 11:17:2)

Compensation awarded by an industrial tribunal may be recoverable by execution, or attachment of earnings if the County Court so orders.

Anyone may appear in person or be represented if he so wishes, by counsel, a solicitor, a representative of a trade union or employers' association, or any other person.

11:2:5   *The Industrial Arbitration Board*
The standing Industrial Court established by the Industrial Courts Act 1919 will be renamed the Industrial Arbitration Board (s124).

It is a permanent body staffed by members appointed by the Secretary of State comprising:

1   A president with the status of a High Court judge
2   Representatives of employers and employees
3   Independent persons

One or more of the persons appointed must be a woman. The Board sits in divisions, usually comprising three persons:

1   An independent chairman, with the powers of an umpire in cases of disagreement between the other two members
2   One person to represent employers, and one person to represent employees

The Secretary of State may refer:

1   Any existing or apprehended dispute or difference to the Board for settlement, if both sides agree, or,
2   Ask the advice of the Board on any matter relating to or arising out of an industrial dispute

The Board also considers references concerning non-observance of the "fair wages resolution" 1946 (see 3:7), but it has no power to make an award. If the Board finds that the contractor was acting in breach of the resolution, then the government department concerned must effect a remedy.

Any award made by the Board does not bind the parties, but it is invariably accepted. The Board regulates its own procedure, hears opposing arguments and allows legal representation to the parties, if it thinks fit. The ultimate decision is not usually backed by reasons.

11:2:6   *The Commission on Industrial Relations*
This statutory body is composed of (s120):

1   Not less than six nor more than fifteen members, appointed by the Secretary of State
2   One member who acts as chairman and one or more as deputy chairmen

Its main function is investigating and advising on issues referred for consideration, the judicial function being the task of the Industrial Court.

The Secretary of State acting alone or jointly with another Minister may refer to the Commission any question concerning industrial relations whether generally, or in a particular industry, or a particular undertaking or, more specifically, the following matters (s121):

1   The way in which employers and employees are organised for the purposes of collective bargaining including amalgamation

and cooperation between bodies organised to further collective bargaining

2   The need for procedure agreements where they do not exist or any matter for which a procedure agreement can provide. A procedure agreement deals with the procedure for negotiating about terms and conditions of employment

3   Whether an organisation of workers is to be granted recognition and negotiating rights so that it may carry out collective bargaining

4   Disclosure of information by employers to employees and trade union officials for the furtherance of collective bargaining

5   What facilities exist for training persons in industrial relations or collective bargaining

The Commission's findings must be reported to the Secretary of State and any other Minister jointly responsible for the reference and they may publish the report if they believe publication to be appropriate (s122). An annual report must be submitted to the Secretary of State, laid before Parliament and published. The report must review the development of collective bargaining during the year, with reference to any particular problems of special importance (s123).

11:2:7 *Inquiries by the Commission (Schedule 3 Part IV)*
The Commission may hold whatever inquiries they deem necessary or advisable for the performance of their functions by use of the following powers:

1   To examine witnesses on oath or require a declaration of the truth of their statements, but the public must be excluded while such evidence is given if the witness so requests

2   Require any person to give evidence or produce documents relating to matters before the inquiry

3   Require estimates, returns or other information to be supplied by:

(a) any person carrying on any trade or business

(b) any organisation of workers or employers or its officers

provided in every case that the High Court could have compelled the giving of such evidence or production of the document.

    There are sanctions to ensure that the Commission is given all the information it requires. A person, organisation of workers or organisation of employers or body corporate may be fined up to £100 if one of the following wrongs is committed:

1   Refusal or wilful neglect to attend or give evidence as required
2   Wilful alteration, suppression, concealment, destruction or refusal to produce any documents as required
3   Refusal or wilful neglect to supply any estimate, return or other information required or
  (a) making a statement therein known to be false in a material particular
  (b) recklessly making a statement which is false in a material particular

Any information supplied is to some extent confidential and secret. It must not be disclosed except in one or more of the following cases:

1   In a report of the Commission, provided it does not prejudicially affect an individual's interests in relation to his private affairs, or
2   With the consent of the person giving it, or
3   To members or officers of the Commission, or
4   To other persons carrying out the Commission's functions, or
5   To the Secretary of State so that he may carry out his duties under the Act or any other Act, or
6   For the purpose of proceedings before the Industrial Court or criminal proceedings for an offence under the Act

Any person who discloses information in contravention of these requirements may be fined up to £400.

11:2:8   *Appointment of a registrar*
Provision is made for the appointment of:

1   A Chief Registrar of Trade Unions and Employers' Associations
2   One or more assistant registrars for England and Wales
3   One assistant registrar for Scotland

to discharge those duties imposed by the Act upon the Registrar (s63).
The first Chief Registrar was appointed on 1 September 1971 and commenced his duties on 1 October 1971.

The Chief Registrar must lay an annual report before Parliament on his activities (s64). His main function is to ensure that a trade union observes the standards set out in the Act and properly administers its own rules so that the interests of union members and the general public are safeguarded.

11:3 RESTRICTIONS ON EXCLUDING THE PROVISIONS OF THE ACT

As a general rule any type of provision in any agreement will be void if it attempts to:

1   Completely exclude or to some extent limit the operation of any provision in the Act
2   Prevent a person from bringing proceedings before the Industrial Court or an industrial tribunal

The legislature has refused to allow the effect of the Act to be nullified by recourse to the simple expedient of exclusion clauses in contracts of employment or other types of agreement (s161).

There are a few exceptions to this general rule and the effect of the Act may be limited in respect of:

1   Any agency shop agreements (see 11:11)
2   Any approved closed shop agreement (see 11:12)

The protection against an unfair dismissal established in s22 does not cover:

1   Dismissals from employment for the sole reason that a contract for a fixed term of two or more years expires without renewal, if either (s30):
  (a) the employee agreed in writing, before the contract expired, to exclude his protection against unfair dismissal, or
  (b) the contract was made before the commencement date of s30 of the Act (not fixed at the time of going to press) and is not a contract of apprenticeship
2   An exclusion of s22 under the terms of a collective agreement, where the Industrial Court recognises that the agreement provides a dismissal procedure as beneficial as that conferred by s22, though not necessarily identical (s31)
3   Cases where a conciliation officer investigates an alleged unfair

dismissal by agreement between the parties to the dispute instead of presenting a complaint to an industrial tribunal (s146)

11:3:1 *How the Act affects the Crown and Crown employees*

The Act applies to Crown employees in the same way as other employees. "Crown employment" is defined as employment under, or for the purposes of, a government department, including employment by associations established for the purpose of the Auxiliary Forces Act 1953, but excluding:

1 Members of the naval, military or air forces
2 Any women's service administered by the Defence Council
3 National Health Service employees

Any reference in the Act to an "undertaking" usually means a business, but in relation to a Minister of the Crown it means either his functions or those of the department of which he is in charge (s162).

11:4 REGISTRATION AND RECOGNITION OF AN ORGANISATION AS A TRADE UNION OR EMPLOYERS' ASSOCIATION

The term "organisation of workers" means a body of employees, whose principal objects include regulating relations with an employer (s61). A body of employees which is entered on the Special Register is also an "organisation of workers," although regulating relations between employer and employee need not be its principal object (see 11:4:3).

A *federation of workers' organisations* is a body consisting of constituent or affiliated organisations of workers, with the principal object of regulating relations between employers and employees (s61).

A federation of workers' organisations is also an "organisation of workers" for the purposes of the Act.

11:4:1 *Eligibility for registration as a trade union*

Any organisation of workers will be eligible for registration as a trade union if it is:

1 An independent body
2 With power to alter its rules and control its own property and funds without the consent of any parent association (s67(1))

The organisation must forward to the registrar

1 A copy of its rules
2 A list of its officers
3 The names and addresses of any branches
4 A return which includes, a revenue account indicating income and expenditure for the last year, a balance sheet as at the end of that period, such other accounts as the registrar may require. These accounts must give a true and fair view of the matters to which they relate, but they can only be required if the organisation seeking registration has been in operation for one year before making an application to the registrar (s68(3))

If registration is refused an appeal against the registrar's decision may be made to the Industrial Court (s115).

The new statutory definition of a *trade union* is an organisation of workers which is registered under the Act (s61(3)). A federation of workers' organisations is not eligible for registration as a trade union unless all of its constituent or affiliated organisations or those represented are either trade unions or organisations for the time being entered on the Special Register (s67(2)).

11:4:2 *The Provisional Register*
The registrar must institute and enter in a Provisional Register every organisation:

1 Registered as a trade union under the Trade Unions Acts 1871 to 1964 immediately before 5 August 1971
2 Applying for registration before 5 February 1972, on the ground that it is a trade union within the meaning of the Trade Unions Acts 1871 to 1964 (s78)

The registrar must cancel an entry on the provisional register after 6 months and register the organisation concerned as a trade union or employer's association, if he is satisfied that the organisation is eligible for registration. The registrar must inform every organisation not eligible that entry on the provisional register will be cancelled unless:

1 Within 6 months after such notification or
2 Any longer period allowed by the registrar

the rules of the organisation are altered to facilitate registration (s79).

Over 350 unions covering about 90 per cent of trade union membership will have to be entered in the Provisional Register.

11:4:3 *The Special Register*

The registrar must set up a special register. An organisation will be eligible for entry if it is:

1   A company registered under the Companies Act 1948 or
2   An organisation incorporated by charter, or letters patent

Any organisation so registered must also come within one of the two following descriptions:

1   An independent organisation of employees, with objects that include regulating relations between employers and employees, though this need not be the principal activity
2   An organisation of constituent or affiliated organisations or their representatives regulating relations between employers and employees, with each constituent or affiliated organisation being a trade union or entered on the special register (s84)

An appeal may be made to the Industrial Court if the registrar refuses registration on the provisional register (s115).

An organisation entered on the special register will be treated as a trade union with all those concessions which the Act grants to such bodies. There are exceptions to this general rule, but many of these are procedural matters relating to:

1   The definition of a trade union (s61(3) see 11:4:1)
2   Registration of a trade union (s73 and 74 see 11:4:1)
3   Entry of organisations in the provisional register (s78–80, see 11:4:2)
4   A trade union's duty to keep accounts, records, a register of members, make an annual return and report and appoint auditors to audit the accounts (s87 and 88, see 11:8)

The purpose of the Special Register. The Special Register will enable organisations operating under a charter or as a limited company with an important role to play in industrial relations to be treated as trade unions.

407

These organisations require special treatment since they could not be reconstituted to become the type of organisation that would be eligible for registration in the normal manner. They will not be required to reject their present status as chartered or incorporated organisations and transform their nature in order to claim bargaining rights and the other statutory benefits conferred by the Act.

The type of body falling within these provisions includes the Royal College of Nursing, the Royal College of Midwives, the Royal College of Physiotherapy, the British Medical Association and the British Dental Association.

In future, organisations of workers will be unable to register as limited companies (s157).

11:4:4 *Eligibility for registration as an employers' association*
An "organisation of employers" is a body of employers or individual proprietors. A federation of employers' organisations is a body consisting of constituent or affiliated organisations of employers or their representatives. Both of these bodies must have as a principal object the regulation of relations between employers and employees or organisations of workers (s62).

The requirements for registration as an employer's association are the same as those for registration as a trade union (s71 and 72) (see 11:4:1).

11:4:5 *Effects of registration as a trade union or employers' association*
On receipt of a certificate of registration the organisation concerned:

1   Becomes a body corporate (if not already one) with perpetual succession and a common seal
2   With the name specified in the certificate
3   Has vested in it all property held by any person in trust on its behalf
4   Must continue all legal proceedings that are pending in the registered name (s74)

11:5 THE POSITION OF
ORGANISATIONS THAT ARE NOT REGISTERED

Even though the name and status of a trade union will be limited to organisations that have been registered, nonetheless an unregistered body may exist to regulate relations between its members and their employers.

This situation will occur when a new organisation of workers is in the emergent stage. A combination of this type will enjoy some privileges, including protection from proceedings for civil or criminal conspiracy. It may negotiate a legally binding collective agreement. Other privileges granted to registered trade unions by the terms of the Act will not be conceded until registration has been secured.

Only on registration will the following rights be allowed:

1   To commence proceedings or make a claim for appropriate remedies before the Industrial Court or industrial tribunal
2   To operate an agency shop or an approved closed shop
3   Seek recognition as a sole bargaining unit
4   Seek remedial action where a procedure agreement is non-existent or defective
5   Secure for members the right to join and take part in trade union activities
6   To be protected against action for instructing its members to break their contracts of employment in the course of an industrial dispute (s85, see 11 : 20 : 3)
7   Taxation advantages in relation to its pension and sickness funds
8   To receive information from an employer for the purpose of collective bargaining

It has been estimated that if all unions refused to register, lost tax advantages would total £5 million. If a trade union decides to cancel its registration it can hive off its provident fund into a separate organisation, register it as a friendly society and thereby secure registration which will bring with it the required tax concessions.

Unregistered organisations are subject to the same and sometimes wider restrictions and liabilities as registered trade unions regarding:

1   Unfair industrial practices, there being no upper limit to the amount of compensation payable to the injured party as is the case with a registered trade union
2   Legal proceedings, since any funds held except those that cannot be used for financing a strike or other industrial action are liable for the payment of sums awarded against the organisation, without the necessity for bringing in representative action against nominated members of the body

11:6 PRINCIPLES TO BE OBSERVED
BY AN ORGANISATION SEEKING REGISTRATION

The principles discussed in this section must be observed by an organisation seeking recognition as a trade union or employers' association. These do not apply to federations of workers' organisations or federations of employers' organisations.

11:6:1 Application for and termination of membership

Any individual applying for membership of an organisation of workers or employers must not be excluded if it constitutes an arbitrary or unreasonable discrimination, but the applicant:

1   Must fall within the description of employee or employer for whose benefit the organisation exists and
2   In the case of membership of an organisation of workers, he must be appropriately qualified for employment as an employee of that description (s65(2) and s69)

The other principles set out in s65 subsections (3) to (6) and (8) to (10) apply equally to organisations of workers and employers.

A member of the organisation must be allowed to terminate his membership by giving reasonable notice and complying with any reasonable conditions (s65(3)). Further, he must not be excluded by way of arbitrary or unreasonable discrimination from:

1   Being a candidate for any office, or holding office in the organisation
2   Nominating candidates for offices
3   Voting in elections for office
4   Attending and taking part in meetings (s65(4))

The voting in any ballot of members must be secret and every member entitled to vote must be given a fair and reasonable opportunity of casting his vote without interference or constraint (s65(5) and (6)).

11:6:2 Political strikes

A member must not be subject to any unfair or unreasonable disciplinary action by the organisation, such as a fine or expulsion, where he refuses to take part in:

1   Any action amounting to an unfair industrial practice on his part or that of the organisation
2   A strike, lock-out or irregular industrial action short of a strike which is organised or financed by the organisation if it constitutes an unfair industrial practice. This important provision protects employees who refuse to take part in the so-called "political strike" which is not in furtherance or contemplation of an industrial dispute, but some extraneous matter, for example, opposition to the Industrial Relations Act itself which occasioned several, widespread one-day strikes (s65(7) and s69(2))

11:6:3   *Procedure when disciplinary action is taken*
With the exception of non-payment of a contribution required by the organisation's rules, a member must not be subjected to any disciplinary action unless:

1   Written notice is given of the charge
2   A reasonable time is allowed to prepare a defence
3   A full and fair hearing is given
4   A written statement of the finding is given
5   An appeal is heard, or the right to appeal is not exercised in those cases where the rules of the organisation grant a right of appeal (s65(8))

A person's membership must not be terminated unless reasonable notice of the proposal to terminate the membership has been given together with reasons (s65(9)).

11:6:4   *Unfair industrial practice*
It will be an unfair industrial practice for:

1   Any organisation of workers or any organisation of employers
2   Any official or person acting on behalf of that organisation

to take or threaten action against a member in contravention of the principles set out above (s66 and s70). The sanctions for committing this type of unfair industrial practice are set out in section 11:9.

411

11:7 THE OBLIGATORY STANDARD THAT THE RULES OF A REGISTERED ORGANISATION MUST ACHIEVE

The rules of a trade union or employers' association must comply with the requirements of Schedule 4 if registration is to be granted, except in so far as the Registrar allows exemption where special circumstances make compliance with a particular requirement inappropriate.

The basic principles set out in the Act are designed to ensure that members of a registered trade union or employers' association enjoy equal rights as regards taking part in the organisation's activities and are fairly treated in their relations with that body.

11:7:1 *Appointment of officers and officials*
As regards members of a governing body, officers and officials like shop stewards, the rules must make specific provision for their:

1   Election and re-election at reasonable intervals
2   Removal
3   Powers and duties

The rules must also specify:

1   The manner in which elections are to be held or ballots taken, whatever the purpose for holding them
2   Eligibility for voting
3   The procedure for counting and scrutinising the votes and ballot papers
4   Declaration or notification of the result

11:7:2 *Powers and duties*
There must be rules dealing with the following matters:

1   The convening and conducting of meetings so that business may be transacted
2   The manner of altering and revoking the rules themselves
3   Which body or official is able to instruct members on the organisation's behalf as to any kind of industrial action that is to be taken together with the circumstances in which such instructions may be given
4   The manner in which the organisation can be dissolved

5   The circumstances in which a federation of workers' organisations, or a federation of employers' organisations, may enter into agreements on behalf of its constituent or affiliated organisations

11:7:3   *Rules governing membership of an organisation*
The rules of organisation must specify:

1   The descriptions of persons eligible for membership
2   The procedure for dealing with applications for membership, including the right to appeal against refusal of membership
3   The amount of any contribution payable for membership and the basis on which it is assessed
4   Procedure and penalties in case of default in payment of contributions
5   The circumstances in which, and the procedure by which, membership of the organisation can be terminated, other than expulsion for disciplinary reasons
6   A procedure for inquiring into any complaint by a member concerning action contrary to the organisation's rules whether by the organisation itself or an official
7   The right of members to inspect the accounting records and register of members

11:7:4   *Rules dealing with disciplinary action*
As regards disciplinary action against a member by the organisation, the rules must specify:

1   The type of conduct in respect of which disciplinary action can be taken
2   The nature of the disciplinary action possible by way of suspension, expulsion or fine
3   The procedure to be followed, including provisions for appeals against a decision

11:7:5   *Examination and approval*
of an organisation's rules by the registrar
After issuing a certificate of registration, the registrar must examine the rules of the organisation and if they appear to be inconsistent with the requirements of the Act, he must indicate the alteration that must be

made within the period specified to remedy the defect. There may be an appeal to the Industrial Court against the registrar's decision (s115).

If the rules when resubmitted are still unsatisfactory a further period may be allowed for alteration. The rules will be approved by the registrar if resubmitted in a satisfactory form within the time specified (s75).

11:7:6 Cancellation of registration

The registrar may apply to the Industrial Court for cancellation of:

1   Registration as a trade union or employers' association or
2   Entry on the Special Register

where rules based on the principles required by the Act have not been submitted at all or have not been amended as required to remove any inconsistency with those principles.

The Court may allow a further period for compliance or cancel the registration, as it considers appropriate in the circumstances.

A trade union or employers' association may apply to the Industrial Court:

1   To be allowed a further period for altering its rules, or
2   For a direction that the registrar should approve the rules already submitted

The court will act as it deems appropriate (s76).

The registrar may successfully apply to the Industrial Court to cancel the registration of an organisation as a trade union or an employers' association or entry on the special register if it is established that:

1   The registration was obtained by fraud or mistake
2   The organisation has ceased to be eligible for registration because of a change in its rules or circumstances
3   The organisation has refused to comply with any requirement imposed on it by the registrar, but extra time may be given to remedy this default (s77)

11:7:7 Winding up a trade union or employers' association

If it appears to the Chief Registrar that there are reasonable grounds for believing that a trade union or employers' association is insolvent, he may appoint an inspector to examine the body concerned. If the inspector's report confirms this belief, a petition may be presented to the High Court by the Chief Registrar for the organisation to be wound up (s90).

11:8 A REGISTERED ORGANISATION'S DUTY TO KEEP ACCOUNTS AND OTHER RECORDS

Every trade union and every employers' association must:

1 Keep proper accounting records in respect of its transactions, assets and liabilities, to give a true and fair view of its affairs and explain its transactions

2 Maintain a satisfactory system of control of its accounting records, its cash holding and all receipts and remittances

3 Keep a register of its members in the form required by the registrar

4 Send an annual return for every preceding calendar year before 1 June dealing with its affairs to the registrar containing, in accordance with Schedule 5 Part I:

  (a) revenue accounts indicating the income and expenditure of the trade union or employers' association during the period covered by the return

  (b) a balance sheet as at the end of that period

  (c) such other accounts (if any) as the registrar may require
These accounts must give a true and fair view of the matters to which they relate

5 Appoint auditors to audit accounts contained in the annual return and forward a copy of their report to the registrar as part of the annual return

6 Publish an annual report of its activities and

  (a) supply a copy free to members or

  (b) include it in a journal relating to its affairs which is available to members
Every annual report must include a full reproduction of the last annual return. If the preparation of an annual report would be onerous, having regard to the small number of members involved, the registrar may grant exemption, but a copy of the annual return must be supplied instead

7 Inform the registrar within one month of any changes in the rules, officers or address of the principal office

8 Supply any person with a copy of its rules on request, either

free of charge or on payment of a reasonable charge (ss87, 88 and 89; Schedule 5, Parts I, II and III)

11:8:1   *Penalties for non-compliance with these duties*
For refusal or wilful neglect to perform these duties a fine not exceeding £100 may be imposed upon:

1   The organisation concerned and
2   Any officer whose duty it was to ensure compliance with the obligation imposed, unless he can prove that he believed on reasonable grounds that some other reliable and competent person was authorised to, and would, secure compliance

Any person wilfully altering or causing to be altered any documents required for the purposes set out above with intent to falsify it, or enable a trade union or employers' association to evade the duties thereby imposed, will be liable to a fine not exceeding £400 (s91).

11:9   COMPLAINTS TO THE REGISTRAR CONCERNING THE ACTIVITIES OF REGISTERED ORGANISATIONS

A complaint may be made to the registrar by a member of a trade union or employers' association, a former member excluded against his wishes, or a person refused membership, alleging:

1   A violation of the guiding principles governing the actions of that trade union or employers' association (see 11:6) which constitute an unfair industrial practice (see 11:6:6)
2   A breach of the organisation's rules (s81)

11:9:1   *Period within which the complaint must be brought*
The complainant must make his application promptly, before the end of a four-week period beginning with whichever is the latest of the following dates:

1   The date of the alleged wrongful act
2   The earliest date upon which the applicant knew of the wrongful act
3   Determination of the complaint by the organisation concerned in accordance with the rules

If there are special reasons, such as illness, preventing presentation of a complaint, the registrar may entertain a complaint after the four-week period has elapsed.

11:9:2 *Resubmission to and consideration by the registrar*
An application may be deferred until the issue has been considered by the organisation itself under an adequate procedure established by its rules. Resubmission to the registrar is possible:

1   After allowing the organisation a reasonable time for consideration, although they have not yet determined the issue
2   Within four weeks of a final determination by the organisation under its established procedure

If the registrar investigates the matter, he must notify the findings to both sides. If the grounds of the application appear to be well founded:

1   He must attempt a settlement without the question being referred to an industrial tribunal (s82)
2   But if he cannot secure a settlement within a reasonable time then he may present the complaint against the trade union or employers' association to an industrial tribunal (s108)

11:9:3 *Complaint to an industrial tribunal in similar circumstances*
The complaint may be referred by the party aggrieved direct to the industrial tribunal instead of to the registrar. The tribunal will not entertain the complaint if:

1   An application has been made to the registrar and
2   He has dealt with the issue or is in the process of dealing with it (s107)

If the claim is just and equitable the tribunal may:

1   Determine the rights of the two sides in dispute and/or
2   Award compensation payable by the organisation to the complainant, but this must not exceed two years' pay or £4160 (that is two years' pay at the rate of £40 per week) whichever sum is the smaller (s109 and s118). Compensation must be granted where loss of employment results from wrongful termination of or exclusion from union membership

o*   417

11:9:4 *Reference by the registrar to the Industrial Court*

If a settlement is not reached and a complaint is not presented to an industrial tribunal, a serious issue may be referred by the registrar to the Industrial Court. If the Court finds that any complaint made by the registrar is well founded, one or more of the following remedies may be granted, as appropriate.

1 An order determining the right of the original applicant and the trade union or employers' organisation concerned
2 An award of compensation payable by the organisation at fault to the applicant, not exceeding two years' pay or £4160, whichever sum is the smaller
3 An order directing the trade union or employers' association to refrain from continuing the action complained of or taking similar action against the applicant in the future (s103)

11:9:5 *Investigation instituted by the registrar*

The registrar must hold an investigation if he suspects a serious contravention of the principles or rules upon which registration as a trade union or an employers' association is based. If his suspicions are well founded he must prevent a continuance or repetition of the situation by consultation with the organisation concerned by securing a promise to remedy the situation. The registrar may make a complaint to the Industrial Court if remedial action is not forthcoming (s83). When holding an inquiry, the powers of the registrar are the same as those of the Commission on Industrial Relations in a similar situation (see 11:2:7). Information given at the inquiry must not be disclosed except (Schedule 3, paragraph 44):

1 With the consent of the person concerned, or
2 To officers or servants of the Chief Registrar or any other person so that the Chief Registrar's functions may be fulfilled, or
3 For the purposes of
  (*a*) proceedings before the Industrial Court or an industrial tribunal on a complaint presented by the registrar
  (*b*) any criminal proceedings in respect of an offence under the Act

Any person disclosing information in contravention of these provisions will be liable to a fine of up to £400 (Schedule 3, paragraph 45).

The Industrial Court, on receiving the registrar's complaint may make an order directing the trade union or employers' association concerned to refrain from continuing the action complained of and to prevent a continuance or repetition of the breach of the organisation's rule (s104).

11:10 FREEDOM TO JOIN OR REFRAIN FROM JOINING A TRADE UNION

The main aim of the provisions to be discussed under this heading is to secure an employee's freedom of action in determining whether he will join a trade union. If he is not a member he cannot be required by the union to come out on strike or be penalised by the union for refusing to do so. The employer must not take any steps to interfere with the employee's statutory right to choose for himself. More significantly, a trade union and its officials must not bring pressure to bear on an employer by forcing him to take action against any employee joining or refusing to join a union. It is no longer possible to operate a "pre-entry closed shop" whereby a person is excluded from entering a given employment unless he is a member of a stated trade union. The general principle now applicable is that an employer may engage anyone with the skills required for the post that is vacant irrespective of whether he is a member of a union. A post-entry closed shop will be allowed in some circumstances whereby a person must join a specific union after entering a specified type of employment, unless he secures exemption (see 11:12).

The overriding general principle is that an employee has the right:

1. To become a member of whichever trade union he chooses and to take part in its activities outside working hours or within working hours if the employer consents
2. To refuse to join a union or a particular union (s5(1)), but where an agency shop agreement exists he must make a payment in lieu of the union membership fee (see 11:11:1)

These rights are granted to a person:

1. Working under a contract of employment
2. Working under any contract whereby he undertakes to carry out personally any work or services, excluding services of a professional nature
3. Crown employment excluding the armed forces

11:10:1 *Unfair industrial practices*
by an employer connected with union membership
It is an unfair industrial practice for an employer or a person acting on his behalf:

1   To interfere with an employee's rights in deciding whether or not to join a trade union, but the employer or person acting on his behalf is permitted to encourage an employee to join a trade union recognised by the employer as having negotiating rights (s5(3))

2   To dismiss, penalise or otherwise discriminate against him for exercising those rights, for example, refusing to promote him when he is qualified and ready for promotion. An employee is discriminated against if the employer offers him any kind of benefit as an inducement to join or refrain from joining a trade union, if the benefit is granted to those employees acceding to the employer's wishes, but withheld from those who do not accede (s5(4))

3   To refuse to engage a potential employee because he is either a member of a trade union or not a member of a trade union (s5(2))

An employee wishing to exercise his freedom of choice to join an organisation of workers not registered as a trade union (or entered on the Provisional Register) is not protected against an employer's discriminatory acts on the ground that they constitute an unfair industrial practice.

An employee may present a complaint to an industrial tribunal alleging an unfair industrial practice by the employer or his representative in connection with s5. If it is just and equitable the tribunal will:

1   Make an order determining the rights of the parties and/or
2   Award compensation payable by the employer to the complainant if the complaint was well founded (s106)

If the employee making the complaint has been dismissed he is entitled to seek re-engagement.

11:10:2 *The employer's remedy*
if he was induced to commit an unfair industrial practice
The employer may claim that he was induced to take the action com-

plained about against the employee or potential employee because of pressure exercised on him amounting to an unfair industrial practice (see 11 : 10 : 3). The employer may require the third party responsible for the unfair industrial practice to be joined as a party to the proceeding. The third party may be required to make a just and equitable contribution to the compensation awarded against the employer. This may amount to a complete indemnity for the employer. A trade union may be required to pay a contribution to the employer in respect of the conduct of its officials within the scope of the authority conferred on them (s119). These provisions recognise the reality of the situation. Although in some cases it is clearly the employer who is solely responsible for acting unfairly, there are other cases where discriminatory action against an employee results from industrial action organised on such a scale as to be unfair to both the employer and employee.

11 : 10 : 3   *Unfair industrial practice*
by a trade union connected with union membership
It is an unfair industrial practice for any person, including a trade union or other organisation of workers or their officials, knowingly to induce an employer to indulge in an unfair industrial practice against an employee exercising his right to join or refuse to join a trade union, by putting pressure on that employer in the form of threatening, organising or financing a strike, or irregular action short of a strike (s33(3)).

A complaint in relation to such action may be presented to the Indus-there are other cases where discriminatory action against an employee to join its organisation by threatening disruption of work and forcing the employer to require the employee either to join the union or to leave his job.

Irregular industrial action means a concerted course of action by employees other than a strike in contemplation or furtherance of an industrial dispute:

1   With the intention of preventing, reducing or otherwise interfering with the production of goods or provision of services and
2   In breach of their contracts of employment in some or every case or, where they are not employees, in breach of their terms and conditions of service (s33(4))

11 : 10 : 4   *Any attempt to*
take away an individual's rights under s5 is void
Any provision in an agreement, such as a collective agreement, is void,
if it prevents the engagement of a prospective employee on the ground
that he is not a member of a trade union, or a particular trade union, or
that his engagement has not been recommended or approved by a trade
union (s7(1)).

It is an unfair industrial practice for any person, including a trade
union or other organisation of workers, or officials of these bodies, to
knowingly induce an employer:

1   To comply with any provision in an agreement which is void or
    declared to be void by the Industrial Court under s7
2   To enter into an agreement which would be void under s7

by threatening or organising a strike or irregular industrial action short
of a strike (s33(3)(c)).

The Industrial Court may declare this type of provision to be void, on
an application by an employee who proves that the provision prevented
him from securing employment with a particular employer (s7(2) and (3)).
It will not be possible for an informal closed shop to be instituted outside
the provisions of the Act.

11 : 10 : 5   *Reference by the tribunal to a conciliation officer*
A copy of a complaint under s5 presented to an industrial tribunal may
be forwarded to a conciliation officer appointed by the Secretary of State.
This officer must try to promote a settlement of the complaint without
the matter being determined by the tribunal, if:

1   He is asked to do so by the employer and employee concerned,
    or
2   In the absence of such a request the officer thinks that his
    intervention would have a reasonable chance of success
    (s146(2))

The officer must try to secure:

1   Re-engagement on fair terms, if the employee has been dis-
    missed, by the employer who dismissed him or the employer's
    successor or associate
2   Alternatively, where re-engagement is impracticable or cannot

be agreed upon, determination as to the amount of compensation payable by the employer (s146(3))

11:10:6 *Reference direct to a conciliation officer*

Where the employee is no longer employed by the employer allegedly committing the unfair industrial practice under s5 then, before complaining to an industrial tribunal, the conciliation officer may be asked to intervene by either employer or employee in the manner described above (s146(4)). Reference direct to the conciliation officer may encourage an early settlement of the dispute without intervention by the tribunal.

11:11 AGENCY SHOP AGREEMENTS

If a registered trade union represents and is financially supported by all the employees in a given undertaking, it is accepted in principle that all employees working there should be union members or make a payment in lieu of a membership fee. The agency shop provisions recognise the justifiable demands of trade unionists that employees should not enjoy the benefits gained from a trade union's activities in securing higher wages and better terms of employment without making a contribution to support these activities. It is for the employees themselves to decide whether such an agency shop agreement should govern their place of employment and their relationship with the employer.

11:11:1 *Meaning of the term "agency shop agreement"*

More precisely, an agency shop agreement means an agreement made between an employer and a trade union whereby the terms and conditions of their employment include a condition that every employee:

1   Becomes a member of one or more trade unions, or
2   If he so wishes, pays in lieu of membership a contribution equivalent to the union dues, to either
  (a) the union itself, or
  (b) to some charity
      (s6(1) and s11)

When an agency shop agreement is made between one or more trade unions and an employers' association, it binds:

1   Particular employers on whose behalf it was expressly made
2   All employers who are members of the association, though

they are not expressly bound by name, whether or not they were members at the time the agreement was concluded

An employer will be released from the agreement by resigning from the association, unless it was expressly made on his behalf (s6(6)).

It is not an unfair industrial practice for the employer to refuse to employ any person or to dismiss, penalise or otherwise discriminate against an employee refusing to join a trade union recognised by an agency shop agreement or pay a contribution to that union or to charity (s6(2)). Presumably discrimination will cover refusal to promote the employee most qualified for a higher grading.

It will not be an unfair industrial practice for a trade union to call a strike to secure the dismissal of an employee refusing to pay a contribution to the charity or a union.

11:11:2 *Payments by an employee not wishing to join a union*
The appropriate contribution to a trade union in lieu of membership may be either:

1 A periodical payment, not exceeding the amount payable for trade union membership, excluding any contribution that is not payable after giving the stipulated notice to the union, such as contributions to a political fund
2 A periodical payment and an initial payment as well, where a new member on joining the union would be required to pay such a contribution (s8)

Where an employee has agreed to pay appropriate contributions to a trade union in lieu of membership and requests his employer to deduct the contribution from his salary and pay it to the union, then any failure by the employer to do so will not be regarded as a failure by the employee to make the payment. If an employee is already engaged in a unit of employment when the agency shop agreement comes into force, then he need not make a contribution for a period of three months. An employee who is engaged after such an agreement has been concluded need not make a contribution for the first month (s6(3) and s8(5)).

An employee objecting on grounds of conscience to being a member of a trade union or paying contributions to the union in lieu of membership, may, if the union accepts his objection, pay an equivalent sum to some charity, to be determined by agreement between that employee and the union (s9).

424

These provisions will end the situation whereby all employees in a certain undertaking must belong to a union as an essential prerequisite to being allowed to work there. If a substantial number of employees decide not to join the union or to make a payment to its funds then the solidarity of the union and its finances may be seriously affected.

An industrial tribunal must determine a dispute concerning:

1   A claim by the employee that the contribution to the union or charity he is being asked to pay is above the equivalent contribution for trade union membership.
2   The genuineness of his conscientious objection to joining the union
3   The charity to receive any payment to be made
4   The amount of the contribution to a charity that would be equivalent to an appropriate contribution to the trade union (s10)

These provisions attempt to secure a compromise between the right of the individual to choose not to belong to a trade union against his will and his social responsibility as a member of a work group whose standards of living may depend on the effectiveness of the union.

11:11:3   *Procedure for procuring an agency shop agreement*
If an employer is unwilling to enter into an agency shop agreement, the trade union concerned may apply to the Industrial Court specifying:

1   The employees to be covered by the agreement, and
2   The employer and the trade union who would be the parties to an agreement

If the Industrial Court is satisfied that the trade union is recognised by the employer as having negotiating rights or rights corresponding to negotiating rights in respect of the employees in question, then the Commission on Industrial Relations may be asked to organise a ballot to determine whether an agency shop agreement should be made (s11).

The Commission will determine whether the ballot should extend to:

1   All employees specified in the application or should be limited to some of those employees only
2   Employees not specified in the application in respect of whom the trade union or joint negotiating panel has negotiating rights recognised by the employer

It is an unfair industrial practice for an employer to threaten or effect a lock-out in order to knowingly induce or attempt to induce a trade union or other person to refrain from making an application to the Industrial Court for an agency shop agreement (s16).

11:11:4 *Members decide by ballot*
The employer is under a duty to enter into and carry out an agency shop agreement, if it is supported by:

1   The majority of employees eligible to vote in the ballot, or
2   Not less than two-thirds of those who voted (s13)

If the employer fails to enter or carry out an agency shop agreement, the trade union concerned may complain to the Industrial Court. If it is just and equitable the Court may make an order:

1   Determining the rights of the parties and/or
2   Directing the employer to take appropriate action in fulfilment of his duty, except in the case of Crown employment (s102)

The trade union may also call a strike or organise industrial action in support of its claim against an unwilling employer (s16(2)(a)).

11:11:5 *Employees may not want an agency shop agreement*
The result of the ballot may be that neither a majority of employees eligible to vote, nor two-thirds of those who voted, have voted in favour of an agency shop agreement. The Industrial Court must make an order stating that:

1   An agency shop agreement must not be made during the next two years between the employer and the trade union concerned, in respect of employees covered by the application that has been voted against
2   If such an agreement is made it will be void (s13)

11:11:6 *Unfair industrial practice by a rival union*
The conclusion of an agency shop agreement by an employer with a particular union may not be welcomed by a rival union seeking recognition from the same employer. To prevent industrial unrest resulting in this type of situation, s13(2) and s16 provide that it will be an unfair industrial

practice for any person, trade union or other organisation of workers or officials of those bodies to organise or finance a strike or irregular industrial action short of a strike or theatening such action knowingly to induce or attempt to induce an employer:

1   Not to apply for an agency shop agreement in the first place with a particular union

2   Not to enter or carry out an agency shop agreement agreed by a majority of employees

3   To enter into such an agreement after an application to the Industrial Court has been made already in respect of the same body of employees

11:11:7 *Continuance or rescission of an existing agency shop agreement*
It is possible for employees to take the initiative in securing rescission of an agency shop agreement where its continuance no longer has their support. The Industrial Court must ask the Commission to arrange a ballot to determine whether the agreement should be continued:

1   On application by an employee, with the written support of one-fifth of the employees covered by the agreement

2   Provided two or more years have elapsed since the result of the ballot supporting the agreement (s14)

The Industrial Court will rescind the agreement if neither the majority of employees eligible to vote, nor two-thirds of those who voted, favour its continuance. For the next two years an application will not be allowed to consider making a similar agency shop agreement in respect of the same body of employees and any such agreement made will be void (s15).

On the other hand, if the result of the ballot shows that either a majority of employees eligible to vote or not less than two-thirds of those who voted in it have voted in favour of continuing the agency shop agreement, then the Industrial Court will not entertain further applications on the advisability of continuing the agreement for the next two years.

It will be an unfair industrial practice for an employer to institute or threaten a lock-out knowingly to induce an employee, trade union or joint negotiating panel not to challenge an agency shop agreement (s16).

An employer may not welcome a rival union challenging the right of the union with whom the employer negotiates under an agency shop agreement to continue as the true representative of the work force.

11:12 NEGOTIATION OF AN APPROVED CLOSED SHOP AGREEMENT

An "approved closed shop agreement" is an agreement made:

1   With the approval of the Industrial Court
2   Between an employer (or employers) and a trade union (or trade unions) whereby specified employees are required, as a condition of employment, to be or become a member of a trade union, unless specially exempted (s17(1))

An employee falling within this category cannot agree with his employer to refuse to be a member of a trade union with which the closed shop agreement was made (s17(3))

11:12:1 *Special exemption from becoming a trade union member*

An employee may object on grounds of conscience to becoming a member of a trade union in accordance with an approved closed shop agreement. By agreement with the union he may pay a specified contribution to a charity instead (Schedule 1 para. 22). The rules set out in 11:11:2 will apply in this situation (para. 23). Every approved closed shop agreement must include principles for determining an appropriate charitable contribution (para. 21).

11:12:2 *Action that may be taken against a non-union member*

Where an approved closed shop agreement exists, it is not an unfair industrial practice for an employer, or his authorised agent, to: refuse to engage, dismiss, penalise or otherwise discriminate against an employee (except a specially exempted employee) covered by that agreement if:

1   He is not a member of the trade union with which the agreement was made (s17(5))
2   He refuses to become a member by not applying for membership or withdrawing any application made before the end of the relevant period; that is:
   (a) three months from the date upon which the employee came within the scope of an approved closed shop agreement for the first time, or
   (b) one month from the date of employment in a position already covered by such an agreement

3   He has been excluded from membership by
(a) rejection of his application or expulsion from membership and
(b) his appeal has been dismissed or withdrawn, or he has not exercised his right to appeal within the stipulated time (s18)

11:12:3   *Approval of proposed*
closed shop agreement (Schedule 1 Parts I and II)
An initial joint application may be made to the Industrial Court by:

1   One or more employers or organisations of employers, and
2   One or more trade unions

Where it is proposed to make a closed shop agreement, a draft of the proposed agreement must be submitted. It is an unfair industrial practice for any person, including a trade union or other organisation of workers or officials of such bodies, to knowingly induce an employer or employers' association to join in making an application under Part I of Schedule 1, by threatening or organising a strike or irregular industrial action short of a strike (s33(3)).

The Industrial Court will refer the application to the Commission to determine whether, in relation to the employees specified, only a closed shop agreement will achieve all of the following purposes:

1   To enable them to be organised, or continue to be organised as a free association of employees in independent trade unions, so as to be representative, responsible and effectual bodies for regulating relations between employers and employees
2   To maintain reasonable terms and conditions of employment and reasonable prospects of continued employment
3   To promote and maintain stable arrangements for collective bargaining
4   To prevent the frustration of existing or proposed collective agreements

A report on these matters must be published and submitted to the Industrial Court, the applicants and the Secretary of State. The Industrial Court will not proceed further with an application unless the Commission reports that a closed shop agreement is necessary to enable all of the purposes specified above to be achieved. In some cases an agency shop agreement may suffice.

In other cases the Industrial Court will make an order lasting for between one to three months, during which time an application may be made for a ballot amongst the employees to whom the closed shop agreement would apply, if there is a written request for a ballot by one-fifth of those employees. If an effective application for a ballot is not made within the time specified, the Industrial Court will approve the draft proposals.

11:12:4 Holding a ballot amongst employees affected

If a ballot is held and there is a favourable response from :

1 A majority of the employees eligible to vote, or
2 Two-thirds of those actually voting

the Industrial Court will approve the draft proposals for an approved closed shop agreement. Where the result of the ballot does not favour the closed shop agreement, then the Industrial Court will not entertain any application for another agreement in relation to the same body of employees for the next two years.

When an approved closed shop agreement is concluded between a trade union and an organisation of employers, it binds :

1 Particular employers on whose behalf it was expressly made
2 All employers who are members of the organisation, though not expressly made on their behalf, whether or not they were members at the time when the agreement was concluded
3 Employers who are not members of the organisation, who apply to be included in the agreement

11:12:5 Continuance of an approved closed shop agreement (Schedule 1 Part III)

An employee covered by an approved closed shop agreement may apply to the Industrial Court for a ballot to determine whether it should continue to exist if

1 One-fifth of the employees covered by the agreement give written approval to the application
2 The application is made two years or more after the date of the previous ballot, whether that ballot related to establishing or continuing the agreement

If, as a result of the ballot, neither:

1   A majority of employees eligible to vote, nor
2   Two-thirds of those who voted

voted for the continuance of the closed shop agreement, it will be revoked by the Industrial Court.

11:12:6   How these provisions will operate

The provisions on approved closed shop agreements are not:

1   Opening the door to a general application of the post-entry closed shop
2   Allowing the operation of a pre-entry closed shop
3   Intended to cover any particular industry by name, but merely to set up the machinery for assessing whether any industry is entitled to have its claim for recognition as an approved closed shop accepted

It is expected that an approved closed shop agreement will be allowed for seamen and actors. These two industries have common characteristics which distinguish them from other types of employment. Jobs are of short duration and the employee seldom remains with the same employer for two successive engagements. In both cases a number of permanent, full-time employees are supported by a large transient workforce.

11:13   A NEW PROTECTION AGAINST UNFAIR DISMISSAL

The dismissal of an employee frequently causes strike action. An employer may terminate his employee's contract of employment by giving the requisite period of notice required by that contract or paying money in lieu of notice. Previously the employee had no remedy if such dismissal was nevertheless unfair because his employer acted without reasonable cause and severely prejudiced the employee's future livelihood. The Act tries to remedy this situation.

11:13:1   Employees not covered
by the protections against unfair dismissal

In this context, the term "claimant" means an employee asserting that his employer has dismissed him unfairly or that Crown employment has been terminated unfairly. The provisions on unfair dismissal do not cover employees engaged in employment of the types specified below :

1   Where the undertaking had less than four employees (including the claimant) who had been continuously employed for a period of not less than thirteen weeks, unless the reason for dismissal was that the employee exercised or intended to exercise his right to join or refrain from joining a trade union

2   Where the employer is the spouse or a close relative of the employee (that is a parent, grandparent, step-parent, child, grandchild, stepchild, brother, sister, half-brother or half-sister)

3   Where the employee is a registered dock worker under the Dock Workers (Regulation of Employment) Act 1946, unless he is not engaged on dock work

4   Any employment as master or crew member of a fishing vessel, where remuneration is solely a share in the profits of the vessel

5   Where less than twenty-one hours a week are worked in normal circumstances

6   Where the employee ordinarily works outside Great Britain

7   Where the employee works on board a ship registered in the UK, provided

(a) the employment is wholly outside Great Britain and

(b) the employee is not ordinarily resident in Great Britain

8   Where the employee was continuously employed for a period less than two years (104 weeks), ending with the date of termination of the contract of employment, unless the reason for dismissal was that the employee exercised or intended to exercise his rights to join or refrain from joining a trade union. (The phrase "continuous employment" has the meaning assigned to it by Schedule 1 to the Contracts of Employment Act 1963 (see Chapter 13) (s151))

9   Where the employee reached either :

(a) the normal retiring age in the undertaking by which he was employed, or

(b) 60 for a woman or 65 for a man
    before the contract of employment was terminated, unless the reason for dismissal was that the employee exercised or intended to exercise his rights to join or refrain from joining a trade union (ss27, 28 and 29)

10   Where a certificate signed by a Minister of the Crown certifies

that the dismissal was for the purpose of safeguarding national security. In such cases the Industrial Court must dismiss any complaint alleging unfair dismissal (s159)

11 Where there is dismissal from employment under a contract for a fixed term of two or more years, by the term expiring without renewal provided:
  (a) the contract was made before the commencement of s30 of the Act
  (b) it is not a contract of apprenticeship (s30)
12 Where there is dismissal from employment under a contract for a fixed term of two or more years (whether made before or after the Act) by the term expiring without renewal, provided the employee agreed in writing to exclude his rights in respect of unfair dismissal conferred on him by s22 (s30)

11:13:2 *An alternative to the statutory procedure*
The statutory provisions on unfair dismissal do not extend to employees who are protected by a dismissal procedure under a procedure agreement, if it is as beneficial as, though it need not be identical with, the statutory procedure and is recognised as an alternative procedure by the Industrial Court. The dismissal procedure must

1 Be available without discrimination to all employees covered by the agreement
2 Grant a right to arbitration or adjudication by an independent referee, tribunal or other independent body, if a decision cannot otherwise be reached because there is a failure to agree (s31)

The agreement may be revoked by the Industrial Court on the application of the parties or the Secretary of State if:

1 All the parties to it are agreeable, or
2 If it has ceased to provide an alternative method of dealing with unfair dismissal (s32)

11:13:3 *The meaning of unfair dismissal*
In every contract of employment to which the Act applies it will be an unfair industrial practice for an employer to dismiss his employee unfairly (s22). For the purpose of the Act an employee is dismissed if:

1 His contract of employment is terminated by the employer

with or without notice, thus "dismissal" clearly covers both instant dismissal and also cases where the appropriate period of notice is given. An employee will still be regarded as having been dismissed if he gives a written counter-notice of his intention to leave before the time stipulated by the employer

2   Under a contract of employment for a fixed term, that term expires without renewal (s23)

If an employee gives notice and leaves his employment because the employer's attitude has made working conditions difficult, this is not a dismissal for the purposes of s22.

Dismissal is "fair" if the reason or principal reason is

1   Related to the employee's capabilities or qualifications for performing the work he is employed to do :
   (a) "Capability" means his skill, aptitude, health, physical or mental quality
   (b) "Qualifications" means his degree, diploma or other academic, technical or professional qualification relevant to the position held,
2   Related to his conduct, for example insubordination and dishonesty
3   Caused by redundancy
4   That continued employment in the present position would be a violation of the employer's statutory duty; for example, the employer cannot continue to employ a woman in a job that has been declared unsuitable for women workers and consequently prohibited by law

On the other hand, dismissal of an employee is *unfair* if the reason or principal reason was one of the following :

1   That he exercised or intended to exercise his rights to join or refrain from joining a trade union
2   Redundancy, if it can be shown that the circumstances constituting the redundancy applied equally to other employees in the same undertaking holding similar positions, that they have not been dismissed, and that the dismissal was really caused
   (a) because the employee exercised or intended to exercise his right to join or refrain from joining a trade union, or

(b) by a contravention of agreed procedures relating to redundancy, where there is no special reason for so acting

These provisions prevent an employer dismissing a trade unionist under the guise of redundancy. On the other hand, a member of an unregistered organisation of workers may be dismissed in this way

3   Where the employer acted unreasonably in treating a good reason for dismissal as a sufficient reason for dismissal

The burden of proof lies on the employer to establish:

1   The reason or principal reason for the dismissal, and
2   That it was a "fair" reason for dismissal
3   That he acted reasonably in treating a good reason as a sufficient reason (s24)

In determining the reason or principal reason for dismissal no account will be taken of any pressure exercised against the employer by way of threatening or organising strike or irregular industrial action short of a strike, knowingly to induce him to dismiss an employee (s33(1) and (2)).

11:13:4   *What effect will these provisions have?*
Clearly the employer must now inform his employee of the reasons for dismissal in every case so that it can be ascertained whether they are fair. If they are not fair a complaint must be made to an industrial tribunal. Since dismissal is fair, if "related to the conduct of the employee" (s24(2)(b)), this may be relied upon in many cases to justify dismissal, until the phrase has been interpreted judicially. Many fine distinctions will be drawn to determine whether the employer acted reasonably or unreasonably in treating a reason for dismissal as being a sufficient reason.

11:13:5   *Dismissal in connection with a lock-out or strike*
An employee may claim that his dismissal is unfair if he is not re-engaged by the employer, his successor or associate, in the same job, or in a different, but reasonably suitable job, when work is resumed after a lock-out. This rule applies whether the lock-out extends:

1   To all employees or to some employees only
2   Whether the dismissal occurs at the beginning or during the course of the lock-out (s25)

Dismissal is fair if the reason, or principal reason, was that the claimant took part in a strike or other industrial action unless:

1   The employer did not dismiss other employees for so acting, or, alternatively, if after they were dismissed, they were offered re-engagement when the industrial action ended, or

2   The reason for the claimant being dismissed or not being offered re-engagement, was that he exercised or intended to exercise his right to join or refrain from joining the trade union (s26)

This provision prevents victimisation of trade unionists.

11:13:6 *Remedies for an employee who has been dismissed*
If an industrial tribunal finds that:

1   The grounds of the complaint relating to dismissal are well founded

2   It would be practicable and equitable for the complainant to be re-engaged by the employer who dismissed him or by the employer's successor or associate

then it may make a recommendation to that effect.

    Compensation will be awarded to the complainant instead of re-engagement where:

1   Re-engagement cannot be recommended

2   A recommendation of re-engagement has not been implemented

The employer cannot be forced to reinstate an employee that he does not want, but compensation is payable if the dismissal was unfair (s106). An employer may feel that it is worth while dismissing a troublesome employee, even if this means that compensation is payable where it is difficult to establish a good reason. An organisation of workers may strike or take other industrial action to secure re-engagement of an employee who has been unfairly dismissed in the view of the tribunal, and such action will not constitute an unfair industrial practice.

11:13:7 *The amount of compensation recoverable*

The tribunal may award such compensation as is just and equitable in the circumstances, having regard to the employee's loss caused by the employer's action in dismissing him. The sum awarded will take into account:

1   Any expenses incurred by reason of the dismissal; for example, costs incurred in seeking a new appointment
2   Loss of any benefit reasonably expected; for example, an increase in salary following imminent promotion

Any compensation awarded may be reduced where appropriate to reflect the aggrieved party's

1   Duty to mitigate his loss, as by seeking alternative suitable work
2   Own contribution to any loss suffered

If the tribunal finds that its recommendation as to re-engagement has not been complied with, then the assessment of any loss suffered in consequence will be:

1   Reduced, if the complainant unreasonably refused the offer made on the terms stated in the recommendation, or
2   Increased, if the employer unreasonably refused to reinstate the employee (s116)

The compensation awarded must not exceed two years' (104 weeks') pay or £4160 (= 104 × £40), whatever sum is the smaller (s118)

11:13:8 *Reference by the tribunal to a conciliation officer*

Wherever possible the Act seeks to promote a voluntary settlement of differences between employer and employee by means of conciliation. A complaint under s22, presented to an industrial tribunal may be referred to a conciliation officer, who must try to promote a settlement without recourse to the tribunal if:

1   So requested by the employer and employee concerned, or
2   In the absence of such a request, the officer considers that he could intervene with a reasonable prospect of success (s146(2))

If the employee is no longer employed by the employer against whom the complaint was made, the officer must try to promote:

1   Re-engagement on fair terms by that employer, his successor or associate
2   Alternatively, agreement as to the amount of compensation payable by the employer where re-engagement is impracticable or cannot be agreed upon (s146(3))

11:13:9   Reference direct to a conciliation officer

Where the employee is no longer employed by the employer who, it is alleged, unfairly dismissed him, then before the employee presents a complaint to an industrial tribunal under s106 the conciliation officer may be asked by either the employer or employee to make his services available to them in the manner described above (s146(4)). Reference to a conciliation officer may encourage an early settlement of such disputes, without the need for intervention by a tribunal.

11:13:10   An employer's remedy if he was forced to dismiss an employee

The employer may claim that he was induced to unfairly dismiss an employee because of pressure exercised on him amounting to an unfair industrial practice. This consideration is ignored by the tribunal dealing with the issue in so far as it affects the rights of the complainant to seek a remedy (s33(1)). Nonetheless it is an unfair industrial practice for any person, including a trade union or other organisation of workers, or their officials, to knowingly induce an employer to indulge in an unfair industrial practice against an employee, by putting pressure on that employer in the form of threatening, organising or financing a strike or irregular industrial action short of a strike (s33(3)).

The employer may require the third party responsible for the unfair industrial practice to be joined as a party to the proceedings against him by the complainant. The third party may be required to make a just and equitable contribution to the compensation awarded against the employer to the complainant. This may amount to a complete indemnity for the employer. A trade union may be required to pay a contribution to the employer in respect of the conduct of officials acting within the scope of the authority conferred on them (s119). Conway v Wade (see 11:19:3) is a good illustration of this situation.

11:14 LEGALLY BINDING COLLECTIVE AGREEMENTS

For the purposes of the Act, the term "collective agreement" means any agreement in any form which is:

1   Made by one or more organisations of workers with one or more employers (or organisations of employers)
2   And is either (*a*) an agreement prescribing the terms and condition of employment, or (*b*) a procedure agreement (s166(1))

A *procedure agreement* is that part of a collective agreement that deals with:

1   The machinery for consulting or negotiating about the terms and conditions of employment and other questions arising between employers and employees
2   Negotiating rights
3   Facilities for trade union officials
4   Procedures relating to dismissal, other matters of discipline and grievances of individual employees (s166(5))

In future, the parties to a written collective agreement will be conclusively presumed to have intended to create a legally binding contract unless there is a term, however it may be worded, expressly negativing legal enforceability (s34).

This is a reversal of the former legal position, which was that collective agreements were legally binding only if they contained an express declaration to that effect. If only one party to a collective agreement wishes to make it legally binding, the possibility that one side may concede on this point will be a powerful bargaining factor in negotiations. There seems little doubt that trade unions will press for collective agreements to be binding in honour only.

11:14:1 *Who are parties to the collective agreement?*
Terms and conditions of employment may be negotiated by a joint body of representatives of:

1   One or more organisations of workers, and
2   One or more employers or organisations of employers (s35(1))

It is conclusively presumed that the constituent parties of this joint body intended to authorise their representatives to negotiate legally enforceable awards on their behalf (s35(3)). If a collective agreement is concluded by these representatives, then each individual party represented is regarded as being a party to that agreement. An agreement recorded in writing is legally binding on a party represented, in the absence of an express declaration to the contrary (s166(4) and s35(4)).

Since the doctrine of privity of contract states that only the parties to a contract are legally bound by its provisions, these rules are directed towards ensuring that the overriding principle of legal enforceability of collective agreements is not nullified by employers and organisations of workers claiming that they are not legally bound by agreements to which they are not directly a party. The joint negotiating body is given full statutory authority to bind the parties it represents. A works committee or joint negotiating council that makes a legally enforceable agreement thereby binds all the employers and employees represented on the negotiating body.

11:14:2   How will legal enforceability be secured?

It will be an unfair industrial practice for any party to a legally enforceable collective agreement, whether employer, trade union, or organisation of workers:

1   To break any provision that is binding upon him
2   Not to take all reasonably practicable steps to prevent altogether or prevent the continuance of, any action in breach of an undertaking embodied in the collective agreement, such as a strike or lock-out, by persons acting or purporting to act on behalf of the party to the collective agreement (s36)

The sanctions that may be imposed for a violation of s36 are set out in 11:2:2.

It will be interesting to see what is expected of persons responsible for preventing continued breach of a collective agreement when the phrase "reasonably practicable steps" has to be interpreted.

The Industrial Court may entertain proceedings brought by one party against the other:

1   On the construction or effect of the collective agreement
2   To enforce that agreement or claim damages for a breach of it (s129)

11:14:3 *Award and enforcement of compensation*
Compensation awarded against a trade union must not exceed the limits
set out below (s117). The scale increases with number of members belonging to the union:

1   £5000 for membership below 5000
2   £25 000 for membership between 5000 and 25 000
3   £50 000 for membership between 25 000 and 100 000
4   £100 000 for membership of 100 000 or more

For the purposes of s117 a reference to a trade union includes an organisation of workers entered in the provisional register. Unlimited compensation
may be awarded against an organisation of workers that is not registered
as a trade union.

Where an award of compensation, damages, costs or expenses is made
against:

1   A trade union or employers' association including those
     entered in the provisional register
2   Trustees of a trade union
3   Members or officials of a trade union or employers' association
     on behalf of all members

It will be executed against any property belonging to or held in trust
for that trade union or employers' association, excepting a fund which
cannot be used for financing strikes, lock-outs or other industrial action
(s153).

Civil proceedings may be brought against:

1   Any organisation of workers that is not a trade union
2   Any organisation of employers that is not an employers'
     association

Any judgement, order or award made against any such organisations may
be enforced by execution or punishment for contempt against any property
belonging to or held in trust for the organisation, except funds that cannot
be used to finance strikes, lock-outs or other industrial action (s154).

11:14:4 *Collective agreements and the individual employer*
An individual employee cannot sue his employer for pay agreed upon
collectively, since he is not a party to the collective agreement, and the

doctrine of privity of contract prevents any such claim. If a term in a collective agreement is expressly embodied in a contract of employment, it is enforceable against the individual employee refusing to be bound by it. It is possible for an employee's conditions of employment to change automatically with any changes negotiated in the collective agreement governing the employment in question, where such a course has been expressly agreed upon.

National Coal Board v Galley (1958, Court of Appeal)

The Coal Board employed Galley as a deputy at a coal mine, under a written contract, the terms of which provided that his wages and working conditions should be regulated by any national agreement in force for the time being. The Coal Board and the union, of which Galley was a member, agreed that "deputies should work such days or part days in each week as may reasonably be required." When Galley, together with other deputies refused to work Saturday shifts, he was sued for damages by his employers for breach of contract. Galley contended that he was not bound by the national agreement since he was not a party to it.

The court decided that Galley was bound by a term in his contract to work on a Saturday if required, since this provision of the national agreement had been incorporated into his contract of employment.

It is also possible to incorporate terms of collective agreements into individual contracts of employment, by implication, where the employee has agreed to their inclusion in this way, consequently he will be bound by those terms, though he is unaware of their precise nature.

Sagar v H Ridehalgh & Son Ltd (1931, Court of Appeal)

Sagar, a weaver in the defendant's mill, had one shilling deducted from his wages for bad workmanship, in accordance with the common practice prevailing in the mill and throughout the trade. He sought a declaration that this deduction was illegal as being contrary to s3 of the Truck Act 1831, and payment to him of one shilling.

The court decided that although it could not be positively proved that Sagar was aware of this practice when he began to work at the mill, nonetheless, he accepted employment on the same terms as other weavers at the mill. The practice was not rendered illegal by the Truck Act 1831 s3, and the deduction made could not be recovered.

It follows from this case that if an employee joins a concern, he must be taken to know and agree to existing practices, though they are not expressly drawn to his attention when concluding his contract of employment. If there is sufficient evidence that an employer has accepted and acted upon the terms of a collective agreement, those terms may be implied into his employees' contracts of employment, so that he may claim that he is entitled to receive any benefits provided by the terms of that collective agreement.

Maclea v Essex Line (1933)

Maclea claimed fourteen days' wages in lieu of notice for each complete year of service, as provided by the National Maritime Board rules. His contract of employment did not expressly embody this term, nor was it even referred to in his contract. Maclea naturally assumed that this term would be incorporated by implication, as had been the case in respect of other contracts for similar employment by different employers in the past. It was shown in evidence that other employees had made similar assumptions.

The court decided that the agreement between the parties was that Maclea should be engaged upon the terms and conditions of the National Maritime Board for the time being in force, which were to be regarded as binding between the employer and employee. He was entitled to recover the wages as claimed.

It is important to draw a distinction, however, between a contract of employment where the employer and employee agree that the terms will change automatically to reflect any change in the collective agreement, and an understanding that the terms of the collective agreement are to be merely a preliminary stage in the process of wage determination.

Dudfield v Ministry of Works (1964)

Dudfield, a lift attendant, was employed by the defendant Ministry on terms that his wages were to be those agreed upon by the Miscellaneous Trades Joint Council for Government Industrial Employees. An increase of ten shillings a week was agreed upon, but the Ministry refused to pay it because of a government pay freeze.

The court decided that a legally enforceable right was not created by the joint council's decision since it was only intended to be consultative.

Despite a long-standing practice, whereby rates fixed by the council had been accepted by both employers and employees, there was no implied obligation that the employer must always do so. Although the rate to be paid to Dudfield was determined by collective bargaining, it was finally fixed by the employer himself.

It is inappropriate for those terms of the collective agreement that regulate industrial behaviour between the employers and unions to be incorporated into the employee's contract.

Rodwell v Thomas (1944)

A civil servant was dismissed, following an accusation that he had stolen a radio set. The National Whitley Council had established a disciplinary procedure for dealing with serious disciplinary charges not giving rise to any criminal proceedings, and Rodwell claimed that this was a term of his contract of employment which had not been observed.

The court decided that even if the need to follow the disciplinary procedure set out was contractual, it was not necessary on the facts to follow it here. In any case it is not every matter governed by a collective agreement that "can be said to be incorporated into a civil servant's contract of employment, so that on a deviation from any term or condition, there is a breach of contract affording him a cause of action." (Mr Justice Tucker)

11:14:5 Collective agreements
and the Contracts of Employment Act 1963

Although an employer is required to give his employee a written statement of the terms of his employment, this written statement may refer the employee to another document where the relevant terms may be embodied—for example, the terms of a collective agreement. The terms referred to are then effectively incorporated into the contract of employment of each employee concerned. The clause referring to the collective agreement will probably be similar in terminology to this example: "Your rate of wages, hours of work, holidays and holiday pay are in accordance with the provisions of the constitution and the working rule agreement issued by and under the authority of the national joint council."

In such cases it may still be open to the employee to establish that the specific terms of his own contract of employment, or the terms under which he worked, conflicted with the collective terms, with the result that those collective terms are inapplicable.

11:15 REMEDIAL ACTION WHERE A PROCEDURE AGREEMENT DOES NOT EXIST OR IS DEFECTIVE

Though a trade union is recognised as having bargaining rights, it may be necessary to introduce a satisfactory, legally enforceable procedure agreement on such matters as negotiation, the lack of which may be the cause of poor industrial relations.

11:15:1 *When may an application be made to the Industrial Court?*

An application may be made to the Industrial Court claiming that a particular unit of employment or a composite unit extending to two or more associated undertakings or employees, suffers from one or both of the following defects:

1   An unsuitable procedure agreement for settling disputes promptly and fairly or alternatively that a procedure agreement does not exist at all
2   Industrial action contrary to the terms of any procedure agreement that exists, which can be as damaging as a strike

This is an emergency procedure that should be used only as a last resort in rare circumstances when voluntary reform has failed.

The application to the Industrial Court may be made by:

1   The Secretary of State, after consulting the parties affected
2   The employer or any trade union recognised by the employer as having negotiating rights or a party to an existing procedure agreement, provided that notice has been given beforehand to the Secretary of State so that he can offer his advice and assistance to promote a settlement. Any question relating to the issue may be referred to the Commission for examination

The Industrial Court itself will refer the issue to the Commission if there are reasonable grounds for believing that one or both of the defects complained about is causing the impairment of orderly industrial relations, or substantial or repeated loss of working time (s37).

11:15:2   *Solution that may be suggested by the Commission*
The Commission may formulate proposals to remedy any unsatisfactory situation discovered after consulting any employer or trade union likely to be affected. The Commission may suggest:

1   Revision of existing provisions or the introduction of new ones capable of having effect as a legally enforceable agreement
2   Their application to a larger unit of employment or a larger composite unit where necessary, and
3   Who are to be the parties to any further proceedings on the matter, such as (*a*) parties to any existing procedure agreement (*b*) together with employers, employers' associations, or trade unions on the ground that these persons would be appropriate parties to any new or revised provisions

Decision-making in large companies is often centralised and it may be essential to consider the undertakings managed by several associated employers in one single exercise. The Commission is given power to examine the grouping together of undertakings if this is the only way of satisfactorily resolving management and industrial relations problems in cases where pressure may be brought to bear on group management.

The Commission must promote and assist discussions between the parties to the reference to secure their agreement to the new or revised provisions (*s*38, *s*39, *s*40). The Commission's recommendations must be in accordance with any provisions agreed upon, but other provisions may also be included.

If the Commission is satisfied that the purpose for which the reference was made has been adequately fulfilled, they may make a report to the Industrial Court to that effect. The Secretary of State, the employer or the trade union who are parties to the reference may apply to the Court for withdrawal of the reference (*s*39(4)).

11:15:3   *Power of the*
Industrial Court to act on the Commission's proposals
The Commission's proposals must be notified to the parties affected and within two weeks the parties may ask the Industrial Court to consider them. The Court will, as it considers appropriate:

1   Extend the scope of the reference to the larger unit or larger composite unit specified in the proposal, or
2   Leave it unchanged

In the absence of any such application the Court will simply confirm the proposals and extend the scope of the reference in accordance with them (s38). No further application will be considered by the Court within two years from receiving the Commission's report, if it relates to substantially the same unit of employment or composite unit (s42(1)).

Any employer or trade union who is a party to the reference may apply to the Industrial Court, within six months from the time when the Court receives the Commission's report asking for an order:

1   Defining the unit of employment or composite unit to which
     the provisions apply
2   Specifying the parties bound by them
3   Making the provisions legally enforceable

unless an order is unnecessary for securing acceptance and observance of the provisions (s41).

The parties so bound may make a joint application to the Court to revoke the order or vary it in the manner specified and the Court will grant the request. On the other hand, if only one party seeks revocation, the Court will have to be satisfied, subject to a report by the Commission if requested, that the Court order is no longer necessary for securing compliance with the provisions of the procedure agreement (s42).

11:15:4   *Employer's duty to notify*
the Secretary of State of procedure agreements
It is proposed to continue the existing scheme whereby the Secretary of State is voluntarily notified of a procedure agreement by the parties concerned. The Act gives additional powers to make regulations requiring a specified employer to give this type of information within a period of not less than six months. The employer must state:

1   Whether he is party to a procedure agreement or observes an
     agreement to which he is not a party and if so to supply:
     (a) a copy of it, if it is in writing
     (b) prescribed particulars, if it is not in writing
     (c) identify a procedure agreement to which he is not a party, if
         the Secretary of State already has a copy
2   The description and number of his employees covered by the
     procedure agreement and those which are not (s58)

The employer may be fined up to £100 if he fails to supply this information altogether or within the time specified (s59). Any person, not merely an employer, will be liable to a fine of £400 if he:

1   Makes a statement when supplying the required information which he knows to be false in a material particular or recklessly makes a statement which is false in a material particular
2   Supplies a copy of a procedure agreement which he knows to be inaccurate or incomplete (s59)

This information may be used:

1   To judge the extent to which procedure agreements are governing relations between employer and employee
2   To identify those areas where procedures can be improved
3   To support an application to the Industrial Court to secure either a better agreement or a new agreement where one does not exist

11:16 RECOGNITION BY AN EMPLOYER OF A TRADE UNION AS A BARGAINING AGENT FOR EMPLOYEES

A stable and effective bargaining structure is a vital prerequisite to reliable collective bargaining, which in turn will produce more harmonious industrial relations. Two important factors will help to secure the relationship:

1   Willingness by employers to seriously negotiate with one or more bodies where they can be shown to represent a large number of employees whose support they enjoy; that is, recognition of a "bargaining agent"
2   Workable negotiating machinery through which the two sides may communicate and discuss any differences of opinion: that is, the provision of effective procedure agreements

11:16:1 Voluntary recognition preferred

Where possible these questions of recognition of organisations of workers or trade unions for bargaining purposes and the establishment of a suitable bargaining structure is best resolved by the parties themselves. Many factors prevent this happening in practice:

1   Unwillingness of the employer to recognise a union or organisation of workers
2   Rivalry over the right to represent a body of workers
3   Ineffective and fragmentary bargaining proceedures

In a situation of this type where the opposing sides cannot reconcile their differences, or agree on a new and more suitable bargaining structure, the strain on industrial relations may result in frequent strikes. The Act provides for an independent investigation in such cases to promote a lasting solution to the problem.

11:16:2   *Recognition confined to registered trade unions*
It is important to realise that an application to the Industrial Court for a ballot among employees to secure statutory recognition as a sole bargaining agent, will be granted only to an organisation of workers that has secured at this point in time, if not earlier, recognition as a registered trade union. The employer may recognise as a sole bargaining agent an organisation of workers that is not registered if he wishes, but such a body cannot secure statutory recognition.

11:16:3   *What is a sole bargaining agent?*
The term "sole bargaining agent" means an organisation of workers with sole negotiating rights in relation to a unit of employees, except for matters dealt with under more extensive bargaining arrangements, and recognised as having these rights by an employer. An employee within that unit has his terms and conditions of employment determined in negotiations which lead to the conclusion or alteration of a collective agreement (s44).

11:16:4   *Application to the Industrial Court*
An application may be made to the Industrial Court by a trade union, an employer or associated employers, or by a trade union and employer jointly, or the Secretary of State to determine whether:

1   Specified employees should be recognised by their employer as comprising a bargaining unit
2   The organisation of workers or joint negotiating panel concerned should be recognised by that employer as the sole bargaining agent for that unit (s45(2)). A joint negotiating panel comprises representatives of two or more organisations

of workers, established for the purpose of making collective agreements (s44).

An unregistered organisation of workers cannot make an application, but the employer, or the Secretary of State, may make an application on its behalf—usually in cases where the imposition of a bargaining agency by the Industrial Court is necessary to solve conflicting claims for recognition in relation to a unit of employment.

Before the Secretary of State makes an application to the Industrial Court he must consult:

1 The employer concerned
2 Any organisation of workers or joint negotiating panel directly affected

An application will not be entertained by the Industrial Court from a trade union, or employer, or a joint application by trade union and employer, unless the Secretary of State has been notified beforehand. The Secretary of State will advise the applicants and other parties directly concerned to promote agreement. He may refer any question on these matters for examination by the Commission (s45(3) and (4)).

It will be an unfair industrial practice for the employer to institute or threaten a lock-out knowingly to induce any person not to make an application for a sole bargaining agency (s55(8)).

11:16:5   *Reference to the Commission on Industrial Relations*
The Industrial Court must refer the matter to the Commission where:

1 The parties to the issue have failed to reach a settlement by adequate use of conciliation facilities
2 The reference is necessary to promote a satisfactory and lasting settlement of the issue, provided
   (a) the same issue has not been similarly considered within the last two years and
   (b) a further reference would not be justified in the circumstances (s46)

Before making a report, the Commission may apply to the Industrial Court for withdrawal of the reference if a lasting and satisfactory settlement has been reached.

11 : 16 : 6 *Powers of the Commission on Industrial Relations*

If it is necessary to promote a satisfactory and lasting settlement, the Commission may formulate proposals for extending the scope of any reference made to it to an associated employer. The proposals must be :

1 Transmitted to the Industrial Court
2 Brought to the attention of persons affected

Any person affected may apply within two weeks of their publication to the Industrial Court asking them to consider whether they are necessary. The Industrial Court may accept, reject or modify the Commission's proposed extensions, but they will be confirmed in the absence of such an application (s47). The Commission will examine the reference or extended reference and set out its recommendations in a report.

11 : 16 : 7 *Prerequisites to recognition of a sole bargaining agent*

The Commission must not recommend in its report that any organisation of workers or a joint negotiating panel be recognised as a sole bargaining agent unless :

1 Each organisation concerned is an independent organisation of workers
2 It meets with the approval of employees in the bargaining unit and would promote a satisfactory and lasting settlement of the questions in issue
3 The organisation or panel recognised has
  (a) the support of a substantial proportion of employees in the bargaining unit
  (b) the resources and organisation enabling it to represent those employees effectively

The Commission may recommend the formation of a joint negotiating panel and the inclusion of individual organisations of employees if they have :

1 The support of a substantial proportion of the employees comprised in that bargaining unit
2 The resources and organisation to enable them to participate effectively in the work of the panel

Any recognition as a sole bargaining agent or inclusion on a joint negotiating panel may be conditional upon satisfying the following requirements, if the Commission so recommends:

1   Making sufficient trained officials available for collective bargaining
2   Not claiming recognition as sole bargaining agent for another bargaining unit, consisting wholly or in part of the employees of any employer to whom the recommendation relates
3   Not having exclusive negotiating rights in matters dealt with under other more extensive bargaining arrangements that are available such as a national agreement (s48)

11:16:8   *Implementing the Commission's recommendations*
An application may be made to the Industrial Court within six months after receiving the Commission's report by the employer, organisation of workers, or joint negotiating panel concerned, asking for a ballot of employees to decide whether a sole bargaining agent should be recognised. Before making any such application any condition imposed by the recommendation should have been implemented. Further, an application cannot be made by an organisation of workers for the recognition recommended, unless at this point in time it has the status of a trade union. A joint negotiating panel cannot make an application for the recognition recommended unless it is a panel comprised of trade unions (s49). If the majority of employees favour recognition the Industrial Court must make an order:

1   Defining the bargaining unit, and
2   Specifying the employer and trade union or joint negotiating panel to be recognised

The order will cease to have effect if:

1   An organisation specified as being a trade union ceases to have that status
2   A joint negotiating panel ceases to be a panel of trade unions (s50)

11:16:9   *Unfair industrial practices*
in connection with collective bargaining procedures
While an application to the Industrial Court or the Secretary of State

under s45 in connection with recognition of a sole bargaining unit is still pending, it will be an unfair industrial practice for:

1   An employer concerned to organise or threaten a lock-out
2   For any person, including a trade union or other organisation of workers or an official of these bodies to organise or threaten a strike or irregular industrial action in order to further their own wishes on this matter

An action will be "pending":

1   At any time before the Industrial Court has determined not to refer any question to the Commission
2   If a reference to the Commission has been made, but not withdrawn
3   If a period of six months has not expired since the Commission reported to the Industrial Court
4   Before failure to reach agreement by recourse to the Secretary of State's advice
5   Before agreement was reached by consultation with the Secretary of State (s54)

11 : 16 : 10   *Making the concept of a sole bargaining agent effective*
If a sole bargaining agent has been recognised, it will be an unfair industrial practice to attempt to defeat this arrangement:

1   If the employer carries on collective bargaining with some other organisation of employees. Naturally, this does not cover bargaining with a trade union represented on a recognised joint negotiating panel if the panel consents
2   If the employer does not carry out collective bargaining to the extent that might reasonably be expected from a willing employer with the body recognised for this purpose
3   If any person, including a trade union, other organisation of workers or officials of those bodies, procures or threatens a strike or irregular industrial action knowingly to induce or attempt to induce an employer to act in the manner specified above or to recognise as a sole bargaining agent or collectively bargain with a body not recommended for recognition in the Commission's report (s54 and s55)

11:16:11 *Complaint to the Industrial Arbitration Board*

The Industrial Court may receive a complaint from a trade union or joint negotiating panel of trade unions that the employer is not negotiating seriously. The Court may authorise the presentation of a written claim to the Industrial Arbitration Board requesting improved terms and conditions for employees in a recognised bargaining unit (s125). Where necessary the Board may make a binding award which may become an implied term of the individual employee's contract of employment (s127). In the case of Crown employment the only remedy will be an order determining the rights of the complainant and the party against whom the complaint is made (s162), but presumably this will act as a strong inducement to the Crown to implement any order made.

11:16:12 *Withdrawal of recognition of a sole bargaining agent*

A trade union or joint negotiating panel may lose its status as a sole bargaining agent if its members are dissatisfied with its activities. An employee with the written support of either:

1   One-fifth of the employees in a bargaining unit where the employer has conceded a sole bargaining agency without an order from the Industrial Court, or
2   Two-fifths of the employees in the case of a recognised sole bargaining agent under s50, provided two years have elapsed since its recognition

may apply to the Industrial Court alleging that a specified trade union or joint negotiating panel does not adequately represent the employees or a section of them in that unit (s51). It will be an unfair industrial practice for an employer to institute or threaten a lock-out in order knowingly to induce an employee not to make such an application (s55(8)).

The Commission on Industrial Relations will attempt a settlement of matters covered in the application. If after a reasonable time the application has not been withdrawn, the Industrial Court may require a ballot amongst all employees in the bargaining unit to determine whether the trade union or joint negotiating panel should continue to be recognised as the sole bargaining agent. If a majority do not favour continuance of the present arrangements the employer will be ordered to cease recognition of the sole bargaining agent for the next two years at least in respect of the employees voting (s53).

11:16:13 *Division of a bargaining unit into sections*

Alternatively the Industrial Court may require the bargaining unit to be divided into two or more sections, after considering the extent to which different descriptions of employees have interests in common by reason of:

1 The nature of their work
2 Their training, experience and qualifications

A ballot may be held for one section only to determine whether that section should continue to be included in the bargaining unit. If the majority of employees in a section vote against being included in the bargaining unit, the Industrial Court must order the employer to cease recognition of an organisation of workers or joint negotiating panel as a sole bargaining agent, for that section for the next two years at least (s52 and s53).

The Industrial Court will not entertain an application from the same organisation of workers seeking recognition as a bargaining unit if the application covers in whole or part the same description of employees for whom an application has been refused within the preceding two years (s53(5)). A different organisation of workers may seek recognition as a sole bargaining agent in the usual way.

11:17 THE EMPLOYER'S DUTY
TO DISCLOSE INFORMATION CONCERNING HIS BUSINESS

The employer and any associated employer must disclose to trade union representatives (an official or other authorised person) with whom he conducts collective bargaining, all information relating to the undertaking:

1 The lack of which may materially impede bargaining between the parties
2 If it is good industrial practice to make such a disclosure, in accordance with the statutory code of practice currently in force

Such information is to be in writing or confirmed in writing if so required. The Secretary of State may by regulation grant exemption from the requirements in the manner specified. The employer is not required:

1 To produce, allow inspection or copying of any document, except a document prepared for the purpose of conveying or confirming the information

2   To compile information involving work and expenditure out
of all reasonable proportion to its value for collective bargaining (s56)

11:17:1   *Disclosure of information to employees*

It is recognised that employees are entitled to basic information about
the undertaking they work for so that they may judge its progress and
assess its potentiality.

Where more than 350 persons, other than excepted persons, are
employed, whether at the same or several places, the employer, if owner of
the undertaking, must issue a written statement to non-excepted employees
giving information about the undertaking and associated undertakings as
the Secretary of State specifies. He has power to make regulations requiring the information to cover subsidiary and associated companies. The
information must cover the financial year for which the accounts are prepared and it must be issued within six months from the end of that period
(s57). An employee may complain to an industrial tribunal if he does not
receive the required information from his employer. The tribunal may give
the employer a further period of time in which to supply the statement.

An *excepted person* is one:

1   Employed under a contract of employment which normally
involves employment for less than twenty-one hours a week,
or
2   Employed in the undertaking for less than thirteen weeks, or
3   Ordinarily working outside Great Britain and who is outside
Great Britain on the date when the information is issued

11:17:2   *Confidential information need not be disclosed*

Under section 158, the employer's duty to publicise under sections 56 and
57 does not extend to:

1   Any disclosure which would be contrary to the interests of
national security, or contrary to a prohibition imposed by law;
for example, the Official Secrets Act
2   Information communicated to him in confidence
3   Information relating specifically to an individual, unless his
consent has been given
4   A disclosure which would be seriously prejudicial to the
interests of:

(a) The employer's undertaking, or

(b) The national interest, in the case of Crown employment (s162) for reasons unconnected with collective bargaining

5   Any information obtained by the employer for bringing, prosecuting or defending any legal proceedings

11:17:3 *Importance of these provisions to a trade union*

This duty of disclosure will enable trade unions to bargain with some knowledge of the employer's position, presumably on such fundamental matters as the profits and losses being incurred, the extent of orders placed for goods produced, and plans for expansion or reduction of the labour force. The exact nature and scope of these disclosures will depend upon the scope of the code of practice drawn up by the Secretary of State. The code may be revised periodically, consequently it can keep pace with progressive changes of outlook as they occur. By strengthening the hands of the trade unions in collective bargaining these provisions may be amongst the most important new rights acquired by the unions under the Act.

11:17:4 *Remedy where information is not given*

A trade union may complain to the Industrial Court under s102 that an employer has not disclosed or confirmed information required. Where the complaint is well founded, the Court may, if just and equitable:

1   Determine the rights of the parties

2   Direct the employer to make the disclosures as required (except in the case of Crown employment—s162(4))

3   Authorise presentation of a written claim to the Industrial Arbitration Board under s126 (except in the case of Crown employment—s162(4)), requesting improved terms and conditions for employees concerned. The Board may make a binding award which may become an implied term of the employee's contract of employment, if necessary (s127)

A sanction of such strength should persuade the employer to make appropriate disclosures in the first place.

11:18 DISCONTINUING OR DEFERRING
A STRIKE THAT WILL CAUSE AN EMERGENCY

New powers are given to the Secretary of State to intervene in disputes which seriously threaten the national health, safety, economy or livelihood of a substantial proportion of the community. These powers may be more effective than recourse to the Emergency Powers Act 1920 which cannot be used to cope with a domestic emergency caused by a strike if only the national economy is endangered. These new powers may be used to protect the public interest.

11:18:1 A cooling-off period may be imposed

The Secretary of State may ask the Industrial Court to order organisations of workers, and organisations of employers, their officials or other persons involved, not to call, support or threaten, a strike, irregular industrial action or lock-out, within a specified area of employment of one or more industries or undertakings for a period not exceeding sixty days (s139(4)). An order for a shorter period may be extended to a maximum of sixty days (s140(2)). Directions may be given to such persons as union officials to take steps to discontinue or defer specified industrial action while any order remains in force—for example, withdrawing any instructions on industrial action already issued (s139(6)).

During the sixty-day period, the Court may make an order bringing other parties within the scope of the original order, where they are instigating action in relation to the dispute (s140(3)).

An order will not be made against a person who is:

1 Merely taking part in the strike or other industrial action
2 Organising the strike or other action in his capacity as a trade union official acting within the scope of his authority (s139(3))

The order may be made against officials of unregistered organisations of workers. An order must only be asked for if:

1 A strike, irregular industrial action or lock-out has begun or is likely to begin in contemplation of furtherance of an industrial dispute
2 Such action ought to be discontinued or deferred to assist a settlement by negotiation, conciliation or arbitration
3 Industrial action has or would cause "emergency circumstances"—that is, an interruption in the supply of goods or services likely to:
   (a) Be gravely injurious to the national economy
   (b) Imperil national security
   (c) Create a risk of public disorder

(d) Endanger the lives of a substantial number of persons or expose them to risk of disease or personal injury (s138)

An order will not be made by the Industrial Court if these conditions are not met. The order will not compel any individual as such to return to or remain at work. There will not be a sanction against an individual for simply taking part in industrial action.

11:18:2 *A ballot among employees about the advisability of striking*
The Secretary of State may apply to the Industrial Court for an order requiring a ballot to be taken where:

1   A strike or other irregular industrial action has begun or is likely to begin
2   There are emergency circumstances (as defined in 11:18:1) and/or
3   The livelihood of a substantial number of employees in any particular industry is likely to be seriously affected, and
4   There are reasons for doubting that the industrial action has the support of the employees involved

Before making any such application the Secretary of State must, where practicable, consult every employer, trade union, or employers' association who are parties to the dispute (s141). He is not obliged to consult an unregistered organisation but is free to if he wishes.

During the period between the making of the order and reporting the result of the ballot to the Industrial Court:

1   The organisation of workers, and other persons specified in that order who have been responsible for industrial action, must not take or threaten further strike action or irregular industrial action amongst employees eligible to vote in the ballot. Any instructions given on these matters that have been given already must be withdrawn. These orders may be extended to any other organisations or persons if they take or threaten similar industrial action
2   An employer or organisation of employers or other persons specified in the order must not organise or threaten a lock-out (s143).

The result of the ballot must be notified to the Industrial Court and the Secretary of State, but it is not binding. The order relating to the cooling-off period lapses after a ballot has been held, and any organisation or individual may then take industrial action within the limits of the law.

11:19 ACTS IN CONTEMPLATION OR FURTHERANCE OF AN "INDUSTRIAL DISPUTE"

It is often important to determine whether an industrial dispute exists within the meaning of the new statutory definition, since vital statutory protections are given by sections 132 and 134 to parties in respect of any acts done "in furtherance or contemplation of an industrial dispute" which might otherwise constitute an actionable wrong—such as inducing a breach of contract or interference with trade, business or employment.

11:19:1 *Meaning of the term "industrial dispute"*
Section 167(1) defines an industrial dispute as a dispute between:

1   One or more employers, or organisations of employers on the one side and
2   Employees or their organisations on the other side

concerning one or more of the following matters:

1   Terms and conditions of employment including physical conditions
2   Engagement, non-engagement, termination or suspension of employment
3   Allocation of work between employees
4   A procedure agreement and any matter relating to it

There is a large body of case law on the meaning of the term "trade dispute" which was the phrase in use before the passing of the 1971 Act. These cases will continue to be authorities for the precise legal meaning of the term "industrial dispute," if they also come within the broad criteria of s167(1).

11:19:2 *All types of employees are within the scope of the section*
The term "industrial" should be widely interpreted to include action taken on behalf of administrative, technical or professional workers.

National Association of
Local Government Officers v Bolton Corporation (1943, House of Lords)

A dispute arose between NALGO and the Corporation, concerning the Corporation's liability as employer, under s1 of the Local Government Staffs (War Service) Act 1939, to make up the difference in salary between what it paid to employees engaged in the Corporation's work and that received by its employees engaged on military service. The Minister of Labour referred this "trade dispute" to the National Arbitration Tribunal, but the Corporation applied to the court for an order to prohibit any adjudication on this matter by the Tribunal.

The House of Lords decided that if there can be a trade union to which the higher grades of municipal officers can belong, it is not an impossible use of language to say that a dispute concerning their conditions of service is a "trade" dispute. Although administrative, professional and technical officials employed by the corporation are not "workmen" in the ordinary sense, they are persons who have entered into contracts with the corporation, "whether the contract be by way of manual labour, clerical work, or otherwise." The dispute was referable to the National Arbitration Tribunal for determination.

11 : 19 : 3   *Loss of the protection given by s132 and s134*
Although an industrial dispute exists, the act in question may not be done in furtherance or contemplation of it, thus any statutory protection otherwise available is lost.

Conway v Wade (1909, House of Lords)

Wade, a trade union officer acting with his union's authority, told Conway's employer that unless Conway was dismissed a strike would be called. Wade's real motive was to force Conway to settle a fine owed to the union. Conway sued Wade for damages for procuring his dismissal.

The House of Lords decided that Wade's actions were not in furtherance of a trade dispute, either existing or contemplated, but motivated by personal spite to punish him for not paying the fine by securing his dismissal, consequently he was liable in damages to Conway. The whole story put forward by Wade, as to the existence amongst Conway's fellow employees of an objection to his presence and their intention to leave the employment if he continued to work with them, was a fabrication.

11 : 19 : 4 *Situations that are*
not within the legal definition of an industrial dispute
A dispute between employers is not an industrial dispute: it is necessary
that workmen should be involved.

Larkin and others v Long (1915, House of Lords)

Long, a stevedore, refused to join an employers' association of all stevedores in Dublin, the aim of the association being to secure higher rates
from the shipowners. Members of the Irish Transport Union working for
Long came out on strike, in an attempt to persuade him to join the stevedores' association. The union supported the aims of this association, since
it compelled its members to pay the scale of remuneration for dock
labourers adopted by the association. Long sued three officials of the Transport Union (including Larkin, the Union's secretary) and three officials of
the stevedores' association for conspiracy.

The House of Lords decided that the only real dispute existing was that
between Long and members of the stevedores' association and this was not
within the legal definition of an industrial dispute. Though Larkin and
other trade unionists supported the aims of the employers' association, this
fact did not change the character of the original dispute. Long was entitled
to damages and an injunction to restrain the defendants and his employees
from doing any acts to force Long to join the stevedores' association.

11 : 19 : 5 *Inter-union rivalry*
For a real dispute to exist there must be a definite demand by one side
against another, consequently inter-union rivalry does not suffice.

J T Stratford & Son Ltd v Lindley & Another (1964, House of Lords)

Lightermen, working barges in the Port of London, were mainly members
of the watermen's union, but some belonged to the Transport and General
Workers' Union. Bowker & King Ltd resisted attempts by both unions to
be granted recognition, but this was eventually conceded to the TGWU.
Forty-five out of forty-eight union members employed by Bowker & King
Ltd, belonged to the TGWU.

To retaliate, the watermen's union, instructed members not to handle
the barges of Stratford & Son Ltd, a subsidiary of Bowker & King Ltd,
thus bringing to a halt their trade of hiring out barges. An injunction was
sought by Stratford & Son Ltd to restrain continuance of the embargo.

The House of Lords decided there was not a trade dispute, consequently the statutory protections were not available. In the absence of any lawful justification for inducing breaches of the hiring contracts and the contracts of employment of union members, such acts were tortious and an injunction would be issued to prevent their continuance.

There was not a present or contemplated dispute concerning the pay or conditions of employment of workmen, at either Bowker & King Ltd, or Stratford & Son Ltd. It was not suggested that the agreement between the TGWU and Bowker & King Ltd concerning terms of employment was unsatisfactory, nor was any approach made to Stratford & Son Ltd to see whether they were prepared to recognise the watermen's union. There were insufficient grounds for finding that this dispute was connected with the terms of employment of any person.

11:19:6 Immunities from legal action
for persons and bodies involved in industrial disputes

Some of the immunities from actions in tort previously provided by the Trade Union Act 1871 and the Trade Disputes Acts 1906 and 1964 are continued by s132 of the 1971 Act, the earlier legislation having been repealed. There is one very significant difference in the new provisions. Registered trade unions and other industrial relations organisations will no longer enjoy immunity from actions in tort unconnected with an industrial dispute (such as defamation, or negligence)—a protection previously conferred by s4 of the Trade Disputes Act 1906. This section was originally enacted to protect union funds against the need to pay damages to persons injured by tortious acts of the union at a time when such funds were limited.

11:20 INTERFERENCE WITH CONTRACTUAL RELATIONS

Where an employer or employee is induced by any person including a trade union official, to either:

1   Terminate a contract of employment by giving proper notice,
    or
2   Refuse to contract at all with a certain employer or employee

then the party who suffers cannot sue the person procuring the breach of contract. Such an action is lawful and remains so, if the inducement is carried out without recourse to unlawful means. The provisions on unfair dismissal may be relevant in this situation (see 11:13:3 and 11:13:10). An improper motive will not turn a lawful act into an unlawful one.

Allen v Flood (1898, House of Lords)

Ironworkers on repair work of a ship objected to working alongside Flood and Taylor, two shipwrights employed on repairs to the woodwork, because Flood and Taylor had previously worked in a yard where shipwrights repaired ironwork as well as woodwork. Allen, a delegate of the iron-workers' union induced the employer to dismiss Flood and Taylor in order to prevent a strike by ironworkers. The dismissed men sued Allen for inducing a breach of contract maliciously, wrongfully and with intent to injure them.

The House of Lords decided that Allen's threat was a malicious induce-ment to the employer to lawfully terminate the woodworkers' contracts of employment; but Allen had not acted unlawfully, nor had he used unlaw-ful means, like threats of violence, to procure the dismissals, consequently he was not liable.

Allen's action would constitute an unfair industrial practice under s33(3) of the 1971 Act (see 11:13:10).

A tort is committed, however, where one person, knowing of the exist-ence of a contract, intentionally induces or procures a party thereto to break that agreement (as opposed to terminating it by lawful means), without any justification for so acting, thereby causing loss to the other party to the contract. It is not necessary to establish the existence of malice.

11:20:1   Direct inducement to commit a breach of contract
The next case shows how contractual rights came to be protected by the creation of a tortious wrong.

Lumley v Gye (1853)

An opera singer, Johanna Wagner, contracted to sing exclusively for Lumley for a stated period of time. Gye induced Miss Wagner to break her contract and sing for him instead.

The court decided that this was a wrongful interference by Gye with a contract for personal services between Lumley and Miss Wagner, which gave Lumley a cause of action in damages against Gye.

Merely giving the employee advice does not constitute an inducement: some act is necessary which amounts to persuasion at least, as by tempting the employee to break his contract of employment by an offer of a higher salary. If the appropriate period of notice is given terminating the contract of employment, before taking up a better-paid appointment, an action cannot be maintained.

It is not enough that a breach of contract might possibly occur, the inducement must be calculated to cause a breach of contract. Proof of special damage need not be given to support an action for maliciously inducing a breach of a business contract: it suffices if the wrongful act must cause *some* damage.

11:20:2   *Inducing a breach of contract*
in contemplation or furtherance of an industrial dispute
An act done in contemplation or furtherance of industrial dispute does not give rise to an action in tort against the person so acting on the grounds "only" that it:

1   "Induces" another person to break a contract to which he is a party
2   "Prevents" another person from performing his contract
3   "Threatens" that a contract will be broken or will be prevented from being performed, whether or not it is a contract to which he is a party
4   "Threatens" that he will induce another person to break a contract to which that other person is a party or will prevent another person from performing his contract (s132(1))

The existence of an industrial dispute is an essential prerequisite to any claim for protection under this section.

This section re-enacts s3 of the Trade Disputes Act 1906 and the Trade Disputes Act 1965, which overruled the arguments used in Rookes v Barnard (1964, House of Lords). The use of the word "only" in section 132 means that the immunity granted is lost if wrongful means are used to procure breach of the contract of employment—for example, deceit, defamation or intimidation—because then an action will lie in respect of the wrong committed. Further, the protection given by s132 covers all types of contract, not merely contracts of employment, consequently the protection is wider under this new section than under the old law.

11:20:3 *Tortious immunity is*
limited to trade unions and employers' associations
Although actions covered by s132(1) are not tortious it will be an unfair industrial practice for any person other than:

1   A registered trade union or employers' association or an organisation entered in the provisional register
2   A person acting within the scope of his authority on behalf of such a registered body

knowingly to induce or threaten to induce another person to break his contract when acting in contemplation or furtherance of an industrial dispute (s96). It will be appreciated that an organisation of workers or employers that is neither registered, nor seeking registration, will not be protected against legal action if it induces or threatens to induce employees to break their contracts of employment. This new provision in s96 is narrower than s3 of the Trade Disputes Act 1906 which protected "any person" inducing a breach of a contract of employment. This important change in the law has been made necessary by the serious nature of unofficial strikes which have constituted an abuse of the previous widely drawn protections given by the law.

Where an employee gives "due notice" of his intention to take part in a strike, whether the notice is given personally or by someone acting on his behalf, then his actions are not a breach of contract. Such actions cannot be used to support a claim under s96 that some person or body, such as an organisation of workers or its officials, has induced a breach of contract and thereby committed an unfair practice (s147(2)(d)). The real problem here is that if the employees have different periods of notice to give, ranging from, say, one to four weeks, it will be impossible to have concerted and relatively swift strike action. A strike would have to come into force in stages to allow each group of employees to give due notice. Alternatively the strike must be delayed until the longest period of notice has expired.

11:20:4 *The situation that these new provisions hope to remedy*
The British tradition of national bargaining has produced over the years very few major national strikes. The real failure has been in the informal system of bargaining at local or plant level, which often results in numerous strikes being called without union authority and contrary to constitutional procedures agreed with the employer. Although small in

scale and short in duration these strikes are damaging to the economy. With the growing interdependence between different sections of industry, a strike by a handful of employees can throw large numbers of employees out of work. In future, the individual who induces industrial action will be protected only if he is acting on behalf of his trade union.

11 : 20 : 5   *Employee's position when he takes part in a strike*
Where an employee takes part in a strike after giving "due notice" of his intention to do so (whether personally or by someone acting on his behalf), such conduct will not support an action :

1   For breach of contract of employment by the employer against the employee
2   For breach of a contract of employment under s5 of the Conspiracy and Protection of Property Act 1875, which covers a breach of contract, by workers in industries like gas, electricity and water, that involves injury to persons or property
3   In tort against the employee himself or some other person or body—thus an unregistered organisation of workers cannot be sued for the tort of inducing a breach of contract (s147(2))

The Act does not prevent the individual worker from going on strike, and a court cannot:

1   Order specific performance of a contract of employment, or
2   By injunction, restrain a breach or threatened breach of a contract of employment

in order to compel an employee to do any work or attend at any place for the purpose of doing any work. This does not affect the employer's right to claim damages for any breach of contract by the employee.
    Conversely, an employee must not, by injunction, be :

1   Restrained from carrying out his contract of employment, or
2   Compelled to take part in any strike or irregular industrial action (s128)

The contract of employment may include a term excluding or restricting the employee's right to strike and the employer may have a right to dismiss, with or without notice, any employee taking part in a strike.

11 : 20 : 6   *Sympathetic support for an unofficial strike*
It is an unfair industrial practice for any person in contemplation or furtherance of an industrial dispute to institute or threaten to institute a strike, irregular industrial action or lock-out to :

1   Further any unfair industrial practice already being taken by that person, or
2   Assist such actions by another person (s97(1) and (2))

Giving support to an unofficial strike at another undertaking is, by reason of these provisions, an unfair industrial practice, except where the support comes from a registered trade union or employers' association which is supporting action taken by its officials or members, where their actions consist of inducing a breach of contract in contemplation or furtherance of an industrial dispute (s97(3)).

The sanctions for committing an unfair industrial practice are set out in 11 : 2 : 2.

11 : 21   INTERFERENCE WITH
TRADE, BUSINESS OR EMPLOYMENT

An act done by "any person," not necessarily a person acting on behalf of a registered trade union or employers' association, will not be an actionable tort on the ground "only" that it is an interference with another person's

1   Trade, business or employment, or
2   Right to dispose of his capital or labour as he wishes

provided such interference is done in contemplation or furtherance of an industrial dispute. The use of the word "only" means that the immunity granted is lost if any wrongful means are used in the course of such interference; for example, if a body not registered as a trade union induces or threatens to induce employees to break their contracts of employment (s132(2)).

11 : 21 : 1   *Can a member of a trade union be sued for conspiracy?*
Conspiracy connotes both the intention and the agreement of two or more persons to do either :

1   An unlawful act, or

2   A lawful act by unlawful means

If a number of persons combine and cause harm to another they are guilty of a conspiracy, though such action would have been legal if pursued by one person acting alone. A combination of two or more persons wilfully to injure a man in his trade is unlawful and also actionable if damage results.

However, some trade union activities are not treated as conspiracies. Section 132(3) re-enacts s1 of the Trade Disputes Act 1906, by providing that an agreement or combination by two or more persons to do or procure an act in furtherance of an industrial dispute is not actionable as a conspiracy, unless the act would also be actionable if done by one individual.

Consequently, workers can act together to improve conditions of work though their actions cause an employer considerable harm provided the act would be legal if committed by one person only. "A perfectly lawful strike may aim at dislocating the employer's business for the moment, but its real object is to secure better wages or conditions for the workers. The true contrast is, between the case where the object is the legitimate benefit of the combiners and the case where the object is deliberate damage without any such cause." (Lord Wright)

No action lies against an organisation of workers or its officials and members if the real aim of their tortious conspiracy is to protect legitimate objectives, even though injury is caused to the party suing.

Crofter Hand-Woven
Harris Tweed Company v Veitch (1942, House of Lords)

Union members employed in large mills on the island of Lewis demanded higher pay. If this demand was met, the employers, who used yarn woven in the crofters' homes, would have been unable to compete with the Crofter Hand-Woven Harris Tweed Co, who were local producers of hand-woven cloth using cheaper imported yarn. Veitch, a union official, acting in combination with mill owners, instructed dockers at Stornoway, also members of the union, not to handle imported yarn. The Crofter Hand-Woven Harris Tweed Company sought an injunction against Veitch to put an end to the embargo.

The House of Lords decided that the main objective of Veitch, and those acting in combination with him, was the protection of legitimate union interests by protecting the living standards of their members, rather than to harm the Crofter Hand-Woven Harris Tweed Company. Further, this objective had been pursued without recourse to unlawful actions. An injunction was not granted to restrain Veitch's activities.

For a "difference" to be regarded as an industrial dispute rather than a personal vendetta, it is not necessary that a strike, which advances the welfare of union members, should be concerned with the financial terms of their employment.

Scala Ballroom (Wolverhampton) Ltd
v Ratcliffe and Others (1958, Court of Appeal)

The plaintiffs claimed an injunction against officials of the Musicians' Union on the ground that they had conspired to cause injury by boycotting the plaintiff's ballroom. The union objected to a colour bar operated by the plaintiffs against dancers seeking admission. Although the union had coloured members, it could not be shown that the union was furthering any immediate material interest by its boycott.

The court decided that if the union and its members honestly believed that a colour bar was undesirable then the welfare of its members was being advanced by any action taken in pursuit of union objectives, though it was not capable of estimation in financial terms. The imposition of a colour bar on the audience had an insidious effect on the musicians and it was impossible to insulate the musicians from their audience. The injunction was not granted. The defendants had agreed amongst themselves to act in a manner that caused damage to the plaintiffs, but since that purpose was not illegal, it was not actionable as a conspiracy.

11:21:2   When union officials may be liable for conspiracy

Officials of a trade union or unregistered organisation will be liable for conspiracy and outside the protection of s132(3) if their predominant purpose is to injure a party by furtherance of a personal grudge against an individual.

Huntley v Thornton (1957)

On refusing to obey a union order to strike, Huntley was called before the district committee, but he left the meeting in a temper after a disagreement during which he became abusive. The district committee recommended Huntley's expulsion from the union, but the Executive Council refused to support this decision. Nonetheless the district committee refused to regard Huntley as a union member and they informed Thornton, the neighbouring district secretary, of their views, but without stating the opinion of the Executive Council. Huntley secured a job in a nearby district, but he was dismissed following representations from a shop steward acting on Thornton's instructions. An action was brought by Huntley claiming damages for conspiracy and intent to injure him for refusing to obey an unlawful direction to strike.

The Court decided that members of the district committee were liable in damages of £500 for conspiring to injure Huntley in his trade. Their actions were not in furtherance of an industrial dispute, but an unjustifiable means of seeking personal revenge, which had caused damage to Huntley. Their paramount object was to pursue a grudge, consequently they were not protected by statute.

Thornton and the shop stewards who implemented the policy of the district committee were not liable. They were unaware of the Executive Council's decision and did not take part in the tortious conspiracy. Their sole objective was furtherance of union interests, free of any intention to harm Huntley.

11:22 INDUSTRIAL ACTION AGAINST PERSONS WHO ARE NOT PARTIES TO THE INDUSTRIAL DISPUTE

A supplier of goods or services not participating in, directly interested in, or supporting a party to a dispute (an extraneous party) may be induced not to carry out his contract with an employer who is engaged at the moment in an industrial dispute with his employees. This situation is dealt with by s98 and such actions are wrongful. It is an unfair industrial practice for anyone, including a registered trade union or its officials, in contemplation or furtherance of an industrial dispute to:

> Knowingly induce a breach of contract other than a contract of employment, or prevent its performance, where such a contract is known to exist or there are reasonable grounds for believing that it does exist

by threatening, organising or financing a strike or other irregular industrial action.

The sanctions for committing an unfair industrial practice are set out in 11:2:2.

11 : 22 : 1 *When a person is an "extraneous party"*

A person is an extraneous party to a dispute if he is not party to it and has not given material support to one of the parties by taking action in contemplation or furtherance of the dispute. A person is not a party to an industrial dispute, nor will be regarded as having acted in furtherance or contemplation of it, if he:

1   Is an associated employer of the employer who is a party to the industrial dispute, or

2   Is a member of an organisation of employers of which a party to the industrial dispute is also a member, or

3   Has contributed to a fund which may be used to assist the party to the dispute, provided the contribution was paid without specific reference to the industrial dispute in question, or

4   Supplies goods to, or provides services for, a party to the dispute under a contract that was concluded before the dispute began (s98(3))

11 : 23   PICKETING

The right to picket premises peacefully, in order to persuade men not to work, is an important power that strikers may use while an industrial dispute exists.

11 : 23 : 1   *Limitations on the right to picket*

The Conspiracy and Protection of Property Act 1875 s7 limits the right to picket. It is a crime:

1   Wrongfully and without legal authority

2   With a view to compelling any other person to do or refrain from doing a lawful act

to:

1   Use violence or to intimidate that person, his wife or children

2   Persistently follow him

3   Hide any tools, clothes, or other property, or deprive or hinder him in the use thereof

4   Watch or beset his place of residence or work or the approach thereto

5   Follow him in the street with two or more other persons in a disorderly manner

Peaceful picketing is lawful under s134 of the Industrial Relations Act 1971.

It is not an offence, under s7 of the 1875 Act, nor tortiously wrong for one or more persons ("pickets") acting in contemplation or furtherance of an industrial dispute to attend at or near the place where a person:

1   Works or carries on business, or
2   Happens to be, other than his place of residence

for the purpose of

1   Peacefully communicating or obtaining information, or
2   Peacefully persuading him to work or not to work

These provisions do not justify the commission of any criminal or civil wrong, like assault, battery, breach of the peace, obstruction of the highway, nuisance, nor do they legalise trespass on the employer's premises for the purpose of a "sit-in" strike. It is not lawful for pickets to obstruct the delivery of goods to their employer's business premises as by lying down in the road. Such conduct is outside the protection of s134 unless it can be brought within the phrase "communicating information."

11:23:2   Police assistance to control pickets

An employer whose premises are being picketed may contact the police for assistance in controlling the actions of the pickets. It may be that peaceful picketing is lawful only if it is carried out within the limits of any directions given by the police on the spot. There is a tendency to charge pickets with obstructing the police, rather than with a specific wrong, like breach of the peace, outlined above. To prevent an apprehended breach of the peace, a police officer can limit the number of pickets.

Piddington v Bates (1960)

In the course of a peaceful picket during a trade dispute, Bates, a police officer, thought that only two men should be stationed at each door of the premises being picketed. Piddington disagreed and pushed past the police officer. He was arrested and later charged with obstructing a police officer in the execution of his duty.

The Court decided that the police officer reasonably apprehended a breach of the peace which it was his duty to prevent, consequently there was a sufficient justification for the arrest.

A similar situation arose in a more recent case.

Tynan v Balmer (1966)

Forty pickets walked in a circle near the service entrance to a factory at which there was an official strike, the object being to bring traffic to a standstill. A police officer thought that this action was likely to cause an obstruction to the highway, but Tynan as leader of the pickets refused a request to stop these activities.

The Court decided that Tynan was guilty of wilfully obstructing the police officer in the execution of his duty. The pickets were not attending for the purposes allowed by statute. Their object was partially to seal off the highway and to cause vehicles approaching the premises to stop, this being an unreasonable use of the highway and a nuisance at common law.

There were too many persons present to enable the picketing to be peaceful. The circling of pickets prevented, rather than assisted, the communication of information and rendered impossible any persuasion of employees not to work.

11:24 WHEN IS IT A CRIME TO STRIKE?

The criminal law is not usually relied upon at the present time as a means of controlling industrial action but, under s5 of the Conspiracy and Protection of Property Act 1875, it is a criminal offence punishable with a fine and imprisonment, for either employer or employee to wilfully and maliciously break their contract of service or hiring, knowing (or having reasonable cause to believe) that the probable consequences will be:

1   The endangering of human life, or
2   Causing serious bodily injury, or
3   Exposing valuable property to injury and destruction

This covers a strike by employers as well as employees, providing essential services. In view of these provisions and those of the 1971 Act the selective criminal provisions relating to strike action in the gas, electricity and water industries have been repealed (s133) though strike action by employees in these undertakings will often be covered by the various laws discussed in this section.

The Police Act 1964 s47 prevents members of the police joining a trade union, but their interests are protected by a Police Federation. It is a criminal offence, under s53 of the Police Act, to cause disaffection, breach of discipline or withdrawal of labour among members of the police force.

TWELVE

Redundancy and How it
Affects the Employer

THE OBJECT OF THE REDUNDANCY PAYMENTS ACT 1965 IS TO PROVIDE monetary compensation to an employee who loses his job, the amount payable being dependent upon his length of service with the employer. The Act recognises that an employee has a proprietary interest in his job and the principle of the "golden handshake," whereby directors are handsomely compensated for loss of their position in the event of a takeover or reorganisation, has now been extended to the ordinary employee. It is not possible to contract out of the Act.

12:1 MEANING OF "REDUNDANCY"
(REDUNDANCY PAYMENTS ACT 1965 s1(1), s2)

If an employee is dismissed wholly or mainly for one of the following reasons, then he is entitled to a redundancy payment:

1   Where the employer has ceased or intends to cease carrying on the business in which the employee was employed
2   Where the employer has ceased or intends to cease carrying on the business in the place where the employee was employed
3   Where the employer no longer needs the services provided by the employee, though the business has not ceased

The words "wholly or mainly" recognise that there may be more than one reason why an employee has been dismissed, and this situation may give rise to an action before a tribunal (see 12:7). The employer must prove that dismissal was not due to redundancy, and failure to discharge this burden will entitle the employee to establish his claim. In Harrison v Chamberlain Studios Ltd (1966) the employer failed to convince the tribunal that a dismissal was caused by an employee's political affiliations rather than redundancy.

12:1:1 *Meaning of "dismissal" (s3)*
An employee is dismissed for the purposes of the Act and may claim a redundancy payment if his contract of employment is terminated by the employer, with or without notice.

On giving the required notice, reasons for dismissal need not be stipulated, but if the employee claims redundancy pay then the onus is on the employer to show that the dismissal was not because of redundancy: consequently it is advisable for the employer to give his reasons. A claim cannot be made where a dismissal results from misconduct, refusal to obey orders, insubordination or lack of co-operation.

Vincent v William Campbell & Sons (Biscuits) Ltd (1966)

Vincent, employed as a charge-hand in a packing department, refused to transfer to another department where the work involved was substantially the same.

The court decided that the employee was not entitled to a redundancy payment, since she had been dismissed for refusing to obey a lawful order.

An employee wrongfully dismissed may sue for damages at common law, in addition to any claim for redundancy.

An employee is considered to have been dismissed and may claim redundancy payment if:

1   Under a fixed-term contract, that term expires without renewal, unless in the case of a contract for two years or more the employee waives his right to a redundancy payment before the contract expires
2   The business closes down as a result of the employer's death and his contract is terminated, but not where the business is continued and the employee is re-engaged within eight weeks of such death (s23)
3   The employee terminates the contract without notice where entitled to do so because of the employer's conduct

Duckworth v P F Farnish & Co (1969, Court of Appeal)

Duckworth, an experienced joiner, was lent to another company because of lack of work at his employer's place of business. The employee agreed to the transfer which was to be "for a few days only." The employer sent Duckworth's insurance cards and tax form to the other company without informing him. Five weeks later, while still on loan, Duckworth wrote to Farnish & Co terminating his contract and claiming redundancy payment on the ground that there seemed to be no opportunity of continuing the employment.

The court decided that the transfer of the insurance cards and the tax form did not amount to a dismissal of the employee. Duckworth was justified in terminating the contract of employment because of his employer's inability to provide remunerative employment for a period of five weeks. He was entitled to a redundancy payment.

12:2 HOW THE EMPLOYER
CAN AVOID A REDUNDANCY PAYMENT (s2(3) and (4))

An employee is not entitled to a redundancy payment where he has unreasonably refused either:

1   A renewal of his contract on the old terms without any break
    in the continuity of employment, or
2   The offer in writing of suitable alternative employment sufficiently detailed to enable him to appreciate what is involved
    and taking effect not later than four weeks from the termination of the existing contract

If an employee in job A is made redundant, offered a suitable alternative job B by the employer, accepts job B and is then made redundant again, his length of service in job A is added to the time spent in job B when calculating the redundancy pay. This provision ensures that an offer of a new job is a genuine continuation of the employment.

Marriott v Oxford & District
Co-operative Society Ltd (1969, Court of Appeal)

Marriott, an electrical maintenance foreman employed by the Society, was informed by letter that he could not be retained in his present position because of a running down of the business. He turned down an offer of employment at a reduced status with a reduction in wages of £3 per week and sought other employment. Four weeks later he was informed by letter that the reduction would be only £1 per week, subject to review in three months, to be operative the following week. About a month later Marriott secured other work and claimed a redundancy payment from his ex-employer.

The court decided that the original contract of employment had been terminated by the employers within s3(1)(a), entitling Marriott to a redundancy payment. On a true construction of the second letter, an essential term as to wages was repudiated and a new term substituted, to which the employee did not consent. If Marriott had left at the end of the week during which he received the second letter, he would certainly have been entitled to a redundancy payment. He should not be deprived of it because he stayed on for a few weeks at a reduced salary, until he found another job.

479

What is to be regarded as suitable alternative work is determined in relation to the employee concerned not in relation to a class of employees. The employee must establish that either:

1   The alternative work is unsuitable, or
2   His refusal was reasonable, considering issues such as his skills, the type of work offered and the nature of the previous work, wages, travelling problems and family situation, loss of fringe benefits, health or physical disabilities, and lack of permanency in the new work

The employee's personal preferences are not relevant.

An employee under notice may wish to leave before the notice expires, to take up a new job. If the employer agrees to the early departure then the employee's entitlement to redundancy pay is unaffected. The employer may, however, make a written objection. Entitlement to redundancy pay will then be decided by a tribunal in cases of dispute.

12 : 2 : 1   Redundancy situations

If a business is moved to a new site nearby, an employee is not dismissed if offered a position at the new location. In R H McCulloch v Moore (1967) a gas board employee in Sussex engaged on semi-skilled work was offered an alternative position in Scotland, East Midlands, Luton or Reading. Dismissal was held to have been caused by redundancy when he declined the offer made. Many decisions on this point turn on the reasonableness of the employee's refusal to accept employment at a new place.

A major change in the type of work an employee is expected to do constitutes dismissal, as in Wolverhampton Die Castings v Kitson (1967) where an employee, with a cerebral thrombotic condition, was required to complete his work within a given time which had not previously been imposed.

If business requirements necessitate the adoption of new methods, but the overall requirements of the business remain unchanged, no payment can be claimed where personal deficiencies prevent a particular employee from adjusting to the new demands made on him. Payment must be made, however, where new methods alter the nature of the work to be done, as where a motor manufacturer uses plastics in the bodywork of cars in place of wood.

It must be pointed out that many decisions turn on their own facts, but in time established precedents will emerge.

12:3 LAY-OFF AND SHORT TIME
MAY GIVE RISE TO A REDUNDANCY CLAIM (ss5–7)

Sections 5, 6 and 7 of the Act prevent an employer putting employees on short time or laying them off for long periods in the hope that they will give notice and relieve the employer of the need to make a redundancy payment. An employee may claim a redundancy payment even though he has not been dismissed, if he has been either:

1   Laid-off, that is, he has received no wages where his wages are dependent on work done
2   Put on short time, that is received less than half of his usual pay for either:
   (a) Four or more consecutive weeks (head 1), or
   (b) A broken series of six or more weeks in which not more than three were consecutive in a thirteen-week period (head 2)

The employee must give written notice of intention to claim within four weeks after the end of the period of lay off or short time and also give the minimum period of notice required to leave the employment. The employer may by counter-notice within seven days contest the claim, if there is a reasonable prospect of a resumption of normal working, for not less than thirteen weeks, within four weeks from the time of writing. The issue is decided by a tribunal, but to receive payment the employee must have left the employment in question.

12:4 IMPORTANCE OF "CONTINUOUS
EMPLOYMENT" TO A REDUNDANCY CLAIM

To make any claim to payment the employee must have been "continuously employed" for 104 weeks before what is called the "relevant date" (the meaning of continuous employment is the same as in schedule 1 to the Contracts of Employment Act 1963, which is explained in 13:2:2). There are two qualifications: any week worked by the employee before he was eighteen does not count, but a short period between renewal of employment does count (s8).

Lee and another v Barry High Ltd (1970, Court of Appeal)

The two plaintiffs, both minors, entered into deeds of apprenticeship for five years, on the understanding that the employer might transfer his responsibilities to another party during that period. After three years such a transfer did take place and after another year a further transfer was effected to the defendant company. The plaintiffs completed their apprenticeship with Barry High Ltd and worked for two months as regular craftsmen before being dismissed as redundant. They claimed redundancy payments.

The court decided that the claim must fail. The Act clearly stipulates that employment is continuous only if it is with one employer throughout the period in respect of which the claim is made. Here there were three employers and neither of the plaintiffs was employed by the defendants for the requisite two-year period. This type of situation was not intended to be within the scope of the Act.

To establish continuous employment where there has been a change in the ownership of a business, an employee must show a transfer from previous to present owner of the entire property and business, with the previous owner terminating employment and the new owner renewing the employee's contract. Consequently, if the employee is later dismissed, laid-off or put on short time, employment has been continuous for the purposes of a redundancy claim (s13).

If the new owner offers employment which is refused, the employee cannot claim any payment if:

1   The terms of employment are the same as before and without any break in employment
2   The terms differ, but are suitable and made in writing before the change of ownership, provided there is not a break in employment for over four weeks

For s13 to be applicable, the ownership of a business must be transferred, and not merely an asset in it. "The vital consideration is whether the effect of the transaction was to put the transferee into possession of a going concern, the activities of which he could carry on without interruption." (Mr Justice Widgery)

Continuity of employment is unaffected by the following events:

1   Transfer of a business or undertaking by one employer to another (for example, when there is a sale of a business as a going concern)

2   Substitution by statute of one corporate body for another as employer

3   Continuation of a business, after its owner's death, by his personal representatives

4   Change of partners, trustees or personal representatives

5   Where a company's employee is taken into the employment of an associated company

12:4:1   *Meaning of the term "relevant date"*

Where a dismissed employee is claiming a redundancy payment, the relevant date for reckoning back over his period of employment is the date on which:

1   His contract of employment was terminated by notice given by his employer

2   His contract of employment was terminated without notice by employer or employee

3   His contract of employment for a fixed term expired

Where an employee gives notice of his intention to claim a redundancy payment because of lay-off or short time, together with his notice ending the contract of employment, then the relevant date for reckoning back over his period of employment is the end of:

1   The last of the four or more consecutive weeks (under head 1)

2   The sixth week or last week (under head 2) (see 12 : 3)

12:5 COST OF MAKING AN EMPLOYEE REDUNDANT (SCHEDULE 1)

If the employee has established that he is entitled to a payment, it must then be determined how much is to be paid. This is the responsibility of the employer, a detailed task that may be handed to the personnel manager. The recipient must be supplied with a written statement of the method of calculation. Failure to do so without reasonable excuse renders an employer liable to a fine of £20 and £100 on a second conviction.

To calculate the amount of a redundancy payment, first establish the "relevant date" as explained in 12 : 4 : 1. Second, establish the standard "week's pay."

The "week's pay" upon which the calculations are made is the minimum remuneration to which the employee is entitled in the week immediately preceding the relevant date. If this was not a normal week's pay, as a result of short time or lay-off, then the minimum remuneration is calculated by reference to the Contracts of Employment Act 1963, schedule 2 (see 13 : 2 : 4). Where these rules cannot be applied to redundancy, then the following presumptions are made:

1   That the contract of employment has been terminated
2   That the employee was ready and willing to work, but no work was provided
3   That the employee was willing to do work of a reasonable nature and amount to earn the average piece-rate sum
4   That the employee was not absent from work without the employer's consent
5   That the rules relating to a minimum wage apply, even if the employee is outside the scope of the Contracts of Employment Act 1963

The maximum for the "week's pay" is £40.

The third step is to count up the number of years of continuous employment, reckoning backwards from the relevant date. The maximum number of years that can be taken into account is twenty.

The payment depends on the employee's age so separate his years of continuous employment into three categories:

1   Years when the employee was aged over forty but less than:
     (a) sixty, for a woman
     (b) sixty-five, for a man
2   Years when the employee was aged more than twenty-one but less than forty-one
3   Years when the employee was aged twenty-one or less but excluding any period worked before he was eighteen

Multiply the number of years in category 1 by $1\frac{1}{2}$.
Multiply the number of years in category 2 by 1.
Multiply the number of years in category 3 by $\frac{1}{2}$.

Add these figures and multiply by the "week's pay." The result is the redundancy payment due.

Because the maximum number of years is twenty and the maximum for the week's pay is £40, the maximum redundancy payment is £1200.

A payment does not affect entitlement to unemployment benefit, nor is it taxable under Schedule E.

An employee must claim within six months or his personal representatives within twelve months after termination of the employment, unless the issue has been referred to a tribunal already. Non-payment by the employer entitles the employee to make a claim direct from the national Redundancy Fund, provided all reasonable steps short of legal proceedings have been taken to recover the payment. The Secretary of State for Employment may refuse to pay a rebate to an employer refusing to make a redundancy payment without reasonable excuse.

12:6 EFFECT OF A STRIKE ON A REDUNDANCY PAYMENT

If an employee under notice, whether given by himself or his employer, takes part in a strike, the employer can serve a notice asking him to extend his contract beyond the date fixed for its termination by the number of days lost because of the strike. The notice must indicate that any redundancy payment due will not be disputed by the employer, if the employee either:

1   Complies with the request
2   Satisfies the employer that sickness or injury prevents him from so complying

Non-compliance with the notice results in loss of the redundancy payment, unless the employer chooses to pay it. The employee may appeal to a tribunal if a payment is not made. If the tribunal finds that the employee was unable to comply with the employer's request, or that it was unreasonable to expect him to comply, then part or all of the redundancy payment may be awarded to the employee as the tribunal thinks fit (s40).

12:7 TRIBUNALS DEALING WITH REDUNDANCY ISSUES

Disputes concerning the right to and the amount of a redundancy payment or a rebate claim from the national Fund by the employer will be determined by an industrial tribunal, set up under the Industrial Training Act 1964 (s12) and consisting of a legally qualified chairman and two other members, one representing the employers and the other representing the employees. The decision of the tribunal is final, subject to an appeal to the High Court on a point of law. The parties may be legally represented; legal aid is available only on a reference to the High Court. Two matters are presumed by the tribunal, until the contrary is proved:

1   That an employee's employment during a given period is continuous
2   That if the employee is dismissed by his employer this is because of redundancy (s9)

The tribunal determines an employee's entitlement to payment where:

1   He terminates the employment because of short time or lay-off
2   Alternative employment has been offered to a redundant employee, and it must be decided if it was suitable and unreasonably refused

Costs will only be awarded against an unsuccessful party who has acted frivolously or vexatiously. A party seeking an adjournment may be ordered to pay the cost involved even though he has not acted frivolously or vexatiously. A "frivolous" application is made with the knowledge that it is doomed to failure. The term "vexatious" involves the same knowledge, with the added intention of putting the other party to unjustified trouble and expense.

12:8 PERSONS EXCLUDED
FROM THE PROTECTION OF THE ACT (ss11, 14–17)

The Redundancy Payments Act does not cover:

1   Persons with a fixed-term contract for two years or more entered into before 6 December 1965, other than apprentices
2   Registered dock workers
3   Share fishermen: masters and members of a fishing vessel crew if remuneration is solely by a share of the profits
4   Crown servants
5   Employees of the National Health Service, the Forestry Commission and the Nature Conservancy
6   Domestic servants related to their employer
7   Persons employed outside Great Britain, excepting those who "ordinarily" work here or are in Great Britain in accordance with the employer's instructions on the relevant date

8 Independent contractors

9 Employees working less than twenty-one hours per week (on average)

10 Persons whose notice expires after their 65th birthday (for men) or 60th birthday (for women)

11 An employee who is the spouse of the employer

12 An employee entitled to a periodic payment or lump sum in the form of a pension, gratuity or superannuation allowance payable on leaving his employment will be excluded from the right to a redundancy payment altogether, if the sum received is equal to or exceeds the redundancy claim. Where the pension or other payment is less than the redundancy payment otherwise payable, then the redundancy payment is reduced to take the pension into account

13 Employees with a right to a redundancy payment on leaving the employment, provided:

   (a) It is in pursuance of an agreement between an employers' association and a trade union

   (b) It is more suitable than the statutory scheme—for example, in the building industry where continuous employment for long periods may not be possible

12:8:1 *Directors may be able to claim redundancy payments*

A working director who owns shares in the company benefiting from his services may be an employee for the purpose of claiming a redundancy payment.

Nottingham Egg Packers & Distributors Ltd
v McCarthy and Haslett (1967, Industrial Tribunal)

McCarthy and Haslett were shareholders and working directors in the applicant company. They claimed redundancy payments as employees in respect of the termination of their employment when the company ceased to do business.

The court decided that they were employees of the company entitled to redundancy payments. In law a limited company is an entirely separate legal person from the people who own shares in it. Appointment as a director does not make that director an employee of the company, but here the parties worked for the company and were paid a salary for doing so. Their position was consistent only with their working under a contract of service with the company.

Adamson v Arthur Smith (Hull) Ltd (1967, Industrial Tribunal)

In this case the tribunal took the view that a director may claim a redundancy payment if he is also an employee of the company, but his entitlement is based on his rights as an employee, not his rights as a director. It was stated that a test should not be laid down whereby a working director with a minority shareholding is entitled to a redundancy payment, whereas a director with a majority shareholding is automatically disentitled.

THIRTEEN

Termination of the Contract of Employment

THE CONTRACT OF EMPLOYMENT MAY END WITH EITHER EMPLOYER OR employee giving the required period of notice. Even if there is a friendly termination of their relationship, it is advisable that both parties should clearly appreciate their rights and duties regarding such matters as:

1. The precise length of notice required with particular reference to the requirements of the Contracts of Employment Act 1963, if applicable
2. The payment of wages due
3. The effect of the Redundancy Payments Act 1965

There are many cases where the contract is ended automatically by an event over which the parties have little or no control. It is unfortunate that the legal rules governing bankruptcy, winding up, closure of a business, death and illness are not clearer. It may be better to consider what effect these contingencies ought to have on the contract if they arise, and then frame an express clause making the necessary provision for insertion into the contract when it is first negotiated.

On those occasions when it is important to dispense immediately with the services of a troublesome employee, the legal rules governing instant dismissal should be carefully studied. The employer must justify his actions by reference to an established legal principle, otherwise the employee may claim damages for wrongful dismissal. If there is any doubt about the legality of instant dismissal, the employer may either dismiss by giving notice or, if he wishes to get rid of the employee straight away, he may pay wages in lieu of notice. This second alternative can be expensive if a lengthy period of notice is involved, where, for example, the employee is a director with a contract for a fixed period of time that has some way to go.

In some cases refusal by an employee to implement the terms of his contract can cause hardship when the employer finds it difficult to recruit a suitable replacement. The courts will not directly order an employee to carry out his duties as promised, but the employer can adequately protect himself if he engages a highly skilled employee by including restrictive clauses in the contract of employment.

Many of the problems that have been presented to the courts in the cases to be discussed in this chapter have arisen because the employer failed to clarify the legal relationship with his employee when the contract was first concluded. Although the chapter is concerned with the termination of a contract, many of the difficulties encountered are rooted in the negotiation of the contractual terms.

13:1 HOW LONG EMPLOYMENT LASTS

The contract of employment may contain an express term which states that the employment is to continue for a given period, or until the task specified in the contract has been performed. The contract will be terminated automatically at the end of the period specified, or when the task is completed, but not before. Thus neither party can terminate the agreement by giving notice.

Many contracts of employment do not specify the period for which the contract is to last, since the parties contemplate a continuing relationship until some event occurs which brings the agreement to an end, such as dismissal, giving notice, or death of the employee. An indefinite hiring may be terminated by mutual consent or either party giving reasonable notice of termination to the other. What is "reasonable" in this context depends upon the nature of the employment. The Contracts of Employment Act 1963 lays down minimum periods of notice that must be given (see 13:2:1).

In a contract of employment for an indefinite period of time, express terms may clearly set out the grounds upon which the employer may dismiss the employee. In such cases, termination of the contract by the employer is justifiable only if the specified grounds exist, if they are deemed to exclude dismissal for other reasons. Unless he is careful, the employer may effectively take away his right to terminate the contract by giving notice, where the employment offers a post that is permanent and pensionable.

McClelland v Northern Ireland
General Health Services Board (1957, House of Lords)

McClelland could be dismissed from her employment with the Board if guilty of gross misconduct, failure to take an oath of allegiance, or inefficiency rendering her unfit for continued employment. The contract was terminable by the employee giving one month's notice, but the employers were not given a similar power. The defendant employers purported to terminate employment on grounds of redundancy, by giving six months' notice.

The court decided that, in the absence of an express provision for dismissal on grounds of redundancy, the employers could not terminate the contract for this reason by giving notice. The contract embodied express powers of termination and it was not necessary to imply a further power to terminate for redundancy, in order to give the contract the business efficacy that the parties must have intended it to have.

A general hiring for an indefinite time is terminable by reasonable notice, but here the employee was offered a permanent post, carrying a pension or gratuity on completion of a stated number of years' service, plus other pension and sickness benefits. The employer could not claim a right to give notice which would deprive the employee of all the pension and other rights offered by the express terms of the contract.

It seems that by being too precise the employer restricts his freedom to dismiss his employee. It is advisable either to set out an exhaustive list of the grounds of dismissal to cover all contingencies, or to draft a term that gives the employer a discretion to dismiss on other grounds that are not specified. The simplest solution, however, is to make express provision for dismissal by the employer on giving the period of notice as specified in the contract.

13:2 GIVING AN EMPLOYEE NOTICE AND THE EFFECTS OF THE CONTRACTS OF EMPLOYMENT ACT 1963

Where the contract of employment may be terminated by either party giving notice to the other, the length of notice required is usually fixed by an express term in the contract. The termination of the employment may denote a breakdown in the personal relationship between the employee and his superiors, and to avoid unnecessary unpleasantness and dissension it is advisable to include an express term on the question of notice.

In the absence of any such provision, reference may be made to any custom in the trade or industry applicable to persons in the same position as the employee. If a custom does not exist then a "reasonable" period of notice must be given, which is determined by an examination of factors such as the employee's status in the concern employing him, whether the employment was temporary or permanent and the intervals between wage payments. Decided cases have established the following periods of reasonable notice in relation to specific employment: three months for a general manager, one month for a head gardener, and twelve months for a ship's chief officer.

13:2:1 Minimum periods of notice
set out by the Contracts of Employment Act 1963

This Act stipulates the minimum periods of notice that an employer must give his employee in order to terminate employment. The contract of employment may, if required, provide for a period of notice that is longer than the period set out in the Act. Where the employer and employee have not expressly agreed upon a period of notice, an employee may claim that the minimum period of notice stipulated by the Act is shorter than that required by custom or the period that is "reasonable" in the circumstances.

Under s1(1) of the Act as amended by the Industrial Relations Act, the employer must give the following periods of notice:

1   One week to an employee with continuous employment of thirteen weeks or more, but less than two years
2   Two weeks to an employee with continuous employment of two years but less than five years
3   Four weeks to an employee with continuous employment of five years but less than ten years
4   Six weeks to an employee with continuous employment over ten years, but less than fifteen years
5   Eight weeks to an employee with continuous employment of over fifteen years

An employee who has been continuously employed for twenty-six weeks or more must give one week's notice (s1(2)). The employer's common law rights of dismissal without notice (see 13 : 4) remain unaffected. For details of employees within the protection of the Act see 1 : 6 : 5.

13:2:2   *What is meant by "continuous employment" (schedule 1)*
The period of employment, for the purpose of determining the length of notice to be given, is calculated in weeks. A normal working week is one in which the employee:

1   Actually works for twenty-one hours, or
2   Is employed under a contract of employment which involves working in normal circumstances at least twenty-one hours, even though the employee works less than twenty-one hours because he is:
(a) Sick or injured and thereby incapable of work (but more than twenty-six weeks' absence for sickness will break the continuity of employment: if employment is resumed for at least one week during a period of prolonged absence due to sickness, then the employee can be absent for another twenty-six weeks before breaking the continuity of employment)

(b) Absent because work has temporarily ceased—for example, being laid off

(c) Taking paid holiday or unpaid holiday with the employer's consent

(d) Absent by leave or custom such that he is regarded as continuing his employment—for example, a day's absence to celebrate a local holiday

(e) Absent without leave, but not informed by the employer that his services are no longer required

13:2:3   *Effect of strikes and lock-outs on continuous employment*
A period of lock-out will not break the employee's period of continuous employment, but it is not included in the total number of weeks worked.

The period of a strike does not break the continuity of the employee's period of employment, but the period is not included in the total number of weeks worked.

Continuity of employment is unaffected by the following events:

1   A transfer of a business or undertaking
2   Where statute replaces one corporate body by another as the employer
3   Where personal representatives continue a business when the owner dies
4   Where there is a change of partners, personal representatives or trustees employing any person
5   Where a company employee is taken into the employment of an associated company

13:2:4   *Wage payments to the employee under notice (schedule 2)*
The rules to be discussed, which cannot be excluded or limited by contract, deal with the protection given to an employee during his period of notice, where he has been continuously employed for twenty-six weeks or more, to prevent the employer from paying inadequate wages. The employee is guaranteed a minimum rate of payment, irrespective of which party to the contract has given notice. These rules are inapplicable where the contractual notice to be given must be at least one week longer than the period guaranteed by the Act (s2(3)). Naturally, the employee must be paid for all work done, these rules being significant only if he is unable to work during the period of notice for a number of hours sufficient to secure payment to him of the guaranteed minimum rate.

13:2:5 Definition of a normal working week

An employee's rights during the period of notice depend upon the concept of normal working hours per week, though this concept is not defined by the Act itself. The contract of employment usually stipulates a fixed number of hours to be worked each week and these will be considered as the normal working hours, excluding voluntary overtime, but including compulsory overtime provided for by the contract.

13:2:6 Employment with normal working hours

The employee must be paid for the normal working hours during the statutory period of notice, if he is:

1   Ready and willing to work, but not provided with work by the employer
2   Incapable of work because of sickness or injury but sickness benefit or industrial injuries benefit may be deducted when calculating the wages due
3   Away on holiday in accordance with the terms of employment

The employee is entitled to the flat wage rate, irrespective of the work actually done.

If payment varies, as in piecework, then a different set of rules apply for the computation of wages payable during the period of notice, where the employee does not work because of lack of work, illness or holidays. Remuneration is payable at the average hourly rate paid in the four weeks fully completed before notice was given. In determining this average hourly rate, only the hours worked and the remuneration paid in respect of such work must be considered. Thus, if hours during that four-week period include:

1   Payment above the normal rate, as where overtime was worked at a higher rate, then the basic rate is substituted
2   Hours when remuneration was not payable at all, then re-muneration in earlier weeks must be considered to bring the weeks under consideration up to four

From the sum determined there may be subtracted payments by the employer by way of sick pay, or holiday pay. Where it is the employee who has given notice, the employer's liability to pay does not arise until the employee leaves the employment in accordance with the terms of his notice.

13:2:7 *Employment without normal working hours*

Normal working hours may not exist during the period of notice. In that case for each week during that period the employee is entitled to a sum not less than his average weekly rate of remuneration in the twelve-week period counting back from the last full week before notice was given. Any week in which less than twenty-one hours was worked is disregarded, but if this reduces the number of weeks below eight, then earlier weeks must be considered beyond the twelve-week period, until the number averaged is eight.

The employer's obligation to pay is subject to the employee's willingness to do work of a reasonable nature, unless he is absent because of illness, injury, or holiday in accordance with the terms of the employment. Any payment of sick pay and holiday pay in respect of the period of notice will be taken into account and deducted from the remuneration payable by the employer in respect of that period. Where the employee gives notice, the employer's liability to pay does not arise until the employee leaves the employment in accordance with the terms of his notice.

13:2:8 *When the employee cannot claim the guaranteed minimum wage*

The employee is not entitled to the guaranteed minimum wage when during the period of notice:

1   He is absent at his own request or takes part in a strike, or
2   He is dismissed, in which case only the period before dismissal is covered by the guaranteed minimum wage

If the contract of employment is broken by the employer during the period of notice and the employee sues, payments to the employee covering the period of notice after the breach must be considered in mitigation of the damage suffered by him in that period. For example, employee Smith, while working out his four-week period of statutory notice, has received payment for the first three weeks of that period. During the third week he is wrongfully and summarily dismissed by the employer. Damages may be claimed by Smith against his employer, but the wage payments up until the end of the third week of the period of notice must be considered in mitigation of damage suffered.

13:3 DISCHARGE OF A CONTRACT OF EMPLOYMENT

There are a number of circumstances in which the contract of employment may be terminated by some determining event. The legal position in relation to these circumstances will now be discussed with particular reference to the rights of the employer.

13:3:1 *Dissolution of a partnership*

If a partnership is dissolved because of the retirement of one or more of the partners, there may arise a case of wrongful dismissal of any employee engaged for a fixed period of time, so that he is entitled to a claim in damages. If the new firm offers employment on exactly the same terms, the employee waives his right of action by entering the service of the new firm. Failure to accept such an offer, in mitigation of any loss likely to be suffered by the employee, will entitle him to nominal damages only in any action for breach of contract against the partners of the original firm.

Brace v Calder (1895, Court of Appeal)

Brace was employed by a partnership of four members for a fixed period of two years, but after six months two partners retired and the partnership was dissolved. The other two partners continued the business and they were willing to employ Brace on the same terms as before, but he refused their offer.

The court decided that the dissolution of the partnership was a wrongful dismissal of Brace, but, being offered employment on the same terms, he suffered only nominal damages.

If the partnership is dissolved by the death of one of the partners, any existing contracts of employment are terminated only if they depend upon some personal element involving the deceased partner. In trading partnerships the exact composition of the firm is either unknown or unimportant to the employee. Thus his contract of employment is not automatically discharged when one of the partners dies, and it may be enforced against the surviving partners.

13:3:2 *Bankruptcy of the employer*

The bankruptcy of the employer does not automatically terminate the contract of employment, unless solvency was an essential element of the contractual relationship. The employee may wish to leave his employment when the bankruptcy supervenes by giving the appropriate period of notice, since the value of the services rendered to the employer after the date of the receiving order cannot be claimed for as a preferential debt (Bankruptcy Act 1914 s33).

The employee's main concern in this situation is whether he will be paid for services that he has rendered already and compensated for losses suffered because of any breach of contract caused by the bankruptcy, where, for example, he has lost his position without being given the appropriate period of notice required under the contract. When a bankrupt's property is distributed then the wages of clerks, servants, and workmen, if unpaid, are preferential debts for the four months before the date of the receiving order, but limited to £200 per person, together with accrued holiday remuneration. Also ranking as preferential debts are National Insurance and pension contributions payable by statute, during the twelve months prior to the receiving order. Similar claims may be made by employees when a limited company is wound up.

Any claim by an employee in excess of £200 for unpaid wages or damages for wrongful dismissal may be maintained, but the debt will not be treated preferentially.

13:3:3 Winding up a limited company

Where the court makes an order for the compulsory winding up of a limited company, or appoints a receiver or manager on behalf of the debenture holders, then any employee of that company is dismissed, since his contract of employment is discharged. Damages may be claimed for wrongful dismissal if the employee is entitled to notice. A contract of employment is not terminated if a receiver, appointed by the debenture holders out of court, carries on the company business as its agent. Where the company business is sold by the receiver, then the contract of employment will be brought to an end.

If the liquidator or receiver allows an employee to continue at the same work, for the same salary, for the period during which notice of termination of the contract had to be given by the company, then damages are not recoverable by the employee, although technically there has been a breach of contract.

Reid v The Explosives Co Ltd (1887, Court of Appeal)

Following a court action by holders of debentures of the defendant company, a manager and receiver was appointed. Reid, an employee, entitled by his contract of employment to six months' notice, was instructed by the manager to continue his work with the company for a period of six months, at his usual salary. At the end of this period the business of the company was sold and Reid sued for damages for wrongful dismissal without notice.

The court decided that Reid was discharged from his original contract of employment by the appointment of the manager and receiver, and consequently he was entitled to damages for wrongful dismissal without notice. However, by continuing to work for the manager for six months, Reid had been employed in work of equal value to that which he had lost, and consequently no damage was suffered.

If the winding up is voluntary, it does not operate as a notice to the employees that their contracts of employment are discharged, if the business of the company is carried on; consequently they are entitled to notice in accordance with the terms of their contracts. This is not so where the voluntary winding up is caused by the company's insolvency. In that case the contract is discharged, subject to a claim for wrongful dismissal. The voluntary winding up of a solvent company for the purposes of an amalgamation does not operate as a dismissal of the company's employees.

If a contract of employment for a fixed number of years is prematurely terminated by a winding up of the company, then the employee need not comply with any covenants in restraint of trade embodied in that contract. Since the company is unable to perform its obligations under the agreement it cannot force the employee to observe his obligations (Measures Bros Ltd v Measures (1910)).

13:3:4 *Compensation for breach of*
contract caused by bankruptcy or liquidation
If the business of a trader closes as the result of bankruptcy or a limited company goes into liquidation, then an employee under a contract of employment for a fixed number of years is entitled to compensation for the loss of earnings during the unexpired portion of his contract. He is not entitled to commission, however, if it was a payment additional to the salary agreed upon and if the employer has the right to refuse to accept all business introduced by the agent.

Re English & Scottish Marine Insurance Co (1870)

In 1867 MaClure contracted with the English & Scottish Marine Insurance Co to act as their agent for a period of five years, in return for a fixed

salary of £500 p.a. and a commission of 10 per cent on all business transacted which MaClure had introduced. In 1868 the company was voluntarily wound up and MaClure claimed from the liquidator the prospective
value of his salary of £500 and loss of commission during the remainder
of the five-year term.

The court decided that the claim for the loss of salary was allowable,
but not the claim for loss of commission. MaClure could not determine
the extent of the business he transacted with the company. He could not
dictate whether or not the company accepted business introduced by him
in issuing a policy of insurance and taking on the resultant risks involved.
By rejecting the business MaClure introduced, the company could reduce
to nothing the amount of business they concluded through his agency.

13:3:5 *Closure of the employer's business may not terminate the contract*
The contract of employment is not necessarily terminated by the closure
of the employer's business. It is essential to examine the terms of the contract, both express and implied, before reaching any definite decision on
this point. Unforeseen accidents, such as fire or flood, may make fulfilment
of the contract difficult or impossible for the employer, but if he is bound
by a contractual clause expressed in absolute terms he must either perform
his obligations or pay damages to the employee affected.

Turner v Goldsmith (1891, Court of Appeal)

Goldsmith, a shirt manufacturer, employed Turner as an agent, canvasser
and traveller, to sell goods manufactured by Goldsmith or acquired by him
from other sources for resale. The agency was for a fixed term of five years
and Turner's remuneration was payable in the form of commission, as
specified in the contract of employment. At the end of two years Goldsmith's factory was burned down and he did not resume business.

The court decided that Goldsmith was liable to pay Turner damages in
lieu of the commission he would have earned if the contract had lasted
for the full five years. The contract was not limited to goods manufactured
by Goldsmith at a particular factory.

13:3:6 *Termination of a contract by the death of one of the parties*
In a contract for personal services between employer and employee
which can be performed only during the lifetime of the parties, there
is an implied condition that each party shall be bound only while he
is alive. If either party dies then the personal representatives of the

deceased, whether it be employer or employee, are not liable on the contract.

The personal representatives of a deceased employee clearly cannot be expected to continue to perform his contract of employment, even if they are competent to do so. More important, however, they may enforce against the employer any right of action that had been vested in the employee before his death, the vital issue here being a claim for wages that have not been paid.

Stubbs v Holywell Railway Co (1867)

Stubbs was employed by the defendant company as a consulting engineer for a period of fifteen months to complete certain work. Before finishing the work he died.

The court decided that his personal representatives could recover two quarterly instalments of salary which were due but not paid, since a term of the contract of employment provided that he was to be paid by instalments.

If wages are payable, say, monthly and the employee dies after completing three weeks' work, his personal representatives may be able to claim wages for the three-week period by bringing an action under the Law Reform (Frustrated Contracts) Act 1943, if the employer is reluctant to make the payment.

Where the contract is one where personal considerations and confidence are important to both employer and employee, the death of the employer also terminates the contract, unless there is an express term to the contrary.

Farrow v Wilson (1869)

Farrow was employed as a farmer-bailiff by Price Pugh, the contract of employment providing that both sides must give six months' notice. The employer was entitled to give six months' salary in lieu of notice if he wished. The personal representatives of the employer were sued for wrongful dismissal by Farrow, since on the employer's death he was not given notice or payment in lieu of notice.

The court decided that if the employee had died the employer could not have compelled his personal representatives to perform the contract of employment or pay damages. On the employer's death, the employee is similarly discharged from his service by reason of an implied condition to that effect. The actions of the personal representatives did not amount to breach of contract.

13:4 INSTANT DISMISSAL
OF AN EMPLOYEE WITHOUT NOTICE

The circumstances will now be discussed in which the employer is justified in dismissing an employee without giving him the period of notice required under the contract of employment. In these cases of instant or summary dismissal the employee cannot sue for wrongful dismissal.

13:4:1 *Effect of the employee's illness on the contract of employment*
Illness and injury, whether permanent or temporary, may be a frustrating event that terminates a contract. The following factors are important:

1   The terms of the contract
2   The nature of the work
3   Whether a substitute is required immediately
4   The expected duration of the incapacity
5   The length of service
6   Status of the employee

Permanent incapacity. Where illness causes permanent incapacity, it frustrates the commercial purposes of the contract and the employer is justified in summarily dismissing the employee concerned. The employer cannot claim damages for losses suffered by being deprived of the employee's services, which may be extensive in the case of an employee with highly specialised abilities, for example, a director of a company. The case illustrating this point concerns apprenticeship, but the principle extends to a contract of employment also.

Boast v Firth (1868)

Firth, an apprentice chemist, was bound to his employer by an apprenticeship deed for a period of five years, but before the end of this period he became permanently ill and unable to fulfil the terms of his apprenticeship.

The court decided that the employer was not entitled to damages as compensation for loss of the apprentice's services. The illness was an act of God, a sufficient excuse for non-performance of the agreement.

Temporary incapacity. If the illness or incapacity is of temporary duration, the contract of employment is discharged only if the incapacity makes a fundamental difference to the employer: it must go to the root of the contract.

Condor v The Barron Knights Ltd (1966)

Condor, a drummer with a pop group, was contractually entitled to six months' notice. Because of ill health his doctor advised that he should be employed only on four nights a week, whereas the contract of employment required him to work on seven nights a week, if work was available. Condor claimed damages for wrongful dismissal.

The court decided that illness had frustrated the contract in a business sense and Condor's summary dismissal was justified. It was unreasonable to expect the defendants to employ a substitute for Condor to work on the remaining three nights of the week.

The implications in this decision are important. Many highly paid executives are expected to work for long hours under pressure, and inability to cope completely with the demands of the position may justify summary dismissal. This is an important right where a lengthy period of notice is required by the contract of employment and it would be impossible to expect complete performance of all duties by the employee during that time.

Where the terms of the contract of employment are being fulfilled, even an extended absence by the employee will not frustrate it and justify summary dismissal, if the illness does not go to the root of the contract. The employer may terminate the contract only by giving the requisite period of notice. A contract for a fixed term may give rise to special difficulties and it is advisable to include an express term in the contract of employment whereby the employer can terminate the contract if illness lasts more than a stated time.

Storey v Fulham Steel Works Co (1907)

Storey, employed by the defendant company as a manager for a fixed term of five years, became ill after serving for two years. He was absent from work for six months, but in the meantime the company terminated his employment.

The court decided that the company's actions were not justified, since

Storey's illness and resultant absence did not go to the root of the contract. The agreement had a further two years to run and there was no reason for the company to believe that the employee would not recover sufficiently to continue his employment.

13:4:2 Disobedient employees

An employee is bound to obey the employer's lawful orders and refusal to do so justifies instant dismissal. The order must be reasonable, however, and not inconsistent with the type of work that the employee is employed to perform. For example, a lace buyer, earning a high salary, was wrongfully dismissed when he refused to obey an order to fold lace on cards which he considered to be derogatory to the work he was employed to perform (Price v Mouat (1862)).

In deciding whether an order is lawful and reasonable it is necessary to examine carefully:

1   The work to be performed
2   The skills of the employee concerned
3   The circumstances of the individual case

An employee is not bound to serve where he is afraid of the consequent risk to his life, or his health, where, for example, there is infection at the place of employment or his employer is violent.

Ottoman Bank v Chakarian (1930, Privy Council)

Chakarian, an Armenian and a Turkish subject, was in the permanent employment of the Ottoman Bank. He was given temporary employment at Constantinople, but feared that his life was in danger from the Turkish authorities. The bank refused Chakarian's request for a transfer, and when he fled from Constantinople they dismissed him without notice. He claimed damages for wrongful dismissal.

The court decided that Chakarian's flight did not entitle the bank to dismiss him, since it was clear that his personal safety was in real danger. His inability to perform the contract of employment in Constantinople could not be regarded as permanent, and his offer to work outside Turkey entitled him to damages. To order him to remain at his post in Constantinople was not a lawful order.

To warrant dismissal, the employee's refusal to obey the order must be wilful, showing a complete disregard of the essential conditions of the

R

contract of service. A single disobedient act suffices if it manifests an intention by the employee to repudiate the whole contract of employment or one of its essential terms, but it need not in itself be of a grave or serious character.

Laws v London Chronicle Ltd (1959, Court of Appeal)

Laws, an employee of the defendant company, attended a meeting at which her direct superior, Delderfield, quarrelled with the managing director. When Delderfield left in the middle of the meeting she rose to follow him. The managing director said to her, "You stay where you are," but she disobeyed and left the room.

The court decided that her conduct did not amount to such a disobedience of a lawful order and deliberate disregard of the conditions of service as to justify her summary dismissal, on the ground that she had repudiated the contract.

Pepper v Webb (1969, Court of Appeal)

Pepper was employed by Webb as head gardener, under a written contract of employment which could be terminated by either party giving three months' notice. After four months of satisfactory service, Pepper began to lose interest in his work and complaints were made about his inefficiency and insolence. One morning Pepper refused to put some new plants into the garden as requested, and when asked what arrangements he had made for care of the greenhouse during his absence over the weekend he answered, "I couldn't care less about your bloody greenhouse or your sodding garden" and walked away. Pepper was instantly dismissed by Webb without wages or notice. He claimed damages for breach of an express contractual term providing for three months' notice.

The court decided that Pepper's conduct on the morning in question indicated a repudiation of his duties under the contract of employment as a gardener, and that, taken against the background of his previous conduct, it was sufficient to justify summary dismissal. An employee repudiates his contract of employment if he wilfully disobeys the lawful and reasonable orders of his employer, as was the case here. Pepper was told to put the new plants into the garden before they died. Such an order was not unreasonable and there was ample evidence to show that the refusal to obey the order was wilful.

13:4:3 *Employee's breach of his duty of fidelity*

If the employee is in breach of his duty of good faith and fidelity to the employer, which is implied into every contract of employment, then he is guilty of misconduct justifying dismissal without notice. The employee must also account to his employer for money and property received in breach of his duty. It is misconduct justifying instant dismissal if the employee fails to render full and proper accounts to his employer where keeping such accounts is material to the proper performance of the employment in question (see 10:4).

13:4:4 *Incompetent employees*

If a person professes an ability to do a certain type of job, as by applying for a vacant post, he undertakes to possess the skills necessary for the fulfilment of the tasks involved, but if this is not so, then the employer may dismiss him. The employee may be dismissed without notice, or payment in lieu of notice, even though he has done his best to complete the duties imposed upon him. The employee's inability properly to perform the contract of employment amounts to a breach of contract, which the employer may accept as a repudiation of the agreement.

An employee cannot be dismissed without notice for his inability to do work that he never claimed he was competent to perform.

13:4:5 *Negligent employees*

The employer may be under a duty to discharge the employee if his incompetence creates dangers for fellow employees. This raises the difficult question of the degree of negligence necessary to justify instant dismissal. The negligent act must be sufficiently serious to strike at the root of the whole contract. If this is not the case, the employer can only claim damages from the employee for the loss caused by his negligence. The next two cases illustrate the distinction.

Baster *v* London & County Printing Works (1899)

Baster, employed as manager of a printing press, caused serious damage to machinery by forgetting to adjust it before use, and in consequence he was dismissed. He sued for damages for wrongful dismissal.

The court decided that the employee's forgetfulness of the proper method of carrying out his work constituted neglect which justified dismissal. The action for damages failed. "It was argued that mere forgetfulness could not amount to neglect; but I think that to forget to do a thing which it is of great importance you should remember, may show such a careless regard to your master's interests as amounts to neglect." (Mr Justice Darling)

The seriousness of an act of negligence cannot always be determined by an examination of the consequences of that act, since the act may be trivial and the consequences serious. It is better to examine the nature of the act or omission, the type of business concerned, and the position held by the employee, and then determine whether there has been serious incompetence. Though insignificant neglectful acts are insufficient to justify instant dismissal, the employer is free to terminate the contract by giving the appropriate period of notice.

Fillieul v Armstrong (1837)

Fillieul, a schoolmaster, was dismissed from his post for arriving two days after the beginning of term.

The court decided that the dismissal was unjustified, but it would have been otherwise if the plaintiff had continually arrived back late after vacations.

13:4:6 Dishonest employees

A strict view is taken of an employee's dishonesty; even a minor dishonest action during working hours justifies summary dismissal. It is an implied term in all contracts of employment that the employee will be honest.

Sinclair v Neighbour (1967, Court of Appeal)

Sinclair, manager of a betting shop, took £15 from the till, replaced it with an IOU for £15, and returned the money the next day. He used the £15 to make a successful bet. The employee knew that his employer disapproved of such conduct. Sinclair sued for damages for wrongful dismissal.

The court decided that the employer was justified in dismissing Sinclair summarily and thus damages were irrecoverable. As a manager it was his duty to keep the till inviolate, and taking money, even by way of a temporary loan, was dishonest and incompatible with his duties.

A contract of apprenticeship may be terminated by the employer if the apprentice is a thief.

Learoyd v Brook (1891)

Brook contracted with Learoyd to teach his ward the trade of pawnbroker. The apprentice was an habitual thief and when Brook refused to continue the contract of apprenticeship he was sued for its breach.

The court decided that where an apprentice by his own wilful acts prevents an employer from teaching him, the employer can set this up as a defence when sued upon his covenant to keep, teach and maintain the apprentice, irrespective of whether or not the apprentice has performed his obligations under the deed.

Dishonesty outside working hours is a ground for instant dismissal, since the employee's conduct undermines the trust that the employer must place in all his staff.

13:4:7 Misbehaviour by the employee

The employee's misbehaviour may justify summary dismissal. It must be remembered that summary dismissal is an exceptional measure that should be used only in exceptional circumstances, the justification for it depending upon the nature of the employment and the position occupied by the employee. A higher standard may be expected where there is close personal contact between employee and his immediate superior. In general, misconduct involves behaving in such a way that it is inconsistent with the standard of conduct expected from the employee. Decisions reached in other cases are of little value, except as guiding principles. The misconduct must go to the root of the contract and show an unwillingness to observe the conditions of the employment as agreed upon between the parties. Case law on this subject must be approached with some caution, since many earlier decisions are inapplicable in the changed social circumstances of the twentieth century. Misbehaviour on one occasion only does not justify summary dismissal unless the circumstances are exceptional and such that the parties cannot continue on the old terms.

Jupiter General Insurance Co v Shroff (1937, Privy Council)

Shroff, manager of the life insurance department of the appellant company, recommended the issue of an endowment policy, although he knew that a few days earlier the managing governor had refused to insure that particular risk. He claimed damages for breach of contract when he was summarily dismissed as a result.

The court decided that Shroff's conduct justified summary dismissal and the claim for damages failed. "A mistake in accepting a risk may lead to a very considerable loss, and a repetition of such mistakes may lead to a disaster . . . if a person in charge of the life assurance department subject to the supervision of superior officers, shows by his conduct or negligence that he can no longer command their confidence, and if when an explanation is called for, he refuses apology . . . his immediate dismissal is justifiable." (Lord Maugham)

Usually isolated acts of misbehaviour do not justify summary dismissal. The Judicial Committee of the Privy Council in this case took the view that "A single outbreak of bad temper, accompanied it may be with regrettable language, is insufficient ground for dismissal. In such cases we must apply the standards of men and not of angels and remember that men are apt to show temper when reprimanded" (Lord Maugham). On the other hand, if the employee is continually late for work, rude to his superiors or improperly dressed, then the employer may dismiss without notice.

An employee's drunkenness will justify summary dismissal if it is habitual or excessive and directly interferes with his ability to perform his duties properly.

Misbehaviour outside working hours. The employee is free to use his spare time as he pleases, provided that any acts of misconduct do not seriously affect the employee's work during business hours. If his work is detrimentally affected the contract is repudiated. Moral misconduct by the employee in his own time will not justify summary dismissal, unless the employee is engaged in domestic service.

If an employee commits a serious wrong outside working hours, for example, an assault on a fellow employee, such that the employer feels it is unsafe to continue the contract of service, then summary dismissal is permissible.

13:4:8 *Employee's right to wages*
Where an employee is properly dismissed without notice for misconduct, he cannot recover wages for the time during which he worked between the last payment of wages and his subsequent dismissal, unless there is an express term in the contract providing otherwise. The position is the same if the employee had a yearly contract of employment and had already served part of that year. Obviously there is no right to wages in lieu of notice. An employer is liable to an employee for wages accrued, but not yet paid, in respect of past work, though he has been justifiably dismissed, where the contract of employment is severable and not entire.

On the other hand, the contract of employment may expressly allow the employer to retain wages accrued but not yet paid at the time when the employee is dismissed for misconduct, provided the wages so retained can be regarded as liquidated damages, compensating the employer for the employee's breach of contract. Forfeiture of a sum which is so large that it can be categorised as a penalty is not permitted (see 13:5:7). Money may not be deducted from wages due for work done by a child, young person or woman subject to the Factories Act 1961, except to the extent of any damages suffered by the employer. This provision does not apply if the wages have not accrued before the employee's misconduct.

13:4:9 *Employer should give reasons for instant dismissal*
Where the employer instantly dismisses an employee for one of the justifiable reasons discussed above, the precise reason for dismissal should be stated. In an action under s24 of the Industrial Relations Act 1971 (see 11:13:3), the burden of proof that a dismissal was fair lies with the employer. If the employer has decided to dismiss, he should do so at the time when the employee's wrong is committed or when he first hears of it if this occurs sometime after the event. Otherwise, by continuing the employment, the employer will be deemed to have waived his right to dismiss.

13:4:10 *When an employee may leave without giving notice*
The employee also has the right to regard the contract of employment as discharged, leaving him free to terminate his employment without giving the length of notice usually required, in the following circumstances:

1 Where the employer is guilty of misconduct, for example, ill treating or assaulting staff or making improper advances
2 Where the employee's life or health are at risk
3 Where the risks anticipated by the employer and employee are increased as the result of a significant change in circumstances, for example, where the outbreak of war or civil strife in a certain area makes completion of a task by the employee unduly hazardous, and the terms of his contract do not require him to accept such risks
4 Where the employer wilfully neglects to discharge his duties under the contract, for example, not paying wages at the time when they fall due or not providing safe working conditions

An employee cannot summarily terminate the contract by paying over a sum equivalent to his wages in lieu of notice.

13:5 MONETARY COMPENSATION PAYABLE FOR WRONGFUL DISMISSAL

13:5:1 *Anticipatory breach of contract*

When an employer engages an employee, the date of commencement of the contract of employment is often fixed at some time in the future, since the employee may be bound already by an existing contract of employment and obliged to give notice to his present employer. Before the date fixed for the commencement of the contract, either employer or employee may renounce his obligations and make it clear that he does not intend to fulfil the contract when the time of performance arrives. The employer may no longer need the services of the employee because of a decline in business or the employee may have received a better offer. This is called anticipatory breach of contract and the party renouncing the contract may be sued immediately by the other party (the promisee). It is not necessary to wait until the date fixed for performance.

Hochster v De La Tour (1853)

The defendant agreed to employ the plaintiff as a courier for a European tour for a period of three months, beginning on 1 June 1852. On 11 May the defendant informed the plaintiff that his services would not be required.

The court decided that the plaintiff could sue for breach of contract immediately; he was not obliged to wait until 1 June and damages were assessed as at the date fixed for performance.

In this case it was the employer who committed the anticipatory breach, but the result is exactly the same where the employee notifies the employer of his intention to renounce the contract of employment.

The promisee, whether employer or employee, may prefer to ignore the repudiation and allow the party repudiating his contractual obligations a further opportunity to perform the contract up until the time fixed for performance, in the hope that during this period a change of mind will occur. The employee may hope that the employer will see his way clear to honouring the offer of employment made, or the employer may hope that the employee will accept the offer of employment made to him in preference to other opportunities open. The main danger in waiting is that between the date of anticipatory breach and the time fixed for performance, some event may occur, such as the death of the party in default, which makes fulfilment of the contract impossible. The party repudiating the contract, or his personal representative in this example, is then discharged from the contractual obligation and damages do not have to be paid.

13:5:2 *Employee's action for damages against the employer*

After commencement of employment the employer may repudiate a fundamental term of the contract, as in the case of an unjustifiable summary dismissal without notice, entitling the employee to sue for damages or his wages, even though he has not completed his duties in relation to the employment.

The damages recoverable will be measured according to the injuries naturally arising from the breach of contract. Thus the sum awarded must be sufficient to place the employee in the position he would have been in if the breach had not occurred. This principle will cover the majority of contracts and the employee is compensated for the loss of his wages for the period of notice not given by the employer. Thus if the employee has been given a sum representing his wages for the period of notice to which he is entitled, the employer cannot be sued for wrongful dismissal, but there may be a claim for unfair dismissal under the Industrial Relations Act 1971 (see 11:13).

Damages may be recovered for some special injury suffered that does not arise naturally. In this case it must be reasonable to suppose that the injury was contemplated by the employer and employee as the probable result of a breach of contract at the time of making the contract. For example, an employee may recover the estimated amount of any commission or tips that he might have earned over and above his basic wage, if he had been allowed to continue to work for the period of his notice (see 13:5:3 Addis v Gramophone Co Ltd (1909)). A domestic servant may claim for board and lodgings that would have been provided during the period of notice.

13:5:3 *Damages are not increased to* *take into account the employee's injured feelings*

The amount of damages awarded cannot be increased to include compensation for injured feelings suffered by the employee as a result of the manner in which he is dismissed. Nor can a claim be made for monetary compensation, on the ground that dismissal makes it more difficult for the employee to secure new employment than if he had been the party to give notice.

Addis v Gramophone Co Ltd (1909, House of Lords)

Addis, a manager employed by the defendants, was given six months' notice in accordance with the terms of his contract of employment, but at the same time a successor was appointed to act as manager during that six-month period.

The court decided that there was a breach of contract in not allowing the plaintiff to discharge his duties as manager and he was entitled to salary for the six-month period of his notice, plus the commission he would have earned if he had been allowed to manage the business himself. He was not entitled to "compensation either for injured feelings of the servant or for the loss he may sustain from the fact that his having been dismissed makes it more difficult for him to obtain fresh employment." (Lord Loreburn)

13 : 5 : 4   Employee's duty to mitigate his loss

Where the employee is wrongfully dismissed without notice or without payment in lieu of notice, he must try to mitigate the loss that he suffers in consequence by attempting to find alternative employment. If he is successful in securing new employment for the period, or part of the period, in respect of which he can claim damages for wrongful dismissal, then any damages awarded against the employer who dismissed him will be reduced by the amount of the wages so earned. Damages will not be awarded where failure to obtain alternative employment at the same rate of remuneration is the fault of the employee, as in the case of Brace v Calder (see 13 : 3 : 1).

13 : 5 : 5   Employer's action for damages against the employee

The employer is entitled to sue the employee for damages in respect of any breach of duty under the contract of employment which amounts to misconduct. Damages will be recoverable in respect of injuries naturally arising from the employee's breach of contract. The sum awarded must be sufficient to place the employer in the financial position he would have been in if the breach had not occurred. Thus if the employee is unjustifiably absent from work, the employer may recover sufficient damages to compensate him for the value of the work that the employee would have completed had he been present. This may be a much higher sum than the wages paid to the employee, as the next case illustrates.

National Coal Board v Galley (1958, Court of Appeal)

Galley, a deputy employed by the NCB under a written contract, agreed to work on such days as might reasonably be required by the management. Together with other deputies, Galley refused to work essential overtime, because miners were receiving better wages than deputies. The NCB sued Galley for breach of contract in being absent from work on a particular day.

The court decided that since Galley exercised supervisory functions in relation to safety precautions, the measure of damages was the cost of providing a substitute for him (around £4). However, it was further stated in the course of judgement, that damages in respect of the absence of a coal-hewer would be the value of the output lost less the cost of mining it, which might be around £100.

The employer may also recover damages for any special injury which might reasonably be contemplated by the employer and employee when they made the contract as the probable result of its breach. For example, if a firm of accountants employ a highly qualified and experienced tax consultant to deal with their clients' complex tax problems, he might be aware that his failure to observe the terms of his contract would cause the firm to lose the opportunity of taking on lucrative consultancy work.

The employer must take all reasonable steps to mitigate his loss by engaging, where possible, another person to carry out the work of the defaulting employee.

13:5:6 Liquidated or unliquidated damages may be recoverable

Damages are unliquidated where one party to a contract sues the other to recover whatever sum the court holds to be the proper measure of damages, in the circumstances. A contract of employment may provide that, in the event of a breach, the innocent party may recover from the defaulting party a sum stated in the contract itself: this sum is called liquidated damages. This type of arrangement has the advantage of saving the time, trouble and expense of litigation should a breach of contract occur, since only the agreed sum is recoverable, even if the actual loss suffered greatly exceeds the sum fixed by the contract. If damages are to be assessed by the contract itself, it is essential to estimate with precision the monetary effect of any possible breach.

Cellulose Acetate Silk Co v Widnes Foundry Ltd (1933, House of Lords)

Widnes Foundry agreed to erect plant for the Cellulose Acetate Silk Co and pay damages of £20 for every week taken to complete the work beyond the date stipulated. There was a delay in completion of thirty weeks and the actual loss of £5850 was claimed from Widnes Foundry.

The court decided that only £600 was recoverable, being the liquidated damages fixed in the contract itself.

The fact that the results of a breach of contract make an accurate pre-estimation of the damages suffered almost impossible does not prevent the sum fixed from being considered as liquidated damages.

13 : 5 : 7 Distinction between liquidated damages and a penalty

A sum agreed on as payable in the event of a breach of the contract of employment may be liquidated damages or a penalty. The distinction is of vital importance. If the sum is liquidated damages it can be recovered from the party in default, since in essence it is regarded as a genuine pre-estimate of the damage suffered by the innocent party. If the sum fixed by the contract is deemed to be a penalty, then essentially it is a threat held against any party likely to violate the contractual obligations. The intention of a penalty is to attempt to compel performance of the contract by severely punishing the party who refuses to implement it. The defaulting party is made liable to pay an extravagant sum, exceeding the greatest loss that could possibly result from the breach. A penalty is irrecoverable and the injured party is limited to the recovery of the actual loss he has suffered. If an employer wishes to guard against breaches of contract by his employees, a penalty clause in the contract of employment is not the method to use.

13 : 5 : 8 Tax considerations when
paying damages (Finance Act 1960 s37, s38)

The first £5000 of damages for wrongful dismissal is not taxable in the hands of the recipient; consequently this sum must be reduced to take into account the employee's liability to pay tax. If this were not done the employee would receive more in damages than if he had continued to work and pay tax on his earnings. The amount deducted is not paid to the Inland Revenue, but is retained by the employer. Consequently in a case of this type it is cheaper for the employer to break his contract than to keep it, always remembering, of course, that a service is not rendered to him by the employee in respect of the payment made.

In addition, unemployment benefit received by the employee must also be deducted from the damages payable. For example, in Parsons v BNML Laboratories Ltd (1964, Court of Appeal) an award for wrongful dismissal of £1200 for loss of salary and commission was reduced by £320 to reflect the tax that would have been paid on it, and by £59.12½ for the sum received as unemployment benefit. A further deduction should be made in respect of the National Insurance contributions that would have been paid on any salary earned.

Where the damages for wrongful dismissal exceed £5000, the excess is taxable in the hands of the recipient; thus the employer liable for payment must hand over the gross sum. The first £5000 still remains tax free, and consequently it must be reduced to reflect the amount of tax that the employee would have paid on it if he had continued in his employment. The sum deducted is again retained by the employer.

Bold v Brough, Nicholson & Hall Ltd (1964)

In 1962 Bold was summarily dismissed and it was unlikely that he would ever secure suitable employment again. He had a ten-year contract with the company which began in 1959, the salary payable for his services being £4000 p.a. and £500 commission.

The court decided that the plaintiff employee was entitled to £26 312 damages, to enable him to purchase annuities to provide for the gross remuneration he had lost, subject to deductions of £5312 to cover:

1   Actual earnings of £546 since dismissal
2   Potential earnings
3   The possibility of serious illness, which would have given the employer the right to terminate the contract

The first £5000 of the damages would not be taxable in the plaintiff's hands. Thus £800 was deducted to take into account the tax that he would have paid if he had continued to work for the company and pay tax on his income.

In making these calculations to determine the sum to be deducted for tax, little regard should be paid to the employee's private income from investments, since he is free to dispose of them at any time he wishes.

Beach v Reed Corrugated Cases Ltd (1956)

Beach sued the defendant company for wrongfully terminating his fixed-term contract of employment, claiming £48 000 for loss of his gross salary between 1956 and 1966. He received £20 000 gross annually from his investments, but he gave most of this away by covenant. If the whole of Beach's income were taken into account, both earned and unearned, and tax deducted, then he would lose only £4650 because of his wrongful dismissal.

The court decided that only the tax Beach would have to pay on his gross salary of £48 000 should be taken into account. His private income should be disregarded.

13:6 EMPLOYEE CANNOT BE COMPELLED TO FULFIL HIS CONTRACT

A contract of employment is not directly enforceable at the instance of an employer by means of a decree directing the employee specifically to perform those positive promises (or stipulations) that he has contractually bound himself to undertake. It would be impossible for the court to supervise effectively the actions of the employee to ensure that he observed the decree of specific performance. Further, it is undesirable to keep persons tied together in a business relationship when the tie has become odious, thus turning a contract of service into a contract of servitude.

13:6:1 *Injunction to restrain a breach of contract*

An injunction may be granted, however, to restrain the employee from committing some act which is prohibited by the terms of his contract of employment. For example, an injunction will be granted to restrain the breach of covenant in restraint of trade embodied in a contract of employment, where it is reasonable between the parties themselves and consistent with the public interest. In such a case the parties have contracted by way of a negative promise (or stipulation) that a particular thing shall not be done, and this agreement is enforceable by means of an injunction.

Lumley v Wagner (1852)

Miss Wagner agreed by way of a positive stipulation to sing for Lumley at Her Majesty's Theatre during a given period. She also promised by way of a negative stipulation that she would not sing elsewhere without Lumley's permission. Miss Wagner refused to sing for Lumley and agreed to sing for Gye at Covent Garden.

The court decided that the contract to sing at Her Majesty's Theatre could not be specifically enforced since it was an agreement for personal services, but Miss Wagner could be prevented from singing at Covent Garden in violation of her negative stipulation; otherwise persons admiring her singing might go there, to the advantage of Gye and the detriment of Lumley.

In this case Lumley was likely to suffer considerable monetary loss if Miss Wagner sang at Covent Garden, but this is not an essential prerequisite to the granting of an injunction, provided that some monetary loss results. The mere expense and trouble of finding a replacement for the defaulting employee will suffice. Damages will be granted if this is an adequate remedy in preference to an injunction where, for example, the employee does not have any specialised skills and a replacement is relatively easy to find. The employer must decide whether to sue for liquidated damages or seek an injunction to restrain his employee's activities, but he will not be granted both remedies.

13:6:2 *Persuading the employee to fulfil his contract*

The inevitable result of granting the injunction is to persuade the reluctant employee to carry out his contract with the employer, rather than forego lucrative employment for a given period and, in the case of Miss Wagner, the publicity vital to the furtherance of her career. It should be noted that the defaulting employee cannot pay liquidated damages as fixed by the contract of employment to avoid the issuing of an injunction.

The principle in Lumley v Wagner applies to any contract of employment containing positive and negative stipulations, but injunctions are usually issued only against employees with specialised skills earning a high salary or fee, such as a director, engineer or designer. For example, if a company employs a highly qualified and well established engineer for the purpose of furthering a proposed scheme, he may be contractually bound to give the whole of his time to the company's business and not to work for any other person as an engineer while the contract of employment is in existence. An injunction restraining a breach of this contract by the engineer must be limited in its effect to the type of work specified in the contract, namely engineering, thus leaving the employee free to engage in other remunerative activities, though presumably less highly paid, during the period of restraint. There is a reluctance to grant an injunction the effect of which is to compel the employee to perform his contract or starve. Since the employee will usually wish to work in his own specialised field, he will be induced to fulfil the original contract of employment.

13:6:3 *Restraint on an employee's spare-time activities*

If an employee agrees to give the whole of his time to his employer during the term of his employment, a clause that is not unusual in many contracts of employment, this is a purely affirmative contract for personal services. A negative stipulation will not be implied into that contract preventing the employee from serving another employer for the duration of the contract, whether doing similar work or something entirely different.

Whitwood Chemical Co v Hardman (1891, Court of Appeal)

Hardman, the manager of a manufacturing company, agreed to give "the whole of his time" to the company's business. In fact he sometimes worked for other employers and the plaintiff tried to restrain those activities by injunction.

The court decided that the contract of employment did not embody any express negative stipulation. Hardman had only stated what he would do, but a term was not included stating the things he should not do. To read into the contract an agreement not to work for another employer involved implying a negative stipulation from a positive stipulation, and this would not be done.

If an employer wishes to restrain the spare-time activities of his employee, then an express negative stipulation to that effect must be included in the contract of employment, as in the example of the engineer given above. In the absence of such an express negative stipulation, the law is reluctant to impose restrictions on employees which prevent them from increasing their earnings in their spare time, subject to one important qualification. An employee must not be engaged during his spare time in skilled work directly competing with his employer, even if he does not disclose any confidential information. Such actions constitute a breach of the duty of fidelity owed by the employee to his employer, a duty which varies according to the nature of his employment (see 2:11, Hivac Ltd v Park Royal Scientific Instruments Ltd).

13:6:4 *Restraints that will not be enforced by injunctions*
If the restriction imposed on the employee is unduly wide and unreasonable as being in restraint of trade, it will not be enforced by an injunction, for the effect will often be to make the employee fulfil his contract or starve.

Chapman v Westerby (1913)

A contract of employment engaging the defendant as skipper of a trawler for a term of ten years provided, by way of negative stipulation, that he "should not give his time or personal attention to any other business or occupation." An injunction was sought by the plaintiff employer to enforce this undertaking.

The court decided that this promise could not be enforced against the employee since: "It would involve this, that so far as earning his living was concerned the defendant would have to be absolutely idle for a term of ten years or continue this contract of personal service; in other words, it would, for all practical purposes, be granting specific performance of a contract of service, a thing which the court would never do." (Mr Justice Warrington)

13:7 RULES TO REMEMBER WHEN SUPPLYING REFERENCES

An employer is not under any duty to provide an employee with a reference or testimonial, unless there is a term in the contract to that effect. If a reference is given, however, an employer must not defame the employee. A statement is defamatory if it tends to lower the plaintiff in the estimation of right-thinking members of society. The person making the defamatory statement may be liable for damages in tort, for either slander in respect of spoken words, or libel if the defamation is in some permanent form such as writing.

To succeed in any action the employee has the burden of proving that the statement was defamatory and that it referred to him. There must also be publication, that is communication to a party other than the person defamed. No action lies for defamation in an open reference handed to the employee personally, for any subsequent publication must be by the employee himself. In cases of slander there is the additional burden of showing either an imputation of incapacity in relation to the employee's trade, profession or occupation or alternatively special loss, such as loss of a position that might otherwise have been secured.

13:7:1 Defences against actions for defamation
The employer may have one of the following two defences to any action, which if successful will negative liability: first that the statements made about the employee were substantially true, for no one is entitled to a reputation that is unwarranted. This is a defence of justification. Second, there is the more usual and useful defence of qualified privilege, where, for example, an employer provides a reference for the guidance of a potential employer who might offer the employee a situation. Here a statement is made to someone having a justifiable interest in receiving it. An employer

will not be in breach of duty to his employee if the reference is not entirely true, provided it was not made maliciously. The defence of qualified privilege is lost if the employee establishes malice, as by proving one of the following factors, that the employer did not himself believe the statement to be true, or that he made a false statement with spite, or that it was published to someone with no justifiable interest in receiving it.

If an employer gives a good reference, but later rescinds it, the second communication is also privileged. There is a duty to inform the new employer of a former employee's dishonest acts discovered after termination of the employment. Where the employer supplies a reference unrequested he will have to bring in stronger evidence to show good faith than in cases where a reference is requested.

13:7:2 Liability for a false reference
An employer may be sued for deceit by the person misled if he recommends an employee by making untrue statements fraudulently, that is, knowing their untruth, or without belief in their truth, or recklessly not caring whether they were true or false. The reference must be given with the intention that it should be acted upon and it must have been acted upon by the person suing, usually a potential employer. The misconduct of the employee recommended renders the employer supplying the reference liable, even though he acted without malice or hope of gain. Further, following the House of Lords decision in Hedley Byrne & Co Ltd v Heller & Partners Ltd (1963), tortious liability is established where a reference is merely misleading, if for example it contains a careless misstatement, causing monetary loss to the person relying on the reference. The employer should clearly state when giving the reference that he cannot be held responsible for its accuracy; then all responsibility for any careless misstatements embodied in the reference is effectively negatived.

13:7:3 Position of the personnel manager
The writing of references is often one of the personnel manager's most significant tasks. If the rules set out above are followed, legal proceedings for defamation will be avoided. A true assessment of the employee's abilities and weaknesses may be given, however unfavourable, but malicious statements must not be included. Proceedings for defamation may be brought against the employer who authorised his personnel manager to supply references or against the personnel manager himself, or against both jointly, in accordance with the principles discussed in section 9 : 3.

List of Cases Cited

CA = Court of Appeal

CCA = Court of Criminal Appeal

HL = House of Lords

PC = Privy Council

One reference to a report is given for each case: the most generally available report has been chosen. Cases from 1936 onwards are mostly in *The All England Law Reports* (abbreviated as AER preceded by the volume number: there are usually three volumes per year).

Other cases from 1890 onwards are in the third series of Law Reports of the Incorporated Council (see *Introduction*). These are identified by an abbreviation of the name of the court:

AC = Appeal Cases in the House of Lords or the Privy Council

Ch = Chancery Division of the High Court

KB or QB = King's or Queen's Bench Division of the High Court

This abbreviation is preceded by the volume number if there is more than one volume of reports for the court for a particular year.

Between 1865 and 1890, reports are in earlier series of the Law Reports. There was a set of reports for each court, identified by an abbreviation of the name of the court:

AppCas = Appeal Cases

ChD = Chancery Division of the High Court

CP or CPD = Common Pleas Division of the High Court

Ex = Exchequer Division of the High Court

HL = House of Lords

QBD = Queen's Bench Division of the High Court

This abbreviation is preceded by the serial number of the volume. The first series (1865–75) is identified by the additional prefix, LR.

References to other series of reports are abbreviated as follows:

A&E = Adolphus and Ellis

CB(NS) = Common Bench (New Series)

E&B = Ellis and Blackburn

Ex = Exchequer (Welsby, Hurlstone and Gordon, 1847–56)

KIR = *Knight's Industrial Reports*

LGR = *Knight's Local Government Reports*

Lloyd's Reports = *Lloyd's List Law Reports*

LT = *The Law Times Reports*

SJ = *The Solicitors' Journal*

TLR = *The Times Law Reports*

WLR = *Weekly Law Reports*

WN = *Weekly Notes*

For recent cases, a reference is given to a report in *The Times* newspaper.

Some older cases are available in the series of *All England Law Reports Reprints* (abbreviated as AER Reprint, preceded by the years covered by the volume).

NAME OF CASE	DATE	REFERENCE	PAGE
Adamson v Arthur Smith (Hull) Ltd	1967	2KIR 302	488
Addie (Robert) & Sons (Collieries) Ltd v Dumbreck	1929 HL	AC 358	367
Addis v Gramophone Company Ltd	1909 HL	AC 488	514
Adler v Dickson	1954 CA	3AER 397	356
Allen v Aeroplane & Motor Aluminium Castings Ltd	1965 CA	3AER 377	302
Allen v Flood	1898 HL	AC 1	464
Allsopp v Wheatcroft	1872	LR 15EQ 59	90
Appelby v Johnson	1874	LR 9CP 158	26
Ashdown v Samuel Williams & Sons Ltd	1957 CA	1QB 409	362
Attwood v Lamont	1920 CA	3KB 571	98
Automatic Wood Turning Co Ltd v Stringer	1957 HL	AC 544	254
Baker v T E Hopkins & Son Ltd	1959 CA	3AER 225	350
Baker v James Brothers & Sons Ltd	1921	2KB 674	234
Barcock v Brighton Corporation	1949	1AER 251	223

Index